I0235254

ENGLAND AND THE NORTH:
THE RUSSIAN EMBASSY
OF 1613–1614

In the year 7121 [1 September 1612–31 August 1613] the most sinful among men Aleksei Ivanovich Ziuzin, according to his vow, ordered this honorable local icon of all saints painted in Kargopol', [to be placed] in the fortress for the health of all Orthodox Christians.

ENGLAND AND THE NORTH: THE RUSSIAN EMBASSY OF 1613–1614

Edited by
Maija Jansson and Nikolai Rogozhin

Translated by
Paul Bushkovitch

Under the Direction of
Victor Buganov, Institute of the History of Russia
Paul Bushkovitch, Yale University
M. Lukichev, Director, the Russian State Archive
of Ancient Documents

American Philosophical Society
Independence Square Philadelphia
1994

Memoirs of the
AMERICAN PHILOSOPHICAL SOCIETY
Held at Philadelphia
For Promoting Useful Knowledge
Volume 210

Copyright © 1994 by The American Philosophical Society
This book is subsidized by the
John F. Lewis Fund.

Jacket illustrations from:
Portrety, Gerby, I Pechati Bolshoi Gosudarstvennoi Knigi

Library of Congress Catalog Card Number 93-74424
International Standard Book Number 0-87169-210-4
US ISSN 0065-9738

Table of Contents

Preface vi

Acknowledgments ix

Editorial Conventions x

Preliminary Material

   V. Buganov xv

   N. Rogozhin xxix

Introduction 1

Aleksei Ziuzin's Account

   The Instructions 71

   Memoranda 124

   The Report 145

End Notes 182

Appendixes 203

Bibliography 214

Index 223

Preface

The Russian embassy of 1613–1614 to James I of England was one more link in the long chain of political relations of the Russian state with England. This was a political embassy, and the reader of its reports will search in vain for the Muscovy Company business assumed in English historiography to be the core of the relationship between the two countries. To a certain extent foreign policy in early modern Europe (particularly for the Dutch Republic) was predicated on commercial interests, and indeed the Company was one element in Anglo-Russian relations. However, for most of Europe at that time other issues played an equal if not an overriding role in the formulation of policy. From the very beginning of Anglo-Russian relations political issues came into play, ones that involved not only the bilateral relationship, but the whole of northern Europe, Russia, Poland, the Scandinavian kingdoms, and to a certain extent the Empire. In Elizabeth's time growing conflict with Spain above all required the Queen's government to become involved with each one of these powers to a greater or lesser extent, with the aim of finding enemies of the house of Habsburg wherever possible and parrying hostile moves in seemingly distant parts of Europe. James I's political agenda reflected his personal commitment to peace and his general support of Protestantism, as well as his fear of growing Dutch naval strength. All these factors came into the play with England's policy regarding Russia.

The political aspects of Anglo-Russian relations at the end of the sixteenth and beginning of the seventeenth centuries have been for the most part overlooked by Western historians whose interests have centered on the history of the English Muscovy Company. The basic work of T. S. Willan not only focused on the Company but was very skeptical of any suggestion of political interests at play. The natural interest in the Company's history continued by Samuel Baron, Geraldine M. Phipps, and others has tended to reinforce Willan's view, perhaps unintentionally. In part the problem is the general neglect of English foreign policy in the north: standard works like those of R. B. Wernham generally ignore the area, and the writings of Scandinavian, Russian, and Polish historians remain unknown in the English-speaking world. Only Norman Evans has explored any aspect of the political relationship in recent years.[1] Thus the story of commerce, whether to Archangel or Danzig, has appeared to be the whole story. It is not. In Russian historiography the situation is different. Though Inna Liubimenko's pioneering work at the turn of the century also stressed the commercial relationship, Soviet historians of Russian foreign policy in the period do not. For them, the basic emphasis is on the political rivalry with Poland, and other affairs are considered in that context. Thirty years ago Ia. S. Lur'e suggested in a brief article that Anglo-Russian relations in Elizabeth's reign were not primarily commercial, but that idea has gone unnoticed in the West.[2] Our contention is that he was right, but that the full context of England's relations with northern Europe must be considered to make sense of the problem. Although commerce was important, other issues hinging on the configurations of continental alliances dominated politics at Whitehall from two decades before the Spanish Armada to the years immediately preceding England's involvement with the Thirty Years' War. Well outside the narrow confines of Muscovy Company business, the crown was rapidly becoming absorbed with the larger problems of alignment between the Habsburgs and their enemies and the criss-crossing alliances among the Catholic and Protestant states. In short, religious and political issues were instrumental in molding England's diplomacy with the Scan-

1. T. S. Willan, *The Early History of the Russia Company 1553-1603* (Manchester, 1956); Samuel Baron, "Ivan the Terrible, Giles Fletcher, and the Muscovite Merchantry," S[lavic] E[ast] E[uropean] R[eview] 56 (October, 1978), 563-585; id., "The Muscovy Company, the Muscovite Merchants and the Problem of Reciprocity," *Forschungen zur Geschichte Osteuropas* 27 (1979), 133-155; Geraldine M. Phipps, *Sir John Merrick: English Merchant-Diplomat in Seventeenth Century Russia* (Newtonville, Massachusetts, 1983); R. B. Wernham, *Before the Armada: The Emergence of the English Nation 1485-1588* (New York, 1966); id., *After the Armada: Elizabethan England and the Struggle for Western Europe 1588-1595* (Oxford, 1984); Simon Adams, "Spain or the Netherlands? The Dilemmas of Early Stuart Foreign Policy," in Howard Tomlinson, ed., *Before the English Civil War*, London, 1983, 79-102; Norman Evans, "The Anglo-Russian Royal Marriage Negotiations of 1600-1603," SEER 61, 3 (July, 1983), 363-387.

2. Inna Liubimenko, *Istoriia torgovykh snoshenii Rossii s Angliei*, part 1, XVI-i vek, Iur'ev (Dorpat/Tartu), 1912; and id., *Les relations commerciales et politiques de l'Angleterre avec la Russie avant Pierre le Grand*, Bibliothèque de l'École des Hautes Études: Sciences historiques et philologiques 261 (Paris, 1933); Ia. S. Lur'e, "Russko-angliiskie otnosheniia i mezhdunarodnaia politika vtoroi poloviny XVI v.," in A. A. Zimin, V. T. Pashuto, eds., *Mezhdunarodnye sviazi Rossii do XVII v.* (Moscow, 1961); B. N. Floria, *Russko-pol'skie otnosheniia i baltiiskii vopros v kontse XVI—nachale XVII v.* (Moscow, 1973); and id., *Russko-pol'skie otnosheniia i politicheskoe razvitie Vostochnoi Evropy vo vtoroi polovine XVI—nachale XVII v.* (Moscow, 1978).

dinavian states, Poland, and Russia at this time to a much greater extent than is generally realized.

Partly, it must be said, this obfuscation was a result of the nature of the evidence, wherein the Muscovy Company figures so predominantly in the few remaining extant records in England. Indeed, because of that one-sided evidence the interests of the country have usually been portrayed as synonymous with those of the Company. And while it is true that for purely practical reasons of linguistics and cultural experience the company personnel did much of the counseling with the English government concerning negotiations with the Russian state (naturally pressing their own interests wherever possible), and over the years handled much of the hospitality for visiting delegations, it is likewise true that newsletters and ambassadorial dispatches from persons outside the merchant community reveal other aspects of the story. Now with Ziuzin's report to the Tsar translated and published in the West, historians can, for the first time, begin to understand Russian political objectives in conjunction with English foreign policy aims in the early seventeenth century. The complaint about the paucity of documents by one of the pioneers of Anglo-Russian studies, Inna Liubimenko, has been assuaged.

That we can now look at all sides of the question of Anglo-Russian policy in the early decades of the seventeenth century is to a certain extent a tribute to the spirit of *glasnost*. It was, however, some years before the actual advent of *perestroika* that our friend and colleague, Sergei Kashtanov, supplied us with a copy of the rotoprint edition of Ziuzin's embassy report from which Paul Bushkovitch could begin the tedious work of translating Nikolai Rogozhin's Russian edition into English. During a visit to Moscow in September 1989, Viktor Buganov agreed to contribute an introduction based on Soviet archive material and M. P. Lukichev gave the project his blessing. The edition is truly a joint venture.

For some time it had been apparent to us that the motives for an alliance between King James and Tsar Michael were not solely economic, but this was a difficult matter to examine given the limitations of English archives. Now that the official instructions to Ziuzin and the English responses to them are available the picture is clear. We find, as one would expect, that those responses are part of a larger policy framed to deal with all of Europe and Scandinavia. And, not surprising at that juncture, that policy had to a great extent evolved from confessional and political rather than commercial interests.

Acknowledgments

The editors want to express their thanks to all those who helped with the research for this volume, particularly the staffs of the National Library of Scotland in Edinburgh; the Guildhall Library, British Library and Public Record Office in London, the Bibliothèque Nationale in Paris; the Huntington Library in San Marino, California; and the Haus- Hof- und Staatsarchiv in Vienna. They also want to thank IREX (International Researches and Exchange Board) and the American Philosophical Society for their support, enabling Dr. Jansson to meet with the Soviet editors in Moscow regarding the preparation of the volume, and Yale University for providing support through the Enders Fund for work at the Bibliothèque Nationale.

Several individuals aside from the editors contributed to this edition and we want to thank them. Jennifer Spock translated the preliminary materials by V. Buganov and N. Rogozhin. Lisa Martin inserted all the diacriticals in the finished text; Peter Hasler, Secretary Emeritus of the History of Parliament Trust, enlightened us about the hazards of an August sea voyage from Archangel to England; John Ferris offered some suggestions regarding members of James's household. We want to thank Patricia Palm, in Mexico City, who provided the translations of Boisschot's letters to the Archdukes. We also want to particularly acknowledge and thank Norman Evans, Director Emeritus of the Round Room in the Public Record Office, for his comments and suggestions about the volume. N. Lukichev, Director of the Institute of USSR History, granted permission for the project to go forward and encouraged it at every juncture. We are grateful for his support and interest.

The editors wish to thank Leonid Vasil'evich Betin for telling us that the Ziuzin icon was in Vologda, and Natal'ia A. Zolotova, Chief Keeper of the Vologda State History, Architecture, and Art Museum, for granting permission to publish the photograph. We also thank Tatiana U. Stukalova, Research Fellow of the State Historic Museum in Moscow and Olga Dmitrieva, Chair of Medieval History, Moscow State University for their help in transmitting it to us.

Paul Bushkovitch
Maija Jansson
New Haven, Connecticut

Editorial Conventions

Text: The text of Aleksei Ziuzin's report to Tsar Michael in 1614 was published in a small rotoprint edition in Moscow in 1979 (*Posol'skaia kniga po sviaziam Rossii s Angliei 1613–1614 gg.*) transcribed from the seventeenth-century manuscript and edited by Victor Buganov and Nikolai Rogozhin. Paul Bushkovitch translated the present text from the Buganov-Rogozhin edition with the exception of the last nine pages that were only recently discovered in the archives folded in with materials relating to Polish affairs. Those pages were not included in the rotoprint edition and have here been translated by Professor Bushkovitch from photostats of the original manuscript pages. For all but this section we have included page numbers of the rotoprint edition within square brackets in the text; that edition includes the manuscript folio numbers. When a page break occurs in the middle of a word we have designated the new page number at the end of the word. The problems of translations are legion, particularly with a seventeenth-century text. For the translator there could hardly be an alternative to using modern orthography. And, in this case, to aid the reader, the punctuation has been also modernized in keeping with the guidelines in Johannes Schultze, "Rechtlinien für die äussere Textgestaltung bei Herausgabe von Quellen zur neueren deutschen Geschichte."[1] In maintaining consistency with the conventions followed in the Ziuzin text, the editors have modernized the spelling and punctuation of other letters and documents cited in the annotation and introduction, and printed in the Appendix. Abbreviations have been extended where the meaning is clear. Parentheses have been kept as they appear in the texts; editors' interpolations are indicated by square brackets.

Titles of Office: In the interests of economy the editors have shortened the long formulaic title of the Russian Tsar and have indicated this by the addition of [ST] in the text, designating [Shortened Title]. However, the Tsar's title is not shortened in those places where the full title is an important component in court ceremonial and state ritual, for example, in Ziuzin's speech to King James at his first audience (Ziuzin, pp. 171–

---

1. Johannes Schultze, "Richtlinien für die äussere Textgestaltung bei Herausgabe von Quellen zur neueren deutschen Geschichte," *Blätter für deutsche Landesgeschichte* 102 (1966): 1–10.

173). In the cases where we have shortened the title it is in conjunction with present Soviet convention and with apologies to past Russian Tsars.[2]

Names of Persons and Places: The matter of standardizing foreign names in a text translated from the Russian for a non-Russian speaking audience was a challenge to the American editors. For known personages they chose to follow English custom, anglicizing most names, but not all. The system, reflecting current usage, is, in fact, anything but consistent! Duke Karl of Södermanland, for example, is most commonly known in the Anglo-Saxon world as King Charles IX after he assumed the Swedish throne, not as King Karl. Mikhail Romanov is known , of course, as Tsar Michael, but Tsar Fyodor remains Fyodor, not changing to Theodore. Indeed, what Englishman or American has heard of Tsar Theodore?! In cases like this, then, the editors have relied on custom rather than foolish consistency and left the names as they are most commonly known. In most instances, though, where we have anglicized and modernized names of persons, the editors have retained in footnotes (transliterated in Roman letters) old or peculiar spellings given in the original report, as in the case of Baldwin Hamey, who is referred to in the text in the Latinized form, Baldwinus Ameus. For names of persons not often referred to in English secondary works we have used the spelling most common in the person in question's country of origin. For the names of English persons priority is given to the spelling in the English *Dictionary of National Biography*, then in descending order to the *Calendars of State Papers, Acts of the Privy Council*, and so forth. The names of all places are modernized.

2. Various diplomats got into trouble about the Tsar's title. Selden reported (p. 148) the experience of Sir Giles Fletcher in *Titles of Honor* as follows: "[The Tsar's] style contains in it all the emperor's provinces and sets forth his greatness. And therefore they have a great delight and pride in it, forcing not only their own people but also strangers . . . to repeat the whole form from the beginning to end. . . . Myself when I had audience of the Emperor thought good to salute him only with thus much [of the title], viz., 'Emperor of all Russia, Great Duke of Volodemer, Mosko, and Novgorod, King of Cazan, King of Astracan'. The rest I omitted of purpose because I know they gloried to have their style appear to be of a larger volume than the Queen's of England. But this was taken in so ill part that the Chancellor (who then attended the Emperor with the rest of the nobility) with a loud chasing voice called still out upon me to say out the rest, whereto I answered that the Emperor's stile was very long and could not be so well remembered by strangers; that I had repeated so much of it, as might show that I gave honor to the rest, etc. But all would not serve till I commanded my interpreter to say it all out."

See also Sir Jerome Horsey's experience, SP 91/1, f. 86. The problem arose again in Moscow in 1638. See SP 102/49, f. 37 (printed in OSP 9: 49–52 and, for a contemporary translation, see HMC, *Cowper* 2: 177–179).

The most complex problem was the translation of Russian political and administrative terms, names of institutions, and titles of rank. Like other Russian emissaries in the West, Ziuzin and Vitovtov usually tried to give a Russian equivalent for the English term. Since Russian lacked the characteristic structure and terminology of feudalism, titles of rank presented them with considerable difficulty. The only inherited Russian title was prince (*kniaz'*), whose holder was not even necessarily a man of great wealth and position, for Russia lacked a system of primogeniture. Consequently the Russians had trouble with the English titles for earls, lords, marquises, and knights, usually translating the latter as "prince" (e.g., Sir Lewis Lewkenor). Sometimes they used "Lord," transliterated into Russian, but were not consistent even in that usage. The political structure of the English state and its various offices presented equal difficulty. The Privy Council and the House of Lords posed the greatest problem, as both seemed to the Russians to have some characteristics of their own Boyar duma, but not all. The Russians also designated certain Englishmen "near boyar" (*blizhnii boiarin*), a term which in Russia did not refer to a specific title or institution, and seems here to mean an aristocrat or official especially close to the crown. In some cases they seem to mean simply "privy councillor," but in others they mean either an informal relationship or simply an office they did not understand. As far as we were able to determine, their translations of designations of lesser office were also inconsistent, a fact which occasionally made identification difficult. Curiously, the one English institution which presented no difficulty in translation was parliament. That was simply "Assembly of the Land" (*Zemskii sobor*), a usage which may tell us much about their understanding of both institutions.[3]

Ziuzin and Vitovtov's reproduction of English proper names presented similar if lesser problems. English vowels and many consonants do not render well into Russian, and the use of the Cyrillic alphabet prevented them from taking the continental option of reproducing English spelling and leaving the pronunciation to the imagination. English first names that were not those of saints recognized in the Eastern church were a particular tangle. "William" generally came out to "Ul'ian", the Russian variant of Julian. King James himself appears as "James, the son of Andrew," though of course he was the son of Henry Stewart, Lord Darnley.[4]

---

3. The reporter of the 1581 embassy of Pisemskii struggled with the same problems and that text was helpful to the present editors in resolving some issues. In almost all cases its terminology was consistent with the usage in Ziuzin's report.

4. See Zuizin's account, below, n. 191.

The Russians were not questioning his paternity. The name Henry was unknown in Russia, but English Henries in 1581 as here come out as Andrews, perhaps because the translators were speaking Dutch or Low German to one another, where Henry is Hendrik, and the English or German aspirate was essentially silent to Russian ears. As with the problem of terminology, the result regarding the issue of names is that a few of the identifications are somewhat uncertain and are discussed in the notes.

The following are some of the terms that occur with sufficient frequency to merit discussion here:

gentry/gentleman: (*dvorianin, syn boiarskii, zhilets*). There are two separate issues here. In the lengthy accounts Ziuzin gave of the Time of Troubles, he used all the terms of rank current in Russian society at the time, and below the boyar aristocracy there were a number of such ranks which taken together encompassed the lesser landholding class, translated here as gentry. The other issue is the use of these Russian terms to designate rank or social status in England. Here again, a non-specific term seemed best for the English reader.

state/sovereignty: (*gosudarstvo*). In Russian usage of the time the same word, derived from *gosudar'*, the word for sovereign, was used to designate both the condition of sovereignty and the institution. In many cases both are actually meant or implied, and the choice of either produces a somewhat stilted English. The term, however, should not be modernized as it is itself a historical artefact, conveying the embryonic sense among seventeenth-century Russians of the state as an institution distinct from the person of the sovereign.

treasure/supplies (*kazna*). The Russian really means anything properly the property of the ruler, from artillery to the archives. Where appropriate, we have been literal and used the word "treasure"; in other cases where the indications were specific we have translated accordingly.

Finally, a number of titles of rank, Russian, Polish, and others are simply untranslatable (e.g., *okol'nichii, starosta*) and have been left in transcription and explained in the notes.

Dates: In the text dates of years appear according to the Eastern calendar (from the creation of the world). The editors have supplied the Western equivalents in square brackets following the Russian dates. In all cases in the Introduction and the annotation the years are given according to the Gregorian or New Style calendar. However, daily dates are given in both New Style and Old Style according to the nationality of the writer. That is, in the cases of English ambassadors, writing either to London or from London, the days are given according to the English or Old Style calendar which is ten days behind the Gregorian system in use

on the continent. On the other hand the dates of the reports and correspondence from Europeans and Scandinavians are given as they were
written, generally according to the New Style calendar. It should be
remembered that the Russians, however, like the English, used the Old
Style or Julian calendar in the seventeenth century, which means that
the daily dates (as opposed to the years) were the same in both countries,
although the English year began on 25 March and the Russian year
commenced on 1 September, as distinct from the European year which
started in January.

Russia in the System of International Relations from the Second Half of the Sixteenth to the first Half of the Seventeenth Century

V. I. Buganov

The internal disorder of the "Time of Troubles" at the beginning of the seventeenth century was closely bound up with external political factors that reflected Russia's position in the system of European and Asian states and her relations with neighboring countries. In the final analysis, these factors flowed from those problems of foreign affairs which, in the objective path of things, history placed before the Russian state at the end of the fifteenth century. That was the period of the elimination of the fragmentation caused by the appanage system, and the end of the yoke of oppression from the Golden Horde.

The government of Ivan III (1462–1503), the first sovereign of "all Russia," already began to carry out the foreign policy program formed by Moscow politicians up to that time. The policy's first point was a consequence of the incomplete process of regaining the ancient Rus' lands, which were lost during the age of appanage fragmentation and the foreign yoke. Their reunification, which stretched over several centuries, inevitably caused Russia to collide with the Grand Duchy of Lithuania and with Poland, for it was precisely to them that the lands passed, becoming known from the fifteenth to sixteenth centuries as the Ukraine and Belorussia. The Polish-Lithuanian Commonwealth, which came into being as a result of the unification of Poland and Lithuania (the Union of Lublin in 1569), also governed some of the Great Russian lands, and had pretensions to others as, for example, Pskov and Novgorod. Other neighbors, Sweden and the Livonian Order, hankered after them as well.

This position of the Polish-Lithuanian rulers destabilized the internal situation in Russia. Princes of various appanages that belonged to the uncles and brothers of the Moscow rulers, in their opposition to the latter, leaned on help from the West, appealed to it, or hoped for it. The grand princes and then the Muscovite tsars were compelled in the struggle with the remaining appanage figures to consider foreign factors.

The second point of the foreign policy program of Moscow flowed directly from the first: acquiring exits to the seas, primarily the Baltic and Black Seas, which were necessary to a young and growing state. Once, in the time of Kiev Rus', the state had had these outlets, for several coastal areas belonged to it: the Caspian, Azov, Black and Baltic Seas. But they passed to militant neighbors: the Golden Horde and Lithuania, Livonia and Sweden.

The third point of the program was the conclusion of the struggle with the Golden Horde which had oppressed Rus' for no less than two and a half centuries. From the 1420s to the 1460s it broke into a series of khanates: the Crimean in the Crimean Peninsula, Kazan', Astrakhan' along the central and lower Volga, the Great Horde, the Great Nogai Horde and the Lesser Nogai Horde in the Northern Caucasus, on the Caspian steppes beyond the Volga, Siberian and Western Siberian Khanate, and the Kazak and Uzbek to the south of it. A few of them, especially the Crimean Khanate, already from the end of the fourteenth century had become vassals of powerful Turkey, and the Kazan' Khanate strongly vexed Russia with frequent military invasions, raids, stealing of captives, demands for tribute, and ransom.

It is not difficult to notice the triune character of the origin of these problems that stood before the country and its leaders at the turn of the 15th-16th century.[1]

In the course of war at that time Moscow succeeded in returning to Russia various lands in the west and south-west (Briansk, Chernigov, Gomel', Viaz'ma, Smolensk and others with their surrounding areas). That is, ancient Russian possessions along the upper Desna, Oka, Dnieper, and Western Dvina rivers. Simultaneously, serious defeats at the hands of Russia shook the Livonian Order on the Baltic coast, also a long-time enemy.

In the first half of the sixteenth century Russia had to beat off frequent assaults by the Crimean Tatars from the south and Kazan' Tatars from the

---

1. K. V. Bazilevich, *Vneshniaia politika Russkogo tsentralizovannogo gosudarstva. Vtoraia polovina XV v.* (Moscow, 1952); A. A. Zimin, *Rossiia na poroge novogo vremeni (Ocherki politicheskoi istorii Rossii pervoi treti XVI v.)* (Moscow, 1972); A. A. Zimin, *Rossiia na rubezhe XV-XVI stoletii (Ocherki sotsial'no-politicheskoi istorii)* (Moscow, 1982).

east. In the middle of the century she moved to a decisive offensive in the east and included into Russia the Khanates of Kazan' in 1552 and Astrakhan' in 1556, and then Bashkiria and the Urals: the western side after the taking of Kazan, and the eastern, after the campaign of Ermak and the destruction of the Great Siberian khanate in the 1580s.[2] From the end of the sixteenth century Russia included a significant part of Western Siberia. (The beginning was at the end of the fifteenth century, when, as a result of the campaign of Muscovite generals, Moscow acquired the lands along the lower Ob'). The successes of the Eastern policy and the expansion of Russia beyond the "Rock" (as the Ural Mountains were then called) foreshadowed the swift advance of the Russian land and sea explorers—military servitors and traders, peasants and townspeople—into the "land under heaven"—Siberia—with its furs and other wealth. Within a century they had reached the shores of the Pacific Ocean.

In the course of the long Livonian war (1558–1583) Ivan the Terrible and his government attempted to resolve the Baltic problem. However, unlike the successes in the east, in the west, in the final analysis, Russia experienced failure. Despite victories at the end of the '50s and the mid '70s (at which time the Russian army had taken possession of almost all Livonia), the war ended indecisively with the loss of all conquests along the Baltic coast. Among the causes for this were the over-straining of the strength and abilities of the state and people, economic impoverishment, bad harvests and hunger, epidemics and the massive flight of the impoverished people to the borders, and the terrible shock of the *oprichnina*, with its terror and destruction.[3] Moreover, Russia had to fight on two fronts: in the north-west against Livonia, the Polish-Lithuanian State, and Sweden, and in the south against the Crimea and Turkey.[4]

2. V. V. Kargalov, *Na stepnoi granitse. "Oborona 'krymskoi Ukrainy'" Russkogo gosudarstva v pervoi polovine XVI stoletiia* (Moscow, 1974); R. G. Skrynnikov, *Ivan Groznyi* (Moscow, 1975); R. G. Skrynnikov, *Sibirskaia ekspeditsiia Ermaka* (Novosibirsk, 1986); A. A. Zimin and A. L. Khoroshkevich, *Rossiia vremeni Ivana Groznogo* (Moscow, 1982).

3. G. V. Forsten, *Baltiiskii vopros v XVI i XVII stoletiiakh (1544–1648)*, vols. 1–2 (St. Petersburg, 1893–1894); V. D. Koroliuk, *Livonskaia voina* (Moscow, 1954); A. A. Zimin, *Oprichnina Ivana Groznogo* (Moscow, 1964); A. A. Zimin, *V kanun groznykh potriasenii. Predposylki pervoi krest'ianskoi voiny v Rossii* (Moscow, 1986); R. G. Skrynnikov, *Nachalo oprichniny* (Leningrad, 1966). Skrynnikov, *Rossiia posle oprichniny* (Leningrad, 1975). The *Oprichnina* was the private administration and court of Ivan the terrible, set up in the years 1565–1570 as a weapon in his struggle with the boyar aristocracy. [For non-Russian readers the editors suggest reference to R. O. Crummey, The Formation of Muscovy 1304–1613, pp. 161–164, 170–172.]

4. N. A. Smirnov, *Rossiia i Turtsiia v XVI-XVII vv.* vols. 1–2 (Moscow, 1946); A. A.

The collapse of military efforts in the north-west meant failure for Russia in the attempt to decide the Baltic problem. In her hands remained only a scrap of land at the mouth of the Neva. The Russian towns of Ivangorod, Iam, and Kopor'e along the southern coast of the Gulf of Finland were transferred to the Swedes. They were successfully reconquered during the Russo-Swedish war of 1590–1593, but the "Time of Troubles" in the midst of the other shocks and failures, led to the loss of this outlet on the Baltic Sea coast. There remained, for ties with European states, only the White Sea, distant and cold. Here, at the mouth of the Northern Dvina, the city-port of Archangel (1584) was built and it was "the northern window" to Europe until the beginning of the Northern war, when Russia acquired St. Petersburg and other ports on the Baltic.

At the end of the sixteenth and beginning of the seventeenth centuries Russia strengthened her position beyond the Volga, the Urals, and in Western Siberia by way of economic assimilation, the building of towns, and the further advance of traders to the east. In the Northern Caucasus the dependence of Kabarda on Russia which had been lost during the Livonian War was renewed. Georgia became an ally of Moscow.

At the close of the sixteenth century one must recognize the internal situation of Russia to be very complex and unenviable. The fault for that was the economic and social crisis that enveloped the state, the growth of mass discontent of the population because of the disasters and burdens of the time of the *oprichnina* and the Livonian War, with the introduction of brutal enserfment legislation, and the struggle for power at the top (the "crisis at the top").

The position of Russia weakened noticeably in the international arena.

In the life of countries in West and Central Europe the sixteenth century was the beginning of the capitalist era and a struggle of two state-political concepts: a program of "universal monarchy," the "supranational" power of the Habsburgs (the Holy Roman Empire or the House of Austria) on the one side, and national absolutism on the other (France and England). Simultaneously this was the epoch of humanism, the Reformation, powerful anti-feudal peasant and plebeian movements, and of numerous heresies and sects. The complex situation provoked, on the one hand, opposition of the absolutist regimes of England and France to the half-hearted intention of the Empire to unite under its power all of

---

Novosel'skii, *Bor'ba Moskovskogo gosudarstva s tatarami v pervoi polovine XVII v.* (Moscow-Leningrad, 1948); G. D. Burdei, *Russko-turetskaia voina 1569 g.* (Saratov, 1962).

Europe; and on the other, their general struggle with the revolutionary pressure of the lower classes. It is known, for example, that Francis I, a passionate enemy of Charles V, Emperor of the Holy Roman Empire, in essence supported him during the Ghent rebellion of 1539–1540 in the Netherlands by giving passage to his army through the territory of France. But that same France, at first not supporting the Reformation in Germany, later, once its revolutionary wing was defeated by the German princes in subordination to the Holy Roman emperor, abruptly changed position and, in an alliance with the German Protestants, enemies of Charles V, she dealt a terrible blow to the Empire. In 1556 the latter broke up into two branches—the Spanish and the Austrian.[5]

By this time, the Ottoman Empire and the Russian state had become powerful factors of international life. And Europe had to consider this seriously. The Turks continually threatened the possessions of the German Empire. The Turkish danger compelled the Habsburgs, as well as the Pope, to look for help from the Moscow rulers. But those rulers were occupied with a struggle with Lithuania and the Livonian Order for the return of ancient Russian lands, an exit to the Baltic, and also with the khans—primarily the Golden Horde.

In the years of the Livonian War, Germany opposed "the Muscovite danger" (as the Livonian Order—an imperial fief—entered into the sphere of its interests). Emperor Ferdinand I officially sanctioned a trade blockade of Muscovy, that in actuality had been established already by his predecessor, Charles V. The Emperor and Papal Curia assisted the union of Poland and Lithuania in a dual state, the Polish-Lithuanian Commonwealth (1569). But, in concluding peace with the Ottomans in 1568, Austria, which recognized itself as her tributary, in essence untied Turkey's hands in the struggle with Russia, and in the following year a united Crimean-Turkish army completed a campaign in Astrakhan which ended, however, unsuccessfully.

By this time the beginnings of an "eastern barrier" against Russia had formed out of the Polish-Lithuanian State, Sweden, and Turkey. The Empire supported them in every way possible—materially, diplomatically, with mercenaries, and with a trade blockade of Russia. To a significant degree this aided the failure of Russia in the Livonian War. For the Empire, such an outcome was very beneficial.[6]

---

5. B. F. Porshnev, *Tridtsatiletniaia voina i vstuplenie v nee Shvetsii i Moskovskogo gosudarstva* (Moscow, 1976), 9–14.
6. B. F. Porshnev, *Tridtsatiletniaia voina*, 4–21; See also: I. B. Grekov, *Ocherki po istorii mezhdunarodnykh otnoshenii Vostochnoi Evropy XIV-XVI vv.* (Moscow, 1963); E.

The continuation of the struggle of the Habsburgs with national-absolutist England and France concluded at the end of the sixteenth century with the defeat of Philip II, the Spanish king. In the Netherlands, a bourgeois revolution was victorious, and a republic arose. The struggle of Protestantism with the feudal Catholic counter-reformation continued. That struggle placed Protestants in opposition to Catholic states, in particular opposing Sweden and the Polish-Lithuanian Commonwealth. Russia at the beginning of the 1590s benefitted, and regained for herself the land near the Gulf of Finland (Iam, Kopor'e, Ivangorod, Korela). At the beginning of the 1600s she intended to promote demands for the return of Narva and Dorpat (ancient Iur'ev) with their environs.

Again, the "eastern danger" became a problem for the Empire and Russian pretenders came to the fore in the guise of "true Russian princes," pretenders to the Moscow throne. The rulers of the Polish-Lithuanian State and the Catholic courts of Western Europe stood as their support. The goal of this venture, as was admitted by Sigismund III, the Polish-Lithuanian king, was interference in Moscow affairs, the spread of Catholicism in Eastern Europe and in the region of the Baltic Sea.

When the False Dmitrii I was killed in Moscow (17 May 1606), Charles IX, the Protestant Swedish king and uncle of Sigismund III, the Catholic Polish king, informed the new Russian tsar, Vasilii Shuiskii, that the German emperor, the Pope, and the Spanish king were behind Poland's acting against Russia. He repeated similar warnings in the following years saying that the loss of Russia's independence was threatened, and offering help. And at last Shuiskii agreed: the army of Jacob De la Gardie entered the Novgorod lands and began to rob and pillage. The Swedes supplemented the Polish-Lithuanian intervention, which took on an open form from 1609 (the beginning of the siege of Smolensk).[7]

Relations with the Polish-Lithuanian Commonwealth and Sweden, especially with the former, had been brought to the forefront for Russia already at the end of the previous century. After the Livonian War the Russian government in its attempted resolution of the Baltic problem collided with the active opposition of the Polish-Lithuanian politicians, especially Sigismund III. This king, ruler of Poland since 1587, received in 1592 the Swedish crown as well, but lost it six years later. According

---

Donnert, "Rossiia i baltiiskii vopros v politike Germanii 1558–1583 gg.," Is-
toricheskie zapiski, vol. 76 (1965).

7. B. F. Porshnev, Tridtsatiletnaia voina, 21–33.

to the Tiavzino peace treaty of 1595 the Moscow government, fearing hostile activity on the part of Poland, agreed to include in it a clause concerning the Swedish monopoly on trade in the Baltic Sea. It would become a "Swedish lake." Swedish policy along the Eastern Baltic acquired an even greater expansionist character—the eyes of the court of Stockholm were directed toward Russian and Polish-Lithuanian possessions. And on their side, too, the Polish-Lithuanian politicians also dreamed about the Baltic coast.

At the beginning of the 1600s, in the course of negotiations with Swedish and Polish-Lithuanian representatives, Russian diplomats attempted to move forward a resolution to the question of an outlet to the Baltic, sometimes relying on Sweden, sometimes on the Polish-Lithuanian Commonwealth. But these attempts were not crowned with success. After the break in the Polish-Swedish dynastic union Sigismund III did not retain hopes for the realization of plans that were frankly chimerical: mastery of the Swedish kingdom and the political subordination of Russia, in the latter case, with the complete removal from the agenda of the question of the return to Moscow of the Ukrainian and Belorussian lands.

The projects of a sort of "federation" of two governments—the Polish-Lithuanian State and Russia—prepared in the last quarter of the sixteenth century by the Polish-Lithuanian and Russian sides, were not realized, since the ruling groups of both countries pursued differing goals: the ruling elite and gentry of Russia attempted to regain the lands of Ancient Rus', the Kievan inheritance of the Moscow sovereigns; the Polish magnates and gentry wanted not only to preserve their Ukrainian and Belorussian possessions, but also to convert particular Russian lands into an object of feudal colonization. This last they tried to realize during the years of the Russian "Time of Troubles" when military actions were organized in the neighboring Slavic government.

The beginning of the "Time of Troubles" stimulated the aggressive plans of both Poland and Sweden. Their interventions, on the one hand, weakened Russia and the Polish-Lithuanian Commonwealth, on the other hand, they made possible the formation of Sweden as a great power on the Baltic Sea.[8]

The relations of Russia with the Western European states at the end of the sixteenth and beginning of the seventeenth centuries were not so

8. B. N. Floria, *Russko-pol'skie otnosheniia i baltiiskii vopros v kontse XVI-nachale XVII v.* (Moscow, 1973); B. N. Floria, *Russko-pol'skie otnosheniia i politicheskoe razvitie Vostochnoi Evropy vo vtoroi polovine XVI-nachale XVII v.* (Moscow, 1978).

lively. For example, the Russian government exchanged letters with the French court which were sent by courier. The first Russian embassy to France was in 1615–1616 (I. Kondyrev and M. Neverov); the first French one to Russia in 1629 (Baron Courmenin).[9] From the middle of the sixteenth century the Netherlands arranged trading ties with the Russian state. The English and Danes were the rivals to their merchants. The Netherlanders traded even in the years of the "troubles," but after their end, England and the Netherlands set up diplomatic relations with Russia. Kondyrev and Neverov, without the knowledge of France, visited the Netherlands, conducting negotiations with the local authorities. Dutch diplomatic representatives appeared in Moscow later.[10]

In the second half of the sixteenth century Russia engaged in a lively trade with England. But negotiations for a military alliance, which were conducted at the end of the '60s and beginning of the '80s, were never brought to a conclusion; the English side drew back, not wanting to be drawn into a conflict in Eastern Europe. Simultaneously, negotiations for such an alliance took place with Sweden, but these too came to nothing.

Philip II displayed an interest in Russia, dreaming of her help against the Turks and even of converting Russia to Catholicism, and joining her to his possessions. Nicholas von Warkotsch, residing in Moscow in the 1580s as an ambassador of Germany, came forth as *de facto* representative of Spain. He and his adviser, the Netherlander, Van der Walle, an agent of the "Spanish King," tried to incline Moscow politicians against the Turks and the English. But Moscow did not wish to conduct war against the Ottoman Porte, nor to lose trade with England. Tsars Fyodor Ivanovich and Boris Godunov confirmed the privileges of the English merchants. Russia continued trade with the Netherlands, despite the insurrection of local "rebels" against their monarch, the King of Spain.[11]

Relations with Turkey and the Crimea in the second half of the sixteenth century were complex and difficult. Both of these states carried out an openly aggressive policy toward Russia. Suffice it to say, that of the

9. G. Zhordaniia, Ocherki iz istorii franko-russkikh otnoshenii kontsa XVI i pervoi poloviny XVII v., pt. 1 (Tbilisi, 1959); V. D. Preobrazhenskii, "Franko-russkie otnosheniia v XVI-XVII vv.," *Uchenye zapiski Iaroslavskogo pedinstituta*, vyp. VII, Istoriia (Iaroslavl, 1945).

10. V. A. Kordt, "Ocherk snoshenii Moskovskogo gosudarstva s Respublikoiu Soedinennykh Niderlandov po 1631 g.," *Sbornik Russkogo istoricheskogo obshchestva*, vol. 116 (St. Petersburg, 1902).

11. Ia. S. Lur'e, "Russko-angliiskie otnosheniia i mezhdunarodnaia politika vtoroi poloviny XVI v.," *Mezhdunarodnye sviazi Rossii do XVII v. Sb. statei* (Moscow, 1961), 419–443.

25 years of the Livonian war, 21 years were marked by assaults or invasions of Crimean Tatars. Some of them were devastating. For example, in 1571 the Crimean army pillaged all the land to the south of Moscow, reached the capital itself and put it to the torch. In the following year, Devlet Girey, the Crimean Khan, with a huge army, again invaded Russia with the aim of conquest—a real threat to the national independence of the state. An army of the "land" of Prince M. I. Vorotynskii saved the country (an *oprichnina* army had suffered a shameful defeat one year earlier) in a battle lasting several days on the Oka River near Serpukhov, and on the Lopasna River by the village of Moloda, smashing the conqueror. For a while the Crimeans were quiet. Then assaults were renewed along the southern border of Russia. In 1591 they again reached Moscow, but were defeated under its walls. The Great Nogai Horde, attempting to restore independence from Moscow, also carried out raids on Russian lands (in the '70s and first half of the '80s). In the second half of the '80s the Russian government again subjected the Great Nogais to its power.

At the end of the century Crimean and Nogai assaults on Russia almost completely halted. From 1593 on the Crimea and Turkey began a long and exhausting war with the Habsburgs, Hungary, Moldavia and Poland.

A change of course occurred in 1607 when they ceased the above-mentioned campaign and the Crimea concluded an alliance with Poland against Russia stricken by the "troubles." Again raids by the Crimeans followed, in which the Great Nogais took part. Peaceful relations of the Crimea and the Nogai Hordes with Russia were resumed only in 1616–1617.[12]

Trading ties with Turkey were set up in Russia fairly early, from the second half of the sixteenth century. From the end of this century diplomatic contacts began, and the exchange of ambassadors. Right up to 1569, in spite of the absence of any treaty of alliance, relations were more or less peaceful in character. But after the annexation of Kazan' and Astrakhan' by Russia and the establishment of the Great Nogais and Kabardians in vassal dependence to her, the situation changed sharply. There followed new raids by the Crimeans and the campaign of a Turko-Crimean army to Astrakhan' in 1569.[13] The ensuing failure put an end to the attempts of Turkey to fight with Russia for the mouth of the Volga, but did not stop the attempts of the Ottomans to push the Russians from

12. A. A. Novosel'skii, *Bor'ba Moskovskogo gosudarstva s tatarami v pervoi polovine XVII v.* (Moscow-Leningrad, 1948), 17–44.

13. N. A. Smirnov, *Rossiia i Turtsiia*, 1:68–120.

the Caucasus. These continued until the beginning of the seventeenth century; moreover, the sultans gave to the Crimea, their vassal, an active military role. Russian politicians, in opposition to this onslaught, relied on the power of their own state, the rising activity of the Don Cossacks, and conducted negotiations with the opponents of Turkey, the Persian Shah and the Holy Roman Emperor. At that time Moscow in no way put forward plans of war against Turkey itself, which remained a very awesome enemy.[14]

Diplomatic relations were in place with Iran from the middle of the sixteenth century. After the conquest of Kazan' a Persian envoy, Seiidhussein, appeared in Moscow in 1553. In response, Ivan IV directed his envoy to Iran. The representatives of both states discussed questions of importance for them regarding an alliance against Turkey and the Crimea and for this they encouraged the Pope, the Doge of Venice, and the King of Spain. However, wars with their enemies long prevented Russia and Persia from concluding a treaty. Only in 1602 did both sides agree on joint activities against Turkey. For two years the Russian detachment of I. M. Buturlin marched toward Derbent (Dagestan), where there was a Turkish garrison. But failure awaited him. The death of Boris Godunov, the Russian tsar, and the adventures of the pretender prevented the fulfillment of the campaign.

Common interests in opposition to allies of Turkey—the *shamkhal* in Dagestan, Bukhara in Central Asia and Khan Kuchum in Western Siberia—also united Iran and Russia.

In the years of the "Time of Troubles" Russia in practice ignored eastern affairs. True, Abbas I, the Persian Shah, formed ties with both the False Dmitriis and the government of V. I. Shuiskii; his goal was to receive some kind of help in the war with Turkey which Persia was conducting at this time. Thus, he counted on the aid of Russian Cossacks in the Northern Caucasus (the town of Tersk and others) against the Turks, and on income from northern trade.

After the accession of Michael Romanov a Russian ambassador was sent out to Iran and ties between both countries were renewed. Abbas I, at Moscow's request, rendered financial help to Russia. Trade relations were arranged. In the correspondence of the sovereigns with one another friendship and an alliance between Russia and Iran were discussed.[15]

14. N. A. Smirnov, *Rossiia i Turtsiia*, 120–159.
15. A. P. Novosel'tsev, "Russko-iranskie politicheskie otnosheniia vo vtoroi polovine XVI v.," *Mezhdunarodnye sviazi Rossii do XVII v. Sb. Statei* (Moscow, 1981), 444–461; A. P. Novosel'tsev, "Russko-iranskie otnosheniia v pervoi polovine XVII v.,"

The penetration of Russia into the Northern Caucasus after the annexation of the Astrakhan' Khanate in 1556, the incorporation of the Kabardians, and the appearances of Russian towns and garrisons on the Terek river, provoked the dissatisfaction of two strong military-feudal monarchies: Turkey and Iran. The latter warred between themselves over the Caucasus. At first, in the sixteenth century, it was possible to speak of the predominance of Turkey in this region—she had taken almost all of Trans-Caucasia and had reached the Caspian sea, and together with the Crimea she was active in the Northern Caucasus as well. At the beginning of the following century the advantage passed from the weakened Porte to the Safavid state of Shah Abbas.

Russian presence and influence in the Northern Caucasus permitted Moscow to oppose the Turkish-Tatar danger along the southern perimeter of their possessions, to guard the Volga route, and to develop trade with countries in the Caspian region.[16]

The stormy conditions of the "Time of Troubles" in Russia coincided with significant changes in the remaining parts of Europe. In 1606 the war of Turkey with the Habsburgs ended. In Germany an offensive began of the Catholic counter-reformation against the Protestants—Lutherans and Calvinists—who had united their forces in 1608 in the Protestant, or Evangelical, Union. It stood in opposition to the Catholic league, formed in the following year. War became imminent between them and the states which supported them; on the side of the Protestant Union stood England, the Netherlands, France, and Sweden; on the Catholic side were Austria (Germany), Spain, and the Polish-Lithuanian Commonwealth. True, the internal opposition in the possessions of the Austrian Habsburgs (the insurrection of Stephen Bocskay 1604–1606, the struggle for the throne between Rudolph II of Hapsburg and his brother Matthew, the religious disputes) delayed the outbreak of the European war, but not for long. Besides this, they played their role in Russian affairs: in Vienna they awaited with impatience the victorious conclusion of the Polish Lithuanian intervention in Russia, for the success of the Catholic offensive in North-East Europe would become the signal for mobilization in Western and Central Europe. But Russia, it would seem, almost on its knees, continued resistance. In 1609 Sweden arrived to help her. In order to distract Sweden, Habsburg diplomacy encouraged the Danish court in

Mezhdunarodnye sviazi Rossii v XVII–XVIII vv. (Ekonomika, politika i kul'tura). Sb. statei (Moscow, 1966), 103–121.

16. E. N. Kusheva, Narody Severnogo kavkaza i ikh sviazi s Rossiei. Vtoraia polovina XVI-30-e gody XVII v. (Moscow, 1963).

war against Charles IX. The Danish-Swedish war of 1611–1613 ended with Gustav II Adolf's, the new Swedish king's, conclusion of peace with Denmark, and also of a truce with Poland. This allowed both Sweden and the Polish-Lithuanian Commonwealth to be active again in their efforts in Russia. But the entrance into the arena of struggle by the people, who rose up in patriotic war against the foreign invaders, concluded with the expulsion of the Polish-Lithuanian army from Russia. And in 1613 the Assembly of the Land chose Michael Fyodorovich Romanov as Tsar. He became the founder of a new dynasty of Russian tsars, recognized at once by England and the Netherlands. They laid the groundwork for a Russo-Swedish truce that led eventually to the conclusion of the Stolbovo Peace of 1617 that ended Swedish intervention in Russia.

Among the countries of the anti-Habsburg coalition, especially England and the Netherlands, the question of trade with Russia played an essential role. To be exact, those countries received from the Russian market strategic goods necessary for the outfitting of the fleet (canvas, hemp, tar, masts, ropes), as well as other valuable commodities (leather, wax, felt, furs, honey, etc.). Trading operations of both countries with the Muscovites were not broken even during the years of the "Troubles"; on the contrary, they expanded. In the course of embittered rivalry, Dutch merchants pushed the English from first place into second; trade with Russia, from the standpoint of contemporaries, became one of the sources of the economic power of the Netherlands. Russia had great importance for Western Europe for the transit trade from Persia as well.

In the event of its success Polish-Lithuanian intervention in Russia would benefit the Habsburgs by the breakdown of English and Dutch trade in the east. Therefore financial and military help was sent from Austria to Poland, whose emissaries hired mercenaries in Habsburg lands.

Poland, with the help of the Empire, had already attempted to realize her plans of conquest in the east. But even she was forced to resign herself to a truce with Russia at Deulino in 1618. The sending of the army headed by Prince Wladyslaw (the pretender to the Moscow throne from the time of the Russian "regency of seven") and the active support of the Empire did not help.

Russia saved her national independence. But when the price had to be paid, it was not small: the southern and eastern coast of the Gulf of Finland remained in the hands of Sweden; the Polish-Lithuanian Commonwealth kept the Russian lands of Smolensk, Chernigov, and Novgorod-Severskii. Their return became a problem for the future, but while Moscow politicians waited there were more current, pressing affairs.

The Russian government in the years from 1613 to 1615 directed ambassadors to various countries: to the Netherlands—Ushakov and Zaborovskii; to England—Ziuzin and Vitovtov; to Denmark—Bariatinskii and Bogdanov, etc. They notified foreign governments of the ascension to the throne of the first Romanov. After concluding peace with Sweden and a truce with Poland it became clear in Russia that the plans of the Habsburgs and their Polish-Lithuanian allies in the east had suffered a blow. But the Russian state, after the internal and external shakeup, was seriously weakened.

The Habsburgs considered such a situation in Eastern Europe very beneficial for the struggle for an all-European Catholic empire. The Thirty Years War that began in 1616–1618 made possible the end of the repeated attempts of the Polish-Lithuanian State again to grab Russian lands, threatening her with the loss of national and state independence.[17]

In the ambassadorial book published below the activity of the Russian ambassador in England, Alexis Ziuzin is described, which, as was explained above, occurred in very complex international circumstances. The materials of this important mission very clearly and convincingly speak of this complexity. They give valuable testimony of the situation of Russia and England at the beginning of the seventeenth century, when Russia was concluding a difficult period, and the West was occupied by the dawn of its own "Time of Troubles"—the Thirty Years War.

---

17. B. F. Porshnev, *Tridtsatiletnaia voina*, 33–56; O. L. Vainshtein, "Rossiia i Tridtsatiletniaia voina 1618–1648 gg.," *Ocherki iz istorii vneshnei politiki Moskovskogo gosudarstva v pervoi polovine XVII v.* (Moscow, 1947), 12–42.

The "Ambassadorial Book on the Ties between Russia and England 1613–1614" as a Historical Source

N. Rogozhin

Ambassadorial books are among the most important sources for the history of Russia in the period of the formation and strengthening of the centralized state. Quite varied in the character of their information, they have increasingly attracted the attention of historians as a valuable source for the history of foreign affairs, embassy ceremony, historical geography and linguistics. They are also interesting as literature.

In all, more than 760 ambassadorial books have been preserved, which are located in 24 fonds in TsGADA [The Central State Archive of Ancient Acts]. They encompass the period from the end of the fifteenth to the beginning of the sixteenth century. The books in question have been described by the author in his account of the contents of ambassadorial books up to the beginning of the eighteenth century along with a list of their publication.[1] Special literature on the ambassadorial books is fairly meager; their study as sources, in essence, has only begun. In many instances, the subject of study continues to be only the "lists of articles," included in the early embassy books and described below. Therefore, we must first turn our attention to the history of the formation of ambassadorial books, their formulary depending on the period of their formation, on the importance of the embassy in question, and on the location of its activity.[2]

Documentation reflecting activity of the Russian embassies abroad

---

1. N. M. Rogozhin, *Obzor posol'skikh knig iz fondov-kollektsii, khraniashchikhsia v TsGADA* (Moscow, 1990).
2. See: *Oko vsei velikoi Rossii. Ob istorii russkoi diplomaticheskoi sluzhby XVI–XVII vekov* (Moscow, 1989).

became continually more elaborate as the process of diplomatic practice evolved. It included a variety of documents: credentials, responses, treaties and accompanying documents, instructions to the ambassador, news from the Russian representative abroad, and accounts of the ambassador. The composition of the embassy documentation and its increase in volume are closely tied to the general process of the formation and development of a single Russian state. From the end of the fifteenth century as international ties increased there arose the demand for regulation and systematization of diplomatic documents. Precisely at this time the first ambassadorial books appeared, as collations of the documentation enumerated above. Books, as a manner of keeping records, added to and standardized documents which already had become insufficient in addressing the growing demands of the state. "Notebooks," created from the merging of treaties and princely wills, preceded the appearance of books. In the process of the formation of the administration of a single Russian state this mode of record keeping in the first half of the sixteenth century was widely used.

The Foreign Office, formed toward the middle of the sixteenth century, systematized and supplemented the existing documents. Starting in the 1560s, the form of an embassy account became permanent in the shape of "lists of articles" which were given their titles in conjunction with the manner of presentation of material. An active foreign policy, an increase in information, the impossibility to act strictly in accordance with points of instruction, bring the accounts to the point where the reports became more complete and took on the form of journals. Besides this, in the structure of the ambassadorial books, separate material was included that touched directly on the equipment of Russian embassies: lists of gifts, memoranda on the extent of petitions to embassy members, travel instructions for various military governors and their formal replies. Along with various other documents ambassadorial books even have accounts by the actual compilers, in other words, reports of arrivals and departures of ambassadors and couriers; lists of people who were present at diplomatic receptions; short accounts of the decisions of the tsar and boyar duma. Though they are not diplomatic documents, these materials are directly linked to them and present themselves as an inseparable part of the ambassadorial books.

Thus, in the majority of the ambassadorial books we see a logically connected account of diplomatic relations, separated according to countries, in strict chronological succession, and not a collection of separate, unrelated documents. Therefore, these books are a multifaceted administrative source that includes various documents; they have a unique formulary and each of them demands external and internal criticism, and then a general evaluation of the structure of each section of the ambassadorial book.

Scrolls of the foreign office which described foreign ties of the Russian state served as a primary source for the compiling of the ambassadorial books. Inventories of the archive of the Foreign Office for 1614 and 1626 single out, within the structure of that archive, originals of the charters and treaties, scrolls and books, which were all equally to be preserved. However, in the ambassadorial books themselves a considerable number of documents were preserved which did not survive to our day in any other form, either original or copy. As a result, the significance of the ambassadorial books as a historical source is even greater. Moreover, it is therefore possible to trace the interrelation of the ambassadorial books and the scrolls, that is to say, the interrelation of primary and secondary sources, when one or the other collection is more or less full.

The published ambassadorial book relating to the ties between Russia and England in 1613–1614[3] contains materials of the embassy of A. I. Ziuzin and A. G. Vitovtov to England. The book serves as a valuable source for the study of the period known as the "The Time of Troubles" in the answers of the Russian envoys to questions of the English courtiers characterizing the foreign and domestic position of the Russian state to 1613. It also provides the correspondence of the Foreign Office with local military governors giving an idea of the organization of the embassy, of embassy ceremony, and the itinerary and escort of the embassy. The book further contains information of Russian subjects, G. Alfer'ev and his companions, who were sent to England for education during the reign of Tsar Boris Godunov. One entry depicts interest in an attempt on the life of King James I by adherents of the Pope in 1605 ("The GunPowder Plot"), which A. I. Ziuzin incorporated in his list of articles from the verbal accounts of English courtiers. The book is also significant for its vivid portrayal of the ceremonies of the inauguration of London's Lord Mayor and the audience of the Russian envoys with James I, etc.

After his ascent to the tsar's throne Michael Fyodorovich sent A. I. Ziuzin and A. G. Vitovtov to London in June 1613 bearing tidings of this event and additional orders were given to the envoys. They were to request aid against the Polish and Swedish kings, to dispatch to Moscow money, gunpowder, lead, and other military supplies. Regarding the request for monetary aid, A. I. Ziuzin received an evasive answer, but soon after his return to Moscow (October 1614), in December of that same year, came an envoy of the English King, John Merrick. Merrick's me-

---

3. TsGADA, fond 35, opis' 1, delo 3.

diation in the Russo-Swedish negotiations played a definite role in the conclusion of the Peace of Stolbovo in 1617. The embassy of A. I. Ziuzin and A. G. Vitovtov played a not unimportant role in the process of preparing for this.[4]

When A. I. Ziuzin was sent to England on June 20th, 1613 the Foreign Office was administered by the duma secretary, P. A. Tret'iakov. He held that position from June 1613 until May 1618. In 1608–1610 Tret'iakov was a duma secretary in the "Tushino camp" after which he changed to the side of the Moscow boyar government. In 1611 he turned out to be in the camp of Prince D. M. Trubetskoi and the Cossack I. M. Zarutskii, and on 25 January 1612, together with the Moscow boyars, ratified a charter for Iaroslavl' and Kostroma which summoned the inhabitants to obey Prince Wladyslaw. In November 1612 the secretary was a member of the militia of Prince D. M. Pozharskii; during the reign of Michael Romanov he headed the Foreign Office until 1618.[5] S. A. Belokurov named Savva Romanchukov (1613–1624) as the assistant to the head of the Foreign Office during the period under review. He is mentioned among a number of subsecretaries of the Foreign Office from 1594 to 1610, and became the second secretary in the reign of Michael Romanov.[6]

Among the sources which sprang up directly in the course of the embassy, and efficiently reflected its stages, an important place is occupied in the ambassadorial books by the instructions, at the base of which are earlier documents. An instruction, called "nakaz" in Russian, was composed before the departure of the mission. In it are enumerated in detail not only the intended tasks of the embassy, but also its duties, expected norms of behavior abroad, possible speeches, and answers to questions of the foreigners. The instruction set forth the most detailed directions not only regarding the tasks of the embassy, but also the means of fulfilling them. Already in 1911 A. I. Zaozerskii turned his attention to the exceptional importance of the instruction to A. I. Ziuzin as a historical source, as it characterized the standard of Moscow diplomacy at the beginning of the seventeenth century.[7]

---

4. N. P. Lyzhin, *Stolbovskii dogovor i dogovory, emu predshestvovavshie* (St Petersburg, 1857).
5. S. A. Belokurov, *O Posol'skom prikaze* (Moscow, 1906), 106–109; S. B. Veselovskii, *D'iaki i pod''iachie XV–XVII vv.* (Moscow, 1975), 522–523; P. G. Liubomirov, *Ocherki istorii nizhegorodskogo opolcheniia. 1611–1613 gg.* (Moscow, 1939), 295.
6. S. A. Belokurov, *Ukaz. soch.*, 116.
7. A. I. Zaozerskii, "K kharakteristike moskovskoi diplomatii XVII v.," *Sb. St., posviashchennykh S. F. Platonovu* (St. Petersburg, 1911), 335.

The embassy of A. I. Ziuzin, naturally, was not the only embassy. The government of Michael Romanov in 1613 almost simultaneously dispatched embassies to Poland (February)[8], and to the Nogai Tatars (March),[9] to Austria (June),[10] to Turkey (June),[11] to the Patriarch of Constantinople (June),[12] to Denmark (July),[13] to the Crimea (October),[14] and Persia (November).[15]

Ambassadorial books describe all of these embassies. As a whole, the ambassadorial books of these nine countries represent a unique monument of the record-keeping of the Foreign Office at the beginning of the seventeenth century. Instructions were placed in them that had been prepared in the Foreign Office separately for each embassy. They contained complaints against the Polish and Swedish kings with an account of the history of the "Smuta", or "Time of Troubles", a description of the devastation of the Russian state, the announcement of the ascent to the throne of Michael Romanov, and various requests regarding financial, military, and diplomatic help, and regarding the exchange of prisoners, etc. The most detailed instructions were given to the embassies traveling to England,[16] Austria,[17] and Denmark[18] while the instructions to other embassies were an abbreviated variant of one or another degree.

Among the earliest Romanov embassies was the mission of D. G. Olad'in to Poland (February 1613).[19] The decision was made to send him on 2 February 1613, but the ambassador left on 11 March 1613, already cognizant of Michael Romanov's occupation of the throne.[20] The main point of the embassy was the final Russian refusal to invite King Sigismund and his son Wladyslaw to the throne of the tsar, while simultaneously initiating negotiations for an exchange of prisoners. The instructions for D. G. Olad'in and A. I. Ziuzin coincide in their ideological stance and chronological sequence, but textually they diverge signifi-

8. TsGADA, f. 79, op. 1, d. 29 (kniga).

9. TsGADA, f. 127, op. 1, d. 3 (1613—stolbets).

10. TsGADA, f. 32, op. 1, d. 1 (1613—stolbets).

11. TsGADA, f. 89, op. 1, d. 1 (1613—stolbets).

12. TsGADA, f. 52, op. 1, d. 1 (1613—stolbets).

13. TsGADA, f. 53, op. 1, d. 3 (kniga); Tam zhe, d. 1 (1613—stolbets).

14. TsGADA, f. 123, op. 1, d. 1 (1613—stolbets).

15. TsGADA, f. 77, op. 1, d. 1 (1613—stolbets).

16. TsGADA, f. 35, op. 1, d. 3, listy 1–163.

17. TsGADA, f. 32, op. 1, d. 1, ll. 1–137.

18. TsGADA, f. 53, op. 1, d. 3, ll. 1–214.

19. TsGADA, f. 79, op. 1, d. 29; Sbornik Russkogo istoricheskogo obshchestva (Moscow, 1913), 142:310–420 (hereafter cited as Sb. RIO).

20. Sb. RIO, 142:xiii.

cantly since they pursue different goals. For example, A. I. Ziuzin had to stress continually Michael Romanov's election to the Russian throne, while D. G. Olad'in, on the other hand, limited himself to a report to the Poles of the decision of the boyars and all the people to choose a Russian tsar. Probably, the instructions were compiled by various people who possibly used some common source containing an account of the events of the "Time of Troubles."

D. M. Pozharskii, in June of 1612 sent a letter to Emperor Rudolf II with a request to render monetary assistance, and to begin negotiations with the Polish king "so that he would order all sorts of soldiers to withdraw from Moscow."[21] The letter has a sort of introduction with a narration of the "Time of Troubles." As P. A. Tret'iakov may have participated in the letter's composition (see above), one may conclude that an analogous document(s) from it was (or were) used in order to compose the instructions for D. G. Olad'in, A. I. Ziuzin, and others. All three documents have more than a little textual agreement, for example, in the explanation of the causes of the "Troubles."

The letter of D. M. Pozharskii: "And King Sigismund destroyed the treaty of peace and betrayed his oath that had been affirmed with tsar Boris, he promised to such a thief [G. Otrep'ev—N. R.] all kinds of help with people and treasure. . . ."[22]

The instruction for D. G. Olad'in: "And their Grand Duke [Sigismund III—N. R.] in violation of oath sent to the Moscow state a thief, the former monk Grishka Otrep'eva, thinking to bring internecine strife to the Moscow state and to ruin [it].[23]

The instruction to Ziuzin: "And King Sigismund destroyed the treaty of peace and betrayed his oath that had been confirmed with tsar Boris and his servants, and having communicated with the Roman pope, and gave to that thief as help, much money and men. . . ."

Clearly, in meaning all three variations concur or are close, but textually only the letter of D. M. Pozharskii and the instruction to A. I. Ziuzin agree. The instruction to A. I. Ziuzin contains information on the ties of Sigismund III with the Roman pope. Compilers of that instruction took into consideration the spread of Protestantism in England, which had been accompanied by a complete break in relations with Rome.[24]

---

21. *Pamiatniki diplomaticheskikh snoshenii drevnei Rossii c derzhavami inostrannymi*, vol. 2 (St. Petersburg, 1852), 1428 (hereafter cited as *Pamiatniki*).
22. *Pamiatniki*, 1410–1411.
23. *Sb. RIO* 142:327.
24. A. L. Morton, *Istoriia Anglii* (Moscow, 1950), 155–165.

These important elements were reflected in the instruction to Ziuzin.

To continue, the letter of Pozharskii: "A certain thief, a monk, a heretic by the name of Grishka Otrep'ev, fled from the Moscow state to Lithuania and, casting off his monastic habit named himself Tsarevich Dmitrii Uglitskii. . . ."[25]

This information is not in the instructions to D. G. Olad'in.

The instruction to A. I. Ziuzin: "A certain thief, a monk, a heretic by the name of Grishka Otrep'ev, fled away from the Moscow state as a result of his evil work loathsome to God, and casting off his monastic habit, gave a written promise to the enemies, that if he took the throne of the tsar he would be excommunicate from God, and called himself . . . Tsarevich Dmitrii Uglitskii.

The instruction to A. I. Ziuzin was supplemented with information on the promise to G. Otrep'ev to convert to Catholicism in the event that he rose to the throne; this also was calculated to get a negative reaction from the English.

And still another example, from the letter of D. M. Pozharskii: "And to him [False Dmitrii II—N. R.] came to the borderland by order of the king, Roman Rozhynski, Prince Adam Wisniowiecki, Jan-Piotr Sapieha, calling themselves hetmen or colonels, Aleksandr Zborowski, the Tyszkewiczes and other colonels and cavalry captains with many Poles and Lithuanians. And they began to distribute seditious letters in all the Sever lands, to cities and provinces, which named that thief Lord Tsar and Grand Prince Dmitrii.[26]

The instruction to D. G. Olad'in: "And Poles and Lithuanians, the Prince Roman Rozynski, Aleksandr Zborowski, Prince Adam Wisniowiecki, Jan-Piotr Sapieha, with many of your Poles and Lithuanians naming another thief in place of the thief who had been killed, and came with him to the walls of the ruling city of Moscow.[27]

The instruction to Ziuzin: "And to him came to the borderland, by order of the King, many notable Poles and Lithuanians—Prince Roman Rozynski, Aleksandr Zborowski, Prince Adam Wisniowiecki, Jan-Piotr Sapieha, Samuel and Jan Tyszkewicz, calling themselves hetmen and colonels and other colonels and cavalry captains with many Poles and Lithuanians. And they began to distribute seditious letters in all the Sever lands in cities and provinces naming that thief the former thief Dmitrii."

25. *Pamiatniki*, 1410.
26. *Pamiatniki*, 1418.
27. *Sb. RIO* 142:327.

Again, all three redactions of the story are unified in meaning, but the instruction to A. I. Ziuzin almost entirely repeats the letter of D. M. Pozharskii, with insignificant changes and additions: in place of "Tysz-kewiczes," appears "Samuel and Jan Tyszkewicz" and the words "many notable Poles and Lithuanians" are added. The instruction and the letter have, as much as one could tell, textual similarity. Possibly, R. A. Tret'ia-kov composed the letter, then used it in the instructions to other embassies, and it is not to be excluded that he himself corrected the draft of the instructions to Ziuzin.

Introduction

Aleksei Ziuzin's embassy to London in November 1613 added a new dimension to James I's schemes for an alliance with the Protestant kingdoms of the north. Now, for the first time in nearly fifteen years, Russia was again a participant in these maneuvers. Marking the end of the isolation of civil war Tsar Michael looked to England for an alliance that would appeal to James's Protestant proclivities while securing Russia against further depredation by the Poles.

Precedent pointed the way to Whitehall. The newly elected Tsar, first of the Romanovs, was looking for "communication by former custom, when the state of Moscow was in peace and quiet with the English state."[1] Relations between the two countries under Queen Elizabeth, Ivan IV (the Terrible), and Boris Godunov had been for the most part amicable. But those were the years before the political polarization of religion in alliances on the Continent. Now with the Catholic states of Germany and King Sigismund III of Poland in league with the house of Habsburg, including the Spanish Netherlands, James was working more aggressively to bolster English influence with the Protestant princes while at the same time strengthening his ties in Scandinavia, whose interests he saw as synonymous with his own. In 1610 Marc' Antonio Correr reported from London that the success of the Poles was displeasing to James. When affairs in Germany are settled, he wrote to the Doge in Venice, James will see to it that Swedish interests are supported, for the King views them as "identical with his own and those of Denmark, his brother-in-law."[2] Although it has been accepted belief that England had a natural affinity with Denmark even before James's marriage to Anne, that relationship between the two countries had been complicated over the years by Danish commercial ties with the Iberian peninsula and the Spanish Netherlands and by the influence of the pro-Imperial faction at the court in Copenhagen. One month before Ziuzin arrived in England, Sir Stephen Lesieur reported to James that the talk of Christian IV's recent embassy to Spain was endless, "the more for that the papists give

---

1. See Ziuzin, p. 158 and n. 21. Throughout the annotation to this Introduction the references to Ziuzin are to the text and notes of his report that follows on pp. 71–202.
2. C[alendar] S[tate] P[apers] V[enetian] 1610–1613, p. 92.

out to have him on their side."[3] Sweden was perhaps a more straight-forward issue. The English had shipped Irish "idle persons and ill-livers" there since 1609 for employment in the long wars against the Poles and more recently against the Danes.[4] And certainly James's reputation in Stockholm was enhanced following his arbitration of the Peace of Knaerød between Gustavus Adolphus and Christian IV. The Russians, though, because of the actions of the Swedish general, Jakob Pontusson de la Gardie, in Novgorod would discourage an Anglo-Swedish alliance.[5] More importantly, however, for the English, following the Uppsala Dec-laration in 1593 Sweden was firmly in the Protestant camp.[6] James's real concern was Poland. By cultivating a Protestant presence in the north he would prevent the domination of Europe by Catholic forces—the Habs-burgs in the center and south and Sigismund in the north. As a modern Polish historian puts it, "The Polish successes in the war with Sweden and Moscow caused an activization of the Protestant camp and of anti-Polish circles at the London court."[7]

The entrance of the Russians into the political balance at this partic-ular juncture weighed in James's favor. Ziuzin, Tsar Michael's first am-bassador to England, was greeted in London barely three months after the coronation ceremony had taken place in Moscow. Coming as it did at the end of the Time of Troubles, Ziuzin's embassy was a political statement about the legitimacy of the new Tsar and the authority of his govern-ment. One of the dinner toasts to Michael from his ambassadors in

3. S[tate] P[apers] 80/3, f. 29v, S. Lesieur to King James, 6 September 1613.

4. See Ziuzin, nn. 13–15. James refused to become involved in the differences between Denmark and Sweden until he understood the disposition of the Swedish King in that conflict. C[alendar] S[tate] P[apers] D[omestic] 1611–1618 (Docquet), p. 98; England would also support the Danes in 1611 (see ibid., n. 175). See also Samuel Purchas, Hakluytys Posthumus or Purchas his Pilgrims, 20 vols. (Glasgow, 1905–1907), 14: 203–224. Regarding the Irish, see below, pp. 49–51, 63 and 64.

5. See Ziuzin, pp. 103, 174, and nn. 11 and 12.

6. In 1609 Sir Ralph Winwood reported a pro-Polish faction in Sweden, a report that may have encouraged the arrangements for sending Irish soldiers there. Sir Ralph Winwood, Memorials of the Affairs of State in the Reigns of Queen Elizabeth and King James, 3 vols. (London, 1725), 3: 103.

7. Edward Alfred Mierzwa, Anglia a Polska w pierwszej połowie XVII w. (Warsaw, 1986), p. 38. The Pope denied direct responsibility for financing the Poles. Sir D. Carleton reported to W. Trumbull that ". . . the ambassador for Poland is returning [from Rome] having made suit to the Pope for 20,000 crowns . . . pretending his wars in Muscovia to have been chiefly prosecuted at the Pope's instigation; but they say the head of the church is deaf of that ear." H[istorical] M[anuscripts] C[ommission], Downshire, 4: 61. See also SP 84/68, ff. 260–262, Sir R. Winwood to Salisbury, 19 March 1612.

England offered him health and longevity for establishing "the root of his just Tsar's descendants for the heredity of his sovereign family forever unmoved."[8] In England, interest in Ziuzin's mission was connected to the undercurrent of Catholic-Protestant tensions on the Continent. James knew, and the Russian experience verified, that the Orthodox church "of the Greek law" was absolutely antithetical to Rome, and although the Protestant camp was divided between Lutherans, Calvinists, and members of the Church of England, it, too, was united in its antipathy to the Pope. Indeed, according to John Merrick, in 1603 Boris Godunov, on hearing of Catholic plots against Queen Elizabeth called the Pope a dog, and added further that if he were nearer Rome he would "pluck him out of his state by the hair of the head for wronging so worthy a prince."[9] From that perspective James I recognized the possibility of the Russians joining him in a northern alliance against Sigismund III and his allies, the Catholic League of German princes organized by Maximilian, Duke of Bavaria. Indeed, paramount in Ziuzin's instructions for his negotiations in England in 1613–1614 was the securing of military and financial help against the Poles.

During the year and a half immediately preceding Ziuzin's arrival the politics of religion had dominated and molded diplomacy at Whitehall— note some of the high points: The marriage that would eventually (1714) ensure a Protestant succession for England, albeit Hanoverian when the Stuart line died, was negotiated and consummated between James's daughter Elizabeth and Frederick, Elector Palatine.[10] The death of Emperor Rudolf in 1612, after a troubled reign of thirty-six years, gave the throne to his brother Matthias (1612–1619), whose failure to reach an agreement with the Estates of Bohemia would shortly lead to the Thirty Years' War. Sir Stephen Lesieur was appointed English ambassador to Emperor Matthias to press the cause of Brandenburg in the succession of Juliers and Cleves, although he was found unsatisfactory and later recalled.[11] The Pope refused a dispensation to the Spanish Grand Duke for the marriage of his sister to Henry, Prince of Wales.[12] No doubt he

---

8. See Ziuzin, p. 156.

9. Cotton Nero B VIII, f. 39, "A particular of the entertainment and usage by me, John Merrick after my arrival at Moscow, being sent by the Queen."

10. See Ziuzin, n. 24.

11. SP 14/70:67, 75:28 (John Chamberlain, *The Letters of John Chamberlain*, ed. N.E. McClure, American Philosophical Society, 2 vols. [Philadelphia, 1939], 1: 378–380). *CSPV 1610–1613*, p. 92; and see SP 80/3, ff. 51–52, Lesieur to James Reasons that the Emperor has "conceived a dislike against my person."

12. *CSPV 1610–1613*, p. 425.

recognized James's dilemma regarding English policy toward Spain, a policy confusing to both people and parliament. Rumors persisted throughout the year of possible war with Turkey and in Germany "a large party in favor of war against the Turk" remained.[13] Should not Christendom lay aside its own divisions and ally against the infidel? The threat, however, was not considered serious enough. Continental Protestant princes worried more about the Catholic union and a possible alliance between France and Spain than they did about the Sultan.[14] An ambassador from the Elector of Brandenburg came to London to discuss the succession of Cleves.[15] Christian IV of Denmark and Charles IX of Sweden were at war for the course of the year, only achieving a peace in January 1613 through the intercession of James.[16] Their arguments were not about religion per se but they had critical political ramifications regarding Catholic alliances. Throughout the hostilities parties on the Continent had worried about Sweden's relationship to Poland. Would Charles IX in Sweden seek help from his nephew Sigismund? Alternatively, it was rumored that Poland might ally with Denmark and take Sweden.[17] In November 1612 James I's eldest son, Prince Henry, died and it was reported that "the Huguenots are grieved, as they built their hopes on the Prince."[18] (Could they but have known what havoc Henry's younger brother Charles would wreak in 1625 and 1626 by lending ships to the King of France for the siege of La Rochelle.) And once again English marital plans were readjusted, this time proposing Henry's brother Charles, Duke of York, as husband for the second Spanish Infanta; but that plan, too, would change in a matter of months as the wind changed. The Dutch decided to continue their ambassador in Constanti-

13. CSPV 1610–1613, pp. 432, 462.

14. CSPV 1610–1613, p. 433.

15. SP 14/71, 16; CSPV 1610–1613, p. 438. In August 1611 James had negotiated a defensive alliance with Joachim Ernst, Margrave of Brandenburg-Ansbach (Thomas Rymer, ed., Foedera Conventiones, Literae et Cujus Cunque Generis Acta Publica inter Reges Angliae, 10 vols. [np, 1739–1745], 7[pt. 2]: 178); and the following month sent similar commissions to Johan Sigismund, Elector of Brandenburg (1608–1620); Moritz, Landgrave of Hesse (1592–1627); and Johann, Count of Pfaltz-Zweibrücken, the guardian in 1610–1614 of Elector Palatine Frederick V, the later "Winter King" of Bohemia (ibid., pp. 178–179).

16. See Ziuzin, n. 11.

17. See Ziuzin, n. 12. See also SP 84/68, f. 39v–40, Sir R. Winwood to Salisbury, 23 April 1611: "If the kingdom of Sweden shall revolt and return to the king of Poland all the countries in these parts of the world whose strength does consist in the power of navigation shall suffer thereby inestimable damage."

18. CSPV 1610–1613, p. 452.

nople for another four years and were "fitting out a great ship with presents for the Sultan."[19] For them rather than war a compromise with the infidel promised rich trade in Turkish dominions and perhaps freedom from piracy on the high seas. The Dutch Republic was virtually the only country in Europe solvent and powerful enough for state and commercial interests to merge in one policy. England sent Sir Paul Pindar to the Grand Vizier in 1613 more to outmaneuver the Dutch than to mediate peace for the Protestant princes who were worried about the Turkish support of the Prince of Transylvania, Gabor Bethlen (1613–1629).[20]

Throughout the year rumors of a plot against James's life were rampant.[21] Catholics were suspected and, as a result, Jesuits imprisoned. Henry IV's assassination only two years before was a living memory not only in France but in the rest of Europe. On the other side of the world, in Virginia, a Spanish presence continued to threaten the English colonies[22] and by early 1613 as relations with Spain cooled James was looking to France instead of Madrid for a wife for young Charles. At that time Sir John Davies, the King's Attorney, was elected Speaker of the Lower House of the Irish parliament and left London in February amidst growing rumors of Irish-Spanish collusion.[23] Secretary Winwood would later describe Ireland as "not a thorn in our foot but a lance in our side."[24] In February 1613 the English court rejoiced in the public marriage ceremonies of Frederick and Elizabeth, entertaining ambassadors from all the Protestant countries and, of course, from Spain.[25] At the same time the Scots were ordered ready to mobilize at a moment's notice against the Irishmen in the service of Spain; on the Continent the alliance of the Catholic League was renewed with Habsburg support.[26] Rumors about Turkey, the Emperor, and the Dutch dragged on throughout late spring.[27] In May the Danish-Habsburg connection reared its ugly head again when

---

19. *CSPV 1610–1613*, p. 463.
20. SP 14/67:25 (Chamberlain, *Letters*, 1: 311–315).
21. SP 14/61:47, 65:70, 71:17; *CSPV 1610–1613*, pp. 4, 425; *CSPV 1613–1615*, p. 13.
22. *CSPV 1610–1613*, pp. 470, 477.
23. *CSPV 1610–1613*, pp. 491, 507.
24. The comment was made in Winwood's speech in the Lower House, 12 April 1614. Maija Jansson, *Proceedings in Parliament 1614*, American Philosophical Society (Philadelphia, 1988), pp. 429, 433. See Ziuzin, n. 89.
25. The couple was affianced on 27 December 1612 (SP 14/71:70; John Nichols, *The Progresses, Processions, and Magnificent Festivities of King James the First*, 4 vols. [London, 1828], 2: 513–516) and was married on 14 February 1614. (ibid., pp. 541–549).
26. *CSPV 1610–1613*, p. 507.
27. *CSPV 1610–1613*, pp. 519, 520, 522, 528.

a Spanish ambassador in Denmark was reported trying to purchase "naval material" from the Danes, "which the late King Philip used to get from that kingdom during Elizabeth's reign." And to add insult to injury he proposed a match between Charles's old prospect, the second Infanta, and the Prince of Denmark, a union that would have given the Habsburgs a familial foothold in the north in addition to the commercial partnership they enjoyed on occasion.[28] By late spring it was reported that even the Dutch sought an alliance with England against Spain, provided, of course, that it brooked no competition from the English in eastern markets. (James had paved the way of friendship by presenting the Order of the Garter to Count Maurice of Nassau in January.)[29] Nevertheless, always vigilant regarding the Dutch, the English merchants would encourage Russian overtures that might promise them privileges denied the Hollanders in Archangel.

What happened, then, to Ziuzin when he finally arrived in London at the end of this eventful year? After a harrowing two months at sea, followed by five days of recuperation at Gravesend, on the 26th of October 1613, Ziuzin and his entourage were met on Tower Wharf by the Lord Mayor of London, the aldermen, and various delegates from the livery companies of the City. As they disembarked guns from a royal naval ship boomed a salute larger than any in living memory for the arrival of a foreign ambassador.[30] Three days later, at the crack of dawn, royal coaches whisked them through the still uncrowded streets to the King's palace at Whitehall where they viewed the procession honoring Sir Thomas Middleton, the newly elected Lord Mayor of London.[31]

Their reception was extraordinary, wrote Ferdinand Boisschot,[32] ambassador from the Archdukes Albert and Isabella of the Spanish Netherlands, because all the merchants from the companies and the mayor of the City were there, dressed in red velvet gowns, riding on horseback to greet them. Samuel Spifame reported to Louis XIII in France that the Russians' expenses were defrayed and their lodgings were to be provided by the City until the following Lent. King James "does many things that

---

28. CSPV 1610–1613, p. 535.
29. On the earlier rivalry with the Dutch, see SP 91/2, f. 1, Appendix, below. Regarding the presentation to Maurice, see SP 84/69, ff. 7–10, Sir R. Winwood to King James, 26 January 1613.
30. See Ziuzin, nn. 193, 209, and 213. Samuel Purchase recorded that, "I was present both at his arrival at Gravesend, and his honorable entertainment into London" (Purchas, Hakluytus Posthumus, 14: 255).
31. See Ziuzin, pp. 162.
32. H[aus-] H[of-] und S[taatsarchiv], Abteilung Belgien, PC Fz. 61.

look simple," it was said, "but to what he feels is important he pays much attention."[33] The formal audience was even more impressive. Before meeting the King, Ziuzin was shown the Chamber where the Privy Council met and the King's throne, "covered with wrought silver and gilded." The Earl of Dorset said that Ziuzin must sit in the King's place and "not disobey our sovereign in this." For the other ambassadors, he said, "This is not done, that they sit on the King's place. Only for the ambassadors of your great sovereign his Majesty the Tsar."[34]

Later, when again shown the King's throne, this time in the Queen's palace, Somerset House, he was told that "no one besides you has ever been in the King's presence in these rooms."[35]

Specifically, then, what were the issues of this embassy that it raised such an enthusiastic welcome, and why was it so important to both sides? For the Russians, as said before, the embassy was singularly political—to establish an alliance and to announce the election of the new Tsar, Mikhail Fyodorovich Romanov, signaling to the English crown the continuity and legitimacy of the Russian state. Once again a Russian tsar was in the seat of authority, one who sought to reestablish the "fraternal love and strong friendship" that had become a tradition of Russian-English relations. It was, after all, fair turn-about for Boris Godunov's respect shown for James in 1603. The projected marriage between Queen Anne's brother Prince Johan of Denmark, and Boris Godunov's daughter, Kseniya, as well as the Mikulin embassy to London in 1601, were public indications of Boris's "moral and diplomatic support for King James's claim to the English throne."[36] Now, specifically, Tsar Michael wanted two things: first, financial help in order to solidify his own position and to begin rebuilding his defenses and, second, he wanted the English King to negotiate a peace between himself and Poland and Sweden that would put to rest their conflicts with Russia and finally rid the country of those large foreign armies still on her soil. For James a northern Protestant

33. Don Diego Sarmiento de Acuña, Count of Gondomar, to Philip III. *Documentos Ineditos para la Historia de España* (Madrid, 1945), 4: 108.
34. See Ziuzin, pp. 169.
35. See Ziuzin, pp. 176.
36. N. E. Evans, "The Meeting of the Russian and Scottish Ambassadors in London in 1601," *SEER* 55, no. 4 (October, 1977): 523, 527. Privately there were ugly rumors. R. Barne wrote to Salisbury from Moscow in 1602 or 1603 that if he had lived, the marriage between Kseniya and Johan "would have proved a notable cross unto the state of the English nation here. For I understood by our interpreters that were nearest unto him that he had divers times sworn the subversion of the English carrying trade hither" (SP 91/1, f.183- 183v).

political alliance against Sigismund III was paramount; only secondarily would commercial interests come into play in his policy with the Russians.

James was known the world over as the peacemaker of Europe, *rex pacificus*, but the new Tsar had better grounds on which to base his requests than simply the reputation of the English King. Those grounds were the good relations alluded to by Ziuzin that had existed between England and Russia since the days of Edward VI, interrupted only by the upheaval of the Time of Troubles. Naturally the common interests were stronger at some times than at others, and Anglo-Russian relations went through many ups and downs before Ziuzin's embassy in 1613. It was not an isolated bilateral relationship founded solely on trade, and the ensuing sketch of the relationship will reveal how much it depended on the activities of the pivotal northern powers, Denmark and Sweden, as well as Poland and the Empire.

England, Russia, and the North to 1603

The reign of Queen Elizabeth witnessed the gradual involvement of England in the political affairs of northern Europe, an area in which previously it had little interest, save for intermittent relations with Denmark and Catholic Poland. Those relations did not follow the paths of English trade, for extensive English trade through the Danish Sound to towns subject to the King of Poland did not produce extensive diplomatic relations with Poland.[37] Until the years 1577–1580 England's diplomatic relations in the north were almost exclusively with Russia, in spite of the large English trade to the Polish ports on the Baltic. English policy remained oriented toward the affairs of France, Spain, and the Low Countries, while the northern powers were totally absorbed in the Livonian War (1558–1583), a three-sided conflict between Russia, Poland-Lithuania, and Sweden over the lands of the former Livonian Order.[38] This long and destructive war was in turn complicated by occasional Danish participation and the so-called War of the Three Crowns (1563–

---

37. Artur Attman, *Den ryska marknaden i 1500-talets baltiska politik* (Lund, 1944); and Artur Attman, *The Russian and Polish Markets in International Trade 1500–1650* (Göteborg, 1973).
38. The Livonian Order, descendant of the medieval order of the Teutonic knights, was in the sixteenth century still the master of the modern territories of Latvia and Estonia. In the 1550s the Reformation undermined the Catholic Order, leaving the country without an effective government and opening the way to its neighbors' expansionist aims.

1570) between Sweden and Denmark. Elizabeth stood aloof from both conflicts, even though they seriously affected English trade in the Baltic.

England's relations with Russia had indeed originated with purely commercial matters. English merchants had been trading to Russia through the mouth of the Dvina River since Richard Chancellor's voyage in 1553, which had led to the formation of the Muscovy Company in 1555. However, England's trade with Russia was not without obstacles, besides those imposed by geography. Denmark claimed the ownership of the Atlantic between Iceland and Norway, and thus theoretically contested the English right to trade with Russia without Danish permission, but Frederick II (1559–1588) did not raise the issue seriously until 1576. More difficult were the obstacles to the English trade at Narva, which was in Russian hands from 1558 to 1581. Denmark did not object to the Narva trade until 1580, as Denmark was the friendliest of the northern powers to Russia, and ships going to Narva paid tolls to Frederick at the Sound. Sweden and Poland, however, objected both to the trade and the conveyance of military supplies to Russia by this route, and privateers from Danzig and the Swedish fleet regularly harassed and captured English ships.[39]

The Emperors Ferdinand I (1556–1564) and Maximilian II (1564–1576) also objected, in part because they claimed a general suzerainty over Livonia for the Empire, and in part because they supported the Hanse in its disputes with England. Elizabeth's government had succeeded in 1567 in making an agreement with Hamburg that provided an alternative to the Steelyard and Antwerp staple (and simultaneously split the Hanse), but Hanse pressure on Hamburg led to the lapsing of English privileges in 1578. The Merchant Adventurers moved to Emden in that year, and they stayed there until the move to Stade in 1587, where they remained until 1611.[40] Thus the Hanse was a permanent antagonist of England for the whole of the reign, reinforcing the enmity of both Poland (Danzig was a Hanse town) and the Emperor.

The political and religious coalitions of the first two decades of Elizabeth's reign were also unfavorable to England in the north (except for Russia), but did not present much of a problem. Though England had almost no relations with Poland, Denmark, and Sweden until 1576, their political alignments were already largely set and were to complicate

---

39. Attman, *Den ryska marknaden*, pp. 153–344.
40. Richard Ehrenberg, *Hamburg und England im Zeitalter der Königin Elisabeth* (Jena, 1896); G. D. Ramsay, *The City of London in International Politics at the Accession of Elizabeth* (Manchester, 1975), pp. 217–289.

English policy later on.[41] These alignments do not correspond with what might be thought from a general consideration of the area. Most important was the attitude of Denmark, which though Protestant in faith, was consistently in the Emperor's camp from the Peace of Speyer in 1544.[42] For this reason all attempts by England to form a Protestant coalition with the Danish King (Europe's other major Protestant monarch) were condemned to failure from the start. Sweden had no reason to support the Emperor, other than good relations with the Hanse, but was too remote and too weak in this period to make much difference. Furthermore, for most of the period Sweden was hardly a likely Protestant ally. After the deposition of Erik XIV (1568), the desire of King Johan III (1568–1592) for religious union led him toward Poland and the Catholic powers. Whatever its policy, Sweden remained remote from England and diplomatic relations at this time were rare. Poland under Sigismund August (1548–1572) was absorbed by its war with Russia over Livonia, which led to conflict over the trade to Narva. Both the King's policy of de facto religious toleration and his frequent bad relations with the Habsburgs did have the effect of putting Poland at a distance from the other Catholic monarchs, but none of this had any significance for the English. The previous Polish ambassador to England had been in Queen Mary's time, and until 1578 contacts were confined to English complaints about mercantile matters, mainly the seizure of English ships going to Narva by Danzig privateers from 1566 to 1568. After 1576 Poland's kings would be more self-consciously Catholic, leading to a gradual change of orientation. The foundation of the Eastland Company

41. Gustav Vasa tried to marry his son Erik (later King Erik XIV) to Elizabeth ca. 1558–1560. Ingvar Andersson, *Erik XIV's engelska underhandlingar: studier i svensk diplomati och handelspolitik,* Skrifter utgivna av Vetenskapssocieteten i Lund 17 (Lund, 1935). Two Danish missions, in 1564 and 1566, by Dr. Albert Knoppert, to prevent English supply of munitions to Sweden, failed. Walter Kirchner, "England and Denmark, 1558–1588," *Journal of Modern History* 17,1 (March, 1945): 4–5; CSPF

42. The pro-Imperial character of Danish foreign policy after 1544 is a commonplace of Danish history, but little monographic literature exists to flesh out the idea. See (for example) *Danmarks Riges Historie,* 10 vols. (Copenhagen, 1898–1905), vol. 3, part 3 (by V. Mollerup) and vol. 4 (by J. A. Fridericia); and for the period 1544 to 1559, Martin Schwarz Lausten, *Religion och politik: Studier i Christian IIIs forhold til det tyske rige i tiden 1544–1559* (Copenhagen, 1977). The apparent absence of any extended study of Denmark's relations with Spain in the period 1570–1618 is an especially serious problem for the historian, who must rely on occasional publications such as that of Charles Piot (below, n. 77).

(1579) meant that England needed a relationship with Poland, with consequences that will be seen below.

Anglo-Russian Relations until 1582

The opening of relations between England and Russia, commercial and diplomatic, marked the reemergence of Russia into West European politics after a hiatus of some twenty years. After the death of Vasilii III in 1533, the years of the boyar regency (1533–1547) saw the gradual withdrawal of Russia from relations with all but its nearest neighbors, Poland-Lithuania and Sweden, and even these relations were scarcely intense. Before 1533 this had not been the case, for Russia had maintained almost yearly contacts with the court of Vienna to find a counterweight to Poland, and had signed a treaty with Denmark in 1516, in part for similar reasons and in part for commercial reasons. In 1524–1525 a Russian embassy had even gone to Spain (stopping briefly in England on the way) to see the Emperor Charles V.[43] During the boyar regency, in contrast, an inconclusive war with Poland (1534–1537) was followed by an entirely passive Russian policy, which maintained minimal relations with Poland and Sweden and none with the rest of Europe. Little changed at first under the new Tsar Ivan IV (1547–1584) because his early moves were in other directions, against the Tatar Khanates of Kazan' and Astrakhan', conquered in the wars of 1548–1556. Thus the arrival of Chancellor in 1553 at first led only to the establishment of commercial ties. Anthony Jenkinson's early trips to Russia and the voyages of Osip Nepeia (1557) and Stepan Tverdikov (1567–1568) concerned such purely commercial matters. Even the beginning of the Livonian War in 1558 did not change the situation at first, Russia's capture of the Livonian port of Narva in that year notwithstanding. The issue of political relations did not arise, even though English ships came in great numbers to Narva, in spite of the Swedish fleet and Danzig privateers.[44]

---

43. A. L. Khoroshkevich, *Russkoe gosudarstvo v sisteme mezhdunarodnykh otnoshenii kontsa XV-nachale XVI v.* (Moscow, 1980); Ia. S. Lur'e, "'Otkrytie Anglii' russkimi v nachale XVI v.," *Geograficheskii sbornik* 3 (1954): 185–187; A. A. Zimin, *Rossiia na poroge novogo vremeni* (Moscow, 1972), pp. 79–94, 169–207, 300–306.

44. T. S. Willan, *The Early History of the Russia Company 1553–1603* (Manchester, 1956); Attman, *Ryska marknaden*, pp. 154–155; Attman, *Russian and Polish Markets*, pp. 73–84; and Samuel H. Baron, "Osip Nepea and the Opening of Anglo-Russian Commercial Relations," *O[xford] S[lavonic] P[apers]*, New Series 11 (1978): 42–63. The minor border war with Sweden (1554–1557) does not change the picture of Russian passivity in the west. Apparently the Nepea mission encountered some

However, by 1567 the war did have an affect on Anglo-Russian relations. In that year Ivan IV proposed to the English envoy Anthony Jenkinson an "offensive and defensive" league that would bring amity and friendship to both countries "without end," a league directed against Poland. The proposal also included a request for a refuge for the Tsar, locked in struggle with his own boyars and nobles in the 1560s. Willan, looking at the relationship from a purely commercial angle, found that the proposal was "embarrassing" and "alarming" to Elizabeth, and failed to see the point both of Ivan's proposal and Elizabeth's response.[45] Ivan did not spell out what the alliance against Poland would mean militarily, but just at this time English ships going to Narva were being attacked by Polish privateers from Danzig.[46] England, as a naval power, could have at the very least protected its own shipping in the Baltic and thus contributed not only to Russia's trade but also to its war effort by bringing much-needed siege supplies to the Tsar. Elizabeth, however, did not respond favorably to the idea, and Burghley's instructions to Thomas Randolph, ambassador to Russia in 1568, adduce as the reason Ivan's hostility to Emperor Maximilian II as well as to Poland and Sweden. As England's own relations with Poland were hostile at that moment, and with Sweden non-existent, Burghley seems to have been moved both by his usual desire for England to remain uninvolved and more importantly by his concern for Maximilian's reaction. The reason is not difficult to discern, for Maximilian's brother Archduke Karl had been a suitor for the

encouragement in Ivan's struggles with the Tatars from Mary's husband Philip of Spain (who was in England in April 1557, at the same time as Nepea): Lur'e, "Russko-angliiskie otnosheniia," pp. 427–428, following the remark of François de Noailles, Bishop of Acqs, ambassador to London in the 1550s, in E. Charrière, *Négociations de la France dans le Levant*, 4 vols.(Paris, various dates), 2: 449–450.

45. Willan, *Early History*, pp. 91–92, 100, where Willan commented erroneously that Elizabeth remained uninterested in a treaty with Russia until 1584. Iurii Tolstoi, *Pervye sorok let snoshenii mezhdu Rossieiu i Anglieiu 1553–1593 / The First Forty Years of Intercourse between England and Russia 1553–1593* (St. Petersburg, 1875), pp. 38–39; Henry R. Huttenbach, "New Archival Material on the Anglo-Russian Treaty of Queen Elizabeth and Tsar Ivan IV," *SEER* 49, 117 (October, 1971): 535–549.

46. Tolstoi, *Pervye sorok let*, p. 38; C. H. Talbot, ed., "Res Polonicae ex archivo Musei Britannici II Pars," *Elementa ad fontium editiones* (Rome, 1967), 17: 36–51; Artur Attman, *The Struggle for Baltic Markets: Powers in Conflict 1558–1616*, Acta regiae societatis scientiarum et litterarum Gothoburgenisis Humaniora 14 (1979): 45–82. Sweden as well tried to limit and control the trade to Narva, but was on good terms with Russia in 1558–1568. A real alliance, however, never emerged. H. Hjärne, *Svensk-ryska förhandlingar 1564–72: Erik XIV's ryska förbundsplaner*, Skrifter utgivna av K. Humanistiska Vetenskapssamfundet 15 (Uppsala, 1897).

Queen's hand (with Burghley's support) since 1563, and was to be one again in 1570.[47] The English reaction reveals the political nature of the objection, and thus reveals a major element in the background of Anglo-Russian relations: the Emperor.

Randolph's embassy resulted in the arrival of Ivan's ambassador, Andrei Grigor'evich Sovin, in England on 27 August 1569. This embassy did in fact result in an Anglo-Russian offensive and defensive league, though the fact has never been recognized by historians. Sovin repeated Ivan's 1567 requests, and on 18 May Elizabeth's government prepared a secret letter for Ivan granting him the request for refuge. The secrecy of this letter, and its rather dramatic contents, have distracted attention from the Queen's other letter of 18 May 1570, which concludes:

> We enter into a friendly and sisterly league to continue forever with you—great Lord and Emperor—as a mighty prince and our dear brother Emperor Lord and Great Duke of all Russia. Which league we will so observe and keep forever, as to bind ourselves and with our mutual and common forces to withstand and offend all such as shall be common enemies to us both and to defend both our princely honors the estate of our realms and countries and to help aid and favor each of us the other with mutual helps and aids against our common enemies as far forth as the effect of these our letters shall stretch.[48]

This statement was not a treaty in proper form, but merely a statement from the Queen, known only perhaps to her and Burghley, who drafted the letter. Ivan's angry reply of 24 October 1570, in which he canceled the Muscovy Company's privileges and announced the fact to Elizabeth with a famous passage asserting that England was clearly ruled by merchants,[49] has misled historians. In the letter Ivan did not say that Elizabeth had rejected his treaty proposal, but merely "you [Elizabeth] have not ended our affairs according as your ambassador [Jenkinson or Randolph in 1567/8] did agree upon, and your letters be not thereto agreeable, for such weighty matters be not ended without some gold or without ambassadors, but you have set aside those great affairs and your Council

---

47. Conyers Read, *Mr. Secretary Cecil and Queen Elizabeth* (New York, 1955), pp. 333–337; J. E. Neale, *Queen Elizabeth I: A Biography* (Garden City, 1957), pp. 142–144, 153–155, 226.
48. Tolstoi, *Pervye sorok let*, p. 91.
49. "muzhiki torgovye," mistranslated as "bowrishe marchaunts," Tolstoi, *Pervye sorok let*, pp. 106–115. It actually means something closer to "trading peasants," a group distinct from legally recognized merchants in sixteenth-century Russia, and thus even more contemptuous.

does deal with our ambassador about merchants' affairs."[50] The crucial point here was that there was no oath affirming the agreement, not that England had rejected his proposal in toto.

Later references to this matter in English documents demonstrate that a secret, oral treaty had indeed been made when Sovin was in England, as Elizabeth's first, private, letter of 18 May 1570 confirms.[51] In 1571 Jenkinson was sent to Russia to assuage Ivan's anger and get the Muscovy Company's privileges back. A memorandum of that year states that he was to take a "letter of a secret league for reciproc[al] reception in case of distress," but also a "letter for an oath and league, written and sent by him [Jenkinson] contains that no aid be given to certain princes and states against him."[52] In 1572 Jenkinson reported his conversation with the Tsar in Staritsa (13 May 1572). After reading the Queen's letters and hearing Jenkinson, Ivan told him that we "do perceive that our secret message unto you committed [in 1567], was done truly according to our mind (although we were advertised to the contrary) and now we are by you fully satisfied." He seemed to be saying that it was the manner of dealing with the issue by the English, not the substance, that so offended him. He repeated his satisfaction, and said that as "our princely, and secret affairs were not finished to our contentation at our time appointed, according to our expectation, we do now leave all those matters, and set them aside for the time."[53] That is, Ivan would not as of May 1572 request an oath from the Queen and a secret letter of confirmation. Consequently Ivan relented and restored the Company privileges.

What can account for the changes in both English and Russian policy in the years 1567–1572? No direct statements exist from either side. If English reluctance to make a treaty in 1567 stemmed from a desire to keep alive the marriage scheme with Archduke Karl, then logically the softening of England's position in 1570 and 1571 would follow from the evaporation of this hope. At the same time England committed itself to very little, and kept its commitments secret. Ivan's desire for the refuge scheme to be secret was understandable, as was his reaction in October 1570 (if not his mode of expression). In early 1570 he had signed a three-year truce with Poland, so the need for an immediate league with

50. What the English at the time thought was meant by the phrase "without some gold" is unclear. The Russian original (as Tolstoi pointed out) means "without confirmation by oath (bez krepostei)." Tolstoi, Pervye sorok let, pp. 109, 114.
51. Ivan's 1576 reference to an Italian and Latin text brought by Sovin suggests that other versions may have been lost: Tolstoi, Pervye sorok let, p. 184.
52. Tolstoi, Pervye sorok let, p. 115.
53. Tolstoi, Pervye sorok let, p. 141.

England against Poland had faded. That truce and the peace of Stettin (December 1570) gradually cleared the Narva trade of Polish interference. War had not begun with Johan III of Sweden, and moreover in early 1570 Ivan had also inaugurated the scheme of investing Prince Magnus of Denmark with a newly created vassal kingdom of Livonia, which seemed to offer the Russian Tsar a cheaper, if more indirect, control over the disputed territory. This led to war with Sweden over Reval by the end of the year, so when the memorandum on Jenkinson's mission was written in 1571, the English presumably knew that they committed themselves not only to aid the King of Sweden, but also (in the indefinite future) the King of Poland. Neither obligation could have been much of a sacrifice for Elizabeth. Ivan as well could afford to be generous, restore the privileges, and temporarily suspend his objections to the form of the league.

Subsequent developments reflect further shifts in the two monarchs' policies and further confirm that an agreement had been made in 1570. In 1574 Daniel Sylvester went to Ivan as a messenger, returning to report the Tsar's lack of satisfaction again with Elizabeth's failure to confirm the agreement in clear enough form.[54] Sylvester then was once again sent in 1575, and the instructions (May 1575) for that embassy incidentally contain the clearest exposition of the problem of the 1570 treaty:

> Whereas we conceive the secret message you delivered unto us from the emperor [evidently in 1572] to stand in two points: The one that he should mislike our refusal to confirm by oath the league agreed on at the time of his ambassador being here, as that it was not subscribed by our councillors' hands:[55] the other, that he found it strange that we should scruple to require like assurance of refuge at his hands . . .
>
> For the first you shall declare unto him, that though we had well hoped that he had conceived so honorably of us that no oath could have drawn us to a more sincere performance of our promise delivered in writing signed with our hand, than the great respect we bear to the maintenance of our princely word, as in honor we are bound; yet the only and chief cause why we yielded not to the confirmation of the same by the oath grew of the great respect we had to have the contents of the said league kept secret (a thing no less earnestly by him required . . .) which with no possibility could have been

---

54. Tolstoi, *Pervye sorok let*, p. 159: "The two points wherein the emperor's majesty find himself not fully satisfied are these: "The first is for that her majesty, having granted to confirm by oath those things which by patent under her hand she has sent him, she will not permit her Council to sign it."

55. The letter of 18 May 1570 promising refuge was signed by numerous councillors.

performed with that solemnity that is usual in that behalf. For the leagues which we confirm by the oath do ordinarily pass our great seal: which can not be done but that the same must run through the hands of so great a number of our ministers as in no possibility they can be kept secret.

And as touching his misliking that the league was not signed by our Council, you may tell him that such things as are signed by our self are never signed by our Council. For that is held a kind of abasement of the state and quality we should to have any joined with us in that behalf.[56]

Thus an oral treaty was made in 1570, and the subsequent anger of Ivan was not at the absence of a "league" but at the form of the agreement, at the lack of an oath. As Ziuzin's account of the Time of Troubles demonstrates, oaths were extremely important to the Russians of the time in the making of agreements. In 1570 Elizabeth had called the refuge agreement "secret," but affixed the Great Seal and the signatures of the Privy Councillors, and thus, as she admitted in 1575, it was not a very secret agreement. The real secret agreement of 1570 was the league (so named in Elizabeth's letter, the refuge agreement was not a league), known only from her private letter drafted by Burghley. No oath or Great Seal was involved here. Ivan interpreted this form of league as insufficient, in part because of his cultural attitude toward oaths, but also perhaps he suspected that the very secrecy of the league would impede its effectiveness. Ultimately this issue was to wreck the whole league, for on 29 January 1576 Ivan told Sylvester that as a result of the English reluctance to confirm the league with an oath he was turning with the same proposals to the Emperor Maximilian.[57]

Later that year Sylvester went back to England, and quickly returned to Russia with Elizabeth's answer. Willan states that "there is no record of Elizabeth's reactions to the Tsar's demands."[58] This is not true. Henry Huttenbach's discovery of a draft treaty with Russia dated the eighteenth year of Elizabeth's reign (17 November 1575–17 November 1576) shows

56. Tolstoi, *Pervye sorok let*, pp. 164–165.

57. Tolstoi, *Pervye sorok let*, p. 183. This report mentions only the refuge, but other sources reveal that negotiations were in progress over a Russian-Imperial alliance. On 24 January 1576, Ivan's representatives, Nikita Romanov-Iur'ev and the secretary Andrei Shchelkalov had met Imperial ambassadors Kobenzl and Prinz and had heard Maximilian's proposals for an alliance which would involve Russia turning away from Livonia to help put Archduke Ernst on the Polish throne and eventually unite against the Turks. *Pamiatniki diplomaticheskikh snoshenii Drevnei Rossii s derzhavami inostrannymi* 1 (St. Petersburg, 1851), pp. 481–586; Hans Uebersberger, *Osterreich und Russland seit dem Ende des 15 Jahrhunderts*, Veröffentlichungen der Kommission für neuere Geschichte Osterreichs 2 (Vienna, 1906), pp. 439–444.

58. Willan, *Early History*, p. 128.

what her response was, and it was to prepare a formal written treaty. The treaty specified not only amity and trade but also, "That as oft as need shall require, and the same be demanded, the one to be ready to aid, and assist the other with men, treasure, munition, and all things necessary for war."[59] This was Ivan's basic demand, and England's agreement represented a further move toward the Tsar over the 1571 letter sent with Jenkinson (above). The proposal never reached the Tsar, for Sylvester was struck by lightning in Kholmogory on the way back (presumably with the draft treaty). After that relations lapsed while Ivan explored the Imperial alternative to the English alliance. The Queen's councillors, however, continued to work at least through the summer of 1577, making increasingly elaborate drafts, adding the qualification that the two future allies should try to convince possible enemies to desist before actually providing aid.[60]

For these years as well little information exists to explain English or Russian policy. Ivan's motivation is not hard to detect: in 1575–1576 he was engaged in a complex struggle to influence the Polish diet to elect either himself, his son, or Archduke Ernst as King of Poland, a struggle that ultimately resulted in the Kobenzl-Prinz embassy to Russia. He seemed to have had little need of England. The English decision, apparently taken in spring 1576, to prepare a written treaty for Sylvester is less clear. Elizabeth and her councillors evidently felt a sudden need for a real alliance with Russia. The only new piece of information which Sylvester had brought back to England had been the news of Ivan's negotiations with the Emperor Maximilian II. Perhaps the English were concerned about the possibility of a Russo-Imperial alliance. Reports from the Imperial court to England in the fall of 1576 were worrisome, and may have affected thinking in England.[61] In any case, Sylvester's sudden death put a stop to the whole process, though some work on the treaty continued into the next year. Perhaps the appointment of Rudolf's brother Matthias as governor-general of the troubled Netherlands in 1577 made the Queen's advisers feel that the new Emperor was to be placated, and thus a Russo-Imperial alliance could be a good thing for England. In any case, relations between Elizabeth and Ivan ceased for several years, and resumed only in 1582, under rather different circumstances.

59. Huttenbach, "New Archival Material," pp. 537, 542.
60. Huttenbach, "New Archival Material," pp. 545–549.
61. C[alendar] S[tate] P[apers] F[oreign] 1575–1577, pp. 370, 384–385.

1577–1595: Growing Involvement

Beginning in 1577 England embarked on a policy of more active engagement with the northern powers. Though commercial interests played some part, the basic reasons were the increasingly threatening situation in the Netherlands, which led England to attempt to secure a friendly configuration of powers on its northeastern flank. As we shall see, this policy was basically a failure in that Denmark was never really secured as a friend and Ivan's death brought a more unfriendly attitude within Russia. Nevertheless, real danger was avoided. The sudden recurrence of English diplomatic activity in the area reflects an importance of northern Europe to England not noticed by modern historians.

Denmark

This diplomatic activity began with Denmark exactly at the moment when the attempt to turn the Anglo-Russian league into a treaty lapsed. In May 1576, Frederick II of Denmark wrote to Elizabeth objecting once again to English trade to Russia around Norway. This time Elizabeth responded, and negotiations took place on this topic in Hamburg (instead of the projected Emden) in 1577. Nothing came of the conference, but contact had been reestablished.[62] A number of other inconclusive contacts followed, and by 1580 the French ambassador to Copenhagen, Charles Dançay could report, *"La reine d'Angleterre envoie souvent devers le roi de Dannemarck et s'efforce plus que jamais de s'assurer de son amitié."* In 1581 Elizabeth informed Frederick that she had awarded him the Order of the Garter, and in 1582 Peregrine Bertie, Lord Willoughby, was sent to make the presentation. Willoughby's instructions also ordered him to discuss the English-Russian trade with Frederick's council. Thus Willoughby's mission might seem a combination of ceremonial and commercial matters.[63] Dançay did not think so. He thought the embassy was political and reported that Frederick

est *diligentement sollicité de l'Empereur, du Roi d'Espagne, et des autres Princes de la maison d'Autriche et de plusieurs autres qui tiennent leur parti, qui pour vrai font*

---

62. The English ambassadors were John Rogers, brother of Daniel, a sort of Danish specialist, and Anthony Jenkinson, presumably because of the Russian issues. Walsingham was interested not only in the commercial issues but in the need for a Protestant alliance: CSPF 1577–1578, pp. 19, 126–130.

63. "Correspondance de Charles Dantzai," *Handlingar rörande Skandinaviens historia* 11 (Stockholm, 1824), pp. 122 (22 October, 1580); Cotton Nero B III, ff. 181–183, 186–190v; Cotton Titus C VII, ff. 213–215, 218–219, 223–224v, 228–235, 237; CSPF 1582, pp. 130–131, 215–217, 247, 254.

*de très grands offres au Roi pour le gagner, et donner l'occasion de favoriser le Roi
d'Espagne contre ceux des Pays-Bas qui se sont soustraits de son obéissance. . . .*

Dançay saw Frederick's opposition to trade to Russia in this light:

*plusieurs ont cette opinion, que le Roi de Dannemarck entreprend d'empêcher le
commerce par l'invention et artifice de ceux qui veulent mettre le Roi en guerre avec
les Anglais et ceux des Pays Bas (29 September 1582).*

As Dançay also suggested, the Danish court was not entirely united on
this topic. The English agent, William Waad, reported of the treasurer
Christoffer Valkendorf that "it is noted in him to favour the Spaniard."[64]
Nevertheless, in 1583 John Herbert was able to make a treaty with
Frederick that seemed to solve the problem of Russian trade around
Norway, for the English promised to pay the sum of one hundred Rose
nobles for the privilege of trading unmolested to Russia, and the Sound
dues were fixed more clearly. Elizabeth accepted Herbert's treaty with
reservations, but it went into effect.[65]

England's relations with Denmark did not end with the conclusion of
a commercial treaty and in fact increased in frequency. These relations
took place against the background of the assassination of William the
Silent (10 July 1584), and the treaty of Nonsuch in August 1585. A
Danish mission to England in 1584 led to Thomas Bodley's embassy of
1585 to the German princes and Denmark to forge a Protestant alliance
on behalf of Henry of Navarre.[66] Frederick showed some initial sympathy, but the pro-Imperial Protestant Elector of Saxony and his own court
dissuaded him. He reported that Frederick was simply afraid of Spain, and
uninterested in an alliance with German Protestants or Navarre.[67] A
further attempt at persuasion by Lord Willoughby in December 1585 also
had no effect, again partly the result of Treasurer Valkendorf's influ-

---

64. "Correspondance," pp. 193, 198; CSPF 1582, p. 216 [2 August 1582].
65. L. Laursen, ed., *Danmark-Norges Traktater 1523–1750*, 2 vols. (Copenhagen, 1912),
    2: 632–644; Cotton Titus C VII, f. 236; CSPF 1583, pp. 389, 410–412, 420–421;
    1583–1584, pp. 99–100, 138–139, 191–192.
66. Cotton Nero B III, ff. 202–205. William Herle told Burghley in July 1585 that the
    King of Denmark would surely support the Queen against Spain, a too optimistic
    appraisal. CSPD 1581–1590, 252–253.
67. CSPF 1584–1585, pp. 415–416, 428, 563–567, 582–584, 636–639; "Correspon-
    dance," pp. 320–322 (10 January 1586); Burghley was concerned in December 1585
    that Frederick should be informed of the victuals bought for the King of Spain's
    navy in the east Baltic. CSPD 1581–1590, p. 293.

ence.[68] At this point Frederick suddenly decided to try to be an intermediary in the conflict between Spain and the Anglo-Dutch alliance. Dançay thought the motive was fear of Spain, and the Netherlanders and Leicester viewed Frederick as simply deceptive or the tool of Philip II.[69] This was undoubtedly an exaggeration, but Noel de Caron reported to Thomas Wilkes that the Danish court was pro-Spanish, and the King's better instincts could not prevail against his councillors.[70] Frederick's chancellor Henrik Ramel came to England in 1586 with the scheme, and Elizabeth had little choice but to go along with it, at least for form's sake, and meetings were actually held in 1587.[71]

By the end of 1587, however, the military situation was serious and Elizabeth had to do something more definite about Denmark. Frederick's refusal to close the Sound to Spanish ships, and the mediation scheme, coming on top of the reports of Denmark's pro-Spanish attitude, led to another mission of Daniel Rogers to Denmark in autumn of 1587.[72] Rogers was commissioned to discuss various matters, including King James VI of Scotland's Danish marriage and Danish shipping complaints against England, but concretely he was only to ask for more aid for Henry of Navarre. This Frederick granted. At the same time Rogers's report referred to secret requests he was to make of Frederick, so secret that they were nowhere written down and therefore there seems to be no extant record of them. The war with Spain was mentioned, to be sure, in his public audience, but only in a bland expression of thanks for the mediation scheme. Rogers judged the secret part of his mission to be a success, and subsequent documents of the Bodley mission give some idea of the contents of the secret discussion at Hadersleben in the winter of 1587–88.[73]

68. CSPF 1585–1586, pp. 89–91, 142–143, 216–218, 249–250, 255–257.
69. "Correspondance," pp. 331–339 (21 April and 18 August 1586); CSPF 1585–1586, p. 238; CSPF 1586–1587, pp. 35–39, 320–321, 324–325, 343–345.
70. CSPF 1586–1587, pp. 252, 256. Leon van der Essen, Alexandre Farnèse, prince de Parme, 5 vols. (Brussels, 1933–34), 5: 76–85.
71. CSPF 1585 1586, pp. 564, 608 609, 632 633, 673 674; Cotton Nero B III, ff. 214–227v; CSPF 1586–1588, pp. 323–324, 335–336; CSPF 1587, pp. 6–8, 60, 83, 161–162, 176–177, 472–482.
72. CSPF 1587, p. 111. William Herle was urging Burghley to make a better understanding with Denmark in January 1587. CSPD 1581–1590, pp. 380, 382.
73. CSPD 1581–1590, p. 425; CSPF 1588 (January-June), pp. 27–28, 33; Cotton Nero B III, ff. 246–249. Available Danish sources add nothing. Even treasurer Valkendorf's correspondent at court knew nothing of the secret discussions. Arthur G. Hassø, Rigshofmester Kristoffer Valkendorf til Glorup (1525–1601) (Copenhagen, 1933), pp. 156–158. The Danish archives for these months contain only an innoc-

Nonetheless, Frederick's secret promises expired with him on 4 April 1588, when he died, leaving his kingdom to his eleven-year-old son Christian IV. A regency headed by chancellor Niels Kaas and treasurer Christoffer Valkendorf took over the government. With the Armada about to sail from Spain England had no idea what attitude the new Danish government would take. In May Rogers was immediately dispatched back to Denmark to sound out the new government, and the results were favorable, as Rogers reported back to Burghley.[74] Howard and Drake could not know all this, of course, for Rogers's reports would have reached London only after they were already at sea. Consequently, when they lost sight of the Spanish fleet in the North Sea on 7–8 August, both Drake and Howard naturally assumed that the Armada was going to Denmark, a friendly port to Spain for those not privy to King Frederick's secret talks with Rogers. On 10 August Drake asked Walsingham to get the Queen to send someone to Denmark so the Spaniards could not refit in Denmark or Norway.[75] The next day instructions were composed for Thomas Bodley, who was to carry out the mission. His instructions incidentally reveal what Frederick had promised: "You shall put the King and the said Governors in mind of the honorable offer made by the late King unto her Majesty, that if her [honor?] or Realme should be assailed, he would come to assist her in person." Clearly young Christian could not substitute for his father, so Bodley was to request the new government not to allow the Armada to refit in Danish harbors.[76]

With the crisis of the Armada past, Anglo-Danish relations entered into a calmer phase, where the main issues were the incidents of English seizures of Danish ships going to Spain and Portugal. In 1590 Georg Schomaker came to England to complain, and later in the year Christopher Parkins stopped in Denmark on his way to Poland and Lübeck to

---

uous letter about Scotland of 10 January 1588: TKUA, Kopibog Latina 1586–1599, ff. 52–53v.

74. CSPF 1588 (July–December), pp. 75–80; HMC, *Salisbury*, 3: 329; Cotton Nero B III, ff. 252–253v, 258v-259v, 267–273v; Lansdowne 57, no. 30; Huntington Library, Ellesmere MSS 1608.

75. CSPD 1581–1590, pp. 526–527, 529. Sir Horatio Palavicino agreed with Drake: ibid., 530. Captain Alonso Vanegas, however, reported that the Duke of Medina Sidonia rejected a proposal to sail the Armada toward Norway as it was "a land of enemies." This conversation implies that at least some Spanish captains assumed Denmark to be a friendly neutral, but the Duke did not. Did he know of Frederick's promise? See C. Fernandez Duro, *La armada invencible*, 2 vols. (Madrid, 1884–1885), 2: 395.

76. Cotton Nero B III, ff. 256–257. Bodley may never have actually gone on this mission: he did go to the Netherlands that autumn.

discuss these problems. In 1592 Paul Knibbe came from the Danish Regents to England to follow up.[77] Nothing of moment was discussed beyond these issues until the majority of Christian IV in 1596.

SWEDEN

As noted above, England had few direct relations with Sweden at this time, but the English kept abreast of affairs, particularly religious affairs. Like many Swedes, the English interpreted King Johan III's religious policy as simply pro-Catholic. In September 1577, Christopher Hoddesdon reported the King's invitation to the Jesuits to found a college in Stockholm. On 12 March 1580, Henry Cobham reported on Francisco de Eraso's mission to Sweden on behalf of Spain, King John's Papist inclinations and, on 4 November 1582, Johan's offer of naval stores to Philip.[78] In that same year Thomas Gorge was sent to Sweden on matters regarding an old debt, and in 1583 Johan sent to Elizabeth, Magnus Brahe, Count of Visingsborg, and Sir Andrew Keith to deal with the matter of the debt, that of the ships going to Russia seized by Sweden, and

77. SP 75/2, ff. 32–57v, 74–76v, 94, 115–115v, 120–120v, 128–132v, 158–168v; Cotton Nero B IV, ff. 2–22, 27–29v, 38, 43–48v. The attitude of the Danish regency to England was not friendly. The missions from the government of the Spanish Netherlands to Denmark in 1589 and 1591 met a favorable response, though one in 1594 did not succeed in getting Denmark to close the Sound to the Dutch and English. The Danes argued that their trade was too important, and offered mediation in the Netherlands. At the same time, Danish royal councillors, especially Barnekov, spoke at some length of their desire to help Emperor Rudolf in his wars against the Turks, and declared that the English supported Turkey. They believed Sir Horatio Palavicino to be the English agent making such contacts, an unlikely object of such suspicions. Charles Piot, "Une mission diplomatique des Pays-Bas espagnols dans le nord de l'Europe en 1594," *Bulletin de la Commission royale d'histoire*, Académie des sciences, des lettres et des beaux-arts de Belgique, 4 ser., t. 11: 437–520.

78. CSPF 1577–1578, p. 443; 1579–1580, pp. 187; 1582, p. 436. This information was not perfectly accurate, though it captured the basic situation. The Jesuit Laurentius Nicolai Norvegus had set up a college in Stockholm in 1576 with Johan's encouragement, but its Catholic character was secret. Eraso was asking for the loan of the Swedish fleet to Philip II, in which he was unsuccessful, and left Sweden in 1579: naval stores were bought in the Baltic for Spain, but whether King Johan offered them cannot be determined. Karl Hildebrand, *Johan III och Europas katolska makter 1568–1580: Studier i 1500-talets politiska historia* (Uppsala, 1898), pp. 290–297; Emil Hildebrand, "Johan III och Filip II: Depescher från det spanska sändebudet till Sverige kapten Francisco de Eraso," *Historisk tidskrift* 6 (1886): 1–50; Oskar Garstein, *Rome and the Counter-Reformation in Scandinavia*, 2 vols. (Oslo, 1964–1980), 1: 174–178.

to ask for mediation in the war with Russia.[79] Sir Jerome Bowes indeed took the offer to Ivan IV, but a truce was made without English help in August 1583. The mediation offer did not change the tenor of information about Johan, as Thomas Tenneker's letter to Walsingham of 16 October 1585 admitted only of less persecution of the Lutherans, not full restoration of their faith.[80] In 1587 the election of Johan's Catholic son Sigismund to succeed Stefan Batory as King of Poland naturally changed the situation of both countries, and eventually England's reaction to them. Daniel Rogers in 1588 again referred to Johan's "inconstancy" in religion,[81] but little mention was made of the country for the next few years. The resumption of the Russo-Swedish war caused comment, but until Sigismund became King of Sweden on his father's death in 1592, Sweden attracted little English attention. Only beginning in 1595, when Duke Karl led the diet to break with King Sigismund over religious and other matters, did Sweden emerge as an object of policy to England.

POLAND 1576–1596

The election of the Catholic Prince of Transylvania, Stefan Batory, as King of Poland in 1575–76 brought a major change in Poland's political fortunes. Batory was able to reverse Poland's defeats at Russian hands in the Livonian War, recovering all the lost territory and establishing Polish rule in the southern parts of Livonia. Ivan was driven entirely from Livonia, now divided between Poland, Sweden, and Denmark. In 1582 the treaty of Iam Zapol'skii between Russia and Poland (made with papal mediation) put a temporary end to this part of the conflict over the Baltic littoral.

Batory's attitude to England was in part the result of his attitude to the two branches of the house of Habsburg. The Vienna Habsburgs were his enemies both because of disagreements over the status of his native Transylvania and because they had provided his rival for the Polish throne in 1575–1576. Spain, however, he considered a friend. The Polish

79. CSPF 1581–1582, p. 400; 1582, p. 200; 1583, pp. 330–331; 1583–1584, pp. 292–293. This was the highest level delegation to England from Sweden since Johan's own trip in 1559–1560 on behalf of his brother taking King Erik XIV's marriage proposals to Elizabeth. It was also the last important Swedish embassy to England in her reign.
80. CSPF 1585–1586, p. 90. Johan expelled Father Laurentius in 1580, and closed the Catholic institutions on his wife's death in 1583. Nevertheless he continued to push for a middle path in religion until his death in 1592, leading many orthodox Lutheran clergy to exile or loss of position.
81. CSPF 1588 (July-December), p. 79.

King at the very beginning of his reign was ready to stop the export of grain (his country's chief export!) to England and the Netherlands to help Philip II, and in 1586 Batory drew up a contingency plan to help the Spanish King in the forthcoming war with England. He planned to occupy the Sound, and supply Spain with food to help the invasion. He suggested that the Spanish fleet land on the Isle of Wight. From the English point of view, the paradox of Batory's reign was that a monarch so hostile to England and so clearly pro-Spanish was responsible for the Eastland Company's foothold in Poland.[82] The relative success of the Eastland Company was the result of Batory's conflict with the city of Danzig. This began at his election, for Danzig had preferred a German Habsburg candidate, and had been in rebellion against the new King from the beginning. Batory responded in 1577 by banning trade through the rebel town and ordering merchants to go to Elbing instead, a few miles to the east but still within the Polish province of Royal Prussia. In 1579 the Eastland Company received a charter from the English crown, and in the next year Dr. John Rogers arrived in Poland to make arrangements for English merchants. In this he was only partially successful, for the King refused to act on the matter, and in November 1581, Rogers made an agreement with the city of Elbing to establish the company staple in that town. From then on until Stefan Batory's death in 1586 Rogers, followed by John Herbert in 1583–1585 (on the way from his more successful Danish mission), tried without success to get royal assent to the agreement with the Elbing magistrates.[83]

The election of Sigismund Vasa as King of Poland in 1587 brought no better a situation from the English point of view. England's war with Spain brought English seizures of ships bound for Spain, a similar problem to that with Denmark. Missions to Poland by Christopher Parkins, with the twin aim of securing the Elbing staple and smoothing over the seizure

82. Ludwik Boratynski, "Stefan Batory, Hanza, i powstanie Niderlandów," *Przeglad Historyczny* 6 (1908): 50–65, 173–194, 322–334; Henryk Zins, *England and the Baltic in the Elizabethan Era,* trans. H. C. Stevens (Totowa, N. J., 1972); J. K. Fedorowicz, *England's Baltic Trade in the Early Seventeenth Century, A Study in Anglo-Polish Commercial Diplomacy* (Cambridge, 1980); and van der Essen, *Alexandre Farnèse,* 5: 75–76.

83. C. H. Talbot, ed., "Res Polonicae Elisabetha I Angliae regnante conscriptae ex Archivis publicis Londoniarum," *Elementa ad fontium editiones* (Rome, 1961), 4: 1–75; Talbot, *Elementa* 17: 95–96, 103–131, 178–239; Zins, *England,* pp. 54–84, Fedorowicz, *England's Baltic Trade,* pp. 34–49. The commercial jealousy of the town of Danzig was another formidable obstacle, one that spilled over into England's relations with the Hanse towns and the Empire.

of Polish ships, failed in both 1591 and 1594–1595. Parkins was not surprised at his failure. In 1589 both he and John Herbert had been at Elbing, and Parkins picked up news of the dispute in Prague between the Polish ambassador, Jan Ostroróg, and the Spanish ambassador, Guillén de San Clemente. San Clemente allegedly objected to friendly letters between Elizabeth and Sigismund, and the papal legate intervened to object to Poland's acceptance of Elizabeth's title, "Defender of the Faith." In 1591 it was the Bishop of Kujawy, Hieronym Rozrażewski, and the Primate of Poland, Stanisław Karnkowski, who blocked privileges for the English merchants, the former asserting that he could not tolerate Protestant ministers in Danzig. The same year the Polish chancellery, presumably under the inspiration of Vice-Chancellor Jan Tarnowski, dropped the title "Defender of the Faith" in letters to Elizabeth, according to Parkins the result of the influence of the Catholic clergy on the King. In 1594 he reported Poland's senate and diet to be entirely under the sway of the "Pope's faction" and he made no progress on the Elbing question. His only success was to assure the Transylvanians of England's friendship, a move that undoubtedly reinforced the friendship of Chancellor Zamoyski, but not of the King.[84] Thus Poland, in English eyes, was just another Catholic power, and Sigismund's 1592 marriage with the Austrian Archduchess Anna, as well as the growing conflict with Sweden, only confirmed this impression. Sigismund's accession to his father's throne in Sweden in 1592 was quickly followed by the restoration of Lutheran orthodoxy at Uppsala in 1593, against the King's wishes. Duke Karl of Södermanland began his rebellion with the Söderköping diet of 1595, and Protestant Sweden was now on a collision course with the Catholic King of Poland. The Eastland Company's agreement with Elbing was in fact never confirmed, and England understood Poland in future years as a hostile Catholic power. For the rest of Elizabeth's reign

84. Talbot, ed., *Elementa* 4: 91–95, 104–124, 146–151, 158–182; 17: 135–137, 149–158. In 1591 Parkins was right: he noticed the change in title on 15 January 1591, and Tarnowski had acquired the office of vice-chancellor only on 7 January, as the result of the defeat of Chancellor Zamoyski in the senate by King Sigismund's party and the clergy led by Primate Karnkowski. Bishop Rozrazewski as well was a supporter of the King. Kazimierz Lepszy, *Rzeczpospolita Polska w dobie Sejmu inkwizycyjnego (1589–1592)* (Cracow, 1939), pp. 230–265. Parkins, like other Englishmen, was struck by the power of the Catholic faction under Sigismund, rather than by the continued semi-toleration of Protestants, especially as the Protestants seemed to have no effect on foreign policy. On Poland's alignment with the Habsburgs and its implications for relations with England, see Fedorowicz, *England's Baltic Trade*, pp. 38–40, and Adam Szelągowski, *Walka o Bałtyk*, 2d ed.(Lwow, 1921), pp. 108–113, 120–123.

Anglo-Polish relations deteriorated rapidly, in large part as a result of the Swedish-Polish conflict.

RUSSIA 1582–1591

The resumption of diplomatic contact between England and Russia in 1582 was the beginning of yet another attempt at an Anglo-Russian treaty, this one being much more serious on the English side than the Russian. The death of Ivan the Terrible in 1584 put a swift end to such endeavors, and inaugurated a period of much more distant and complex relations.

In 1582 the initiative had come from the Russian side. Early in that year, Ivan conceived the notion that he needed a new wife (to be his fifth) and a treaty with England. His war with Poland over Livonia had just come to an end in January 1582, with the truce of Iam Zapol'skii, concluded with the help of the papal mediator, the Jesuit Antonio Possevino. Negotiations were under way with Sweden, to bear fruit in the next year. In June the Tsar instructed his ambassador, Fyodor Andreevich Pisemskii, on the aims of his mission with the help of one Dr. Robert Jacob, an English doctor on Russian service.[85] Ivan wanted not just an aristocrat's daughter, but one with royal blood, and (in Russian terminology) an "appanage princess." Mary Hastings, daughter of the Earl of Huntingdon, fitted the bill according to Dr. Jacob, so Pisemskii was ordered to take a look at her and get a portrait. The marriage question was to lead into the treaty, whose provisions were a bit vague: it was to be a treaty of alliance, but the details were to be worked out by an English embassy to Moscow. Pisemskii was also ordered to tell the Queen that the Danes were unjustly claiming Pechenga and the Kola peninsula and preventing English trade there.[86] Pisemskii left the Dvina mouth on 11 August, in a convoy of English and Dutch ships escorted by two English men-of-war (to protect them from the Danes) and made landfall at Scarborough on 16 September 1582. From there they went on by land, arriving in Tottenham High Cross (where they stayed because of plague) on 27 September. Negotiations began. Their first audience was on 4 November, but real discussion began on 17 December in Greenwich, with Secretary Walsingham, Leicester, Christopher Hatton, and Lord Hunsdon. Pisemskii opened the discussion with a review of Anglo-Russian relations, noting that the previous friendship had not led to a

---

85. Willan did not use the long account in SRIO 38. Willan, *Early History*, pp. 161–164.
86. SRIO 38: 3–14.

treaty. He then stated that King Stefan Batory was the Tsar's enemy, and was supported in this by the Pope and the Emperor. The Tsar requested a treaty of friendship, which would obligate both sides to send men, and if that was impossible, military supplies in time of war. Clearly the obligations would be mainly on the English side, but Pisemskii hinted, noting Russia's favor to the Muscovy Company, what would be the Russian return. Later on at the banquet that day the English asked him what truth there was in the rumor that the Pope had reconciled Ivan and Stefan. Pisemskii replied, "The Pope may say what he wants when no one is there; but if he had reconciled our sovereign with the King, then our sovereign would not call the Lithuanian [i.e., Polish] King his enemy, and would not write to his sister, your sovereign Queen Elizabeth, that he was his enemy."[87] While the Russians waited for Elizabeth's reply, George Barne of the Muscovy Company, who was in charge of their logistic arrangements, told them that the King of Denmark was trying to prohibit trade by both English and Dutch to Russia.

Their next formal audience was on 20 January 1583, but they had no reply until 10 March on the treaty proposal. On that day their translator brought the Russians (now in London) the reply that the Queen was in general in favor of the idea, but wanted to specify that she should request any enemies of the Tsar to cease their actions before she joined in hostilities on any level. The formal reply came on 19 March with that provision, agreeing to the proposal and adding some details about trade: the whole basically a copy of the unsigned treaty of 1576–1577.[88] The Russians replied that the proposals did not explicitly call the Tsar "brother," and that it also requested a monopoly of trade for the English in Russia, excluding all other western merchants, which could not be granted. The English response was that the reply would be rephrased, and the monopoly issue would be referred to the Queen. Another audience with the Queen took place on St. George's day, the traditional day of the Garter Feast, and it was purely ceremonial. The final audience was at Greenwich on 26 May, and the Queen repeated her position of 10 March. As no agreement could be reached, Elizabeth announced to Pisemskii that Jerome Bowes would be sent to Russia to handle the matter.[89] After this the Company representatives, Thomas Randolph

---

87. *SRIO* 38: 38–39. English translation of Pisemskii's speech to the Queen: Tolstoi, *Pervye sorok let*, pp. 190–192. A memorandum for this meeting shows that the English did not expect an alliance proposal: ibid., 194–195.

88. *SRIO* 38: 43–48.

89. *SRIO* 38: 48–58.

and George Barne, presented various merchant complaints, including the alleged privileges of the Netherlander Jan de Wale. Pisemskii left on 15 June, with a corrected copy of the English proposals (Ivan was called brother), and arrived home after a rough passage on 26 July 1583.[90]

In addition to the treaty business, Pisemskii brought up the marriage, and recorded the results in a secret addendum to his report. It turns out that he met privately with Elizabeth on 18 January on the subject. The Queen was not enthusiastic. She asserted that Mary Hastings was not beautiful enough for the Tsar, and asked what might be the conditions of such a marriage. Only on 5 April did she agree to the portrait, and on 17 May Thomas Randolph brought Pisemskii to an attic that looked on the garden of Sir Thomas Bromley (the Lord Chancellor), where he was able to see the Tsar's prospective bride in the company of Sir Thomas. A little later Lady Bromley and the Countess of Huntingdon brought Pisemskii to see Mary at closer range in the garden. The Queen and Pisemskii discussed the matter briefly at the final audience (26 May), and the portrait arrived on 13 June.[91]

English motives can be reconstructed again only circumstantially. The end of Archduke Matthias's protectorate in the Netherlands in 1581 meant that the Emperor was no longer a consideration. Furthermore the English were afraid of the sudden involvement of the Pope in Russian affairs. Henry Cobham saw danger in the presence of a Russian ambassador in Rome and in Possevino's mission.[92] In October 1582 he reported from Paris on further of Possevino's intrigues to bring the Russians under the authority of the Pope and to ally them with the Emperor against the Turks.[93] This information, which seems to have reached Cobham from Italy, was accurate, for it reflected exactly Gregory XIII's purpose in directing Possevino to mediate the Russo-Polish peace. None of this could bring joy in London, and the question about the Pope's mediation put to Pisemskii at the meeting on 17 December reflected this concern. Furthermore England was not now close to war, as she would be in 1587–88, and did not need northern allies so greatly. Elizabeth could afford to place conditions and to argue about commercial issues.

In this situation Elizabeth was ready to make a treaty, though not just

---

90. *SRIO* 38: 58–64.
91. Throughout Elizabeth seems to have had two concerns: first, that Mary's children could not be the heirs to the Russian throne, as other heirs already existed, and second, regarding the extent to which her position would be properly dignified (the Tsar's previous wives had no royal blood, as did Mary). *SRIO* 38: 65–70.
92. *CSPF 1581–1582*, pp. 93, 124–125, 152, 644.
93. *CSPF 1582*, pp. 380–381.

any treaty, and Bowes's instructions reflected these concerns. He was empowered by the Queen to sign any treaty that fitted his instructions, so that the situation of 1570 would not be repeated. The instructions specified that the Queen should not be required to open hostilities against any prince who was Ivan's enemy without first asking said prince to cease and desist his activity. Bowes was told that "you shall pray our good brother the K. to conceive well of our meaning therein." This does not seem to mean that Bowes was to refuse even to compromise on this point, but merely to explain thoroughly the Queen's position. Bowes was to state that Mary Hastings was not well enough for a marriage to the Tsar, and to discourage him from further such projects. He was also to offer the Queen's services to mediate the war with Sweden. A separate memorandum instructed Bowes to pass on the merchants' complaints about various exactions and the trade of Jan de Wale as well as the injustice of the King of Denmark's exactions at Wardo.[94]

The history of the embassy is also unique in that a detailed Russian record of the negotiations is matched by Bowes's own much shorter account published in the first 1589 edition of Hakluyt's *Principall Navigations*. The history of this publication is rather complex for the first printing was almost immediately withdrawn and an anonymous account was substituted, the one that appears in the 1598–1600 edition and most modern republications. The main difference between the two is that the anonymous version completely omitted any account of political negotiations and described only the trade discussions. As we shall see, Bowes' own version did mention the discussion of a league (omitting the secret marriage discussions), but devoted much less attention to it than the Russian official record.[95]

The Russians were aware of Bowes's arrival by 7 August 1583, and sent the usual officials to meet and bring him to Moscow, where he arrived on 15 October. On the eighteenth the sub-secretary Savva Frolov came to ask him not to mention the secret business (the marriage) at his audience, which took place on the twenty-fourth. On 6 November Bowes had his first meeting with the officials assigned to talks with him, Nikita Romanovich Iur'ev-Zakharin (i.e., Romanov: the grandfather of Tsar Michael), Bogdan Bel'skii, the ambassadorial office secretary Andrei

94. *CSPF 1583*, pp. 374–378, 406–407; *CSPF 1583–1584*, pp. 294–295; Tolstoi, *Pervye sorok let*, pp. 201–221.
95. Robert M. Croskey, "Hakluyt's Accounts of Sir Jerome Bowes's Embassy to Ivan IV," *SEER* 61, 4 (1983): 546–564; Richard Hakluyt, *The Principall Navigations, Voiages, and Discoveries of the English Nation* (Cambridge, 1965 [reprint of 1589 edition]), pp. 491–501.

Shchelkalov, and Savva Frolov.[96] At this very first meeting, the issues arose which had already been a problem at the time of Pisemskii's mission: the English desire to discuss issues beforehand with any enemy of Russia before joining a military effort, and the English desire for a monopoly of trade by the northern route. The Russians would concede neither, and on the first point only offered specifically to mention King Stefan of Poland as the potential enemy. Bowes rejected the idea.[97] Then the boyars pressed him a little on the trade issues, saying that the English rivals were the Dutch (at Kholmogory) and the French (on the Kola peninsula), and both were friendly with England, so why should Elizabeth object to their trade? Bowes simply said no concession on this point was contained in his instructions. On 1 December Iur'ev-Zakharin and Bel'skii came alone to Bowes's lodging to discuss the secret matters, the marriage. Bowes responded that his orders were to speak with the Tsar alone on all this. On 8 December he had further discussions, where the Russians presented reasons against the English position on the treaty: England would have Russian support against the Pope or anyone else, and Russia's enemies were Poland, Sweden, and Denmark. Bowes described his mistress's enemies as (besides the Pope), the Emperor and the King of Spain, "a friend such as many could be bought at market for a penny." Denmark he presented as friendly, recounting the presentation of the Order of the Garter to Frederick; and Sweden he claimed as friendly. Long discussion of the trade followed, with the Russians stressing the advantages that they had from Jan de Wale in particular, who brought goods the English did not have to sell. Another inconclusive meeting.[98]

On 13 December he came to the palace to see the Tsar in person. Bowes told Ivan that Mary Hastings was not well and did not want to change her religion, to which Ivan gave a conciliatory reply. At this point Bowes made a serious error, for he blithely mentioned that the Queen had at least ten female relatives who were even more beautiful. Ivan asked for names, but Bowes did not give any. There then followed an argument between Bowes and his Russian counterparts, before the Tsar, about what exactly Bowes had said in the negotiations. This got nowhere, and Ivan then gave the Englishman a long historical defense of

---

96. Tolstoi, *Pervye sorok let*, pp. 231–235.

97. *SRIO* 38: 86–93; Hakluyt, *Principall Navigations*, pp. 491–494.

98. *SRIO* 38: 93–103; Hakluyt, *Principall Navigations*, p. 494. Bowes claimed later that he did not name any of the Queen's enemies, but if the Russian record was accurate, he was either incompetent or deceptive. The Emperor in 1584 was not an enemy, even if not a friend, and Denmark was scarcely friendly, in spite of the 1583 treaty.

the Russian decision to allow the Dutch to trade, and the audience ended.[99]

Five days later he was back again, and Ivan told him that he had been told Bowes wanted to see him alone again, which Bowes denied. Ivan then reminded him that it was not Russian custom for ambassadors to speak privately to the Tsar without his boyars, apparently implying that he was doing him a great favor. Bowes replied that he had done so at the court of France, and received the sharp reply that French customs were irrelevant in Russia. Ivan then repeated his position on the details of the projected treaty and asked Bowes in more detail about the other relatives of the Queen whom he had mentioned. Bowes would (and probably could) not give much answer, other than to promise to send portraits. On 1 January 1584, the Russians proposed concrete language for the treaty which would restrict but not abolish the trade rights of non-English merchants in the north, and a partial concession on the issue of prior negotiations with Ivan's enemies: the prior discussions should take place at the last minute, to prevent Ivan's enemies from being warned. Bowes did not comment on the latter part, apparently accepting it, but still objected to the trade clause. Ivan in turn said that he would have to send an ambassador to England to make a final agreement; and he sent to ask about the ten royal female relatives Bowes had mentioned, although Bowes denied ever mentioning them. The meeting dissolved in procedural debates.[100]

Another January meeting, on the fifth, with the Tsar was equally fruitless, for Ivan asked Bowes why he was unwilling to negotiate and referred everything back to the Queen if, in fact, as ambassador he was empowered to do the opposite. Bowes merely repeated that those were his instructions, and Ivan clearly became angry, lectured him on diplomatic protocol, and then implied that the problem was not with the Queen's position but with Bowes's clumsiness. Bowes then complained about the treatment of his embassy at various times—food and other matters, and Shchelkalov's doings—and was dismissed. That same day a sort of final summary was sent by Bel'skii and Frolov, who read him a list of his misrepresentations of various facts, his own earlier statements and Pisem-

---

99. *SRIO* 38: 103–112. In the course of the discussion Bowes also told Ivan that Elizabeth could send the army of Johan Casimir of the Palatinate to help the Russians. In Bowes's account only the commercial business is mentioned. Hakluyt, *Principall Navigations*, p. 494.

100. *SRIO* 38: 112–119; Hakluyt, *Principall Navigations*, pp. 494–495. Bowes does not mention the Russian concession on the alliance, saying that the articles proposed were the same as from Pisemskii.

skii's negotiations. On 11 January an expanded group of boyars met Bowes and admitted that his treatment had defects, but defended Shchelkalov in the matter. Again on 19 January Ivan met Bowes, this time in a more conciliatory mood: on the trade he stuck to his position, but he admitted that he had no real enmity to Denmark, and the treaty need not extend beyond an alliance against Poland and Sweden. Bowes this time responded in kind, admitting that Elizabeth's relations with Poland and Sweden were none too friendly, but referring the matter to a future embassy from the Tsar. (According to Bowes he did admit that Poland was no friend to Elizabeth.) Undoubtedly to his embarrassment, Ivan brought up the marriage again, but Bowes again simply suggested that this was a matter for the future embassy. On 8 February Bowes finally told the boyars that the treaty was conditional on the English monopoly in the north, but when his bluff was called would not make a treaty. (Bowes put this exchange as occurring on 13 February and with the Tsar, but the content of the exchange was the same.) On 13 February he met privately with the Tsar with no result on the marriage issue, and four days later with Bel'skii and Frolov, who brought him a text of an agreement. Apparently it did not fully concede a monopoly and, in addition, Bowes raised a new issue: that of the Tsar's right to Livonia. Here the negotiations ended, for Ivan died on 18 March 1584.[101]

The new government did not get its internal matters settled enough to give Bowes its own ideas until 14 May. This was only to confirm the old charter of privileges of 1572, and no mention was made of an alliance or further privileges, though Bowes claimed that Tsar Fyodor did mention the alliance at the final audience, stating a wish for such an alliance as existed in his father's time. This could only be the 1570 oral agreement. Bowes left Moscow on 30 May, boarded an English ship and sailed for home on 12 July.[102]

Bowes's surviving reports give a rather different impression of the events, but they concentrate on the events after Ivan's death. He stressed the malevolent attitude of Shchelkalov and Nikita Romanov, both being as well of the "Dutche" (that is, German, or Imperial) faction. This was not imagination, and the second, anonymous, account of the mission in Hakluyt added that when Ivan died Shchelkalov sent to tell him, "your English emperor is dead." Nevertheless, it was not the whole story. Bowes was extremely inflexible in the negotiations, and offended the Russian protocol as well. He repeatedly said things that undermined his own

101. *SRIO* 38: 119–133; Hakluyt, *Principall Navigations*, pp. 495–499.
102. *SRIO* 38: 133–145.

position, like the suggestion that Elizabeth might send Johan Casimir's army to Russia. Bowes badly botched the marriage issue, giving Ivan the idea that Elizabeth might find an alternative to Mary Hastings when the Queen had made it clear in the instructions that he was to put an end to these discussions. The instructions also do not say that he was not to make any compromise whatever on the two points at issue of the alliance and trade. They merely say that he was to convey the Queen's position, and he was given a mandate to negotiate and sign a treaty in the Queen's name. There is nothing in the instructions that would have prohibited him from signing the compromise version offered by Ivan in January or on 13 February. In January the Russians had conceded the idea of prior discussion, but Bowes insisted on the trade monopoly. As Bowes does not seem to have had any reason to push the Muscovy Company's interests so strongly (and incompetently), his attitude can only be put down to an inflexibility of personality fatal in a diplomat. This was the reason why his letters and his account emphasized the hostility of the "Dutche" faction, Nikita Romanov and Shchelkalov.[103]

If Bowes had been a different man and made a treaty before Ivan's death, the new government would probably have done little with it, for his description of the orientation of the government of Fyodor Ivanovich is fairly accurate. Only Boris Godunov seems to have been to any extent favorable to English traders and to an English alliance, but he was not yet in control. The years of Fyodor's reign (1584–1598) were ones of continual factional battles at court, and these battles had implications for foreign policy. For one thing, the government was often preoccupied with internal problems, and for another, factions hostile to or uninterested in England remained influential until Boris's accession to the throne in 1598. The result was a series of fruitless English efforts to improve relations which finally came to an end with the Horsey mission

103. 'Dutch' here probably means German, rather than Hollander, for de Wale seems to have been the only Dutchman in Moscow, and the embryonic Dutch republic had no relations with Russia yet. De Wale also identified himself to the Russians as a subject of the King of Spain, not as Dutch. Lur'e, "Russko-angliiskie otnosheniia," pp. 435–438. We also know from Fletcher and other sources that Romanov and Shchelkalov did support an Imperial alliance. The anonymous Hakluyt account speaks of Dutch merchants, but as Croskey has shown, it is a very dubious source, cobbled together by Hakluyt himself or some other from Bowes's account and information apparently from Horsey. It also refers to the German physician Bomelius as Dutch. The text of the second anonymous account: Richard Hakluyt, *Principal Navigations, Voyages, Traffiques, and Discoveries of the English Nation*, 10 vols. (London, 1927–1928 [reprinting the 1598–1600 edition]) 2: 251–263.

of 1590–1591, and diplomatic relations did not resume until 1598, with the mission of Francis Cherry.

The history of the English missions in 1585–1591, fruitless as they were, does reveal clearly the structure of the problem. Right after the coronation of Tsar Fyodor, Bowes was sent back to England and Horsey as well, with a message for the Queen. In December 1584, the Russian court sent Reinhold (Roman) Beckman to England with a message of complaint about Bowes and his behavior as well as about the misdeeds of various English merchants. His stay in London in the spring of 1585 passed in recriminations about both Bowes and the English merchants in Russia, and accomplished little, but Horsey was sent in 1586 to try to patch up the problems. On 1 January of that year Tsar Fyodor had already given Rowland Howard and some other merchants (not the Muscovy Company per se) a privilege confirming that they might trade without paying customs, but otherwise with less favor than before. Horsey was able to get this confirmed again in February 1587, taking the credit for himself. That summer the English sent Francis Cherry, a Russian merchant, to Moscow to deal with the Anthony Marsh debt affair, which was to continue as a problem for over a decade. At no time in this period does a renewal of the league seem to have been discussed.[104]

That issue of the league came up again only with the mission of Dr. Giles Fletcher in 1588, which gave him the experience to publish the famous description of Russia. No Russian sources survive for this mission, and the English ones are rather fragmentary, but it is clear that Fletcher was to do two things: renegotiate the Anglo-Russian league and bring the Company privileges back to what they had been. As the Company was already a supplier of naval store to England, its privileges in 1588 were not only a commercial matter. Fletcher's results, according to his report, were mixed but not entirely unsuccessful. He wrote, "Concerning the matters of league and friendship betwixt your Highness and the Emperor, it is received in very kind sort, and profession made of like good will and other correspondency as was before betwixt your Highness and the Emperor's father."[105] As we have seen, this would suggest that an oral

104. SRIO 38: 146–196; Edward A. Bond, *Russia at the Close of the Sixteenth Century,* Hakluyt Society First Series 20 (London, 1856), pp. 153–341, 356–381; Robert Croskey, "The Composition of Sir Jerome Horsey's 'Travels,'" *Jahrbücher für Geschichte Osteuropas* 26, 3 (1978): 362–375; A. A. Sevast'ianova, "Zapiski Dzheroma Gorseia o Rossii v kontse XVI–nachale XVII vekov: Raznovremennye sloi istochnikov i ikh khronologiia," in V. B. Kobrin ed., *Voprosy istoriografii i istochnikovedeniia otechestvennoi istorii: Sbornik trudov* (Moscow, 1974), pp. 63–124.

105. Bond, *Russia,* p. 349. On the commercial aspects of the mission see also Samuel H.

agreement of friendship and mutual defense was made, but not committed to paper. In the situation of 1588, it would imply that military supplies could be sent to England without obstruction, something that was already proceeding under the auspices of the Muscovy Company's usual purchases of naval stores. As far as the Company itself went, the privileges were restored to the Company, not just to individuals associated with it, and the trade to Persia opened to the Company. This attitude on the part of Fyodor's government was not, however, as significant as it might seem, as Fletcher reported. He complained at great length of his "hard entertainment," the cause being the various alliance projects under way with the Emperor: Fyodor's ambassador was trying to make an alliance against Poland, and there was talk of alliance of Russia with Spain against the Turks. These reports by Fletcher captured the essence of the political situation. At the death of Stefan Batory in December 1586, the Habsburgs had put forth Archduke Maximilian as candidate for the throne, but he had been defeated by the supporters of Sigismund Vasa early in 1587. Russia had supported the candidacy of Maximilian, obviously fearing a joint kingdom of Poland and Sweden. This meant a return to the policy of Ivan III and Vasilii III, alliance with the Habsburgs rather than with England. Indeed in April 1588, as Fletcher was leaving England, the Russians sent an embassy to Prague that offered Rudolf the possibility of the Russian throne for Maximilian after the death of Fyodor, thus bypassing Tsarevich Dmitrii. This offer was made in the name of Boris Godunov and "other lords," and explained Fletcher's report that Boris was now no friend of England or the Company. Thus on the issue of relations with England Boris, though earlier he had assured Horsey of his friendship both for his own person and for England, now seems to have joined England's other enemies at the Russian court, Nikita Romanov and Andrei Shchelkalov.[106] Fletcher returned to England in the summer of 1589.

Baron, "Ivan the Terrible, Giles Fletcher, and the Muscovite Merchantry: a Reconsideration," *SEER* 56, 4 (October, 1978): 563–585.

106. Bond, *Russia*, pp. 342–351; Joseph Fiedler, "Beziehungen Osterreichs zu Russland in den Jahren 1584–1598," *Almanach der kaiserlichen Akademie der Wissenschaften*, Vienna, 16 (1866): 255–278; Tolstoi, *Pervye sorok let*, pp. 288–312. The Russian mission produced a return mission of Nicholas Warkocz from Prague to Moscow which did raise the idea of a Russian league with the Habsburgs, including Spain. A copy of Warkocz's relation was translated into Spanish and sent on to Madrid. L. P. Lapteva, ed., "Donesenie avstriiskogo posla o poezdke v Moskvu v 1589 godu," *Voprosy istorii* 6 (1978): 95–112; and the Russian account in *Pamiatniki diplomaticheskikh snoshenii* 1: 1101–1222. See also Uebersberger, *Osterreich*, pp. 535–541.

The last major diplomatic effort by England in Russia at this time was the Horsey mission that left London in summer 1590. Again, the sources for this embassy are all English and mostly emanate from Horsey himself. This was a real low point in relations between the countries. Horsey, who seems to have been more than a bit disreputable, was the object of various accusations in Russia and became virtually persona non grata. The accusations were mostly protocol and business matters, and may have been (as Horsey thought) the result of Shchelkalov's malevolence, but Horsey attracted the antagonism also of Bowes and the Company. There may well be truth to some of the accusations. He had great difficulty performing his tasks, and had only one secret meeting with Boris Godunov. Notably his messages to the Tsar no longer contained any reference to any league or amity. Evidently Fletcher's treatment had been more convincing than verbal promises of a league. And without Ivan the Terrible on the throne, England could not be sure of a friend in Russia. The complaints Horsey brought were entirely about the treatment of Fletcher and trade disputes, the Marsh affair, and others. Horsey was never received by the Tsar. The complaints were ignored, and he finally left in summer 1591, having accomplished nothing whatever. He attributed all this to the influence of Shchelkalov, but there seem to have been other factors. In 1587–1590 the struggle over the Polish throne had brought Russia and the Empire together, and their talks continued through the 1590s. At the same time the intrigues at the Russian court had reached a more dangerous stage, for Tsarevich Dmitrii perished in May 1591. Boris Godunov secretly assured Horsey of his favor to Horsey and England, but was unable, so Horsey reported later, to show it openly. If this story is true Boris may have been motivated by his imperial plans or by the affair of the Tsarevich, either enough to require secrecy. Boris's later policy as Tsar after 1598 does suggest that he was concealing a more favorable attitude to England than he expressed in 1590–1591.[107]

After the summer of 1591 messages and royal letters continued to go back and forth, but no embassies of any importance were exchanged until 1598. Trade continued, but diplomacy ceased. The collapse of Anglo-Russian relations after the death of Ivan IV in March 1584 demonstrates the political nature of the relationship, based on common interests that were not merely commercial. Commerce went on, year in year out, but the political relationships were subject to much greater fluctuations. Originally the result of Ivan's desires for allies against Poland in 1569, the

---

107. Bond, *Russia*, pp. xcix–cvii, 252–256 (Horsey's Travels), 356–375; Tolstoi, *Pervye sorok let*, pp. 364–403.

oral agreement for a league was never translated into a written treaty, though England was ready to do so by 1576. It was the desire on the part of Ivan and his advisors to explore the Imperial option that seems to account for their loss of interest in England between 1576 and 1582. Exactly at that time, however, the increasingly threatening situation for England made necessary the stabilization of its relations with northern Europe, so Elizabeth responded to the renewed Russian offer of 1582. Bowes's incompetence seems to account for the failure of the negotiations in 1583–1584, but Ivan's death rendered Bowes's failure irrelevant. Fyodor was a weak ruler captive to increasingly violent factional struggles among his boyars, and England's chief friend at court, Boris Godunov, was not about to sacrifice his chances for the future by sticking to an unpopular English alliance. He also may have been less committed to the idea than Ivan IV. The change of Tsar in Russia left England with no real friends in the north.

The End of Elizabeth's Reign

The last years of Elizabeth's reign were dominated by the war with Spain, a growing success for the Dutch but a stalemate for England. France's short-lived intervention in the war (1595–1598) brought little change, and the inexorable advance of the Dutch armies was not matched by English victories at sea. In the north, Duke Karl of Södermanland's revolt against King Sigismund kept both kingdoms occupied with one another until the outbreak of the Russian Time of Troubles in 1604. England's relations with northern Europe revolved now around Denmark and Russia, both intertwined by Russo-Danish marriage negotiations. In both cases the revival of diplomatic ties after the hiatus in the early 1590s was the result of the policies of new rulers, Christian IV and Boris Godunov. In the background of all this activity was the Empire.

Denmark 1596–1603

The revived contacts of Denmark with England were a direct consequence of the majority of Christian IV in 1596. In the previous years there had been low-level Danish messages complaining about English seizures of Danish ships, but Christian decided to move in a new direction and bring Denmark back into a more active role in the European political scene. His first act was to send the historian and chancellor, Arild Huitfeldt, and the nobleman, Christian Barnekov, to England as ambassadors in fall 1597. Though they were empowered to discuss shipping claims, their primary purpose was to offer Christian's mediation in the Anglo-Spanish war. This was the burden of Huitfeldt's speech at his first audience before the Queen on 7 September 1597, which seems to be lacking in the English records. Elizabeth's answer was entirely negative, blaming Spain for the conflict and holding out no hope for Christian's proposal. The mediation issue was discussed further on 14 and 16 September, but had no more result than the shipping claims. In October the two Danes went on to the Netherlands with the same mission, and received the same answer from the Dutch authorities.[108]

Elizabeth's government did not receive the Danish mediation proposal as a friendly offer, and was even more incensed by Christian's seizure of English ships in the Sound to make up for Danish losses. The instructions to Lord Zouche and Christopher Parkins on their embassy of June-July 1598 show that the English interpreted the move as political, the result of Spanish intrigue or at least sympathy for Spain in the war. Zouche and Parkins were to emphasize that Spain was importing grain, naval stores, and munitions from the Baltic area. The English were to remind Christian that if Denmark aided Spain by allowing such trade, she was not really neutral. Only trade in grain could be conceded. At the same time, the English did not give up on Denmark, for they asked Christian to encourage discussion of the Imperial Mandate of 1597 against English trade at the Imperial Diet. The ambassadors were to stress the need for Protestant solidarity, and the ambitions of Spain. The mission was not without success, it seemed. Parkins reported to Cecil that the actions against the English merchants "have been procured by one onlie of the Nobles, who had been verie familiar with the King of Spaigne his Ambassador at his being heare." Christian agreed, as a pure favor to Elizabeth, not as admission of wrong, to return the English ships and compensate goods already lost, on 10 July, 1598. The conflict seemed settled.[109] However, this was not the case, and Parkins had to return to Denmark in the fall of the same year to try to obtain monetary compensation from the Danish king. Parkins succeeded in getting the money, some 40,000 talers, and could tell Cecil that this controversy was now at an end and a new Danish embassy would shortly arrive in England.[110]

Nils Krag did indeed arrive shortly, in December 1598, for the next round of discussions. Most of his time was spent in fruitless argument

108. Holger F. Rørdam, *Historieskriveren Arild Hvitfeldt* (Copenhagen, 1896), pp. 198–221, tillaeg 121–152; SP 75/2, ff. 192–226v; Cotton Nero B IV, ff. 56–62. The Dutch clearly informed England of their negotiations with Huitfeldt and Barnekov, as the basic documents are in SP 75/2, ff. 231–240v.

109. SP 75/3, ff. 3–50v, 94–97v; Cotton Nero B IV, ff. 158–169v. Rymer, *Foedera* 16: 344–347.

110. SP 75/3, ff. 51–64v, 72–76v.

with the commissioners appointed by the English crown to discuss complaints against English privateers, and nothing was solved. The argument remained this time on the legal level, without accusations from the English side that Denmark was inclining toward Spain. Krag also objected to English fishing off the northern coast of Norway. The rest of 1599 was spent in intensive Anglo-Danish discussions of these problems, complicated by the Danish seizure of English fishing vessels in the summer. Thomas Ferrers went to Denmark in July and August 1599, followed immediately in September by one of Elizabeth's most experienced diplomats, Sir Stephen Lesieur. Neither mission produced any result, and over the winter a new proposal emerged for a meeting of commissioners of both sides in Emden.[111] This proposal led to such a meeting in May-June 1600, in Emden, that was aborted almost from the start. Contrary winds delayed the English delegation, and the Danes left, declaring that their commission from the King had expired. After the English returned home, a memo in Christopher Parkins's hand tried to explain the situation, concluding that the Danes really did not want to negotiate, for they were satisfied with the status quo in spite of the English privateers. They could always seize English fishing boats and raise the sound tolls. England's need was to protect its merchants. Thus, it seemed that the whole issue of the war had become secondary to commercial issues. After this fiasco, the next year was quiet, and only in 1602 did Stephen Lesieur again go to Denmark to try to arrange another meeting of commissioners from both sides, this time at Bremen.[112]

The 1602–1603 meeting at Bremen, the last action of Elizabeth's reign concerning Denmark, included a new element, one that clarifies much of the background of these otherwise arcane disputes about the law of the sea. The new element was the presence of the Emperor Rudolf II's representative, Ehrenfried von Minkwitz, and the issues raised by the Imperial Mandate of 1597 against the Merchant Adventurers.

---

111. Krag: SP 75/3, ff. 67–68v, 79–87v, 90–90v, 98–107v. Cotton Nero B IV, ff. 63–155; Rymer, *Foedera* 16: 354–359; "Niels Krags Relation om sit Gesandtskab til England 1598–1599," anonymous translation from Latin, *Nye Danske Magazin* 4 (1823): 173–216. Ferrers: SP 75/3, ff. 138–145v, Lesieur: ff. 154–174.

112. SP 75/3, ff. 185–201v, 204–205v, 208–210v, 213–216v, 223–224v, 227–228v, 231–232v, 237–224v, 251–264v. Lesieur was also instructed to try to mediate Danish-Swedish differences, as part of a general English attempt at conciliation of Denmark over the Russian marriage proposals, about which more below: Sven Ulric Palme, *Sverige och Danmark 1596–1611* (Uppsala, 1942), pp. 355–357. Palme does not seem to have realized how bad general Anglo-Danish relations were, though he grasped that the English feelers to Denmark were the result of a need to conciliate Russia.

The issue of that Imperial Mandate went back for some years. England's dispute with the Hanse had continued since 1567, and in 1582, while the English staple was at Emden, the Hanse towns had managed to get the Imperial Diet to issue a Mandate that declared the Merchant Adventurers an illegal monopoly and expelled them from the Empire. The Spanish ambassador to the Emperor backed the Diet's decision. Emperor Rudolf, however, had refused to ratify the mandate. Apparently his councillors were not convinced that the damage to German commerce was very great, and feared worse consequences if the mandate were ratified. Rudolf also seems not to have wished to offend Elizabeth, and in the early 1580s his relations with Spain were cool, as he was unhappy with the direction of Spanish policy in the Netherlands under Granvelle and Parma. Unfortunately the Anglo-Spanish War reactivated resistance to the English among the Hanse towns. In 1591 a Hanse diet had renewed its charges, and at the 1594 Imperial Diet the 1582 Mandate was again published. This time it was the College of Electors, not the Emperor, who stopped its implementation. In late 1596 the chief of the Hanse towns, Lübeck, renewed its pressure on the Emperor, again with the support of the Spanish ambassador, Guillén de San Clemente, as well as that of Archduke Albert in the Netherlands. All this seems to have worked, and on 26 May 1597, Rudolf ratified the Mandate into law.[113] Elizabeth answered with a new decree on privateers (27 September 1597), and until 1601 there matters stood, with the English increasing their actions against Hanse ships.

Cecil was aware that the dispute was at least in part a political dispute arising from Spanish "intrigue" not only in Prague, but also in the Hanse towns and Denmark, especially during the Spanish embassy to those parts in summer and autumn 1597. English agents in the Hanse towns kept him fully informed of this aspect of the problem. So little is known of Rudolf's foreign policy that it is difficult to assess his reasons for the sudden flexibility of his position in 1602. The appointment of Minkwitz in November 1601 as a special commissioner to deal with the problem

113. Ehrenberg, *Hamburg und England*, pp. 158–211; Ludwig Beutin, *Hanse und Reich im handelspolitischen Endkampf gegen England*, Studien zur Geschichte der Wirtschaft und Geisteskultur, VI (Berlin, 1929), pp. 3–46. Wernham also notes the shift of Rudolf and his government against England in the early 1590s. R. B. Wernham, "Queen Elizabeth I, The Emperor Rudolph II and Archduke Ernest, 1593–94," in E. I. Kouri and Tom Scott, eds., *Politics and Society in Reformation Europe* (London, 1987), pp. 437–451. Beutin also suggested that Rudolf needed financial support from the Hanse towns for his war against the Turks that began in 1592. *Hanse*, p. 11.

certainly signified a turn in policy. Minkwitz was an experienced diplomat who had even served his master in Russia, helping to pressure Sweden in the negotiations for the Tiavzino treaty of 1595. He was skeptical of the Hanse merchants' claims that the Merchant Adventurers were ruining them. He found no such signs in the Hanse towns, and reported that they were clearly prosperous and trading in English cloth.[114] In spite of his skepticism about the Hanse towns, Minkwitz was basically on the side of Denmark and the Hanse. The English seem not to have realized the change in attitude in Prague and in the fall of 1602 came to Bremen for simultaneous negotiations with both Minkwitz and the Danish commissioners. Nothing came of the negotiations. The English commissioners, Robert Eure, John Herbert, Daniel Dun, and Stephen Lesieur, confronted a fairly distinguished Danish delegation, Manderup Parsberg, Arild Huitfeldt, and Dr. Jonas Carisius. Nothing was accomplished, for the Danes took a very hard line, insisting not only on the wrongs of English privateers, but also on fishing rights and Danish control over the sea passage to Russia. The English attempt to raise the general issue of Denmark's favorable attitude to England's enemies (i.e., Spain) was met with silence. Minkwitz was extremely reluctant to negotiate, and did not begin until March 1603, seemingly cooperating with the Danes. The problem was undoubtedly in Prague, for his appointment came hard on the heels of the fall of Rudolf's chief councillors, Wolfgang von Rumpf and Count Paul Sixt von Trautson, in October 1600. This was the beginning of the crisis of Rudolf's reign. The result created great delays in business and allowed for the increasing influence of Catholic Karl von Liechtenstein in the Imperial Privy Council and elsewhere. In any case the whole discussion was cut short by the death of Queen Elizabeth on 24 March 1603.[115]

SWEDEN AND POLAND 1595-1603

In the last years of Elizabeth's reign relations with Poland and Sweden were determined not by English desires but by the Swedish revolt against

114. Paul L. Hughes and James F. Larkin, *Tudor Royal Proclamations*, 3 vols. (New Haven, 1969), 3: 183–185; SP 82/4, ff. 55–68v; 81/8, 74–75v; Beutin, *Hanse*, pp. 33–34; A. A. Zimin, *V Kanun groznykh potriasenii* (Moscow, 1986), p. 189.

115. Most of the records of this phase of Anglo-Danish relations have been printed from Cotton Nero B V in Rymer, *Foedera* 16: 429–436, 438–446, 451–452, 460–473, 478–487. SP 75/3, ff. 265–265v, 270–271v; SP 82/4, ff. 144–153, 170–171v, 177–178v; SP 84/5, 1–9v, 56–63v, 71–72v, 75–78v. Felix Stieve, "Die Verhandlungen über die Nachfolge Kaiser Rudolfs II in den Jahren 1581 bis 1602," *Abhandlungen der historischen Klasse der königlichen bayerischen Akademie der Wissenschaften* 15, 1 (Munich, 1880): 1–160.

King Sigismund. The 1595 Diet of Söderköping had begun the process of revolt and Sigismund was determined to stay in power against all odds. Hindered by the lack of enthusiasm of his Polish subjects, he managed to mount a naval expedition to Sweden in 1598, in part with English ships requisitioned in the harbor of Danzig. The expedition was a complete failure, and in 1598–1600 Karl consolidated his hold on Sweden, Finland, and the Swedish possessions in Estonia. He did not stop there, and in fall 1600 invaded Polish Livonia, beginning a war that lasted until 1629.[116]

The first move in the new Polish situation came from Sigismund, apparently at the instigation of the Admiral of Aragon, Francisco de Mendoza. This was part of a general Spanish effort in the north in 1597, which had led also to the publication of the Imperial Mandate against the Merchant Adventurers (see above). Sigismund was persuaded to send to the States General and to England an ambassador to complain of English and Dutch actions, and settled on one Paweł Działyński, who became famous in the annals of Elizabeth's reign. Działyński's behavior was certainly peculiar. In the Hague he lectured the Dutch on the virtues of obedience to kings, and suggested that they fight the Turks rather than Spain. In England Działyński deeply offended Elizabeth at the audience in Greenwich, though the precise nature of the offense is not clear. In the days after the incident he presented Poland's claims against England over the seizure of Danzig ships going to Spain, and received the usual answers, similar to those given to Denmark. The incident in Greenwich remained an obstacle to relations with Poland for decades.[117]

116. The Polish-Swedish war over Livonia formed the background to much of northern politics in this period. After initial Swedish successes, Karl was routed by the Poles at Kirchholm in 1605. Swedish involvement in the Russian Time of Troubles on the side of Tsar Vasilii Shuiskii in 1609–1610 was partly motivated by Karl's need for an ally against Poland. The Kalmar War (1611–1613) with Denmark distracted Sweden, and the involvement in Russia did the same for Poland, but in 1616–1617 they were at one another again. This time the young King Gustavus Adolphus was more successful. Riga fell in 1621, and the rest of Livonia by 1625. Swedish moves into Royal (Polish) Prussia led to the stalemate that ended at Altmark in 1629 under the mediation of France, anxious for Sweden's participation in the Thirty Years' War.

117. Talbot, Elementa 4: 186–210, 17: 160–165. H. Ellis, Original Letters Illustrative of English History, 3 vols. (London, 1824), 3: 41–46. "Sir R. Cecil to the Earl of Essex: An Account of the Queen's Reception of the Polish Ambassador, 26 July 1597." Działyński also urged England not to sell siege supplies to Russia in view of the approaching expiration of the Russo-Polish truce in 1598. Fedorowicz believes the Spanish initiative to have been only in the minds of the English, though

England's response was to send George Carew to Poland the next summer, with the result that he arrived right in the middle of Sigismund's attempt to recapture Sweden. Carew spent most of his effort on the shipping questions, and had no more success than did his colleagues in Denmark, but at least he seems to have assured himself that the attitude of Działyński was more hostile than that of King Sigismund. He also tried to appeal to Chancellor Zamoyski on the issue of Elizabeth's title, but to no avail. Part of the problem was that Carew had followed Sigismund to Sweden, and shortly after the temporary reconciliation of Sigismund and Karl (Treaty of Linköping, 28 September 1598) had received letters from Karl to Elizabeth asking for her favor. According to Carew, the "Papist" faction among the Poles, led by Vice-Chancellor Tylicki, had taken Carew's receipt of the letters as hostile. This interpretation was not wrong, for his reports to the Queen were very favorable to Karl.[118]

Later events confirmed this pattern. Relations with Poland almost ceased, not to resume until the accession of James. In 1599 Karl sent James Hill and Johannes Nicolai to England to make a treaty with Elizabeth, offering ships and naval stores in return for English troops. Elizabeth assured Karl of her favor, but did not think the time right for a treaty. The mission of Sir Richard Lee in Russia and Sweden (1600–1601) included similar vague promises of alliance but nothing concrete for Karl. In 1602 John Merrick was instructed to convey the Queen's favor to Karl, and her permission to recruit troops, but no more. There matters stood until 1603, when the English commissioners at Bremen responded to a letter from Karl's secretary Bertold Heinzken which apparently asked for English mediation of the growing dispute with Denmark. The commissioners replied that Elizabeth naturally favored harmony between Sweden and Denmark, thus prefiguring King James's role in settling the Kalmar War in 1613.[119]

Szelągowski pointed out the role of Mendoza long ago. Fedorowicz, *England's Baltic Trade*, p. 41; Szelągowski, *Walka*, pp. 121–122.

118. Talbot, *Elementa* 4: 212–216, 218–251; 17: 166–169. Carew's reports were strengthened by Karl's transmission of a short defense of his position by Peder Nilsson, presumably now preserved as SP 95/1, 90–95. Nilsson's tract came with James Hill in 1599 (see below). Tor Berg, *Johan Skytte: Hans ungdom och verksamhet under Karl IX's regering* (Stockholm, 1920), p. 173.

119. Palme, *Sverige och Danmark*, pp. 341–344; HMC, *Salisbury*, 11: 202, 204, 207, 264. SP 91/1, ff. 177–178, 189–189v. Little is known of Merrick's mission.

RUSSIA 1591–1604

In the early 1590s Anglo-Russian relations were devoted to the Anthony Marsh affair and other commercial matters, a consequence of the collapse of political relations after the death of Ivan the Terrible. Political relations resumed with the 1598 mission of Francis Cherry. These relations were resumed at English initiative, and they had nothing to do with trade issues. In 1596 Russia had confirmed the Muscovy Company's privileges, apparently to the surprise of the English. Cherry's embassy was not to discuss the Company, where there was no issue, but to address England's relations with the Ottomans, an issue that had arisen, as far as London was concerned, in 1595. In the autumn of that year John Merrick had returned to London with the news that the Russian court had been informed by the papal legate and the Imperial ambassador that Elizabeth had been supporting the Turks in their war against the Empire (1592–1608). The next year's news of the confirmation of trade privileges must have reassured the English government, but the Imperial Mandate of 1597 seems to have changed the situation. England needed to combat these rumors, for the Mandate against the Merchant Adventurers had commercial intent and consequences to be sure, but also was thought to be the result of Spanish intrigue. The English desire for good relations with Russia was the consequence of the deterioration of relations with the Emperor as well as with Denmark. Unfortunately for Elizabeth, Cherry arrived precisely at the beginning of a new Russian attempt at an arrangement with Emperor Rudolf.[120] This move involved an attempt at a Habsburg-Godunov marriage, with the intent not only of raising Boris's prestige but also of providing an ally against Poland. Russia had been

120. SP 91/1, ff. 105–105v; HMC, Salisbury, 9: 112, 227; The Imperial ambassador was presumably Nicholas Warkocz, whose third mission to Russia came in December 1594 to March 1595, in the last month joined by legate Alessandro Komulović. Pamiatniki diplomaticheskikh snoshenii 2: 1–290, 10: 393–432; Uebersberger, Österreich, pp. 561–562; Huntington Library, Ellesmere MSS 1620, 1621; J. Payne Collier, The Edgerton Papers, Camden Society 12 (London, 1840), pp. 288–301; Willan, Early History, pp. 219–231, Phipps, Sir John Merrick: English Merchant-Diplomat in the Seventeenth Century (Newtonville, Massachusetts, 1983), pp. 20–24. Spain as well courted Russian friendship, hoping for help against England. In 1594 Philip II tried to get Spain's ambassador to the Emperor, Guillén de San Clemente, to convince Russia to seize the English ships at Archangel, taking advantage of the Russian mission to Prague in that year. The Emperor's Vice Chancellor Kurtz advised against it, and time ran out in any case, for the Russians had to leave in early spring. Philip tried again with the same result. V. Meysztowicz, ed., "Documenta Polonica ex Archivo Generali Hispaniae in Simancas," Elementa ad fontium editiones 19 (Rome, 1968), pp. 63–64, 71–72.

traditionally supportive of the Habsburg candidacy for the Polish throne, and as late as 1595 Rudolf's emissary Minkwitz had helped Russia to make the Tiavzino treaty. By 1598 the Emperor and King Sigismund were increasingly friendly; Russian-Imperial talks did not break down until spring, 1600.

During this period Elizabeth sent two missions to Russia, both apparently exploratory. The first was the bungled mission of Dr. Willis in 1599, which aroused only the suspicions of Vasilii Shchelkalov, the Russian Secretary of the Foreign Office. It is notable that Shchelkalov's questions to Willis (aside from protocol matters and the issue of Willis's medical competence) revolved around the use of English ships to support King Sigismund's 1598 expedition to Sweden against Duke Karl. Willis tried as best he could to convince the Russians that the ships had been requisitioned, bringing a letter from the Queen and one from Carew, signed also by Cecil, both asserting the English case. Again, England was eager to reassure the Russians of her lack of sympathy for Sigismund, but Shchelkalov remained suspicious.[121] The failure of the Willis mission led to the mission of Sir Richard Lee in 1600–1601. This, like the two before it, had no commercial side. Lee was instructed once again to reassure the Russians that England did not support either the Turks or Sigismund's struggle in Sweden. In addition, he was to suggest an English marriage for Boris's son, but not to oppose actively the Habsburg project. In this last regard he seems to have exceeded his instructions, with the inevitable complications for English diplomacy.[122] Lee's mission was in any case overshadowed by the last major embassy to England from Russia before 1613, the Mikulin mission of 1600–1601.

Mikulin passed Lee in Archangel on his way to England. His mission was largely ceremonial and political, for his first task was officially to inform Elizabeth of the accession to the Tsar's throne of Boris Godunov.

---

121. *SRIO* 38: 269–275; Norman Evans, "Doctor Timothy Willis and his Mission to Russia 1599," *OSP*, New Series 2 (1969): 39–61. HMC, *Salisbury*, 10: 212, 236–237, 371. B. N. Floria, *Russko-pol'skie otnosheniia i baltiiskii vopros v kontse XVI-nachale XVII v.* (Moscow, 1973), pp. 63–89. Was Shchelkalov, like his brother in 1584, a supporter of the Habsburg alliance? After the idea's collapse in 1600 he was edged out and then formally replaced in 1601. Floria, ibid., pp. 146–147.

122. N. E. Evans, "The Anglo-Russian Royal Marriage Negotiations of 1600–1603," *SEER* 61, 3 (1983): 363–387; *SRIO* 38: 364–410; SP 91/1, ff. 156–156v; HMC, *Salisbury*, 9: 344, 430; 10: 13, 76, 169–172, 175, 180, 227, 275–276, 318, 436–437. Neither Russian nor English records give a full account of the proceedings, beyond a rather unclear reference to discussions of Anglo-Danish relations (*SRIO* 38: 403). The evidence that he exceeded his instructions on the marriage issue comes from a later Muscovy Company petition. Evans, "Anglo-Russian," pp. 370–371.

He was also to repeat the 1596 confirmation of the Muscovy Company's privileges, a non-controversial issue by 1600. More important, he was to convey the Tsar's desire that all Christian monarchs ally against the Turks, and also his satisfaction that the rumors of Elizabeth's pro-Ottoman attitude were false. At the same time, Mikulin was to convey to Christian of Denmark, if he were to stop in Denmark, his dissatisfaction with Danish interference in Anglo-Russian trade. At the time Mikulin's instructions were written, Russia was still committed to the Habsburg alliance, though Emperor Rudolf's rejection of that alliance in May 1600 made much of Mikulin's activity irrelevant. The embassy passed without incident. The Russians had a friendly meeting with King James's ambassador from Scotland, presumably relying on their instructions to be friendly to any successor to Elizabeth. James's Danish marriage would make him particularly attractive to the Russians after the closure of the Habsburg option, though at the time no one in London could know that Boris would turn to the Danes. The Essex affair in spring 1601 made for more excitement in Mikulin's report than any negotiations, and the one suggestion that may have been made to him about an Anglo-Russian marriage he left unmentioned in his report.[123]

The next few years saw movement back and forth, but little of substance. Boris's foreign policy was directed toward an alliance with Denmark against Sweden, as Duke Karl carried his struggle against Sigismund into Livonia in early 1600, just as the Habsburg plan collapsed. Boris nearly succeeded in arranging a marriage with the Danish royal house before his own death, and that meant, until early 1603, he was no longer interested in England. The accession of Christian's brother-in-law, King James of Scotland, to the English throne meant that Boris could have good relations with both countries, but Denmark at this point was clearly the more important. Trade questions were secondary. James's first mission to Russia, that of Sir Thomas Smith (1604–1605), was sparked by rumors of moves against the Muscovy Company privileges, and was headed by Smith as Company representative, as well as royal emissary. However, the instructions to Smith passed over commercial questions in a few lines and devoted several pages to reiterating the innocence of the English in the face of the charge of provoking the Ottomans to war, and to a long disquisition on the peace negotiations with Spain, stressing James's pacific desires and the respect paid him by the princes of Eu-

123. SRIO 38: 278–363; SP 91/1, ff. 141–142v; HMC, Salisbury, 10: 371; 11: 347–348, 386–387; Evans, "Anglo-Russian," p. 374, and "Meeting," pp. 517–528; Phipps, Merrick, pp. 27–31.

rope.[124] If Smith told all this to the Russians, here may well be the origins of Ziuzin's mission to James the peacemaker. After Smith's mission, political relations collapsed as a result of the Time of Troubles.

In the last years of the reign of Elizabeth, Anglo-Russian relations were in a period of relative calm. The Muscovy Company continued to trade with little difficulty, and political relations were marked by a mismatch of needs. Boris sought alliance with powers moderately hostile to England, the Empire and Denmark. At the same time, England was increasingly isolated in the north and needed Russian friendship, hence her pursuit of even a rather questionable marriage project. There was a tenuous basis for that English move, for Russia had no relations with England's principal enemy (Spain) and England was on unfriendly terms with Russia's principal antagonist (Poland). Boris had no desire to antagonize England, but his needs and interests lay elsewhere with powers unfriendly to Elizabeth, Denmark, and the Empire. The result was relations that were correct but ultimately cool, a very different situation from the period of the reign of Ivan the Terrible, or the more complex situation after 1613. The events of this period demonstrate once again that England's relations with Russia cannot be understood outside of their northern European context. The crucial factors were the relations of Russia and England with Denmark, Poland, the Empire, and Sweden, not just Anglo-Russian trade interests.

England, Russia and the North 1603–1613

James came to England in 1603, bringing with him from Scotland his Danish wife and three children, Henry, Elizabeth, and Charles.[125] The children were as warmly welcomed as the parents, being the first living direct heirs to the English throne since the death of Edward VI in 1553. However, aside from the family James brought with him experience in government and an interest in peace-keeping, an interest perhaps born of necessity in dealing with the factious Scottish nobles responsible for his father's murder and his mother's exile.

Thirteen years before assuming the English crown, in 1590, James had

---

124. SP 91/1, ff. 177–178; 196–202; HMC, *Salisbury*, 11: 172, 421–422, 630; 16: 185–186, 459; 17: 69; Sir Thomas Smith, *Sir Thomas Smithes Voyage and Entertainment in Rushia* (London, 1605); Phipps, *Merrick*, pp. 50–61.

125. I.e., the future Henry, Prince of Wales, b. 1594; Elizabeth, Queen of Bohemia, b. 1596; Charles, King of England, b. 1600.

sent an embassy to Denmark, the Protestant princes of Germany and to England. His ambassadors, William Stewart and John Skene (later Lord Curriehill), were to seek a means of peace between England and France and Spain. Failing that, they were instructed to negotiate an alliance among Denmark, Scotland, and the German princes that would "assist the peaceful party against the obdurate."[126] The embassy was portentous. If it were to be said that there was a pervading direction to James's foreign policy when he was King of England, it would be described as confessional rather than commercial. The impetus to those policies, in James's words, was compromise and peace: "Let Whitehall (fit emblem for her purity) be her chief palace and let it say *aedes alma salus*."[127] Regarding Russia and the north a Protestant peace policy worked, but with regard to the Habsburgs compromise on one part was necessary to ensure the other. For example, the first major achievement of the new King was the signing of the Treaty of London in 1604 ending the long and costly war with Spain but also bringing the Catholics into a friendly camp. (Parliament would not allow such a thing to happen twenty years later.) He had already signed an agreement with the United Provinces the year before.

English relations with Poland under Elizabeth had been tense, and the 1597 Działyński incident had aggravated the Queen. Sigismund III corresponded with James in the early years of his reign although he sent no embassy to London from 1603 until 1615.[128] Under the new monarch Sigismund, like other Catholics, had hoped for more religious toleration in England.[129] No doubt he expected that toleration would be the natural outcome of the Somerset House conference and the ensuing peace of London.

James was not interested in prohibitions against Catholics per se; he spoke openly in parliament of the Roman church as the "mother church," although he acknowledged that it was increasingly "defiled by

126. *Calendar State Papers Relating to Scotland, 1574–1603*, p. xiv, and National Library of Scotland, MS 2912.

127. *The Peace-Maker Or Great Britain's Blessing framed.* . . . (London, 1618); for the treaty with Spain see Rymer, *Foedera* 7, 2: 117. See also, SP 94/30, f. 226, where the Spanish comment on James as peacemaker and ". . . the motto of *Beati Pacifici* with which your Majesty has and does adorn his escutcheon of arms."

128. See above, note 117. *CSPD 1611–1618*, p. 296. In 1603 Sigismund sent Stanisław Cikowski, a Polish Calvinist, to greet James with his accession to the English throne. This embassy reestablished correct, if not warm relations between the two countries: Mierzwa, *Anglia*, pp. 22–57.

129. SP 14/6:37.

some infirmities." His real concern was with radical Catholic ideology and political thought formulated by theologians like Suarez and often put into practice by Jesuits. The Pope, he pointed out in the same speech to parliament in 1603/4, "claimed an imperial civil power over all kings and emperors, dethroning and decrowning princes with his foot, as pleaseth him." [130] The Gunpowder plot of 1605 confirmed James's fears of the radical elements and propelled him into a more aggressive pro-Protestant stance that in 1608 would culminate in the formation of the Protestant Union. The introduction of a mandatory oath of allegiance in England only further widened the gap between Whitehall and Rome.

SWEDEN

Sweden's preoccupation from 1595 with deposing Sigismund III from the Swedish throne and James's concern with a union of England and Scotland kept these countries somewhat isolated from one another in the years directly after James's accession to the English throne. It was not until the creation of the Ulster Plantation that relations between England and Sweden resumed in any degree.

Sweden in 1610 was described by a Dane (with, of course, some natural bias!) as a large and barren country where the common people were "most brutish." The nobility, "such that remained unexecuted," seldom came into court, fearful of antagonizing the crown if they did. The King's word was law, and ever since his most recent illness Charles IX was reported to be "more furious than he has been in divers years before," vacillating wildly in his opinions, never to "long continue in one and the same mind."[131]

Charles IX actively pursued an English alliance, aware of Sweden's precarious position between Denmark and particularly Poland which until 1599 had ruled Sweden. Sweden's constant need for mercenaries, coupled with the English necessity during the early years of the settlement of the Plantation of Ulster for a place to which unruly Irish could be exiled at little charge to England, formed the basis of a reciprocal arrangement as early as 1609. By English royal commission that year Sir Robert Stuart and his brother were to transport one thousand men to Sweden.[132] Andrew Greep warned Secretary Salisbury that the quality of the men sent might jeopardize the success of the scheme. "These Irish-

130. *Journals of the House of Commons* (London, 1742-), 1: 144.
131. SP 75/4, f. 160–160v, John Selbie to Salisbury, 21 April 1610; SP 95/1, ff. 164–165v, Anon. to Salisbury, 4 April 1610.
132. SP 95/1, f. 156–156v.

men," he said, "being such seditious and mutinous people that his Majesty shall have cause rather to fear than to trust them."[133]

The plan was a machiavellian device, in fact, "to rid away from the
King of England the unprofitable members of his dominions."[134] And, as
Greep had warned Salisbury about the nature of the Irishmen that were
being sent, so another person, whose name is now lost, warned the
Swedish King about them. Charles IX, when he was told of their "continual disloyalty to their true and lawful King, his Majesty of Great
Britain," found the name "Irish" distasteful.[135] The distaste did not linger
long, however, and in an atmosphere of necessity, as the military preparation of Denmark and Poland escalated, Charles sought more Irish
mercenaries. In April 1610 he granted a commission to Colonel Byngley
to bring over one thousand additional soldiers from Connaught.[136] There
was little opposition at home; many Englishmen saw the plan as a good
one. Thomas Lichfield wrote to Salisbury that the numbers of idle Irish
once landed in Sweden would be "safer kept from return to their country
than if they were in the strongest prisons in England."[137] Eventually
these Irish mercenaries formed the regiments of the King of Sweden's
forces recruited to assist the Russians against the Poles.[138] By autumn
1610 the Swedes had vacated Livonia and shifted the bulk of their armies
to the western parts of Russia around the area of the castle of Ivangorod.
There, according to Sir James Spens's report, 6,000 men served against
the Poles. 4,000 of them were in Swedish regiments composed of a little
more than half (about 2,200) Irishmen; the rest were French and Dutch.
Spens wrote from Stockholm about the success of this campaign and the
consequent need for replacements. "I need not speak of the inconvenience [that] may fall if the Poles should prevail," he wrote to Salisbury,
adding what service it would be to his country to relieve her of a thousand or two Irishmen "without charges to the King's Majesty."[139] The
success of the Irish in these campaigns, however, was not altogether
without question, and rumors proliferated of their mutinous behavior and
their leaving the Swedes to join their Catholic brothers the Poles. The

133. SP 95/1, f. 156–156v, A. Greep to Salisbury, 28 July 1609.
134. SP 95/1, ff. 164–165v, W. Stuart to Salisbury, 4 April 1610.
135. SP 95/1, f. 166, T. Lichfield to Salisbury, 6 April 1610.
136. SP 95/1, f. 166. Regarding Byngley, see below, p. 63.
137. SP 95/1, f. 166, T. Lichfield to Salisbury, 6 April 1610.
138. SP 95/1, f. 168.
139. SP 95/1, ff. 170–171, Sir J. Spens to Salisbury, 30 Sept. 1610; and see also SP 75/1,
    ff. 115–116, R. Engelsted to Salisbury, 25 October 1608.

general report was that their pay was meager and the war, like the country, was cold and miserable.

While the Swedes contracted with James to remove unwanted Irishmen, they also pursued a perhaps more edifying attempt to make a real military alliance with him. This was the first important political contact since 1604, and seems to have been prompted by James's authorial pride. In August 1609, James had sent Andrew Keith the younger to Sweden to give King Charles the English King's latest tract against the Pope, presumably his *Premonition to all Christian Monarchies* of 1609. Charles took the opportunity to respond to James's act of dubious kindness by sending an embassy to England in the following year. The ambassadors, the aristocrat Gustav Stenbock and the learned Johan Skytte, were empowered to treat with the Dutch on the same trip and for the same purpose. They arrived in England on 13 July 1610, finding a greeting similar but also simpler than that of Ziuzin four years later. The burden of their message was the injustice of King Sigismund, and their need for help against this Catholic tyrant. Charles hoped that he could join what he conceived to be an Anglo-Franco-Dutch alliance against the Habsburgs, in return for which he hoped for English help against Sigismund. More concretely, the Swedes hoped that they would be allowed to recruit soldiers in England (while Sigismund should be forbidden) and that James should mediate the struggle of the two Vasas over the Swedish throne. Other Swedish concerns were not neglected. Charles asked that the English persuade Christian of Denmark to keep his promises and that James make an alliance against Russia, should the current Swedish-Russian agreement collapse, as it in fact soon did. James, who handled most of the negotiations himself in Latin, was only forthcoming in part. He was evasive on the French and Dutch alliances, referring the matter to his allies. He did announce that he recognized Charles as the rightful King of Sweden, but did not want to mediate the dispute with Poland as he felt Sigismund to be a hopeless and jesuitical Catholic, since he had failed to appreciate the copy of the *Premonition* that James had sent him. Better defeat him in battle, he advised. As to Christian, James was surprisingly negative about his brother-in-law. He lost his temper and said that Christian was still a young man and could easily commit stupidities. On the Russian question, James asserted that his subjects' interests in Russia (presumably the Muscovy Company) were too small to make a military alliance with Sweden worth his while. Skytte's attempt to convince him that a Polish victory in Russia would help the Catholics to threaten Protestantism left James unmoved. This is an attitude that James would soon change, but the interview in question took place on 24 July, while the crushing Polish victory over the Russo-Swedish army at

Klushino (24 June 1610) was presumably still unknown as neither side had mentioned it. Surely it would have been a powerful argument for the Swedes. After the interview with James, Stenbock and Skytte met with Cecil and Northampton to tie up details and deal with matters of trade, returning home moderately satisfied with their results.[140]

While the wars continued on Russian territory concern was expressed among the Protestant princes that with the army of Sweden otherwise engaged a vacuum was created for the King of Poland's entrance into that country. Spens warned that the wars "shall draw all to Russland" and therefore "it was good for the general cares of princes [of] our religion that the King of Denmark were not permitted . . . to be an occasion to the King of Poland to get entry into Sweden."[141] Spens wrote again to England in December 1610 warning that if the Russian wars proved prejudicial to the anti-Catholic princes of Europe the issue would become trying, "because it is a matter of policy and estate."[142] His fear was not ungrounded. On 4 April 1611 Christian IV of Denmark declared war on Sweden.

The goodwill between England and Sweden prior to what would become known as the Kalmar war provided a precedent for amity that would eventually encourage the Swedes to depend on King James to arbitrate a settlement with Denmark. In the meantime, however, the rest of Protestant Europe lay in fear lest Charles IX should in desperation seek help from his nephew Sigismund III of Poland or, alternatively, that Charles should be taken over by Poland with the support of the Polish regiments already amassed in Russia. Maurice of Orange thought that Sweden, even under the new King, Gustavus Adolphus, after Charles's death in 1611, "would yield itself absolutely unto Sigismund rather than be taken by the King of Denmark."[143] Charles IX's death may have delayed the peace process. Until Gustavus Adolphus II could be crowned

---

140. The Swedes wanted England to observe their blockade of Polish Riga. Cecil hesitated here, while Northampton seems to have been more accommodating, and the result was a compromise relatively favorable to Sweden. This embassy left almost no trace in English records: see SP 95/1, ff. 158–158v, James to Charles IX, 22 September 1609 sending Andrew Keith and the book; f. 160, letter of credence from Charles IX for Stenbock and Skytte; ff. 174–175v, letter of Stenbock and Olof Stråle from the Hague to Cecil thanking him for his friendship and warning of the result of Polish victories in Russia, 6/16 November 1610. The basic source is the report to Charles IX by Johan Skytte printed in Berg, *Johan Skytte*, pp. 231–259.

141. SP 95/1, ff. 181–182, Sir J. Spens to Salisbury, 23 December 1610.

142. SP 95/1, ff. 177–177v, Sir J. Spens to Salisbury, 8 November 1610.

143. SP 84/68, ff. 254–255v.

no treaty could be promulgated. James was anxious that the peace be concluded as quickly as possible to preclude the further entrenchment of the Poles in Russia, and even in Finland. For Spens had reported in 1612, after a visit to Finland, that the Finns "love the Pole" better than they do the Swedish King, and if, he wrote, the Finns fall in with Sigismund then all of Russia will go to the Poles. Moreover, he said, that if he himself had not given them hope of King James's love and his care to make peace, then "they had sent for the king of Poland before this."[144]

Even before the actual outbreak of hostilities Sweden had sent the 1610 embassy to Amsterdam seeking support. The Dutch, not wanting to antagonize the Danes by allying with the Swedes in their complaints regarding Danish sound tolls, even then suggested that King James be asked to intervene in order that "the extremity of the sword" might be avoided.[145] After the outbreak of the conflict it was only King James who remained acceptable to all sides as a mediator.

A "contract" of peace was signed on 20 January 1613 between the warring parties in the Treaty of Knaerød, with King James a guarantor.[146] Sir Ralph Winwood wrote of the importance of the peace to both England and Europe, saying that with Sigismund's marriage to two sisters of the late Queen of Spain, one after the other, "the power of these two kings combined together—the one, master of the northern part, the other of the southwest of the world—cannot be but formidable to all the princes of Europe."[147]

DENMARK

Christian IV, although not able to read English, certainly spoke and understood enough of the language to have had a good time during his visit to England in 1606. His brother-in-law, James, and sister, Anne, laid on lavish banquets and costly entertainments for his pleasure.[148] He would come again in July 1614.[149] However, regardless of warm personal relationships within the family, Denmark's foreign policy was more am-

---

144. SP 95/1, f. 199, King James to Sir J. Spens, 17 September 1612.
145. See also SP 75/1, f. 116, R. Engelsted to Salisbury, where it is reported as early as 1608 that Finland "lies open now for the Poles."
146. See Ziuzin, n. 12.
147. SP 84/68, f. 262, Sir R. Winwood to Salisbury, 19 March 1612. Sigismund married Anna (1592–1598) and then Constantia (1605–1631), both daughters of Archduke Karl of Styria. Their sister Margaret was the wife (1598–1611) of Philip III of Spain.
148. Nichols, *Progresses* 2: 54–93.
149. Nichols, *Progresses* 3: 13–19. In 1610–1611 Dr. Jonas Carisius was ambassador to England, SP 14/57: 110, Sir Thomas Lake to Salisbury, 21 October 1610.

biguous than James may have preferred. Power politics and commercial interests generally kept Christian in the Habsburg camp. For him compromise was not an issue. In May 1610 he suggested "most secretly" that James might consider the marriage of his daughter Elizabeth to the Dauphin of France.[150] Actually Henry IV had earlier (in 1603) proposed a similar scheme, that time of a double marriage of the Dauphin and Lady Elizabeth and Prince Henry and the eldest daughter of the King of France, also named Elizabeth.[151] Such marriages would unite Catholic and Protestant powers and provide good ground for building a league, he said. But the suggestion may have been proffered only to test the wind. In the autumn of the same year James informed Christian IV of Charles IX's offer of his son as a husband for Elizabeth. James recognized that if he were to pursue that course "such an alliance [would be] to embrace a quarrel." The results of such a match could only have brought double problems: "much anxiety to his mind as a loving father and much inconvenience to his estate as a King."[152] The offer was declined.

As early as August 1610 Sinclair expressed to England Christian's concern that in the event of a war James not help the Swedes. The Swedish embassy to England of that year suggests that Christian did have something to fear. The unresolved issues from the meeting between Sweden and Denmark at Flabäck in 1603 were beginning to rankle Christian. Four points were in contention: the controversy regarding the territory of Lapland, the matter of Sonnenburg in Estonia, the toll raised in Sweden on Danish goods and, perhaps most importantly to Christian, the matter of the three crowns on the Danish escutcheon. (Later it was actually reported that the war arose over Charles's use of the emblem of the three crowns and his styling himself "King of Norvegia.") Some effort had been made to mediate the problem of the tolls with the Dukes of Brandenburg and Brunswick, respectively, but the Swedish commissioners never appeared at the scheduled meetings.[153]

The Danes claimed the situation had worsened since 1608; the Swedes spoiled ships in the seas of Denmark, commanded incursions into Norway, and encouraged the Finns to turn against Denmark. With this list of

150. SP 75/4, ff. 165–166, A. Sinclair to King James, 12 May 1610. Later Charles I would marry the French princess, Henrietta Maria.
151. S. R. Gardiner, *History of England from the Accession of James I to the Outbreak of Civil War 1603–1642*, 10 vols. (London, 1886), 1: 107.
152. SP 75/4, ff. 191–195, Instructions for Denmark, 4 September 1610.
153. SP 75/4, ff. 220–221, Christian IV to King James, 4 November 1610; SP 84/68, ff. 39–40, Sir R. Winwood to Salisbury, 23 April 1611; Palme, *Sverige och Danmark*, pp. 365–498.

grievances in mind, coupled with Sweden's absence at the scheduled meeting of commissioners, Christian announced that he "referred his cause to God alone."[154] Three years later, on 4 April 1611, he sent a Herald of Arms to Charles IX, proclaiming war on Sweden. Clearly he blamed Sweden for putting him in an untenable situation whereby he could not choose otherwise, "lest we will lose a great part of our lands and royal dignity."[155] Sir Ralph Winwood reported to Salisbury that the cause of the outbreak of war was "personal animosity" rather than "reason of state."[156] Christian sent to Holland for 4,000 or 5,000 mercenaries but offered so little pay that none of that country who could find work at home would accept service in Denmark.[157] After a year of conflict Christian was anxious for peace. The English had helped him with mercenaries, but they had also provided the same for the Swedes. An argument could be made that arming both sides provided the best assurance of neutrality. In any event when Sir Robert Anstruther proposed to Christian that James mediate a peace, Christian was amenable within certain limits. Diplomacy became all. Christian declared that Denmark could not enter into a truce with Sweden for certain "great and weighty reasons." However, because the King's Majesty of Great Britain and the whole world would in the process see that the fault was not in the Danes, they could give Anstruther power to answer in their absence. He wrote "that we by no means will agree to make truce but let thus be done: everyone shall keep peace . . . and so upon both sides all manner of hostility to be discouraged and ended." And so the matter was remitted "unto the hands of his Majesty of Great Britain."[158] The Swedes were also happy for English mediation. In the Hague it had been said before the Danish capture of Kalmar in 1611 that those who were in the fortress the preceding night had a vision of angels, which were interpreted to be "the angels of England."[159] After all was said and done, in January 1613, it was reported from Denmark that both the Kings of Denmark and Sweden "do rest content and are to send and give humble and hearty

---

154. SP 75/4, f. 220.
155. SP 75/4, ff. 247–247v. Palme, *Sverige och Danmark,* pp. 499–620.
156. SP 84/68, ff. 260–262, Sir R. Winwood to Salisbury, 19 March 1612.
157. SP 84/68, ff. 27–29, Sir R. Winwood to Salisbury, 8 March 1611; ibid., ff. 34–40v, passim.
158. SP 75/5, f. 3, Christian IV to Sir R. Anstruther, 8 August 1612; see also ibid., ff. 14–18, Instructions for Anstruther, and ff. 27–27v, Sir R. Anstruther to Sir T. Lake.
159. SP 84/68, f. 111, Sir R. Winwood to Salisbury, 20 August 1611.

thanks to his Majesty of Great Britain for the care his Majesty had taken of their good and welfare."[160]

While the peace negotiations were going on rumors spread of collusion between the Dutch and the Swedes against the Danes in the Sound. The Hollanders were angry about the "high and heavy tolls and impositions" levied by the Danes and then raised higher to support the war with Sweden.[161] After the signing of the peace, for which the province of Holland and particularly the town of Amsterdam were most thankful, the Sound tolls levied by the Danes continued to be a problem. At the same time the connection between Denmark and Spain appeared again to upset the political balance in Europe. Sir Ralph Winwood wrote to James from the Hague in March 1613 of the "extraordinary provision and preparation by sea of the Spaniard." Although opinion was generally that the preparation was for use against Dutch East Indies shipping, there were those who claimed that "the King of Spain would privately possess." A secret embassy had been sent from the Archduke into Denmark, and Winwood wrote that "some secret intelligence (with practice against these countries), is abrewing between Spain and Denmark."[162] As a result, the Dutch wanted a defensive alliance with the Hanse towns. Winwood became alarmed when he saw the treaty the Hollanders proposed because "the whole drift" of it was framed expressly against Christian IV, James' brother-in-law who, since Knaerød, had become the "nearest and dearest" ally of England.[163] Tensions escalated when it became known that the Dane, Lord Ulfeldt, had been sent by Christian on an embassy to Spain. The Dutch, Winwood reported, thought that only King James could rectify the situation. James's response in April 1613 was to move the princes of the Protestant Union "for the strength and continuance of their league" to include the Dutch States.[164] The Queen Regent in France conceived "a strong jealousy" regarding that

---

160. SP 75/5, ff. 59–60 (and see Ziuzin, n. 11). Leo Tandrup sees English policy as moved by the desire to prevent complete Danish dominance in the north emerging as a result of the poor Swedish performance in the war: Leo Tandrup, Mod triumf eller tragedie: En politisk-diplomatisk studie over forløbet af den dansk-svenske magtkamp fra Kalmarkrigen til Kejserkrigen med saerligt henblik pa formuleringen af den svenske og isaer den danske politik i tiden fra 1617 og isaer fra 1621 til 1625, 2 vols., Skrifter udgivet af Jysk Selskab for Historie, nr. 35 (Aarhus, Universitetsforlaget, 1979), 1: 187–223.

161. SP 75/5, ff. 79–82, the States General to the Land States of Denmark, 15/25 May 1613.

162. SP 84/69, ff. 43–46, Sir R. Winwood to King James, 3 April 1613.

163. SP 84/69, ff. 43–46.

164. SP 84/69, ff. 43–46.

plan and against the States of Holland, saying they had made "some confederacies for mutual assistance" and that the Protestants "shall always have the good wishes and prayers of these men for the advancement of their cause."[165] In May of the same year Winwood reported that "the animosities and defiances between the States and the King of Denmark daily do multiply."[166] Finally, on 11 July 1613, Christian reduced the tolls to their level before the Kalmar war.

James's lifelong personal interest was in the broad issues on which a balance of power could rest during the first two decades of the seventeenth century. He was little concerned with "such affairs of other states as are merely civil and peculiar to their own policy." James was seen as the "mirror of Christian princes, taking unto him[self] a general care of God's cause (whereof lieutenant he is)." He carried "a provident and watchful eye" over all that professed the same faith, "lest they should reap tares for wheat."[167]

When Ziuzin and his party arrived in London in the autumn of 1613, how much did the English know about recent events in Russia? On what knowledge could James base his response to the Tsar? Almost from the time of his accession to the English throne in 1603 and certainly from the period following Boris Godunov's death in 1605, news from Russia reached England only sporadically, and that generally by a circuitous route, often long after the events had occurred. Even so, however, the news reports when they arrived were reasonably accurate if lacking in specific details. Aside from the regular ambassadorial network that reported from various courts in Europe, the Muscovy Company merchants had assured that connections with Russia would not be broken during that unsettled period. They, as well as the English and Scottish mercenaries who had joined the Swedes, initially to help the Russians, provided sound intelligence. *Exactly* what information the English had, however, will never be known because of the loss of so many of the documents relating to the period. The English report of the Ziuzin embassy itself and most of the records of the Muscovy Company, whose ships carried the ambassadors and whose members knew intimately the political situation surrounding the embassy, are believed to have been burned in seventeenth-century fires. The historian can assume with some certainty, then, that there was rather more factual information available

---

165. SP 84/69, ff. 229–233v, Sir R. Winwood to Salisbury, 31 January 1612.
166. SP 84/69, ff. 62–63, Sir R. Winwood to King James, 11 May 1613.
167. SP 84/69, ff. 122–124, Sir R. Winwood to Salisbury, 5 September 1611 (printed in *Memorials* 3: 290).

to James than we can currently piece together from the accounts in newsletters and ambassadorial dispatches from Italy and the Continent.[168]

Communication in the other direction, from England to Russia, was without doubt worse. Years of war and the resulting social dislocation had isolated the Russians during the Time of Troubles, leaving them in many instances unaware of changes in foreign politics and ignorant about what alliances had been forged and what treaties signed in the interim. It was natural, then, that before setting out for England Ziuzin was specifically instructed by the new Tsar to try "to find out by all means and by asking all people" what was the current state of England's alliances.[169] Was King James at peace or at war with the Swedish King Gustavus II Adolphus? And where did he stand with Christian IV of Denmark, his brother-in-law? Which other countries were supporting the Danes and how—with men or with money? And had James had any communication with Poland? Obviously England's relationship with Scandinavia (as well as Poland) and, in this case, particularly Sweden, would have a bearing on that crown's response to Tsar Michael's request. If James was not to be offended it was necessary for the Russian ambassadors to know what tack to take. And for them the stakes were high; only a mediated peace or a decisive military victory could secure the Russian throne and the country itself against further depredations: the first taking diplomacy and time; the second, money and soldiers.

Although details of the current political configurations were unfamiliar to Michael, the English merchants, John Merrick and others, brought political news with them to Archangel in June 1613. From their reports Tsar Michael learned of James's role in the Peace of Knaerød.[170] No doubt that knowledge encouraged him to appeal to James for similar negotiations on his own behalf with Sweden and Poland. He discovered also, however, that "the soldiers whom the Swede had collected against

---

168. Travel literature and historical tracts (such as SP 91/1, ff. 215- 217v) were also formative in creating a vision of Russia and the Russians. Both Giles Fletcher and Sir Thomas Smith were knowledgeable from their visits and their accounts were quoted by others as, for example, Robert Johnson, *Relations of the Most Famous Kingdoms and Commonwealths throughout the World* (London, 1616). Recent scholarship points to the possibility that Fletcher was familiar with Baron Sigismund von Herberstein's *Rerum Moscoviticarum Commentarii*. See Samuel H. Baron, "Herberstein's Image of Russia and its Transmission through Later Writers" in Gerhard Pferschy, *Siegmund von Herberstein* (Graz, 1989), pp. 245–273.
169. See Ziuzin, p. 72.
170. See Ziuzin, pp. 146–147.

the Dane had not been disbanded," causing those who lived in Archangel to "live cautiously."[171] These reports from the merchants centered on Scandinavian interests but important as they were, news of Sigismund in Poland was more critical to the Russians, and that news was not forthcoming. James later told Ziuzin that Sigismund's injustice, his violation of oath, and his destruction and blood shedding were known, and that on that account the English "have no communication with him about anything."[172] But when Ziuzin and his entourage left Archangel in August 1613 they had no idea where the English stood vis-à-vis relations with Sigismund or, for that matter, aside from their part in the Peace of Knaerød, where the English stood vis-à-vis the Swedes and the provision of mercenaries for their army. For King James and the English who were preoccupied with the Roman Catholic-Protestant dichotomy the situation in Russia was yet another chapter of the same story.

RUSSIA

Gustavus Adolphus, who succeeded Charles IX on the Swedish throne in 1611, is the Protestant protagonist in the Russian story. Although James knew of the events described by Ziuzin in his first speech to James as "the treason of their Swedish General, Jakob Pontusson" [de la Gardie] and about the Swedish "injustices to the Moscow state" and the taking of Novgorod in July 1611,[173] communication between England and Sweden remained open. The attitude of England in the northern conflict, however, might be described as less pro-Swedish than anti-Polish.

The problems of succession began in Russia in 1598 when Tsar Fyodor Ivanovich died childless and were resolved only in 1613 with the election of Mikhail Fyodorovich Romanov as Tsar. During the intervening Time of Troubles various factions of noblemen, two pretenders to the throne (the False Dmitriies) and the king of at least one foreign power actively sought to fill the political vacuum.[174] After the assassination of the first false Dmitrii in May 1606, Vasilii Shuiskii, a boyar "with princely lineage," emerged as ruler over a divided and broken state. His

---

171. See Ziuzin, p. 142.
172. See Ziuzin, p. 174.
173. See Ziuzin, p. 174.
174. This brief summary of the standard account of the Time of Troubles is taken primarily from Robert O. Crummey, *The Formation of Muscovy 1304–1613* (London, 1987), pp. 205–233; and the classic, S. F. Platonov, *Ocherki po istorii smuty v moskovskom gosudarstve XVI-XVII vv.* (St. Petersburg, 1910). An English translation of Platonov's own shorter version is S. F. Platonov, *The Time of Troubles*, trans. John T. Alexander (Lawrence, Kansas, 1970).

position was untenable. Within a year a second false Dmitrii, with a motley crew of supporters, Polish noblemen, Russian boyars (including the Romanovs) and cossacks, and soldiers of fortune, crossed into Russian territory and moved toward the capital, threatening Shuiskii's position. Unable to consolidate power within the country, Shuiskii was forced to turn for support to Russia's traditional enemies—the crowns of Poland and Sweden. He called on Sigismund III to withdraw those Polish subjects in the pretender's forces, but the request resulted in a meaningless arrangement, "worth less than the parchment on which it was written." However, Shuiskii's negotiations with the then Swedish King Charles IX (who was Sigismund's uncle) bore fruit, and it was agreed that Swedish troops would join Russian forces in fighting the Poles. It was a grave miscalculation. The intervention of the Swedes only served to provide the pretext for a major Polish invasion in 1609, this time openly led by Sigismund. Shuiskii's Swedish allies were of no help. Sigismund's forces, combined with the Polish soldiers already there whom Shuiskii was trying and hetman Stanisław Żółkiewski, defeated the Russian-Swedish army at Klushino (24 June 1610). Most of de la Gardie's mercenary troops went over to the Poles, and he retreated ignominiously toward Finland. On 17 July the Moscow mob demanded Shuiskii's abdication. He was packed off to a monastery and the Russian state left leaderless again. Smolensk was besieged by the Poles, and the Swedes were camped on the outskirts of Novgorod, less interested now in defending that city than in conquering it.

It was out of this desperate political scenario that the temporary boyar government in Moscow conceived of a plan to offer the Russian throne to Prince Władysław of Poland, Sigismund's son. Although he was a foreigner and a Roman Catholic he was young, and through the Polish crown had some military and financial means. The Polish hetman, Żółkiewski, who negotiated the conditions under which Władysław could accept the crown, agreed that Władysław would forsake Roman Catholicism and convert to Eastern Orthodoxy. Thus, the main hurdle to the Prince becoming Tsar had been surmounted: he would disavow all allegiance to Rome. But the boyars, and indeed Żółkiewski himself, were unprepared for Sigismund's reaction to the plans. He had become convinced that the conversion of Russia to Catholicism was his mission, and that the Polish crown was the source of power by which he could carry it out. The extremity of Sigismund's position provided at last a rallying point for the population of the Muscovite state. Even though there would be another three years of fighting, the tide had turned. The response to Sigismund's strategy for Polish supremacy and Roman Catholicism in Russia came in the form of a kind of volunteer army led by the noblemen of Riazan' under the direction of Prokopii Liapunov.

By the summer of 1611 the Russians who had supported the armies of various pretenders, the cossack detachments, and certain private soldiers were united in a strategy to defeat and oust the Poles. The going was not easy. Within a year the cossacks murdered Liapunov, leaving the united forces without leadership. On 3 June 1612 Smolensk fell to Sigismund's troops and in mid-July the Swedes took Novgorod—a major step beyond their original agreement to assist the Russians! However, the momentum of the volunteer army was not lost. With new headquarters at Iaroslavl', Prince Dmitrii Pozharskii assumed the leadership and, with an eye to the future, began building an administration, bringing together as much as possible of the old nobility and ecclesiastical hierarchy as well as summoning representatives from the people to create a *zemskii sobor* (Assembly of the Land). At the same time Pozharskii was consolidating his military position, and by October 1612 had recaptured Moscow and most of central Russia. With his military position secure and victory in hand Pozharskii and his associates, knowing from bitter experience the necessity of a legitimate political solution, summoned the *zemskii sobor* to select a Tsar to rule over all Russia. Despite war weariness the people responded enthusiastically:

> In January 1613 delegates to the zemskii sobor began arriving from all corners of Muscovy. They represented all major groups of free men—nobles, clergymen, towns people, and peasants. Precisely how many of them were there is not clear: the protocols of the assembly record 177 names, and as many as 500 men may have taken part.[175]

On 7 February 1613 a body roughly comparable in size to the Lower House of the English parliament of the same period chose Michael, the young son of Metropolitan Filaret Romanov, to be Tsar of all Russia. That choice was confirmed two weeks later by a group of leading noblemen assembled for the purpose. That he was chosen or elected was important to the Russians, although King James underplayed this fact in emphasizing Michael's hereditary qualifications through the Romanovs. Heredity and succession were touchy issues with James, the first outsider to assume the English throne since William the Conqueror, he was defensive about his own lineage.[176]

---

175. Crummey, *Muscovy*, p. 231.
176. It would be publicly questioned in a Polish work entitled *Alloquia Osiecensia*, written by Gaspar Cichocki and published in Cracow the following year. See Ziuzin, n. 277.

There was an audience in London for Russian news. "Official" news-letters were addressed to Robert Cecil, Earl of Salisbury, and later, after his death in 1612, were sent to Sir Thomas Lake and Sir Ralph Win-wood, Secretaries of State. But general correspondence, too, the unoffi-cial letters, often contained accounts of the political machinations during the Time of Troubles. Let us look briefly at the kind of comment that reached England at this time and on which James and his advisers based their political assumptions.

After a fourteen-month stay in Stockholm, Thomas Chamberlayn, mercenary, was sent with a Swedish regiment to support Shuiskii against the Poles in Moscow in the spring of 1610. In a letter to Cecil he vividly described that campaign, the entrance of the Polish hetman, Żółkiewski, into Moscow and the reemergence of the second False Dmitrii. By July Shuiskii had abdicated and in October Chamberlayn was in Smolensk where, he wrote, the Russians were "content to make the King emperor and his son to succeed," provided that he not introduce "papistry, as in particular no Jesuits, priests, monks, or friars."[177] But the Russians still had doubts, he wrote, and given an alternative would rather be com-manded "by any nation but them [i.e., the Poles]." Chamberlayn wished "our noble Duke of York" were there to decide the issue. (Could he have known that Charles was then just ten years of age?) He went on to say that a Polish ambassador was soon to go to England to treat of a marriage,

---

In fact, the negotiations planned to be held at Stettin in 1615, where England was to mediate a peace between Poland and Sweden, would be threatened by James's reaction to that book, which denounced his right of succession to the English throne. Earlier (8 March 1610) in clarification of points made in Dr. Cowell's book, James's message to Parliament was that "the King takes himself to be beholding to no elective powers, depends upon no popular applause, that he derives the lines of his fortune and greatness from the loins of his ancestors." Elizabeth Read Foster, *Proceedings in Parliament 1610*, 2 vols. (New Haven, 1966), 2: 49. On the problems arising from the Cichocki book see Mierzwa, *Anglia*, pp. 42–43; A. Kraushar, "Poselstwo Dickensona do Zygmunta III," *Miscellanea historyczne* 32 (1909): 1–16; and HMC, *Trumbull*, 5: 345–347 (J. Dickenson to Sir R. Winwood, 25 September 1615). The book questioned James's claim to the English throne and contained "offensive epithets and passages at the expense of the religious beliefs of the King of England." James's first proclamation to his English subjects attempted to offset this kind of criticism and publicly to establish his claim. See James F. Larkin and Paul L. Hughes, eds., *Stuart Royal Proclamations*, 2 vols. (Oxford, 1983), 1: 1–4, "A Proclamation declaring the undoubted Right of our Sovereign Lord King James to the crown of the Realmes of England, France, and Ireland."

177. T. Chamberlayn to Salisbury, n.d. (SP 88/3, ff. 42–47v; Talbot, *Elementa* 6: 116–121). The letter is undated and the events therein may have taken place before Shuiskii's abdication in July 1610.

but the diplomat to be sent was "a great papist, not generally affected to our nation." And the Duke of Lorraine, he wrote, brought financial help to Sigismund as well as, he believed, religious support, the writer having understood that the Duke "was at Rome before he came unto the King." Lastly, he commented at length on the behavior of the Irish mercenaries under Captain George Byngley. These were the Irishmen sent to Sweden in a punitive action against Catholics in Ulster. An account of Lord Chichester's services on behalf of the English plantations in the north reported that he had "done his best for the reformation of religion," besides cutting off "bad and disloyal offenders . . . he has sent away 6,000 of the same inclination and profession to the wars in Sweden."[178] The Irish, "pressed for hearing mass and living as Catholics according to the Pope's religion in Ireland," were unhappy serving in Sweden, a country whose service Chichester found they "do not affect."[179] In 1610 the Lord Deputy of Ireland, Lord Chichester, advised that the men sent for the service of the Swedish King might be employed instead "in the service of Russia."[180] The same year the Irish in Ulster were described by Sir Edward Brabazon in a letter to Salisbury, as the "catapillars of this kingdom," and he proposed that they be removed for the service of Denmark.[181]

After the overthrow of Shuiskii, when Sigismund's plans to press his own claims to the Russian throne were known abroad, a small flurry of newsletters reached London. Chamberlayn again reported to Salisbury, this time on the "immutability" of the Polish King's resolutions. "He plans to be crowned Tsar before returning in the summer," he wrote, "although not before he has taken Smolensk."[182] In April 1611, Patrick Gordon wrote that the Polish forces around Smolensk were weakened and unfit to assault the city. However, hearing that Gabor Batory, nephew to King Stefan Batory and Prince of Transylvania (1608–1613), had overrun Moldavia and had an army assembled in Transylvania, the Poles were now "more obstinate" than before in their desire to take Smolensk, seeing that there might be troubles at home. It was believed that "malcontented Poles and Muscovites who change their mind with

178. C[alendar] S[tate] P[apers] I[reland] 1611–1614, pp. 479–480 (Lord Chichester's Services, May 1614); and see above, pp. 49–50.
179. CSPI 1608–1610, p. 272 (Sir A. Chichester to Salisbury, 17 August 1609).
180. CSPI 1608–1610, p. 371 (Rembrances . . . 29 January 1610).
181. CSPI 1608–1610, p. 407 (Sir E. Brabazon to Salisbury, March 1610).
182. T. Chamberlain to Salisbury, 22 January 1611 (SP 88/2, ff. 7–8v; Talbot, Elementa 6: 95–97).

fortune" might readily join Batory in an invasion of Poland.[183] Gordon also reported that Sigismund had already written to James of his success in Russia, declaring that the English merchants trafficking there should now pay to him the customs they had in former times paid to the Grand Dukes.[184] James may well have received the letter itself from Sigismund before the arrival of Gordon's account in his own letter. It was believed in Warsaw, Gordon informed Cecil, that Sigismund had isolated himself from the nobility and senators and was "governed by Jesuit counsel." The Polish ecclesiastics were pressing the religious issue by speaking out against dissenters. They demanded that churches accidentally destroyed by fire in Wilno should not be repaired, and they were expelling Protestant preachers out of those villages in Prussia that were subject to the Polish King. Certainly the Venetians writing from England knew how the suspicions of the princes of the Union "were strengthened with regard to the Bavarian League . . . nor does the agreement between the Emperor and Matthias trouble them little, nor yet the success of Poland in Russia."[185]

By summer 1611 Sir William Stuart, in the service of the Swedish King, had arrived at Narva with his troop of Irish mercenaries, intended to fight in Russia against the Poles. In less than a month so many of the Irish under his command had gone with the enemy that he complained to Salisbury that he needed more recruits to regain the strength of his regiment. This time he asked for only English and Scottish.[186] In the autumn that year James Hill, a Scottish mercenary, wrote to Salisbury from Moscow that the cruelty of the Poles makes the Moscoviters so "hard-hearted" against them that they would be glad for any other prince. And because the land is so wracked, he wrote, it is open for any prince to take as a prize, and none, he thought, could do it better than King James or the King of Denmark; and for James "it would be a

---

183. P. Gordon to Salisbury, 28 April 1611 from Danzig (SP 88/3, f. 19; Talbot, *Elementa* 6: 103–104). The rumor was false: Batory intended to invade Moldavia that spring, but instead was himself defeated by the combined forces of the princes of Moldavia and Wallachia in July of that year.

184. Sigismund to James I, 23 February 1611 from Smolensk (SP 88/3, f. 9; Talbot, *Elementa* 6: 97–98).

185. *CSPV 1610–1613*, p. 64. The agreement mentioned here was the agreement of 10 September 1610, in which Matthias made many concessions to Rudolf. By the end of the year the agreement collapsed, leading to the final defeat of Rudolf, his abdication of the crown of Bohemia in favor of Matthias, in summer 1611.

186. SP 91/1, f. 222. See Appendix, below.

thousand times more profitable unto England as Virginia."[187] Shortly
before Christmas that year the diet at Warsaw granted a large subsidy and
"it was decided to continue the Russian war for nine years."[188]

At the beginning of the new year, on 6 January 1612, Gordon again
wrote to Cecil, this time from Königsberg, of Sigismund's determination
in Poland. He also reported that Johann Sigismund, the Elector of Brandenburg, had been entertained in Warsaw in a "most kindly and broth-
erly" way and with the consent of the whole estates was given *feudum
ducalis Prussia* and he, as *beneficarius regis*, swore the oath of fidelity.[189]
Little did either of them know then that in the following year the
balance in the German states would be shaken by Johann Sigismund's
rejection of Luther for Calvin and Wolfgang Wilhelm of Neuburg's conversion to Catholicism.

In the spring of 1612 James apparently sent a letter to Sigismund
regarding the English trading companies at Elbing and in the northern
part of Russia, around Archangel, no doubt at the instigation of English
merchants who prevailed on the government to ensure that the ports
stayed open even during the Polish invasions. We do not have a copy of
the letter itself. However, an undated memorandum that may refer to the
letter in question notes that James had written not only to Sigismund but
also to the King of Sweden offering to send his ambassador to mediate
peace between them. The last two paragraphs of the memorandum are
concerned with the English merchants in Danzig and the liberty of trade
there, the same topic discussed by Sigismund and Gordon and reported
on 12 April 1612.[190] Gordon wrote that following the delivery of the
letter Sigismund had a long discussion with him concerning English trade
in his dominions.[191] Apparently Sigismund was already considering the
northern Russian state as within his purview—a critical bit of intelligence relayed by Gordon. Sigismund told Gordon that the Dutch had
"offered great sums of money to have the privileges due to the English
company in Moscow given to themselves." And Sigismund said that he
had refused out of consideration for the English, although it is not at all
clear precisely why the English were given deferential treatment at this

187. J. Hill to Salisbury, 25 October 1611 (SP 88/3, f. 36–36v; Talbot, *Elementa* 6:
    112–113).
188. SP 88/3, f. 36v (Talbot, *Elementa* 6: 113); HMC, *Downshire*, 3: 193.
189. P. Gordon to Salisbury, 6 January 1612, Königsberg (SP 88/3, f. 53; Talbot, *Elementa*
    6: 121–122).
190. SP 88/3, f. 48 (Talbot, *Elementa* 6: 121–122).
191. P. Gordon to King James, 20 April 1612, Königsberg (SP 88/3, f. 55–55v; Talbot,
    Elementa 6: 125–127).

point. Certainly the Poles wanted no open breach with England, but that they would protect Polish-Dutch relations opens further questions about them at that time. To complicate the story further, the same letter reported that Sigismund was ready to march into Russia with the support of 4,000 Dutch soldiers (under their own colonels) for which he had made no financial provision. And it was mused in Warsaw that "other nations are subject to mutiny if they do lack present pay."

But a Dutch presence in Russia was conceived as a threat in most circles in London. The English merchants, with an eye to the Persian trade and the shipment of goods to Europe out of the northern Russian ports, were deeply concerned that the Dutch not strengthen their foothold in that area. By early spring of 1613 these merchants would parlay their commercial interests into a political proposition for an English presence in Russia.

In the meantime it was reported in London that the "old question for Cleve" had brought a division of German princes along religious lines, and that if their combination in a league would come to pass, at last there would be "less intermingling betwixt Protestants and Papists, and so sever the sheep from the goats."[192] A few months before Adrian, Baron of Flodorf, had written to James that he had learned from the Elector of Brandenburg of *"les extorsions, ambition et injuste invasion des Polonnois (ennemys et oppreseurs de la vraye Chrestiene) sur les Moscovites"* and all, he said, *"avecq desir d'agrandir le nombre des Jésuits . . . en tous les monastères de Moscovie."*[193] It was rumored that Philip III would enter the Low Countries and put forward his second son for Emperor. Did this signal to the English that the twelve-year truce so recently signed with Spain and the Archdukes was already a failure? And further, it was reported that in Moscow the Polish King was driven "to most miserable distress" for his "discontenting" the kingdom with Jesuits.[194]

It was sometime in the early spring of 1613 before news reached England of the Russian recapture of Moscow and the "irrecoverable defeat" of Sigismund the previous October.[195] In the meantime the merchants of the Muscovy Company had prevailed on James and the Privy Council to consider the idea of an English presence in the northern ports of Russia. That plan has been discussed elsewhere, and there is extant at

---

192. HMC, *Buccleuch & Queensberry*, 1: 240–241, Sir C. Montagu to Sir E. Montagu, 6 February 1613.

193. See Ziuzin, p. 125.

194. HMC, *Downshire*, 4: 19, Sir J. Throckmorton to W. Trumbull, 19 January 1612/13; and see p. 16; see also Winwood, *Memorials* 3: 439.

195. HMC, *Downshire*, 4: 19.

least one substantial (although undated) contemporary tract on a "Scheme for Acquiring Land in Russia," primarily for trading purposes.[196] The motives of the project may have been connected with the Muscovy Company's desire for the security and protection of their own commercial interests. The plan itself, however, evolved as a private undertaking, certainly by James Hill and Arthur Aston, and probably Adrian Freiger, who left Hamburg together for St. Nicholas at Eastertime the previous several "avises or intelligences" in hand "that the Moscoviters desire to have our sovereign King to their protector";[197] the project is discussed in Ziuzin's report, below.[198] The mercenaries claimed that they had gone to Russia with James's knowledge, although Ziuzin was instructed to tell the English that those men carried with them no credential from the English crown. One must wonder after reading the Ziuzin account whether James knew very much at all about the project that had been conceived by mercenaries and sold to him as a broad political venture in response to "the distressed and perplexed estate of that famous country and people exposed at this present to imminent danger as well of invasions from enemies abroad as of intestine broils and seditions at home."

If the cipher in the letter from John More to Sir Ralph Winwood written in early February 1613 were known, the identity of the individuals involved would be further confirmed. More wrote that "our Muscovy merchants are dealing with * to set them a course to induce 4 to undertake the protection of that country upon good conditions of dominion in case we prevail. . . ."[199] At the time Foscarini, the Venetian ambassador in London, reported that James was interested but the Council was divided on the issue. He described it as a scheme whereby the Muscovites asked for "troops and orders to drive out the Poles" in ex-

---

196. See Samuel H. Baron, "Thrust and Parry: Anglo-Russian Relations in the Muscovite North," *OSP* 21 (1988): 19–40; Chester Dunning, "James I, the Russia Company, and the Plan to Establish a Protectorate Over North Russia," *Albion* (Spring, 1989): 206–226 and, by the same author, "A Letter to James I Concerning the English Plan for Military Intervention in Russia," *SEER* 67 (1989): 94–108; I. Lubimenko, "A Project for the Acquisition of Russia by James I," *E[nglish] H[istorical] R[eview]* 114 (April, 1914): 246–256; Phipps, *Merrick*, pp. 68–73. For the tract, see Cotton Nero B XI, ff. 381–384.

197. For the first quotation regarding the "avises," see SP 81/11, f. 210 (J. Hill to Salisbury, 16 February 1612); the second is from Rymer, *Foedera* 7, 2: 194.

198. See Ziuzin, p. 66. There were thousands of English mercenaries on the continent at this time recruited to serve under Sir Edward Cecil at Juliers. Rymer, *Foedera* 7, 2: 166.

199. See HMC, *Buccleuch & Queensberry*, 1: 124–125.

change for which "they offer to place ports in his Majesty's hands, to depend on his orders, and to pay the troops themselves."[200] A similar scheme was described by Boisschot in November 1613. He connected the proposal with Ziuzin who, he reports, asked James to mediate a peace for Russia with the Poles. If that failed, then James should provide soldiers and ships for the Russians who would in return give him a province on the coast as security for the fleet.[201] The arrangement described as such hardly seems like the protectorate some historians would make it out to be, and in any event the English government was ultimately not interested in the undertaking.

The English government's concern with the project, prior to any comments on its commercial viability, was directed toward the politics of the Scandinavian states: "What jealousy may grow from the n[orthern] princes if the King take upon him the sovereignty [of the northern area] . . . or enter the league defensive?"[202] The crown was not about to jeopardize the good relations with Sweden and Denmark that it had so desperately sought earlier and was just now establishing. Gustavus Adolphus and Christian were known quantities; the situation in Russia was anything but clear.

The Russians in the course of the previous two years had made overtures to one King, one Archduke, and two Princes to restore peace in the kingdom.[203] The Muscovy Company merchants claimed that now some Russian noblemen sought to explore the possibility of help from yet another source, James I. Although there is little extant information concerning the situation, under the circumstances the plan does not strike one as being unusual nor, given the small number of Englishmen who knew the language and the people, was it peculiar that Merrick was the spokesman for it to the English crown. However, according to the commission given to Merrick, what England sought in Russia was primarily a political resolution: "the reestablishment of peace and government therein by our [English] means."[204] James's response to this eventually aborted project is clear in the commission granted to Merrick and his colleague, William Russell, in May 1613.[205] Although latitude was given

200. CSPV 1610–1613, p. 538.
201. HHST, Abteilung Belgien, Pc fz. 76–77, F. Boisschot, 29 November 1613.
202. Lansd. 142, f. 395, and see I. Lubimenko (above, n. 196).
203. Charles IX of Sweden, Archduke Maximilian, Władysław of Poland, and Karl Philip of Sweden. See also James Spens to Salisbury, 11 October 1612 (SP 95/1, f. 213) and SP 81/11, f. 210, Appendix, below, and see Ziuzin, nn. 39 & 63 and pp. 78 and 93.
204. Rymer, Foedera 7, 2: 193.
205. Rymer, Foedera 7, 2: 194.

to them for broad discussion with the Russians there is no mention of trade or customs or tolls in this commission. It dealt solely with political realities, commissioning Merrick and Russell as servants of the English crown to "treat, confer, agree and conclude" with the Russian "Lords, states, General of the army, gentry, and commons, or with such persons by what name or title soever they be called as do at this present represent the body of that state" about the "defense and protection of that country and dominion." Another commission issued to them at the same time reflected the Muscovy Company agenda.[206] By that they were authorized to negotiate the renewing or confirming (or both) of the traditional immunities, privileges, and liberties within Russia.

When news of the recapture of Moscow by Pozharskii's troops in October 1612, and the ouster of the Poles from that city, finally reached London in the spring of 1613, it was reported that Sigismund had been beaten out by the Russians "with much ado to save his own life by the speed of a good horse."[207] It was conjectured then that if the Russians could retake Smolensk in the summer, Sigismund would truly have lost, and "his masters the Jesuits shall not have any cause to brag of their conquests, but with scorn and shame may pull in the horns of their pride and boastings."[208] The arrival of the news of the Polish defeat when the English were in the midst of their discussions about sending some sort of deputy governor to Russia no doubt took the steam out of the arguments. In any event, Merrick and Russell sailed for Russia, commissions in hand, landing in Archangel in June 1613 unaware that five months earlier a new Tsar had been elected.[209] Their arrival was well timed, though, to brief Aleksei Ziuzin on his embassy to James and to arrange for his passage on their return to England in August in Muscovy Company ships.

In the meantime it had also been rumored in Sweden that the Russians had retaken Smolensk from the Poles. In the same newsletter, sent from Stockholm to London at the end of September 1613, there was evidence that although "the empireship of Moscovy is known to be a thing of great wealth and dignity," the Swedes were not overly enthusiastic about getting their young Prince Charles further involved.[210] The Russians themselves, wrote Thomas Fisk, were in "great disorder" about the possibility

206. Rymer, *Foedera* 7, 2: 193.
207. HMC, *De L'Isle and Dudley*, p. 97; see also HMC, *Buccleugh & Queensberry*, 1: 241, Sir C. Montagu to Sir E. Montagu, 6 February 1612/13.
208. HMC, *De L'Isle and Dudley*, p. 97.
209. James probably did not hear of Tsar Michael's election until August 1613. See SP 91/1, f. 240, Appendix, below.
210. SP 95/2, ff. 7–8, T. Fisk to Sir T. Lake.

of a formal Swedish presence in the country and the Swedes found the expenses high in just maintaining "those Dukedoms and regions" of which they were already in possession, let alone taking on Russia.[211] For James, though now aware of Michael's election, the other news only confirmed the still unsettled conditions in Russia.[212]

By this time, however, the Swedish General, Jakob Pontusson de la Gardie, had entrenched himself in Novgorod to stay until the conflict would be resolved by the peace of Stolbovo in 1617. Smolensk had been taken by the Poles in July 1611 and was not recaptured until 1654, only to be formally returned to Russia in 1667, fifty years after the Truce of Deulino that in 1618, at least for a time, provided some respite from the fighting.

Thus, at the time of his election Tsar Michael's legacy was a war-torn country still occupied by the forces of two foreign powers. His first tasks were to reestablish the machinery of government for the stabilizing of domestic affairs and to reinstitute normal diplomatic relationships for the rebuilding of a coherent foreign policy. During his first few months as Tsar, Michael sent ambassadors to Denmark, Germany, Holland, and England. He hoped for real support by way of money and soldiers.

When the embassy arrived in London King James was on progress, and consequently was not present for the welcoming ceremonies at Tower Wharf. The audience, however, high on the agenda for his return to the City, was scheduled for 7 November 1613. In the meantime Ziuzin and his secretary were treated to the Lord Mayor's festival, and they witnessed the bonfires of the Guy Fawkes day celebrations. Later, after the formal audiences were over, in the dreary winter months in London, Ziuzin was often found "surrounded by merchants," having given "the greatest satisfaction" in the matter of commerce.[213] It was reported in March that James sent Patrick Gordon to Sigismund to sound out his willingness to negotiate, a gesture signaling James's desire to work toward a peace among Christian princes.[214]

Ziuzin's embassy was counted a success by both sides, although it fell short of offering an immediate loan to the Tsar.[215] As it was, the embassy opened diplomatic relations and prepared the way for a second Russian mission to England the following year that would result in James again

211. SP 95/2, ff. 7–8.
212. See Appendix, below, p. 00, SP 91/1, f. 240, Sir Thomas Smith's letter to Viscount Rochester, August 1613.
213. CSPV 1613–1615, pp. 81, 84.
214. CSPV 1613–1615, p. 97.
215. SP 91/2, f. 1, Appendix, below.

sending Patrick Gordon to Poland, this time to begin work on the peace treaty that would eventually be signed in Stolbovo in 1617.

It was reported that Ziuzin left England sometime in late May or June arriving in Archangel on 3 July 1614. Shortly thereafter James bestowed a knighthood on Merrick and sent him immediately to Russia with a commission in hand ordaining him ambassador with all the concomitant powers to begin the peace negotiations between Michael Fyodorovich and Gustavus Adolphus.[216] The Secretary of State wrote within the year to Merrick that King James would support the Tsar's peace initiative in every way short of war, for, laying the blame on parliament, he said he could not bear the cost of going to war for him if that peace failed.[217]

Paul Bushkovitch
Maija Jansson
New Haven

The account of the Russian Embassy to England in 1613–1614

[The Instructions]

[p. 40][1] On the 20th of June of the year 7121 [1613] the Sovereign Tsar Grand Prince, Mikhail Fyodorovich, of all Russia ordered the gentleman [*dvorianin*] and viceroy [*namestnik*] of Shatsk, Aleksei Ivanovich Ziuzin, and the Secretary, [*d'iuk*] Aleksei Vitovtov, to go to the English King James as ambassadors for his sovereign business and for that of the land. And they were to go to Vologda, and to the Dvina, to the new city of Archangel. And Aleksei Ivanovich and the Secretary, Aleksei, were to go to Vologda without delay.

And when they come to Vologda he [Ziuzin] is to take from the Governors [*voevody*] Prince Mikhail Temkin-Rostovskii and Grigorii Pushkin, boats so that they will be able to journey on. And it has been written to the sovereign Governors, Mikhail and Grigorii, about their departure.[2] And they are to go onto the Dvina, to the new city of Archangel; and when they come to Vologda they are to report it to Tsar Mikhail Fyodorovich [ST].[3]

And when they come to the Dvina they are to say to the Governor, Nikita Mikhailovich Pushkin, and to the Secretary, Putilo Grigor'ev, that they should be sent to England on English ships that will come from England. And that it has been written to them about this matter from

---

216. See Rymer, *Foedera* 7, 2: 202.
217. Papers of the Marquis of Bath, Whitelocke Collection, volume 1, f. 182 (Sir R. Winwood to Sir J. Merrick, 5 October 1615). See also, SP 103/61, f. 20–20v.

Tsar Mikhail Fyodorovich; it has been ordered [p. 41] to them to prepare the English ship on which they will sail.[4] And Aleksei Ivanovich and the Secretary Aleksei are to go on that ship to England. And on what day they will come to Vologda, and how they will leave Vologda; and how they will come to the new city of Archangel, and on what day they will leave the new city of Archangel to go beyond the sea; and with whom they will go on the ship, and how many people will be with them on the ship with Aleksei and the Secretary—how many Russians and how many Germans[5]—Aleksei Ivanovich and the Secretary Aleksei must write to Tsar Mikhail Fyodorovich [ST] in Moscow.[6]

And a letter has been sent from Tsar Mikhail Fyodorovich [ST] with him about his passage to the Danish King, Christian. And if something on the sea should bring Aleksei and the Secretary to any of the towns of the Danish King and the rulers do not want to allow them to go to the English King, then Aleksei and the Secretary Aleksei are to show them the Sovereign's letter to the Danish King, Christian.[7] And if the King is in any place not far away, then Aleksei and the Secretary are to send to the Danish King Christian the sovereign's letter [p. 42] and themselves are to ask to go to England. And they are to say to the Danish King's officials that the Great Sovereign Tsar and Grand Prince, Mikhail Fyodorovich, of all Russia has sent them to the English King, James, to announce his [the Tsar's] sovereignty,[8] and about other good business; and to their sovereign King, Christian, Tsar Mikhail Fyodorovich [ST] has sent ambassadors, as well as to King James.[9]

And on the sea they should take great care that they nowhere encounter the Poles or the Lithuanians or the Swedes, so that they might pass safely.

And when they have come to Archangel and have gone by sea and come to England they are to find out by all means, and by asking all people, whether the English King James is at peace or not at peace with the Swedish King[10]; and if the Danish King Christian is at peace with the Swedish King or not. And if he is not at peace and there is war between them will it continue, in what places is it and who is the stronger, the Danish King than the Swedish or the Swedish King than the Danish? And have there been battles between them anew; and if there have been, where, and who has defeated whom; and who has taken towns from whom? And in the future what is expected, peace or war? And does the English King James stand with the Dane against the Swede, and does he [James] help him? And if he stand with him, with what does the English King James help the Dane?[11] Or is King James at peace with the Swede, and how long has it been, and for how long and on what terms? And which Kings are helping against the Danish King, and who is helping with what—with men or with [p. 43] treasure? Or has the Danish King

Christian made peace with the Swedish King and, if he has made peace, for how many years? Or has he made a truce or an eternal peace, and what were the terms?[12]

And now the English King James and the Danish King Christian—have there been communications anew with the Polish King, Sigismund; and if there have been, what were they about?[13] And whatever they find out about all this they are to write down for themselves and, in general, take care of this affair.

And the undersecretary who will be with them[14] is ordered to carry the letters when they come to the King's court. And when they come to his palace and the King's chamber the Secretary Aleksei [Vitovtov] will take the letter and carry it, and when Aleksei [Ziuzin] makes his bow to the King and asks about his health, then Aleksei Ivanovich [Ziuzin] will take the letter from the Secretary and give it to the King.[15]

And when the King asks about the health of the Sovereign Tsar and Grand Duke of all Russia, then Aleksei Ivanovich should say:

"When we came from our Great Sovereign and our Tsar and Grand Duke, the Autocrat of all Russia, the Great Sovereign, his Imperial Majesty (Tsar) in his great and glorious Kingdoms (God willing), was in good health."[16]

And after that Aleksei Ivanovich is to make a speech and say[17]:

"By the love of God, glorified in the Trinity, the Sovereign Tsar and Grand Duke, Mikhail Fyodorovich, of all Russia, and Sovereign and Ruler of many States, has ordered to be said to you, Great Sovereign, his beloved brother, King James: It is known to you yourself, Great Sovereign, our brother, that before now there was strong fraternal love and friendship between the Great Sovereign Tsar and Grand Duke Ivan Vasil'evich, the Autocrat of all Russia, of blessed memory,[18] and his son the Tsar, the Great Sovereign and Grand Duke, Fyodor Ivanovich,[19] [p. 44] the Autocrat of all Russia, of blessed memory, the Tsar and Grand Duke, Boris Fyodorovich,[20] of all Russia, and our beloved sister, Elizabeth, of blessed memory.[21] And after this the Tsar and Grand Duke, Vasilii Ivanovich [Shuiskii], of all Russia, had loving communication with you, our brother.[22] And when in the time of the Tsar and Grand Duke, Boris, the Moscow state suffered many injustices through violation of oath from the Polish King, Sigismund, and the lord councillors [pani rada], and the Tsar and Grand Duke, Vasilii Ivanovich, wrote about the injustice from the King and lord councillors to you, his beloved brother, truly, in his letter [sent] with your merchants, John Merrick and his associates.[23]

"And that after that, in the time of Tsar Vasilii [Shuiskii], there happened from King Sigismund, the King of Poland, and the lord councillors, according to their evil intention, many injustices and destruction to the Moscow state against their many oaths. And we now announce truly their injustices and evil design to you our brother according to your love for us. When the Tsar, Ivanovich [Shuiskii] [ST] of all Russia, became the Sovereign Tsar and Grand Duke, Autocrat of all Russia, in the Moscow state and in all the states of the Russian Tsardom [Tsarstvie] he sent to Lithuania, to King Sigismund, his emissaries, Prince Grigorii Volkonskii and the Secretary, Andrei Ivanov, announcing to him his own sovereignty and reminding him of his[24] injustices—how he had violated his oath and violated his agreement of peace and had caused such wicked confusion and fruitless bloodletting among men—and how he would send to him his ambassadors, instructing them truly how to [p. 45] correct such great injustices that had come from his side; and how he should pay for many unaccountable losses that had been perpetrated by him on the Moscow state. And Sigismund, the King of Poland, with those emissaries wrote to Tsar Vasilii and ordered that he was sending to him his emissaries about all sorts of good business; and that he would truly send his decree to his ambassadors, who at that time were in Moscow, that they should make and establish a treaty about all sorts of good business. And King Sigismund sent to Tsar Vasilii, his emissaries, Stanisław Witowski, the wójski of Parcew, and Prince Jan z Drucka Sokoliński, his secretaries and gentlemen,[25] with credentials with his royal signature and seal."[26]

The Secretary Aleksei [is to say]:

"And the King himself and the lords councillors, intending to ruin the Moscow state more than before, strove to make confusion in the Moscow state and to spill blood in vain. And they ordered the rumor to be spread in all the border areas of the Moscow state that the thief[27] who had been the sovereign in Moscow had left Moscow and was with them in Poland, and that in his place supposedly some Lithuanian was killed. And designing and investigating they sent to the border of the Moscow state, to the land of Sever,[28] another thief, by birth a Jew, calling him by his previous name, Dmitrii,[29] as if that same person who was in Moscow had run away from murder in Moscow. And to him came to the border on the King's command many noble Poles and Lithuanians, Prince Roman Rózyński and Alexander Zborowski and Prince Adam Wiśniówiecki [p. 46] and Jan Piotr Sapieha, and Samuel and Jan Tyszkiewicz, who called themselves generals and colonels, and other colonels and captains with many Poles and Lithuanians; and they began to send subversive letters into the whole land of Sever, to cities and towns, calling that thief the previous thief Dmitrii. And many cowardly cossacks and boyars' slaves, poor people of the towns of the border and of Sever, believed these subversive letters; and others who saw that there would be ruin and war from the Poles and Lithuanians joined that thief.

"And there began to be among men dissension and bloodshed more than before. And many Sever towns and those from the Polish border began to surrender to that other thief because of the great war and ruin from the Poles and Lithuanians. And then that thief, having collected together with Poles and Lithuanians many Russian thieves and cossacks, tried to go to the ruling city of Moscow and, having come near Moscow, stood in a camp and let loose war into the provincial cities. And they began to ruin the Moscow state and to burn large and small villages and to take people prisoner and to kill and rob some, and to spill blood in vain without mercy, and to attack the ruling city of Moscow. And the ambassadors of King Sigismund who were at that time in Moscow, Mikolaj Oleśnicki, the castellan of Małogoszcz, and Aleksander Gosiewski, the *starosta* of Wieliż, and the emissaries Stanislaw Witowski and Prince Jan Sokoliński, according to the order of King Sigismund, though they saw such ruin to the Moscow state, did no good—sent nothing to the King about his injustice and they did not restrain from bloodshed the Poles and Lithuanians who [p. 47] had come with the thief, and they spoke of many high measures and presented demands for towns and uncountable treasure which is impossible even to write.

"And speaking much with our boyars, meeting for many days, they decreed a truce between Tsar Vasilii and the Polish King, Sigismund, again for a short time, for four years, on the basis that Tsar Vasilii would release to Lithuania the Governor of Sandomierz and his daughter[30] and all the Poles and Lithuanians who had been arrested in Moscow in the act of their injustice.

"And the King was supposed to remove immediately, to the last man, from the Moscow state, the Poles and Lithuanians who were with the thief; and in the future they should not make war against the state of Moscow and should not send men by war, or by any other measures against the state of Moscow. And about the great affairs, about a treaty to amend these broken affairs and the losses that were made to the state of Moscow by the King, there should be sent to a congress on the border from both sides great ambassadors, and that they should make and establish a treaty about every good affair. And to all this Tsar Vasilii kissed the cross to King Sigismund on the treaty of truce; and for the King, his ambassadors and emissaries kissed the cross to Tsar Vasilii.[31]

"And these ambassadors and emissaries of the King were sent away from Tsar Vasilii with honor according to the previous custom and with them were released the Governor of Sandomierz, Jerzy Mniszech, with his daughter and his friends, and many noble Poles and Lithuanians who had been held in the Moscow state for their injustice. And at that the Governor of Sandomierz, Jerzy Mniszech, and his son, *starosta* of Sanok, and

Zygmunt Tarło, and the other great lords gave an oath and kissed the cross for all the Poles and Lithuanians who were released: [p. 47] that they would not join that thief who stands near Moscow, and that they would not unite with the Poles and Lithuanians who were with that thief, and that they would do no evil to the Moscow state. And Tsar Vasilii sent his people to accompany them to the border.

"And the Governor of Sandomierz with his friends broke their oath: when they left the ruling city of Moscow they communicated with that thief who stood at that time near Moscow, and with the Poles and Lithuanians who were with that thief, and they killed many of the Russians who were sent to accompany them and took some prisoner. And the ambassadors of King Sigismund themselves, Mikołaj Oleśnicki, the castellan of Małogoszcz, with his associates, and the Governor of San-domierz, with his friends and with his daughter, came to the camp of that thief; and when he had come into the camp of that thief the Governor of Sandomierz married his daughter to that thief,[32] and was with him in the camp and taught him every manner of evil and told that thief the customs of the previous thief, the unfrocked monk. And, according to his evil counsel and design that thief tried to capture the Moscow state with all measures, with various battles and by an assault on the city. And by God's grace that thief did not receive his wish at Moscow and, coming from Moscow, they beat many of his Poles and Lithuanians and expelled them from the camp; and that thief, running away from his camp with the Poles and Lithuanians from Moscow, stopped in the city of Kaluga, two hundred and ninety versts from Moscow, and began to communicate with the Lithuanian King Sigismund about all sorts of evil designs for the ruin of the Moscow state.

"And King Sigismund did not preserve in any way the new truce and oath of his ambassadors that they had [p. 49] made in Moscow in the presence of Tsar Vasilii and strove for great bloodshed, not only that after the treaty of his ambassadors and after their oath to bring the Poles and the Lithuanians from the Moscow state, he himself came with soldiers and artillery to the city of Smolensk of the Moscow state, with many Poles and Lithuanians and mercenaries of other lands, and besieged the city of Smolensk.[33] And he ordered them to fire at the city from the artillery and attack the city of Smolensk with various assaults and mines, forgetting his own oath and that of his last ambassadors.

"And Tsar Vasilii, seeing the King's injustice, had sent against the King to Smolensk his brother, the boyar and general, Prince Dmitrii Ivanovich Shuiskii, with many Russian soldiers. And with Prince Dmitrii he sent the General Jakob Pontusson de la Gardie,[34] of the Swedish King, Charles,[35] whose Germans[36] served Tsar Vasilii for pay. And the

Polish King, Sigismund, heard that Tsar Vasilii had sent against him with his brother, Prince Dmitrii, many Russian and German soldiers, so he sent against Prince Dmitrii the crown hetman of Poland,[37] Stanisław Żółkiewski, and with him many lords councillors and his entire court with all the Polish and Lithuanian soldiers and the mercenaries of various lands. And the Swedish King Charles's General, Jakob Pontusson, forgot his oath and betrayed Tsar Vasilii and went over, along with all the Germans on the field of battle, to the Poles and Lithuanians. And the boyar Prince Dmitrii Shuiskii left for Moscow."

And Aleksei Ivanovich [Ziuzin] is to say:

"And the hetman Stanisław Żółkiewski [p. 50] sent to the King at Smolensk that Prince Dmitrii, with all his men, had gone to Moscow. And the King ordered the hetman to go to Moscow with all his men, and the King ordered the thief who was in Kaluga and the hetman, Lord Jan Sapieha, with the Poles and Lithuanians who were with the thief, to go with all their men to Moscow too. And they stood on both sides of Moscow, and on one side the crown hetman of Poland, Stanisław Żółkiewski, and the colonels and the captains with many men, and on the other side, with the thief, the other hetman, Jan Piotr Sapieha, with many Poles and Lithuanians. And Jakob Pontusson with the Germans went to the Novgorod region and Tsar Vasilii, caring for his land, sent his own court with the boyars and the generals, many soldiers to Great Novgorod and to Pskov. And in Moscow remained few soldiers, boyars, and generals.

"And some boyars and generals who were in the provinces, Mikhailo Saltykov and his associates, having forgotten God and their souls, on which they had sworn an oath to Tsar Vasilii, betrayed him and went to the Lithuanian King, Sigismund, and, designing with them, the Lithuanian King, Sigismund, wrote and ordered, together with hetman Stanisław Żółkiewski, to Moscow, to the boyars and generals, and to the soldiers and lesser gentry of all ranks, to the effect that he, taking care for Christendom and wanting to calm the Moscow state and remove bloodshed, had come to the border of the Moscow land and had sent hetman Żółkiewski to Moscow supposedly not for war but for agreement on a good cause: that all the Moscovites should take to the sovereignty the King's son, Prince Władysław,[38] for the peace of Christendom. And his son would rule in the Moscow state just like the previous [p. 51] Great Sovereigns in the Moscow state, and in no way would violate any customs.

"And the King sent a letter of articles in his hand and with his seal to the boyars describing how his son would be the ruler of the Moscow state. And in the letter the King wrote that his son would be the ruler in the

Moscow state in our faith of the Greek law, and in all things would be as the previous Moscow Great Sovereigns. And that there should be no Poles and Lithuanians with him in Moscow nor in offices in Moscow or the provinces and that there should be no Poles and Lithuanians in border places, and that he should in no way disturb our orthodox Christian faith of the Greek law, and that he should not put Catholic churches in Moscow or in the provinces, and that he should make no mockery of our faith and hold in honor also the patriarch of Moscow and the metropolitans and the archbishops and the whole clergy. And in addition, many of the affairs of the land were written in that letter in articles, how the Prince was to rule and govern in all affairs according to that treaty.[39] And many people of the Moscow state who were at that time in Moscow, hearing such a letter from the King, believing it contained truth and seeing such oppression from the Poles and Lithuanians, and being besieged and not being able to endure deprivation and hunger, began to waver; and the boyars and the generals and people of all ranks, of whom there were only a few in Moscow, petitioned the Sovereign Tsar and Grand Duke Vasilii Ivanovich, of all Russia, that he should leave his sovereignty for the quiet of Christians. And Tsar Vasilii left his sovereignty for the quiet of Christians so that Christian blood would not flow for him.[40]

"And the boyars and the generals and the gentry and people of all ranks, those few who were in Moscow [p. 52] because of the pressure and insult and the siege of the Poles and Lithuanians and not enduring the deprivation and hunger of the siege, elected to the Moscow state King Sigismund's son, Władysław. And they made a treaty with the Polish hetman, Stanisław Żółkiewski, with all the articles about how the Prince should rule.[41] And they strengthened it with signatures and oaths. And the Polish hetman, Stanisław Żółkiewski, and the colonels, and the captains swore an oath for Sigismund, the King of Poland, and for his son, Władysław, and for all the Polish and Lithuanian land: that before Władysław would come to the ruling city of Moscow that the hetman with all his men would leave the Moscow state to their previous places and remove all the soldiers from the Moscow state and would detach hetman Jan Piotr Sapieha from the thief who stood in Kaluga and send him from the Moscow state. And having captured that thief and his wife, Marinka, he would give them to the boyars of the Moscow state and he would do no harm to the city and regions of Moscow, and he would not send his men to war, and that the King should depart from Smolensk for Lithuania. And according to that treaty and its ratification the great lord our father, Metropolitan Filaret of Rostov and Iaroslavl' and, as ambassadors, the boyar Prince Vasilii Vasil'evich Golitsyn with his associates and some gentry and people of all ranks, went to King Sigismund at Smolensk from Moscow.[42] And in Moscow the traitors of the Moscow state, the boyar Mikhailo, the son of Gleb Saltykov, with his [p. 53] advisors who accompanied him at the King's side began to govern and rule in all things, having come from the King according to the orders of King Sigismund."

The Secretary Aleksei is to say:

"And the crown hetman of Poland, Stanisław Żółkiewski, violating his oath, did not leave Moscow with his soldiers, and designing together with the traitors of the Moscow state, with Mikhailo Saltykov and his associates according to the King's command, by deception, as if to guard against the thieves, let Poles and Lithuanians and Germans inside the stone walls of Moscow.

[p. 53] "And they surrendered the Tsar and Grand Duke Vasilii Ivanovich and the great boyars, his brothers, to that hetman Stanisław Żółkiewski, keeping it secret from everyone, and the hetman sent them to the Polish King Sigismund in violation of his oath. And they did not capture the thief who was in Kaluga, but rather let him go from Moscow on purpose to the Sever towns to make war. And seeing such evil deeds, the most holy Germogen, Patriarch of Moscow and all Russia, unmasked these traitors and their evil deeds and wrote letters to all the towns from himself, saying that ruin is being wreaked on the state of Moscow and destruction on our Christian faith of the Greek law.[43]

"And the King did not keep that treaty which was made with hetman Stanisław Żółkiewski and ratified by oath, and broke the oath of the hetman and the colonels and the captains. [He] detained the great ambassadors of the state of Moscow with him, and did much dishonor and oppression to them at Smolensk; and putting them in chains, he sent them to prison in Poland and Prussia, which is never done to ambassadors in any states, but which Sigismund did to these ambassadors.[44] But the Poles and Lithuanians who were in Moscow, when they entered the city put their own officials in the offices in Moscow and in the provinces. And in Moscow [p. 54] and the provinces they began to collect many taxes in money and in kind and to commit great exactions and outrages on all sorts of people of the state of Moscow, and to insult our true Orthodox faith of the Greek law, and to make Catholic churches in Moscow, and began to bring the people of the Moscow state by force into the Latin faith. And the Poles and the Lithuanians took for themselves the keys of the city and the munitions in the city, and the munitions in the treasury—gunpowder, and lead, and cannonballs, and all sorts of artillery supplies.

"And at the city gates and in the streets at the grillwork gates they placed their guards—Poles, Lithuanians and Germans—and began to bring people according to our faith to the oath to Sigismund instead of his son Władysław, in Moscow and in the provinces. And our boyars and generals and all sorts of people of the Moscow state, seeing the great injustice of the King, wrote to King Sigismund and sent to him to say that King Sigismund should adhere to justice and to what hetman Stanisław Żółkiewski had sworn his soul to the whole Moscow state for him and his son Prince Władysław, that he should soon give his son Prince Władys- ław to the Moscow state in our Orthodox Christian faith of the Greek law, and he should leave the town of Smolensk, and do no oppression, and order his army to leave the state of Moscow, and not allow the ruin of the Moscow state and the spread of his Latin faith in the Moscow state.

"And Sigismund the Polish King and the lords councillors, forgetting the hetman's oath and ignoring our request, [p. 55] more than before began to design all manner of evil against the Moscow state, and did not quickly give his son Prince Władysław in our faith to the Moscow state, and did not withdraw from Smolensk, and took Smolensk in violation of his oath and killed many boyars and gentlemen and all manner of people of the male and female sex, including infants, and spilled much innocent blood.

"And his Poles and Lithuanians and Germans in Moscow by his com- mand burned our ruling city of Moscow and desecrated the churches of God and the monasteries, and reviled the honorable icons and many miracle working curative relics, and deposed Patriarch Germogen with great dishonor from his throne and put him in prison and starved him. And they killed boyar Prince Andrei Vasil'evich Golitsyn and other boyars and gentry and all sorts of servitors, and merchants and tradesmen and lesser gentry, a numberless multitude of the male and female sex, including infants, and spilled much innocent blood.[45] And they sent our Tsar's treasury, a great collection from old time of our previous Tsars, our ancestors, and our Tsar's valuables and all our Tsar's property to the King, and grabbing some they divided it up.

"And the Poles and the Lithuanians settled down in the ruling city of Moscow. And in Moscow they seized your, our beloved brother's, mer- chants and tradesman, Mark the Englishman and his associates, who at that time were in the ruling city of Moscow.[46] And [they] took all their goods, and robbed them, and held them under strong guard and afterward killed them in an unchristian fashion.

"And seeing such great disasters and the ruin of the Moscow state, and the Lithuanian [p. 56] King Sigismund's injustice and evil design, and hearing that they had sent Tsar Vasilii to the Lithuanian King and that they had settled down in our ruling city of Moscow, in all towns of the Moscow state our boyars, and generals, and *chashniki, stol'niki, striapchie,*[47] and gentry and all sorts of servitors and lesser gentry communicated with one another and took counsel and swore an oath that they would all stand together against King Sigismund and his son Władysław for our true Orthodox Christian faith of the Greek law and for the Moscow state against the Poles and Lithuanians and they did not want the King and the Prince for the Moscow state.

"And they assembled together and stood near Moscow two years and besieged the Kitaigorod[48] and the Kremlin, and fought the Poles and Lithuanians in attacks and in their sallies forth. And first they took the Great Stone City[49] and in that success they killed numberless Poles and Lithuanians and Germans and captured more than four thousand alive. And the other Poles and Lithuanians sat in the Kitaigorod and the Kremlin and sat there an entire year. And our boyars and soldiers attacked the Kitaigorod and the Kremlin from all sides and bombarded them from guns, and everyday killed Poles and Lithuanians.

"And last year, in August of 7120 [1612], King Sigismund sent to the Poles and Lithuanians besieged in Moscow for help the Lithuanian hetman Karol Chodkiewicz, with many Poles, and Lithuanians, and Germans, and mercenaries of various lands in order to get the besieged out of Moscow or [p. 57] [to] supply reinforcements and bring supplies to the city and thus strengthen them and encourage them. And our boyars and generals and all sorts of soldiers did not let him get [in]to Moscow but had a battle, and fighting with them they did not dismount their horses three days and nights. And by the grace of the God and the prayers of the most holy Mother of God they smashed the hetman and took more than ten thousand living prisoners.[50] And the hetman ran away to Lithuania with few men and sent to the King that the King himself should assemble an army and go, and that he himself had been beaten. And the King on the hetman's message immediately began to collect an army. And our boyars and generals, hearing of the King's preparations, and that when he had collected his army he would march to Moscow himself, attacked the Kitaigorod from all sides and by God's grace took the Kitaigorod and the Kremlin and killed more than fifteen thousand Poles and Lithuanians, and the others. Lord Mikołaj Struś, the *starosta* of Chmielnik and Lubecz, who was there in Moscow in the place of the hetman, and the colonels, and captains, and all sorts of servitors were taken prisoner alive—about ten thousand. And when our boyars and generals and all sorts of soldiers had by God's grace cleansed our ruling city of Moscow of the Poles and Lithuanians, at that time the King came himself to the Moscow state and with him hetman Karol Chodkiewicz with many Poles and Lithuanians and Germans and mercenaries of various lands. And our boyars and generals sent many generals against the King, and with them gentlemen and boyars' sons and all sorts of soldiers. And the generals fought with the King near Volokolamsk[51] two days not dismounting from their horses, and killed many of the King's men, and took more than ten thousand alive. And the King after that battle left for Poland with great [p. 58] fear. And they killed many Poles and Lithuanians in the towns and fortresses where the Poles and Lithuanians sat in the state of Moscow."

And Aleksei Ivanovich [is to say]:

"And when the boyars, and the generals, and all the Christloving soldiers of the Moscow state had freed themselves of all evils and defeated all enemies of their faith, they gave praise to God for the gift He had sent and prayed to the all-gracious God and the most holy Mother of God and all the saints to enlighten their hearts, that they might ask someone to take the scepter of rule of the Russian Tsardom of the Moscow state. The metropolitans, and archbishops, and bishops, and all the sanctified council of the Russian Tsardom prayed and begged. And the sovereigns' children, the Tsars and Tsarevichi of various states who served in the Moscow state, and the boyars, and *okol'nichie*, and gentry, and all sorts of servitors, and the merchants and the multitude of the whole people of all the towns of our great Russian Tsardom petitioned our sovereign mother the nun, Marfa Ivanovna, and us the Tsar Mikhail Fyodorovich [ST], that the Great Sovereign our mother the nun, Marfa Ivanovna, should bless us, the Great Sovereign, and we, the Great Sovereign, should take pity on our whole state of Moscow, and be the lord Tsar and Grand Duke, Autocrat of all Russia over the great state of Vladimir and Moscow and Novgorod and the Tsardoms of Kazan', Astrakhan', and Siberia and all the great and most glorious states of the Russian Tsardom according to the family of our great sovereigns the Tsars of Russia. For [p. 59] we, the Great Sovereign, praise the lawful spouse of the worthy Great Tsar Ivan Vasil'evich [ST], and [mother] of our the Tsar Fyodor Ivanovich [ST], the Tsaritsa and Grand Duchess Anastasia Romanovna-Iur'eva [aunt] of her nephew Fyodor Nikitich Romanov-Iur'ev.

"And by the will of the all-generous God glorified in the Trinity and according to the family of the Great Sovereigns, Tsars of Russia, and according to the blessing of our Great Sovereign mother the nun, Marfa Ivanovna, and on the prayer and request of the metropolitans, archbishops, bishops, and the whole sanctified council, and on the petition of the Tsars and Tsarevichi who serve in the Moscow state, and the boyars, and *okol'nichie*, and gentry, and generals, and all the servitors and officials, and the multitude of all the people of all the towns of all the great Russian Tsardom, we, the Great Sovereign Tsar and Grand Duke Mikhail Fyodorovich Autocrat of all Russia, have come to rule in our great states, Vladimir, Moscow, and Novgorod, and the Tsardoms of

Kazan', Astrakhan', and Siberia, and all the great and most glorious states of the Russian Tsardom.

"[And] remembering the previous fraternal love and loving communication between the Great Sovereign, our grandfather of blessed memory, the Tsar Ivan Vasil'evich [ST], and our uncle the Great Sovereign of blessed memory, the Tsar Fyodor Ivanovich [ST], and the Tsar Boris Fyodorovich [ST], and the Great Sovereign of glorious memory our loving sister Queen Elizabeth; and [remembering] at last the loving communication of Tsar Vasilii with you, the Great Sovereign, [p. 60] our brother,[52] we have sent to you, the Great Sovereign our brother the beloved King James, our gentleman and viceroy Aleksei Ivanovich Ziuzin and our Secretary Aleksei Vitovtov to report our sovereignty and our health; and to ask about your, our brother's, health; and to speak about other good and great things which will arise between us sovereigns and our great states to the good and peace of Christians; and to declare to you the many injustices of the Polish King, Sigismund, and the Swedish King, before our state of Moscow. And you, Great Sovereign our beloved brother King James, should be in fraternal love and strong friendship with our Tsar's majesty and stand together with us against all our enemies, remembering the previous fraternal love and strong friendship with the Great Sovereigns the Tsars and Grand Dukes of Russia our ancestors and your fraternal loving communication with Tsar Vasilii Ivanovich [ST]. And you should order your advisors to speak with our ambassadors about all good things. And for the perfection of fraternal love and strong friendship you should send to our Tsar's majesty your own great ambassadors, instructing them truly that you, the Great Sovereign, should in the future be in fraternal love and strong friendship with our Tsar's majesty forever, unshakably, and stand together against all our and your enemies."[53]

And when they have made the speech, they are to give the speech in writing if they are so requested.[54]

And when, after the formalities, the King [p.61] will invite them to the palace and send to them someone of his councillors with an answer, and they begin to ask what kind of orders on what matters there are from Tsar Mikhail Fyodorovich [ST] [that] they should declare.

And Aleksei Ivanovich and the Secretary Aleksei are to say, if they learn that the English King is not at peace with the Swede and helps the Dane against the Swede[55]:

"The Great Sovereign our Tsar and Grand Duke Mikhail Fyodorovich Autocrat of all Russia, and sovereign and holder of many states, wishing to visit your Great Sovereign King James with his Tsar's fraternal love, remembering the previous loving communications and strong fraternal love between the Great Sovereigns of blessed memory the Tsars and Grand Dukes Autocrats of all Russia, Tsar Ivan Vasil'evich [ST], and with his son of blessed memory Tsar Fyodor Ivanovich [ST], and Tsar Boris Fyodorovich [ST], and the great Sovereign of glorious memory your Queen Elizabeth, and afterward with Tsar Vasilii Ivanovich [ST], has sent us—me, the gentleman and viceroy of Shatsk, Aleksei Ivanovich Ziuzin and the Secretary Aleksei Vitovtov—to announce his fraternal love and strong friendship and harmony and his new sovereignty to your great Sovereign King James. And he has ordered us to declare his fraternal and friendly love to his beloved brother your King James and to describe the injustices and violations of oath of the Polish King Sigismund and the Swedish King to the state of Moscow. And that his Tsar's majesty, remembering the previous [p. 62] loving communications and fraternal love and strong friendship of the Great Sovereigns the Russian Tsars his ancestors with your Great Sovereigns, wishes to be in fraternal love and strong friendship and treaty with your Great Sovereign King James. And your Great Sovereign King James, for that reason, should be in fraternal love and strong friendship and treaty with our Great Sovereign, his Tsar's majesty.

"But for the perfection of fraternal love now your Great Sovereign King James should show his original heartfelt loving friendship to our Great Sovereign his Tsar's majesty and should help us against our enemy, the Polish King Sigismund with treasure, money and gold, and goods, and all kinds of artillery supplies, as much as is possible for him, the Great Sovereign [King James]. And that he should stand together with our sovereign against the Swedish King Gustav[us] Adolph[us] for their many injustices and violations of oath,[56] and should not communicate with them to any ill of our Great Sovereign and his great states. And your sovereign should write to the Danish King Christian that he, the Danish King, Christian, should stand together against the Swedish King with our Great Sovereign, the Tsar's majesty. And our sovereign, his Tsar's majesty has also written with his ambassadors in a letter to the Danish King Christian about the injustice of King Sigismund and the Swedish King.[57] And our Tsar Mikhail Fyodorovich [ST], seeing such fraternal friendship and love and help against the Polish King from your[58] King James, the Great Sovereign, in return [p. 63] will give your sovereign his Tsar's love and will stand together against his enemies."

And if the King's advisors begin to say:

"[That] they[59] said in their speech at the audience from their own sovereign to their sovereign King James, and read out the injustice of the Polish King and the Swedish King's General, Jakob Pontusson, and said that their sovereign King James should be in fraternal love and strong friendship and unity and treaty with Tsar Mikhail Fyodorovich [ST]. And now they have announced by order of their own sovereign to them, the advisors, that their sovereign King James would help them against the Polish King Sigismund with treasure, and stand together against the Swedish King, and that their sovereign King James should send to the Danish King Christian so that he should stand together with their own sovereign against the Swede.

"And do they have any genuine instruction from Tsar Mikhail Fyodorovich [ST] on how their sovereign King James is to help the sovereign against the Polish King with treasure?[60] And what sort of treasure? And in what manner is he to stand with him against the Swedish King, and has there been any instruction about making and ratifying a treaty and unity?"

And Aleksei Ivanovich and the Secretary Aleksei are to say:

"Our Great Sovereign, his Tsar's majesty, has sent us about this matter to his beloved brother, your sovereign King James, and we spoke about that at the audience, and now we have announced it to you his advisors by our sovereign's command. And you should report our words to your sovereign King James, and your sovereign [p. 64] should order an answer made to us."

And if the King's advisors begin to say:

"That the Polish King Sigismund has written or sent to their sovereign King James and justified himself in everything before Tsar Boris and Tsar Vasilii and the Russian states,[61] saying that they [the Russians] treacherously killed him whom they called the unfrocked monk[62] and who ruled the Russian state after Tsar Boris, and [that] they wanted to kill the Polish ambassadors Mikołaj Oleśnicki and Aleksander Gosiewski, and the Governor of Sandomierz and his friends at that time, and stole all their property and kept them under guard for a long time in the state of Moscow; and killed many other Poles and Lithuanians; and to rule the Moscow state they elected Tsar Vasilii, and afterward removed Tsar Vasilii from the state and elected to rule the Moscow state the King of Poland's son, Prince Władysław, and swore an oath to him; and after that they did not want him to rule and wanted to kill the Poles and Lithuanians who were in Moscow.

"And the Swedish King wrote to their sovereign [James] and sent justifying himself before the Moscow state that his General, Jakob Pontusson, served the Moscow state and fought against the Poles and Lithuanians and cleansed Moscow of the Poles and Lithuanians; and the boyars and generals wrote to the Swedish King Charles that he should give them as a sovereign one of his two sons, whomever he chose, and the Swedish King Charles wanted to give his son to rule the Moscow state.[63] And [p. 65] [then] the boyars and all sorts of people of the Moscow state again did not want his son as sovereign of the Moscow state, and by that dishonored him. And this same is known to them from others and to the sovereign King James, [who] hearing such injustices of the King, helped him."

And Aleksei and the Secretary Aleksei are to say:

"Even if the Polish King Sigismund and the Swedish Charles, and the present King Gustav[us] Adolph[us][64] have written to your sovereign King James, or ordered [to be written], justifying themselves, then they have written lies and covered up their evil deeds, and in the future no truth is to be expected from the Polish and Swedish Kings. It is known, I assume, to your Great Sovereign and to you all, that the Polish King always writes bad things to the Pope against all Christian states; and he [the Pope] wants that, so that he may establish by his evil designs the popish faith in all Christian states so that all Christian sovereigns should be under papal obedience and pastorate. And the injustices of the Swedish King have also been known to you for a long time, and how constant and strong he is in his truth.

"And we have reported from our Great Sovereign his Tsar's majesty to your sovereign King James at the audience, orally and in writing, what sort of genuine injustices have been done to the Moscow state from the Polish King and the lords councillors.

"And now we report truly to you, the royal advisors, the many injustices of the Polish and Swedish Kings: how by God's judgment our Great Sovereign his Tsar's majesty, our uncle of blessed memory, Tsar Fyodor Ivanovich [ST], died, left the earthly kingdom, and went to [p. 66] eternal blessedness; and after him Tsar Boris Fyodorovich [ST] came to rule the great states of the Russian tsardom by the election of the people of all ranks of the Russian states, and he was in brotherhood and love and communication with your Great Sovereign King James more than all other Great Sovereigns. And during the rule of Tsar Boris Fyodorovich [ST] in the year 7109 [1600–1601] in the third year after the death of the sovereign Tsar Fyodor Ivanovich [ST], Sigismund, the Polish and Lithuanian King, sent to Tsar Boris Fyodorovich [ST] his great ambassadors, Leon Sapieha, the chancellor of the Grand Duchy of Lithuania, with his associates. And these ambassadors agreed with the boyars on a truce between our Great Sovereign Tsar Boris Fyodorovich [ST] and Sigismund, the Polish and Lithuanian King, and between their great states, for twenty-two years, from the year 7109 [1600–1601] to the year 7131 [1622–1623].[65] And Tsar Boris and King Sigismund ratified this truce by their souls, giving an oath that in the years of the truce the sovereigns and the states would be in peace and friendship and love, and make no war or unfriendliness, and not to send anyone into the land of the Moscow state, and not allow passage through the Polish and Lithuanian land to any soldiers, and not to help enemies with people or money.

"And soon after this ratification a certain thief and monk, a heretic named Grishka Otrep'ev, escaped from the Moscow state to Lithuania because of his evil deeds, loathsome to God [p. 6] and throwing off his black robe, he gave a written promise that if he took [the] Tsar's throne he would be cut off from God; and [Otrep'ev] called himself the son of our Tsar Ivan Vasil'evich [ST], the Tsarevich Dmitrii of Uglich, though the Tsarevich Prince Dmitrii of Uglich had died thirteen years before.

"And when that thief, the unfrocked monk, came to Lithuania, then, by the advice and design of Jerzy Mniszech the Governor of Sandomierz, [the] Princes Adam and Konstanty Wiśniówiecki, and the *starosta* of Ostriany, Michal Ratomski, and many other Poles and Lithuanians, joined the thief. And they brought that thief, the unfrocked monk Grishka, to King Sigismund, calling him the sovereign's son as if they truly knew that he was the son of our Great Sovereign Tsar Ivan Vasil'evich [ST], Tsarevich Dmitrii of Uglich.

"And the thief petitioned the King for help to become sovereign of the Moscow state. And King Sigismund, violating the decision of peace and his oath made with Tsar Boris by his soul, communicated with the Pope of Rome[66] and gave the thief much money and men to help him against Tsar Boris and the Moscow state. And the lord councillor of the crown of Poland, the Governor of Sandomierz, Jerzy Mniszech, agreed by the King's command to give him his daughter Marina and much money in aid, and himself went with soldiers by the King's command to the border of the Moscow state. And that thief Grishka Otrep'ev, and the Governor of Sandomierz with many Poles and Lithuanians, went to the border of the Moscow [p. 68] state into the Sever towns secretly. But Tsar Boris, knowing the agreement of peace between himself and King Sigismund and its ratification, kept no additional soldiers in the Sever towns by the Lithuanian border. And that thief took some of the Sever towns by surprise and began to besiege other towns of the Moscow state.

"And the boyars of our Moscow state sent as a messenger to the crown of Poland and the Grand Duchy of Lithuania and the lords councillors the thief Grishka's uncle, Smirnoi Otrep'ev, to unmask the thief. And Tsar Boris for this purpose also sent his emissary, Postnik Ograrev. And in the years 7111 [1602/3], 7112 [1603/4], and 7113 [1604/5] our boyars and officials wrote from our state about the apostate heretic and unfrocked monk Grishka Otrep'ev many times to the Polish and Lithuanian border cities, to the rulers and *starostas*. And the clergy, the patriarch, metropolitans, archbishops, and bishops wrote to the Polish and Lithuanian clergy many times, unmasking that heretic with proof of the apostate's origin and what sort of person he was, and how and why he escaped across the border, and how Tsarevich Dmitrii died; and that the Polish King Sigismund and the lords councillors, spiritual and temporal, *starostas* and rulers, since they knew this, should not believe the thief and should not violate the peace, and in no way should help the thief and should not send their soldiers into our Moscow state in violation of their oath. And the Polish King Sigismund and the lords [p. 69] councillors, spiritual and temporal, and the *starostas* and rulers did not believe all this and began more than before to entice the people of the Moscow state and to help the thief, wanting to sow confusion in the Moscow state.

"And the King began to write letters to sow confusion among all sorts of people to all the towns of the Moscow state, calling the thief the Tsarevich Dmitrii of Uglich, the son of our Great Sovereign Tsar Ivan Vasil'evich [ST], and asking them not to oppose him.[67] And because of these letters in the far border towns ignorant simple people from the Don, the Volga, and the Iaik, thieves and cossacks, began to be in confusion and to join the thief. But many people of the Moscow state, remembering God and their souls, were loyal to Tsar Boris, swore an oath to him, and since they knew the truth of the death of Tsarevich Prince Dmitrii Ivanovich, stood against the thief and the Poles and Lithuanians, and fought against them in many places, killing many Poles and Lithuanians.

"And at the same time, by God's judgment, Tsar Boris Fyodorovich [ST] died,[68] and in the Moscow state arose division and internecine warfare and bloodshed; some believed the confusion and many joined the thief, and capturing the boyars and generals in the army and the towns, took them to the thief.[69] And by the action of the enemy and the design and aid of the Polish and Lithuanian King Sigismund, that thief came to the ruling city of Moscow. And by evil intrigue, the action of the devil, that thief, apostate, and heretic reached the throne of Tsar, and was named the sovereign of Moscow. [p. 70] And many Poles and Lithuanians and the Don and Volga atamans and cossacks came with him to the ruling city of Moscow. And the thief became the sovereign of the Moscow state, sent many boyars and generals and all sorts of people to prison in the towns, and executed some. And then, by the King's command, Jerzy Mniszech came from Lithuania with many Poles and Lithuanians, and by his treaty the Governor of Sandomierz brought with him his daughter Marina and gave her to him as his wife.[70] And with the Governor of Sandomierz the ambassadors Mikołaj Oleśnicki, the castellan of Małogoszcz, and Aleksander Gosiewski, the King's gentleman, came from the King to the thief, congratulating him on his sovereignty and declaring the King's friendship for him, and that he had acquired the sovereignty of the Moscow state by his royal help, and that he should in return cede to him cities and lands of the Moscow state. And in Moscow the Poles and Lithuanians by order of the thief began to do much insult to our Christian faith and wreak much violence on the people of the Moscow state. And that thief Grishka had intended with the Poles to kill the metropolitans, archbishops, boyars, generals, and all sorts of the better people by deceit, and send away some to Poland and Lithuania, and destroy God's churches and smash our Orthodox Christian faith of the Greek law and place Roman churches and establish the Roman faith.

"And the Moscow state is large and wide and from far places, from Siberia and Astrakhan' and other places it takes two years to get to Moscow, and many soldiers [p. 71] were at that time in such faraway places. Those people of the Moscow state who were in the Moscow state and knew about the thief could not stand against him because all the soldiers were away. But when the soldiers and people of all ranks came together from far away, they joined together with one thought and reproved the thief and put him to an evil death.[71] And those Poles and Lithuanians who tried to defend him and began to kill Russians were killed by the plebeian people of the land for their many acts of arrogance. The boyars of the Moscow state protected the Governor of Sandomierz and his daughter and friends the Wiśniówieckis and many other Poles and Lithuanians from death. And no dishonor of any sort was done to the King's ambassadors and they were honored and fed according to the previous ambassadorial custom without diminution.

"And soon after the murder of the thief the boyars and generals of the Moscow state and all ranks of soldiers and civilians elected to the Moscow state and all the states of the Russian Tsardom a sovereign from among the boyars, from the clan of the Suzdal' Princes, Prince Vasilii Ivanovich Shuiskii. And when the Tsar and Grand Duke Vasilii Ivanovich of all Russia had become the sovereign he sent to Lithuania to King Sigismund his ambassadors, Prince Grigorii Volkonskii and the Secretary Andrei Ivanov, announcing to him his sovereignty and reminding him of his injustice, how he had violated his oath and broken the treaty of peace and caused such evil confusion and pointless bloodshed among men; and that he should send to him his own ambassadors, instructing them truly how he would correct the great injustices which had been committed from his [p. 72] side, and pay for the many uncountable losses which had been inflicted on the Moscow state. And Sigismund the Polish King sent and ordered with those ambassadors to Tsar Vasilii that he would send to him his own ambassadors about every good thing; and he would truly send an order about how they should make and establish a treaty about all good things.

"And King Sigismund sent to Tsar Vasilii his ambassadors Stanisław Witowski, the wójski of Parcew and Prince Jan z Drucka Sokoliński, his secretaries and gentlemen with their credentials signed by his royal hand and his seal.[72] And the King himself and the lords councillors, designing to further destroy the Moscow state, strove to spread confusion in the Moscow state and shed blood in vain, and so ordered the story be spread in all the border regions of the Moscow state and on the Don to the cossacks to the effect that the thief who had been the sovereign in Moscow had escaped from Moscow and was living with them in Poland and that a certain Lithuanian had been killed in his place. And, designing and searching they sent to the border of the Moscow state, to the Sever land, another thief by birth a Jew, calling him by the former name Dmitrii,[73] as if the one who had been in Moscow had escaped from murder from Moscow. And to him in the border came by the King's order Poles and Lithuanians and Germans: Prince Roman Różyński, Alexander Zborowski, Prince Adam Wiśniówiecki, Jan Piotr Sapieha, Samuel and Jan Tyszkiewicz, calling themselves hetmans, and colonels, and other colonels, and captains with many Poles and Lithuanians.

[p. 73] "And they began to send letters sowing confusion into all the Sever land to cities and places, calling that thief the previous thief Dmitrii. And many cowardly cossacks of the Sever border towns and boyars' slaves, poor people, believed these letters of confusion; and some seeing that destruction and war were coming to them from the Poles and Lithuanians, joined him. And there began to be dissension and bloodshed among men even greater than before. And many Sever towns and those of the Polish border began to surrender to that other thief because of the great war and destruction from the Poles and Lithuanians.

"And then the thief, collecting the Poles and Lithuanians with many others, with the Russian and Ukrainian cossacks, strove to go to the ruling city of Moscow. And when he came close to Moscow he made a camp and let loose war upon the provincial towns. And he began to destroy the Moscow state, to burn the villages large and small and to take people prisoner, and to kill and rob some and to spill blood mercilessly and cruelly and to besiege the ruling city of Moscow. And the ambassadors of King Sigismund who were then in Moscow, Mikołaj Oleśnicki of Małogoszcz and Aleksander Gosiewski, the *starosta* of Wieliż, and the emissaries Stanisław Witowski and Prince Jan z Drucka Sokoliński, by the order of King Sigismund, though seeing such destruction to the Moscow state, did nothing of good—did not send to the King about his injustice, and did not prevent the Poles and Lithuanians who came with the thief from shedding blood. And they spoke arrogantly and demanded towns and uncountable treasure, so much there is no room even to write it down. And having said a great deal, [p. 74] and met our sovereign with the boyars for many days, they ordered a truce between Tsar Vasilii and the Polish King Sigismund and between their states for a short while, for four years on the condition that Tsar Vasilii would release to Lithuania the Governor of Sandomierz and his daughter and all the Poles and Lithuanians who had been held in Moscow for their injustices.[74] And the King was to immediately remove the Poles and Lithuanians who were with the thief from the Moscow state to the last man and in the future not make war on the Moscow state; as for the greater business a treaty to correct the interrupted affairs and the losses to the Moscow state, they should send from both sides great ambassadors to a meeting on the border and make and establish a treaty about all good things.

"And Tsar Vasilii made an oath to all this on the truce and the King's ambassadors and emissaries swore for the King. And the King's ambassadors and emissaries were sent away from Tsar Vasilii with honor, according to the previous custom, and together with them the Governor of Sandomierz, Jerzy Mniszech, with his daughter and friends and many noble Poles and Lithuanians who had been held in Moscow for their injustices were released. And at that the Governor of Sandomierz, Jerzy Mniszech, and his son the *starosta* of Sanok and Zygmunt Tarło and other of the best lords swore an oath for all the Poles and Lithuanians who were released, that they would not join the thief who stood near Moscow, and with the Poles and Lithuanians [p. 75] who were with the thief they would not join together and would do no harm to the state of Moscow. And Tsar Vasilii sent his people to accompany them to the border. And the Governor of Sandomierz and his friends violated their oath by the King's command, and when they were leaving the ruling city of Moscow they got in touch with the thief who stood before Moscow and the Poles and Lithuanians who were with the thief, and they killed and captured many of the Muscovite escort that was sent with them. And King Sigismund's ambassadors, Mikołaj Oleśnicki, the castellan of Małogoszcz, with his associates, and the Governor of Sandomierz with his daughter and friends came to the thief in the camp before Moscow. When they had come to the camp the Governor of Sandomierz married his daughter to this second thief and stayed with him in the camp and instructed him in every evil and taught him the customs of the previous thief, the unfrocked monk.[75] By his evil council and design that thief tried to assault the state of Moscow by various measures—battles, and an assault on the city. And by God's grace the thief did not get his way at Moscow and killed many of the Poles and Lithuanians who left Moscow and expelled them from the camp. Then the thief with the Poles and Lithuanians left the camp at Moscow and stayed in the town of Kaluga ninety versts from Moscow, and began to communicate with King Sigismund about an evil design to destroy the Moscow state.

"And King Sigismund strove for great bloodshed [and] did not keep the new truce and oath of his ambassadors [p. 76] and emissaries which they had ratified in Moscow under Tsar Vasilii [which said] not only that he was to remove his Poles and Lithuanians from the Moscow state according to the treaty and oath of his ambassadors; but he himself came with his army and artillery to the Moscow state's town of Smolensk and with many Poles and Lithuanians and mercenaries of various lands. He besieged the town of Smolensk, bombarding it with his artillery, and tried to take by storm and with mines, ignoring his own oath and that of his ambassadors. And Tsar Vasilii, seeing the King's injustice, had sent against the King at Smolensk his cousin the boyar and General Prince Dmitrii Ivanovich Shuiskii with many Russian armies; and with Prince Dmitrii he sent the Swedish King Charles's General, Jakob Pontusson, whose Germans served Tsar Vasilii for hire. And the Polish King Sigismund heard that Tsar Vasilii had sent against him a great Russian and German army with his cousin Dmitrii, and [himself sent] against Prince Dmitrii the crown hetman of Poland, Stanisław Żółkiewski, and with him many lords councillors and his whole court with all the Polish and Lithuanian armies and with the mercenaries of various lands.

"The Swedish King Charles's general, Jakob Pontusson, having forgotten his oath to Tsar Vasilii, got in touch with the crown hetman Stanisław Żółkiewski, turned traitor, and went over with all his German troops on the battlefield to the Poles and Lithuanians. And the boyar [p. 77] Prince Dmitrii Ivanovich Shuiskii with all his soldiers withdrew toward Moscow. Hetman Żółkiewski sent to the King before Smolensk that Prince Dmitrii with all his troops had retreated to Moscow. And the King ordered the hetman to go before Moscow with all his troops, and ordered the thief, who was in Kaluga, and hetman Jan Sapieha with the Poles and Lithuanians who were with the thief, to go before Moscow and to stand before Moscow from both sides—from one side hetman Stanisław Żółkiewski with the colonels and captains with many soldiers, and from the other side with the thief the hetman Jan Sapieha with many Poles and Lithuanians. And Jakob Pontusson with his Germans went by the King's orders to the Novgorod area. And Tsar Vasilii, protecting his land, sent his own court, many soldiers with boyars and generals, to Velikii Novgorod and Pskov. And only a few boyars and generals and soldiers remained in Moscow.

"And some boyars and generals in the provinces, Mikhail Saltykov and his associates, forgetting God and their souls on which they had sworn to Tsar Vasilii, turned traitor and joined the Lithuanian King

Sigismund. Designing with them, the Lithuanian King Sigismund wrote and ordered together with the hetman Stanisław Żółkiewski to the boyars, generals, and all ranks of soldiers and civilians in Moscow to the effect that he, supposedly out of pity for Christendom and wanting to calm the Moscow state and remove the bloodshed, came himself to the Moscow border; and that he had sent hetman Żółkiewski before Moscow not for war but for a treaty about good things; and that the Muscovites [p. 78], for the peace of Christendom, should take the King's son Władysław to the sovereignty. And that his son would rule the Moscow state in our Orthodox Christian faith of the Greek law and in all things be as our previous sovereigns in the Moscow state and violate no commandments.[76]

"And the King sent a letter of articles over his signature and seal to the boyars stating how his son would rule the Moscow state.[77] And in the paper the King wrote that his son would be in our faith of the Greek law and in all things like the previous Moscow Great Sovereigns. And under him Poles and Lithuanians would not be in Moscow or provincial towns, nor in offices in Moscow or in provincial towns or border areas, and no harm would be done to our true Orthodox Christian faith, and no churches of the Papist faith would be built in Moscow or the provinces, and no insult to our faith and that the Moscow patriarch and the metropolitans and archbishops and all the clergy would be held in honor. In addition many other affairs of the land were written down on that paper by articles, how the Prince was to rule the state and how he was to conduct affairs by that treaty.

"Many people of the Moscow state who were in Moscow at that time heard the King's letter and believing that it contained truth and seeing such pressure from the Poles and Lithuanians and being besieged, could not any longer bear the need and hunger and began to waver. And the few boyars and generals and all ranks of men who were in Moscow petitioned Tsar Vasilii Ivanovich [ST][p.79] that for the peace of Christendom and the end of the spilling of Christian blood he should leave his sovereignty. "[p. 79] And Tsar Vasilii left his sovereignty.[78] And the boyars and generals, and the cup-bearers and stol'niki and great gentlemen and gentlemen from the provinces, and boyars' sons, and musketeers, and cossacks, and all the serving people were at that time in far places against the Swedes and in Siberia and other far countries and did not know what had been done with the sovereign in Moscow. And removing the sovereign from the sovereignty, the Moscow boyars and generals and gentlemen and people of all ranks, those few in Moscow, because of the pressure and the siege of the Poles and Lithuanians, elected to the Moscow sovereignty King Sigismund's son Władysław, and made a treaty with the crown hetman, Stanisław Żółkiewski, with all the articles describing how the Prince was to rule, and ratified it with signatures and oaths.

"And the crown hetman Stanisław Żółkiewski, and the colonels, and captains swore an oath for Sigismund, the King of Poland, and his son Władysław, and the whole Polish and Lithuanian land: that before the Prince Władysław should come to the ruling city of Moscow the hetman with all his people would leave the Moscow state, and remove all soldiers from the Moscow state, and remove the hetman Jan Piotr Sapieha from the thief who stood in Kaluga and send him away from the Moscow state. And when they had caught that thief and his wife Marina they should give him to the boyars of the Moscow state. And they should do no harm to the towns and places of Moscow and not let their own people go to war. And the King should leave Smolensk [p. 80] for Lithuania and do no harm to Smolensk. And according to that treaty and ratification the Great Sovereign our father metropolitan Filaret of Rostov and Iaroslavl' and as ambassadors the boyar Prince Vasilii Vasil'evich Golitsyn with associates and gentlemen and people of all ranks went to King Sigismund at Smolensk from Moscow.

"And in Moscow traitors of the Moscow state who had come from the King, the former boyar Mikhailo the son of Gleb Saltykov and his advisors who had been with him by the King, began to govern and to hold everything by the King's orders. And the hetman of the Polish crown Stanisław Żółkiewski, violated his oath and did not withdraw with his soldiers from Moscow; but intriguing with the traitors of the Moscow state, Mikhailo Saltykov and his advisors, by royal command he brought Polish and Lithuanian and German soldiers within the stone walls of Moscow by deceit, as if for defense against the thieves.

"And the traitors of the Moscow state, Mikhailo Saltykov, and his associates gave over Tsar Vasilii Ivanovich his brothers the great boyars to the hetman Stanisław Żółkiewski, keeping it secret from everyone; and he sent them to the Polish King Sigismund in violation of his oath. And they did not catch the thief who was in Kaluga, but intentionally let him go from Moscow to the Sever towns. And the most holy Germogen, Patriarch of Moscow and all Russia, seeing such evil deeds, reproved those traitors in their evil deeds and sent letters from himself into all the towns, saying that great destruction to the Moscow state and insult to the Christian faith by the Poles and Lithuanians [p. 81] was taking place.[79]

"And the King did not hold to the treaty that had been made with hetman Stanisław Żółkiewski and ratified by oath and he violated the oath of the hetman and colonels, and captains. He held the great ambassadors of the Moscow state by himself and did them much dishonor and oppression at Smolensk; and he brought them by his will to swear allegiance to himself rather than his son Władysław, and putting them in chains he sent them to prison in Poland and Prussia, and thus King Sigismund did to the great ambassadors something that is not done to ambassadors ever in any states Christian or Muslim.[80] And he did not soon give his son for the Moscow state as the treaty demanded nor did he leave Smolensk. And the Poles and Lithuanians who were in Moscow went into the city and put their administrators over Moscow and the provinces and into the chancelleries and began to collect many taxes and monetary incomes and unreasonable taxes in kind in Moscow and the provinces, and to lay great burdens and violence on all the people of the Moscow state and to insult our true Orthodox faith of the Greek law, and to make churches of their Papist faith in Moscow and to bring the people of the Moscow state to their Papist faith by force. And the Poles and Lithuanians took the keys of the city and the artillery of the city gates and walls, and the artillery in the treasury, the gunpowder, lead, and cannonballs, and other gunnery supplies, and placed their own Poles, Lithuanians, and German mercenaries as guards at the city gates and the street gates and began to bring people in Moscow and the provinces to an oath [p. 82] of allegiance to the name of King Sigismund rather than his son Prince Władysław.

"And the boyars and generals of the Moscow state and all sorts of people, seeing the King's great injustice, wrote and sent to tell King Sigismund that he should stand on the justice which his crown hetman Stanisław Żółkiewski swore by his soul to the whole Moscow state for him and his son Prince Władysław; to the effect that he should soon give his son Władysław for the Moscow state and in our Orthodox Christian faith of the Greek law, and withdraw from the city of Smolensk and commit no oppression, and order his soldiers to leave the Moscow state and not allow the Moscow state to be ruined.

"And Sigismund, the Polish King, and lords councillors forgetting the hetman's oath and our petition began to plot even greater evil against the Moscow state. He did not give his son Prince Władysław for the Moscow state in our faith, did not withdraw from Smolensk, and took Smolensk in violation of his oath and mercilessly killed many boyars and gentlemen and many men and women, even suckling infants, and spilled much innocent blood.[81] And the Poles, Lithuanians, and Germans who were in Moscow by his royal command burned the ruling city of Moscow and desecrated the churches and monasteries and insulted the honorable icons and healing miracle-working relics [p. 83], and removed Patriarch Germogen from the throne with great dishonor and starved him in prison. And they killed the boyar Prince, Andrei Vasil'evich Golitsyn, and other boyars, and gentlemen, and boyars' sons, and all sorts of serving men and merchants, and all sorts of traders and civilians—a numberless multitude of the male and female sex even to suckling infants, and spilled much innocent blood. And they sent to the King our Great Sovereign's treasury, a great collection from the ancient years of the previous Tsars, and the Tsars' vessels and all sorts of the Tsars' property; and they stole some for themselves and divided it up, and the Poles and Lithuanians settled in the ruling city of Moscow.

"And seeing such great disasters and the destruction of the Moscow state, and the injustice of the Lithuanian King and his evil designs, and hearing that they had sent Tsar Vasilii to the Lithuanian King, and settled in the ruling city of Moscow, the boyars, and generals, and cup-bearers, and *stol'niki, striapchie,* and gentlemen, and all sorts of soldiers and civilians communicated with one another and made a council and swore an oath that they would all stand together against King Sigismund and his son Władysław for our true Orthodox Christian faith of the Greek law, and for the Moscow state against the Poles and the Lithua-nians and not want the King or the Prince for the Moscow state.

"And when they had collected together and come to Moscow they stood there two years and besieged the Great Stone City and the Kitaig-orod and the Kremlin. And in assaults and forays out they killed many Poles and Lithuanians and first took the Great Stone City and [p. 84] killed a numberless amount of Poles and Lithuanians and Germans, and captured more than four thousand alive, and the rest of the Poles and Lithuanians sat in the Kitaigorod and the Kremlin, and they sat a whole year. And the boyars and all sorts of soldiers assaulted the Kitaigorod and the Kremlin from all sides and bombarded the city with cannon and every day killed many Poles and Lithuanians.[82]

"And in August of the year past 7120 [1612] King Sigismund sent to the Poles and Lithuanians besieged in Moscow the hetman of the Grand Duchy of Lithuania, Karol Chodkiewicz, with many Poles and Lithua-nians and German mercenaries to help them in order to bring out the besieged from Moscow, or give them reinforcements and supplies so as to strengthen and encourage them. And our boyars and generals did not allow the hetman to get to Moscow, [they] met him and fought a battle with him and they fought three days and nights never leaving their horses. And by the grace of God and the prayers of the most pure Mother of God they totally defeated hetman Karol and took more than ten thousand prisoners alive. And the hetman escaped to Lithuania with a few men and sent to the King that he himself should collect troops and come, and that he [Karol] had been defeated. And the King on hearing the hetman's message began to assemble an army. And the boyars and generals heard of the King's assembly of troops and that he planned to come to Moscow himself, so they assaulted the Kitaigorod and the Kremlin from all sides and by God's grace they took the Kitaigorod and the Kremlin and killed many Poles and Lithuanians, more than fifteen thousand. And the others, Lord Mikołaj Struś, the *starosta* of Chmielnik and [p. 85] Lubecz, who was in Moscow in place of the hetman, and captains, and all sorts of other soldiers they took alive, about ten thousand men.

"And when by God's grace the boyars and generals and all sorts of soldiers had cleansed the ruling city of Moscow of Poles and Lithuanians, and the King at that time invaded the Moscow state himself with the hetman Karol Chodkiewicz and with many Poles and Lithuanians and, bragging, wanted to further destroy our Moscow state, then the boyars and generals sent many generals against the King, and with them sending all sorts of soldiers. And the generals fought with the King near Volokolamsk[83] for two days not getting down from their horses, and they killed many of the King's men and took more than a thousand prisoners. And from that battle the King went back to Poland with great fear. And in the fortresses and towns where the Poles and Lithuanians remained they killed them and drove the Poles and Lithuanians from the Moscow state.

"And we declare to you truly the injustices of the Swedish King to the Moscow state when, by God's just anger, under Tsar Vasilii Ivanovich [ST], by the design of Sigismund, the Polish King, and the lord councillors, there began to be confusion and unsteadiness among men. [And] when King Sigismund sent into the Russian state the thief, with Poles and Lithuanians, and called him Tsarevich Dmitrii in the place of the first thief who had been killed, Grishka Otrep'ev, to destroy the Moscow state, and much Christian blood [p. 86] began to flow because of them.

"And Tsar Vasilii, seeing the confusion and unsteadiness among his people from the King and the thief, and not thinking to stand up against the Poles and Lithuanians with his own Russian people, he sent to Great Novgorod his relative, the boyar Prince Mikhail Vasil'evich [Skopin]-Shuiskii. And he ordered him to communicate with the Swedish King, Charles, about mercenaries, so that Charles,[84] according to the treaty and its ratification that was made by the Great Sovereign Tsar [ST] Fyodor Ivanovich with the Swedish kingdom in the year 103 [1595],[85] should show his love and allow mercenaries to be hired from his own Swedish and from other lands, with whom Tsar Vasilii could stand against the Poles and Lithuanians.

"And King Charles, after communication with the boyar Prince Mikhail Vasil'evich [Skopin]-Shuiskii, sent soldiers to be hired—French and Swedes and others—with his General, Jakob Pontusson de la Gardie, to Great Novgorod to the boyar Prince Mikhail Vasil'evich [Skopin]-Shuiskii. And Prince Mikhail gave wages to Jakob and the mercenaries ahead and for the past time from when they had assembled and come to him, and besides that gave them many gifts. And he agreed with Jakob Pontusson de la Gardie by oath and signature that Jakob Pontusson de la Gardie, with all his soldiers who had come with him, would stand against the Poles and Lithuanians and fight alongside them for Tsar Vasilii and the whole Moscow state valiantly until death and would commit no treason. And the boyar Prince Mikhail Vasil'evich, with the Russian soldiers, and General Jakob, with the German mercenaries, left Great Novgorod together and on the way killed Poles and Lithuanians in many places [p. 87] and before Moscow they drove all the Poles and Lithuanians from their camp.

"And in Moscow Tsar Vasilii received General Jakob and the mercenaries with honor and ordered them to be paid in full right away according to the treaty, and beyond the set pay he granted them money: the general and the colonels, captains, and private soldiers by his great Tsar's grant, everyone his deserts, and beyond that he ordered them to be given sufficient provision and in all things showed his Tsar's mercy toward them. And Tsar Vasilii had sent to Smolensk against the King his brother, the boyar and general Prince Dmitrii Ivanovich Shuiskii, with many Russian soldiers, and so he sent Jakob Pontusson de la Gardie with the mercenaries whom he had brought to Moscow along with Prince Dmitrii.

"And the Polish King Sigismund, hearing that Tsar Vasilii had sent against him many Russian soldiers and mercenaries from other lands with Prince Dmitrii his brother, sent against Prince Dmitrii the crown hetman Stanisław Żółkiewski, and with him many lords councillors and his own court with all the Polish and Lithuanian soldiers and mercenaries of other lands.

"And when the boyar Prince Dmitrii Ivanovich began to fight with the hetman, and regiment began to close and fight against regiment, then the Swedish King Charles's General, Jakob Pontusson de la Gardie, forgetting the oath that he had sworn to Tsar Vasilii that he would fight to the death and not [p. 88] commit treason, betrayed Tsar Vasilii. Having communicated with Żółkiewski, [he] went over to Żółkiewski with all the mercenaries whom he had with him, and stood with him against Prince Dmitrii and the Russians. And Prince Dmitrii with all his soldiers went back to Moscow, and Jakob Pontusson de la Gardie with all the Germans went to Great Novgorod. And Tsar Vasilii, hearing that Jakob had betrayed him and gone to Novgorod, sent to Novgorod his boyars and generals, his court, and many soldiers, gentlemen, and boyars' sons against Jakob. And Jakob, fearing the sovereign's men, had gone into his own land.

"And hetman Stanisław Żółkiewski, knowing that Tsar Vasilii had sent soldiers from Moscow to Novgorod, came to Moscow with all the men who were with him by the King's orders. And the thief who was in Kaluga, and with him hetman Piotr Sapieha with Poles, Lithuanians, and Russians, came to Moscow by the King's order and besieged Moscow from two sides.

"And what happened before Moscow for our sins—how Tsar Vasilii left the sovereignty and how they elected the Polish Prince Władysław, and how there was a treaty with the hetman about that, and how and what the hetman and the Poles plotted with the traitors of the Moscow state according to King Sigismund's orders, what they did to Moscow—that we have already told your sovereign truly by the order of our sovereign at the audience.[86] And how after the destruction of Moscow the boyars, and generals, and people of all ranks, seeing the King's injustice and evil design [p. 89], and the destruction of the ruling city of Moscow, and the great bloodshed and the defiling of the holy churches of God, and the insult to the icons and miracle-working relics, made a council and went to Moscow against the Poles and Lithuanians: and from Novgorod the boyars and generals and all sorts of soldiers came to Moscow for the same reason.

"And at that time the Swedish King, Charles, sent his General, Jakob Pontusson de la Gardie, with many men to the Novgorod land. And General Jakob came not fighting and making no quarrels and stopped not far from Novgorod and sent emissaries to Moscow to the boyars and generals, saying that supposedly his sovereign King Charles, knowing the injustice and violation of oath by the Polish King Sigismund to the Moscow state, had sent him to defend the Novgorod area from the Poles and Lithuanians. And that the King [Charles] had ordered Jakob to say to the boyars and generals [that] if they wanted to take to the Moscow sovereignty his son, either of the two Princes, then he would not hold on to whichever son they would want and would give him to the Moscow state.[87] And the boyars and generals of the Moscow state, consulting with the whole land, ordered that a reply be made to Jakob Pontusson de la Gardie from Novgorod. And knowing his injustice and violation of oath they ordered that the offer of a Prince be refused, for he could not be trusted and his untruth was known, and he should return to his own land.

"And the boyars and generals and all sorts of soldiers and civilians took firm counsel about this and swore an oath that they wanted no [p. 90] unbeliever not of the Greek law of whatever state as sovereign of the Russian state, and that they would choose for the Moscow state a sovereign of our faith of the Greek law, whomever God gave, since they saw from the Polish King and Prince much destruction to the state and insult to the faith. And Jakob Pontusson de la Gardie wrote after that to the boyars and generals and all sorts of men in many towns of the Moscow state that they should not elect a sovereign for the Moscow state from any other state, but should elect to the Moscow state a sovereign of the Moscow clans, who would be a relative or in the family of our previous Great Sovereigns, the Russian Tsars, and that their sovereign the Swedish King would be in love and friendship with our sovereign.

"And after that Jakob Pontusson de la Gardie, being close to Novgorod and rendering people unaware while he was communicating with Moscow, took Novgorod by stealth and did much evil. And now in Novgorod he holds Metropolitan Isidor and the boyar and General Prince, Ivan Odoevskii, in captivity. And you, our brothers, may judge yourselves the great injustice and violation of oath of the Polish King Sigismund and the lords councillors and the great injustice of the Swedish King and the great shedding of innocent Christian blood from both. Is this a proper thing that King Sigismund does—that violating the oath that he swore with by his royal soul he committed such shedding of Christian blood in our Moscow state, and spilled much innocent Christian blood on both sides? And in the future how are we to communicate between our Great Sovereigns by ambassadors and emissaries if the ambassadorial oath [p. 91] is not strong or permanent?

"And your great King James, seeing and hearing so great an injustice of the Polish King and the lords councillors to our Great Sovereign and to his whole Moscow state, and the great shedding of innocent Christian blood, and the injustice of the Swedish King and his General, Jakob Pontusson de la Gardie, should now show his fraternal heartfelt love for our Great Sovereign against the Polish King Sigismund and the lords councillors and help him with treasure, money and gold, and goods and all sorts of artillery supplies, as much as will be possible. And against the Swedish King your Great Sovereign King James should stand together with our great sovereign. And your sovereign should send to our great sovereign, the Tsar's majesty, his ambassadors or emissaries, about all this, instructing them truly how his royal highness should in the future be in fraternal love and friendship, in unity and agreement with our Great Sovereign, the Tsar's majesty, forever and unshakably. And he should order specifically to his ambassadors and emissaries to say to the Tsar's majesty how his royal highness should stand together with our Great Sovereign, the Tsar's majesty, against the Swedish King. And our Tsar Mikhail Fyodorovich [ST] orders that with your ambassadors and emissaries a treaty should be made and established by his own advisors about the affairs between the Great Sovereigns, however is proper and right.

"Now we are not instructed to make an agreement nor to make an agreement with the King's advisors."

[p. 92] And if the King's advisors or confidantes say to Aleksei or the Secretary Aleksei:

"You have said to us by the order of your sovereign, the Tsar's majesty, in your conversations, that our sovereign, his royal highness, should help your Great Sovereign the Tsar's majesty, out of fraternal love, with his royal treasure against his enemies the Polish [and] King Sigismund, and that his Royal Highness should stand together with your great Tsar's majesty against the Swedish King, Gustav Adolf. And we declare to you by the loving advice of our sovereign King James, his Royal Majesty: that our sovereign, his Royal Highness, orders help to your great sovereign out of fraternal love against his enemies the Polish King, Sigismund, and the Swedish King, Gustav Adolf, and allows in his state for soldiers to go to serve the Tsar's majesty by the usual custom found in their state, for hire. And your Great Sovereign should order them to be paid their deserts according to agreement and should send them on his sovereign service against his enemies wherever he wishes. And if these mercenaries are needed by the Tsar's majesty, then you ambassadors should make a treaty with the advisors about hiring them and strengthen it with signatures."

And [then] Aleksei Ivanovich and the Secretary Aleksei are to say:

"It is known to your Great Sovereign and you, his majesty's advisors, that the Moscow state is wide and extensive and there is a multitude of soldiers in it. But now, because of our sins, the Devil's action, and the confusion and evilly clever [p. 93] design of King Sigismund, because of the war and destruction by the Poles and Lithuanians many towns and places in the state have grown poor and for that reason there is great poverty in the state, it is not possible to give a salary quickly to the soldiers of the Moscow state, because it is not possible to collect taxes quickly for the soldiers of the Moscow state.

"And our Great Sovereign, the Tsar's majesty, hoping in your Great Sovereign's fraternal love, has ordered us, the Tsar's majesty's ambassadors, to ask from his Royal Highness against his enemies the Polish and Swedish Kings, the aid of his Royal Highness's treasury, whatever there might be to pay his soldiers. And your sovereign's mercenaries are not needed by our Great Sovereign; and at the present time they do not need to go, for many country districts and villages and the peasants in them have grown poor, and there is nowhere for soldiers or their horses to find food, and nothing to give them. And your sovereign, his Royal Highness, if he wishes to be in fraternity and heartfelt love and friendship with our Great Sovereign, the Tsar's majesty, he should help our Great Sovereign, the Tsar's majesty, against the Polish King, as much as he can."

And if the King's advisors should say that their sovereign's soldiers would go by sea to Poland and Lithuania, not through the Moscow state, and would not go by the land of your sovereign, then Aleksei Ivanovich and the Secretary Aleksei are to say:

"If your sovereign King James would do this from fraternal love and friendship of our Great Sovereign, to order his soldiers to go [p. 94] against Poland and Lithuania by sea from his country, not passing through the Moscow state, then our Great Sovereign, the Tsar's majesty, has nothing to give for hire for your sovereign's soldiers at the present time. And we have no instructions about this."

And if the King's advisors should say that their sovereign King James, showing to your Great Sovereign fraternal heartfelt love and aid, would send several thousand of his own soldiers to war against his [the Tsar's] enemies in Poland and Lithuania at his own expense, and your sovereign should at the same time act against the Polish and Lithuanian land, so that they should both come at the same time, [then] Aleksei Ivanovich and the Secretary Aleksei are to say:

"Your Great Sovereign, his Royal Highness is acting as every great Christian sovereign should by sending his soldiers against the Polish King from fraternal love and friendship for our Great Sovereign, the Tsar's majesty, and wishing to avenge the injustice against him. And our Great Sovereign, the Tsar's majesty, in response to his loving brother your Great Sovereign, will return him fraternal love and friendship wherever possible. And now your Great Sovereign, his Royal Highness, should order us to leave as soon as navigation is possible, without delay, for our own Great Sovereign, the Tsar's majesty; and should send his own ambassadors or emissaries together with us to the Tsar's majesty; and should instruct them truly about all such matters, how the Great Sovereigns should be in fraternal [p. 95] love and friendship and stand together against the Polish and Swedish Kings. And our Great Sovereign, the Tsar's majesty, will order his advisors to speak about these matters with the ambassadors or emissaries of your sovereign and to establish what sort of business there should be between the Great Sovereigns; but we have no instructions to treat military affairs or to make an agreement."[88]

And if King James' advisors should say:

"You have told us that our Great Sovereign should help your Great Sovereign, the Tsar's majesty, against his enemy the Polish King with treasure, and stand together against the Swedish King with your sovereign, but you say that you have not been instructed by your sovereign to make an agreement about so great a matter and that our sovereign should send to your Great Sovereign his own ambassadors or emissaries about a treaty, instructing them truly how these matters are properly to be be-

tween the Great Sovereigns. And our Great Sovereign King James, remembering [the love] of your previous Great Sovereigns, the Russian
Tsars, with the English Great Sovereigns, wishing now that he should be
in fraternal love and friendship with the Great Sovereign Tsar Mikhail
Fyodorovich [ST] and stand together with your sovereign against the
Swedish and Polish Kings, and will help with treasure. And you should
now confirm in writing against the help that our sovereign will send, that
your sovereign will pay back that treasure to our sovereign according to
the treaty with the ambassadors of our sovereign, however our sovereign
wishes."

[p. 96] And [then] Aleksei and the Secretary Aleksei are to say:

"Our Great Sovereign the Tsar and Grand Duke Mikhail Fyodorovich
Autocrat of all Russia sent us to his loving brother your Great Sovereign
King James, remembering the fraternal friendship, love, and communi-
cation of our ancestors, the previous Great Sovereign Tsars and Grand
Dukes with the great sovereigns your English Kings and Queen Elizabeth,
to announce his sovereignty and declare the injustices of the Polish King
Sigismund and the lords councillors and the Swedish King, and so that
your sovereign King James would now show his original heartfelt fraternal friendship and love for our Great Sovereign, and help him against the
Polish King Sigismund with treasure, money and gold, and goods, and all
sorts of artillery supplies, and stand together with our sovereign against
the Swedish King because of his injustices. And now we hear from you,
the advisors, that your great sovereign King James wishes to be in fraternal friendship and love and communication with our Great Sovereign,
the Tsar's majesty, and to help against the Polish King with treasure and
stand together against the Swedish King. And for this we praise your
Great Sovereign King James; and in return our Great Sovereign, the
Tsar's majesty, will show his Tsar's fraternal love and friendship for your
sovereign where possible. And the Tsar's majesty will be in fraternal
friendship and communication with his beloved brother your Great Sovereign King James over all other sovereigns.

"And as to what you now say, whatever help now your sovereign will
provide in treasure for our Great Sovereign, in that matter of treasure we
should agree in writing with you that our [p. 97] Great Sovereign would
pay back in the future that treasure [which he will receive]. Then your
advisors should tell us exactly by the command of your sovereign how
many thousand rubles, and what kind of treasure or goods or artillery
supplies your sovereign wishes to give to our Great Sovereign against the
Polish King, and in what fashion your sovereign wishes to stand together
with our Great Sovereign against the Swedish King."

And if the King's advisors will press Aleksei Ivanovich and the Secretary Aleksei to make and establish an agreement about these matters, then Aleksei Ivanovich and the Secretary Aleksei are to say that they have no instructions to make an agreement, and no instructions on how and what to agree to; and they are definitely not to agree but to ask for ambassadors that their sovereign King James should send to their sovereign ambassadors about all these matters.

And if the advisors [blank space] should say that our Great Sovereign his royal majesty, from fraternal love and friendship for his brother, your Great Sovereign, would send a loan of ten thousand rubles against the Polish King, then Aleksei and the Secretary Aleksei are to say:

"I think that you know yourselves how our Great Sovereign's Moscow state is wide and populous, but now by our sins it is poor in treasure because of King Sigismund and the lords councillors and the Swedish King in violation of their oath. And many soldiers have grown poor, and with this help, ten thousand, how will they stand against such wicked enemies and [p. 98] avenge their injustices? And your sovereign King James from loving fraternal friendship and love for his brother our Great Sovereign, the Tsar's majesty, has helped him against his enemies with treasure, and goods, and gunpowder, and lead, and sulphur, and other military supplies, as much as possible, by which our Great Sovereign would be able to stand against his enemies and avenge their injustices. And our Great Sovereign, the Tsar's majesty, in return for such fraternal friendship and love will repay your Great Sovereign with his loving fraternal friendship and love and even beyond."

And Aleksei Ivanovich and the Secretary Aleksei are definitely to find out this: "How many thousand rubles does King James wish to send to the sovereign and what sort of treasure, and how does he wish to stand against the Swede, and will he send his ambassadors or emissaries to the sovereign? And convince the advisors by all means that King James should help with treasure and goods and artillery to the sum of a hundred thousand, and at the least to the sum of eighty or seventy thousand, and if need be to the sum of fifty thousand rubles."[89]

And if the King's advisors offer help to the sovereign in treasure to the sum of fifty thousand rubles, but want to confirm this by writing and oath, that King James will pay this sum in the future to the sovereign, then Aleksei Ivanovich and the Secretary Aleksei are to say:

"That our Great Sovereign, the Tsar's majesty, has sent us as ambassadors to his loving brother your Great Sovereign to announce his sovereignty and to remind him of fraternity, love, and communication [p. 99]; and [to ask] that your Great Sovereign at the present moment should help our Great Sovereign against his enemies the Polish King Sigismund and the lords councillors and the Swedish King. And we have not been instructed to come to an agreement on this by our Great Sovereign, as we said before, and we can put nothing in writing without the order of our sovereign. And your Great Sovereign, his royal highness, with that treasure should send to our Great Sovereign, the Tsar's majesty, his ambassadors or emissaries with us soon; and instruct them truly how the Great Sovereignties are to be in loving fraternal friendship and love and communication forever and unshakably, and how they are to stand together against any enemy. And our Great Sovereign, his Tsar's Majesty will order his Sovereign's boyars to speak with the ambassadors or emissaries of your Sovereign and establish how affairs between them, the Great Sovereigns, are to be and how it is fitting between their great states."

And Aleksei and the Secretary Aleksei are definitely to speak and by all measures convince King James to send treasure to the sovereign together with his ambassadors or emissaries; but they should definitely not make a written agreement or swear an oath. And in the conversations with the royal advisors they are to say:

"In the time of the Great Sovereign Tsar Fyodor Ivanovich [ST], Rudolf, the Roman Emperor, sent to the Tsar's majesty with help against his enemies his ambassador Nicholas Warkocz, and Tsar Fyodor Ivanovich [ST], from fraternal [p. 100] friendship and love, sent to Emperor Rudolf with his own ambassadors the *duma* gentleman, Mikhail Ivanovich Vel'iaminov, and the Secretary Afanasii Vlas'ev with sables and other furs more than fifty thousand rubles, and there was no written agreement between the Great Sovereigns on that treasure.[90] And now, too, your Great Sovereign King will help our Great Sovereign the Tsar's majesty against the sovereign's enemies with treasure, and send with them to our Great Sovereign his ambassadors or emissaries; and our Great Sovereign, the Tsar's majesty, knows by that what love to return to your sovereign."

And Aleksei Ivanovich and the Secretary Aleksei are definitely to insist on this by all means, and say firmly that with the treasure he [James] should send his ambassadors or emissaries. And they should definitely not give anything in writing. [p. 100] And if the King's advisors should offer treasure to the sum of [blank] thousand, but do not wish to send it without a written agreement, then Aleksei and the Secretary Aleksei are to stand firm and to speak strongly by all means that God may give them, that he should send the treasure with the ambassadors and that they should not make a written agreement. And if it is in no way possible to convince them of this, then Aleksei and the Secretary Aleksei are to beseech them as a final measure:

"[That] then we will take by ourselves, beyond the instruction of our sovereign, a written agreement on that treasure which your sovereign will send to our Great Sovereign, the Tsar's majesty; and your sovereign [p. 101] will send that treasure with us without delay. And Aleksei and the Secretary Aleksei are to give a written receipt from themselves when they receive the treasure, looking at the price of each item according to the list sent with them that describes the price of each item. And they are to insist to the King's advisors that their sovereign King James, wishing to be in fraternal love, friendship, and agreement with the Great Sovereign, the Tsar's majesty, should send that treasure with his ambassadors or emissaries together, and order that price to be set at which merchants buy the goods in the state among themselves or at which they buy the goods from the merchants for their sovereign King James, so that the merchants should not wish any advantage. And our Great Sovereign, the Tsar's majesty will in return repay your Great Sovereign with his Tsar's love where it will be proper."

And if the King's advisors say that King James is sending to our Great Sovereign with the treasure, his ambassadors or emissaries, and [they ask] is there for them a credential letter of the sovereign? Then Aleksei and the Secretary Aleksei are to say:

"That your Great Sovereign the King should send his ambassadors or emissaries to our Great Sovereign the Tsar's majesty and we have our sovereign's pass for your ambassadors or emissaries with us, and we will give them the pass which has been sent with us."[91]

And if the King's advisors say to Aleksei and to the Secretary Aleksei that their sovereign King James will send to the Polish and Swedish King his ambassadors about [p. 102] all their injustices that they have done to the Moscow state in violation of their oath, and that they should in the future cease all their injustices and do no evil to the Moscow state, and [that] sending to Tsar Mikhail Fyodorovich [ST] ambassadors and emissaries they should establish peace as before. And if King Sigismund and the Swedish King, Gustav Adolf, on the King's message wish to send their ambassadors or emissaries with his ambassador to Tsar Mikhail Fyodorovich [ST], then do they [Ziuzin and Vitovtov] have any order from the Tsar's majesty as to where and in what city or place the ambassadors of Sigismund and the Swedish King should meet with the ambassadors of the Tsar's majesty for an agreement about all the good things which will arise between them, the Great Sovereigns and the Great Sovereignties, and to make a treaty about all these good things?[92]

And Aleksei [Ivanovich and the Secretary Aleksei] are to say:

"Our Great Sovereign, the Tsar's majesty, remembering the strong love and friendship and unity of the previous Great Sovereigns the English Kings with the previous Great Sovereigns our Russian Tsars and

Grand Dukes, wishes in the future to be in fraternal love and strong friendship and unity with his brother your sovereign King James above all other sovereigns. And that your sovereign King James, showing his love and good will to our Great Sovereign, the Tsar's majesty, wishes to send his ambassadors to King Sigismund and the Swedish King Gustav[us] Adolph[us], and write to them about their injustices to the Moscow state and that they should refrain from such bloodshed and correct themselves before our Great Sovereign. [p. 103] And King Sigismund and the Swedish King Gustav[us] Adolph[us] should send to our Great Sovereign, the Tsar's majesty, their ambassadors to conference to speak about all the matters that relate to peace between the states and to quiet and good agreement and harmony. And now your Great Sovereign, his Royal Highness, should send us back to our Great Sovereign and send his own ambassadors to our Great Sovereign the Tsar's majesty without delay, instructing them truly how in the future the Great Sovereigns should be in fraternal love and strong friendship and unity and agreement. And to King Sigismund and to the Swedish King, Gustav[us] Adolph[us], your Great Sovereign should send his ambassadors and emissaries soon and write to them about their injustices, so that they should refrain from such evil deeds and not spill Christian blood with violence and do not evil to the Moscow state, and correct themselves before our Great Sovereign, the Tsar's majesty, and send to our Great Sovereign their ambassadors or emissaries to speak about all good things, how they might remove the blood between the Great Sovereignties and establish quiet and peace. And when King Sigismund and the Swedish King, Gustav[us] Adolph[us], send to our Great Sovereign their ambassadors or emissaries together with your sovereign [p. 104] Royal Highness's ambassadors or emissaries to a conference, and our Great Sovereign the Tsar's majesty, [will] order his boyars to speak with the ambassadors of your sovereign and the ambassadors or emissaries of the Polish King, Sigismund, and the Swedish King, Gustav[us] Adolph[us], about all things, and to decide how and what matters are proper between their Great Sovereignties."[93]

And if the King's advisors begin to speak to Aleksei and to the Secretary Aleksei about the Polish and Swedish Kings separately, that their sovereign King James will help the sovereign against the Polish King but wishes to send ambassadors or emissaries to make peace with the Swedish King, then Aleksei and the Secretary Aleksei are to say to the royal advisors:

"That their sovereign King James wishes to help our Great Sovereign the Tsar's majesty against the Polish King with treasure, and our Great Sovereign, the Tsar's majesty, [p.105] receives this from your Great Sovereign with great love, and in return our Great Sovereign, the Tsar's majesty, will return your Great Sovereign his Tsar's fraternal friendship and love where possible. And that your sovereign wishes to send his ambassadors to the Swedish King about his injustices and that he should correct himself before the Tsar's majesty [repeated], then your Great Sovereign should send us back to the Tsar's majesty without delay and should send his own ambassadors with us to the Tsar's majesty, instructing them truly how the Great Sovereigns are to be in love and communication and agreement."

And if the King's advisors should say to Aleksei and to the Secretary Aleksei that their sovereign King James desires and wishes that all the Christian sovereigns should leave off all their mutual grievances and be in love and unity and stand together with all their forces against the Muslims, then the Alekseis are to say:

"Our Tsar, Mikhail Fyodorovich [ST], always cares for and works toward that all Christian sovereigns should be mutually in love and unity [p. 106] and that all Christian sovereigns should stand together against the Muslims; but now our Great Sovereign's great enemies are the Polish King Sigismund and the Swedish King Gustav Adolf; and unless he deals with them and avenges their injustices he cannot stand against anyone besides them."

And if Aleksei Ivanovich and the Secretary Aleksei come to England and truly discover that the English King James and the Danish King Christian have made peace with the Swedish King for many years and ratified it by oaths and writing, and between them war is not to be expected, then they are to say to the King at the audience, and after the audience with the advisors they are to read out, the injustices of the Polish and Swedish Kings and [say]:

"That King James, remembering the fraternal loving communications of our previous Great Sovereigns the Tsars of Russia with his predecessors, the English Kings and Queen Elizabeth, and now wishing to be in fraternal friendship and love and communication with Tsar Mikhail Fyodorovich [ST], has helped against the Polish King Sigismund with treasure, money and gold coin and goods, and all sorts of artillery supplies.

"And to the Swedish King Gustav[us] Adolph[us], King James should write in his own name that he should refrain from his injustices, and whatever towns of our Great Sovereign he has taken in violation of his oath he should return to our Great Sovereign after sending ambassadors or emissaries, and should be with our Great Sovereign, the Tsar's majesty, in friendship and love like that peaceful agreement made in the time of our Great Sovereign [p. 107] Tsar and Grand Duke Fyodor Ivanovich Autocrat of all Russia with the Swedish Kingdom and the Swedish King should stand together with our Great Sovereign against the Polish King and should be in peace and quiet with our sovereign."

And the Alekseis are definitely to speak to the King's advisors about all the things written in this Instruction, and to speak about all these matters considering the situation there and what is most advantageous to the sovereign and the land and to the honor and advancement of the sovereign's name.

And if the King's advisors begin to speak about commercial matters, that the Tsar's majesty should allow English merchants and traders to go to trade by way of the sovereign's land to Persia and Bukhara and to other states to the east, then the Alekseis are to say:

"When their sovereign King James sends to our Great Sovereign Tsar Mikhail Fyodorovich [ST] his ambassadors or emissaries together with them, and if he would order his ambassadors to speak to the Tsar's majesty about all these matters, then the Great Sovereign, the Tsar's majesty, they think would for his beloved brother King James, allow his merchants and traders to go through his states to Persia and Bukhara and other states to the east."[94]

And if the King's advisors should speak to them about the English merchants, that the sovereign should grant that they should come [p. 108] to the Moscow state to the port of Archangel in ships alone, and that no merchants of other states should be allowed to come to the port, then they are to say:

"That their sovereign King James should order his ambassadors to speak to our Great Sovereign the Tsar's majesty about this, and our Great Sovereign from his beloved brother King James would grant to the merchants that they might come to his states to the port and trade freely in all sorts of goods without tolls. And we say this to you, that many Great Sovereigns send to Tsar Mikhail Fyodorovich [ST] with great petition that the Tsar's majesty should permit the traders of their states to come to the port with their goods and trade in his states. And our Great Sovereign the Tsar's majesty from love of his brother King James refuses many traders of various states and does not allow them to come to Archangel, but the Tsar's majesty only allows some few men to come for trade to the port who bring goods for the Tsar's treasury."[95]

And if the King's advisors begin to say to [the Alekseis] that previously the Russian Great Sovereigns favored their subjects, the merchants and traders, and gave them Tsar's charters for toll-free trade, with their sovereign's [p. 109] red seals[96]; and now will Tsar Mikhail Fyodorovich [ST] favor their sovereign King James' subjects the merchants and traders? Will he order the charters of grant of the previous Great Sovereigns, the Russian Tsars his ancestors, to be rewritten in his own sovereign's name?

Then Aleksei Ivanovich and the Secretary Aleksei are to say:

"[That] our Great Sovereign Tsar Mikhail Fyodorovich [ST], having become sovereign Tsar and Grand Duke and Autocrat of all Russia in his great and most glorious states of the Russian tsardom, and wishing to be in fraternal love and friendship with his beloved brother your Great Sovereign King James above all other sovereigns, has sent us his ambassadors to your Great Sovereign King James to announce his sovereignty and remind him of fraternal love and friendship. And our Tsar Mikhail Fyodorovich [ST], a sovereign and holder of many states, from fraternal friendship and love for his beloved brother your Great Sovereign King James, favors your great sovereign's subjects, the merchants and traders, and permits them to come to his great states and to the port and to trade freely in all sorts of goods without tolls; and [he] orders his Tsar's charters of grant be given them by the previous custom, and will keep them in his Tsar's favor by the previous custom."

And if the King's advisors begin to say to Aleksei and the Secretary Aleksei that they said to their sovereign King James, in their own sovereign's [p. 110] name, in the speech and the conversations with them, that [regarding] those subjects of their sovereign, Mark the Englishman[97] and his associates, who were in Moscow and whom supposedly the Lithuanians, robbing and stealing their goods, killed. And they know now for sure that Russian cossacks killed Mark the Englishman at the time that they took the Kitaigorod from the Poles and Lithuanians, and those cossacks who killed him took his property[98]; and the sovereign should show his favor and order those goods which were taken from Mark to be found and given to the traders. And [then] Aleksei Ivanovich and the Secretary Aleksei are to say:

"That they know for sure that when by Sigismund's royal command the Poles and Lithuanians burned and destroyed the ruling city of Moscow and stole everyone's property, then they seized in Moscow your sovereign's subjects, Mark the Englishman with his associates. And the Poles and Lithuanians robbed them of all goods and property, and they held Mark himself up to the capture of the Kitaigorod under strong guard and great oppression in the English yard in the Kitaigorod. And when by the grace of the all-powerful God glorified in the Trinity the boyars and generals of our Moscow state took the Kitaigorod from the Poles and Lithuanians, and at the capture they killed many Poles and Lithuanians and Germans who occupied the Kitaigorod for the King, from that time there is no news of Mark the Englishman. [p. 111] And it is not known if the Poles and Lithuanians killed him at the time of the capture or if the mob killed [him] at that time by mistake, since at that time they killed many Russian Muscovite people who had been forced to remain in Moscow by the Poles and Lithuanians. And you yourself can understand, that when a city is taken by the sword, then brother does not spare brother.

"And Mark already had no more goods or property, for what goods and property he had the Poles and Lithuanians took; that, I think, you know yourselves without us. And whatever traders of your sovereign King James there were in the Moscow state in the provincial towns and not in Moscow, these all traded in all sorts of goods with all sorts of people freely and were not insulted, and everywhere people honored and cared for them as before."

And if there be any ambassadors at the English court from the Pope or Emperor, or the Spanish or the French King, or Venice, or the Princes of the sea coast [Netherlands?] or of any other Christian state, and if the Alekseis should happen to see them at the King's court, and they should begin to speak of the Polish King Sigismund and the Moscow state—by what manner the confusion and enmity between the Polish King and the Moscow state has arisen—or if they should begin to justify the Polish King Sigismund before the Moscow state, then the Alekseis are to speak with them about the Polish King's and the lords councillors' injustices to the Moscow state in accord with what has been truly written above in this Instruction, and [p. 112] [they are to say]:

"That they should themselves consider whether it is proper for such a great Christian sovereign to act in violation of his oath. And if an oath sworn by the sovereign's soul is not strong, then in the future what can be trusted? And how will Great Sovereigns communicate with one another when the oath of embassies is not strong and not firm? And that these ambassadors or emissaries, hearing the many injustices of King Sigismund before the Moscow state, and the shedding of Christian blood in violation of many oaths, should write about this to their own Great Sovereigns. And that their sovereigns, the Pope of Rome, and the Emperor, and the Kings of Spain, and France, should take care of Christianity and endeavor to reprove the Polish King, Sigismund, in his many injustices and the spilling of innocent blood and should try to make him refrain from bloodshed. And all great Christian sovereigns should be in brotherhood and love and unity.

"And our Great Sovereign Tsar Mikhail Fyodorovich [ST], by the blessing of our Great Sovereign his mother the nun Marfa Ivanovna, and at the request and petition of all sorts of people of the Moscow state, having become the Great Sovereign Tsar and Grand Duke, Autocrat of all Russia, in his great and most glorious states of the Russian tsardom, above all cares and endeavors that Orthodox Christians (who for several hundred years have suffered in Muslim hands, and hope for aid sent from the all-powerful God and from the great Christian sovereigns to liberate them from the hands of the Muslims) and that all Christian sovereigns, strengthening themselves mutually in love and unity and agreement [p. 113], should stand together in common against the Muslim sovereigns."

And if the ambassadors or emissaries of the Pope or Emperor or the Kings of Spain or France or of Venice should say to the Alekseis that Tsar Mikhail Fyodorovich [ST] has sent them, the ambassadors, to King James about fraternal love and unity and an agreement; and [that] the Pope and the Emperor and the Spanish and French Kings now are mutually in unity with King James and stand together against the Turk; and does Tsar Mikhail Fyodorovich [ST] want to be in love and unity with the Pope and the Emperor, and the Spanish and French Kings and stand together against the Turk?

And [then] the Alekseis are to say:

"Our great sovereign Tsar and Grand Duke Mikhail Fyodorovich of all Russia cares for this and endeavors strongly that all Christian sovereigns should be in love and unity among themselves and stand together against the Muslims. But now the wicked Polish King is an enemy to our Great Sovereign, the Tsar's majesty, and his great states; and now if the Pope and the Emperor, and the Spanish and French King and the Doge of Venice have established unity and an agreement between them, then they should send their ambassadors or emissaries to the Polish King, Sigismund, and to the lords councillors, reproving them in their injustices before the Moscow state, and saying that he should cease such bloodletting and put away all sorts of evil designs against our great sovereign and his great states.

[p. 114] "And all Christian sovereigns should stand together against the Muslims so that in the disagreement and division and dispute of Christian sovereigns among themselves the hand of the Muslims should not be raised. And the Christian states should not be in decline in the face of the evildoers. And to Tsar Mikhail Fyodorovich [ST] the Pope and Emperor, the Spanish and French Kings should send their own ambassadors and emissaries about all matters, instructing them truly about an agreement and unity and with what they will send their ambassadors or emissaries to the Polish King and to the lords councillors. And our sovereign, the Tsar's majesty, will order all his boyars to make a treaty with them about how the great sovereigns should be in love and unity and an agreement; and they will stand together against all their enemies."

And if the King's advisors will begin to say to Aleksei and to the Secretary Aleksei [that] it is known to them that after the boyars and generals of the Moscow state cleansed the Moscow state from the Poles and Lithuanians, King Sigismund came to Moscow himself and with his son Prince Władysław, and gave his son Prince Władysław for the Moscow state. And the boyars and generals and people of all ranks did not want his son Prince Władysław for the Moscow state, did not take him, and thus dishonored him.

[p. 115] And Aleksei and the Secretary Aleksei are to say about this to the advisors:

"When Sigismund the Polish King, in 7119 [1610/11] and 7120 [1611/ 12], violating his own and his crown hetman, Stanisław Żółkiewski's, oath, detained the ambassadors of the Moscow state, Metropolitan Filaret and the boyar, Prince Vasilii Vasil'evich Golitsyn, with their associates in Poland and took the city of Smolensk, and did not give his son Prince Władysław,[99] according to the hetman's treaty in our Greek faith, to the Moscow state and wanted himself, the King, to take possession of the Moscow state for Poland, and burned and destroyed the ruling city of Moscow, and insulted our Orthodox Christian faith, and ruined the churches of God and many monasteries. And the boyars and generals and all sorts of people of all sorts of ranks of all towns of the whole great Russian tsardom assembled together and established among themselves a strong council of good union, and ratified it by oath that they would stand firmly against the Polish King, Sigismund, and his son, Prince Władysław, because of the many injustices and bloodshed, and would fight them to the death; and that they did not want for the Moscow state the Polish King Sigismund's son, Prince Władysław, or anyone of foreign faith from any state, only of the Greek faith. And that they would choose for the Moscow state a sovereign of the Greek law, whomever God would give.

"And when, by the grace of our all-powerful God glorified in the Trinity and by the prayers of the most pure Mother of God, the boyars and generals of the Moscow state and all sorts of people defeated the Lithuanian [p. 116] hetman, Karol Chodkiewicz, and took the ruling city of Moscow from the Poles and Lithuanians; and the Polish King Sigismund hearing this, came himself to Moscow and with him hetman Karol Chodkiewicz with many men and, they say, Prince Władysław was with him too. And many deserters and prisoners told the boyars of the Moscow state in interrogations that the Polish King definitely was coming to destroy the Moscow state and to rescue the Poles and Lithuanians in Moscow and not to give his son to the Moscow state. And he had no thought of giving his son, Prince Władysław, to the Moscow state.

"And even if King Sigismund at that time wanted to give his son to the Moscow state, we had already sworn an oath that we did not want his son for the Moscow state, and not even to think about how it might be done in violation of oath, and that all would rather die than have King

Sigismund and his son now or in the future as sovereign in the Moscow state.

"And the boyars and generals of the Moscow state wrote to King Sigismund many times that he should not come to the Moscow state for his injustices and not bring his son with him. And King Sigismund, forgetting the aid of God, and raised up with pride and bragging that he would completely destroy the Moscow state and kill or take prisoner all of us, the Orthodox Christians, came to the Moscow state with his own and mercenary forces in great number, and enraged like a lion he wanted to swallow us all up. And the boyars and generals of the Moscow state [p. 117], seeing his evil design and raised up pride, put their trust in the almighty God and the grace of the most pure Mother of God, seeing their own justice before Him, sent from Moscow the generals with many men against the King.

"And by God's grace and the prayers of the most pure Mother of God the generals and soldiers of the Moscow state met the King at Voloko-lamsk, ninety versts from Moscow, and defeated the Polish King, and took many prisoners and weapons. And the King returned home from that battle with great shame. And now the boyars and generals and people of all ranks of the Moscow state from small to great have sworn an oath that we all do not wish the son of the Polish King Sigismund nor anyone else from any states for the Moscow state, only our just sovereign chosen by God, our Great Sovereign Tsar and Grand Duke Mikhail Fyodorovich of all Russia, and we do not even think of anyone else, and that we will all lay down our heads for the Orthodox Christian faith and our just sovereign."[100]

And if the King's advisors start to ask Aleksei and the Secretary Aleksei about Tsar Vasilii (that the rumor has come to them that Tsar Vasilii is in Lithuania with his brothers) and is he now alive. Then Aleksei and the Secretary Aleksei are to say:

"By the evil design and violation of oath of King Sigismund his het-man, Stanisław Żółkiewski, entered Moscow by deception and sent Tsar Vasilii off to Poland to King Sigismund, hiding him from everyone, and now we [p. 118] know for sure from deserters and many prisoners that Tsar Vasilii and his brother Prince Dmitrii have died in prison from great need and oppression by the King. And only his brother, Prince Ivan Ivanovich Shuiskii, has remained alive, and he is now with the King and the lords in great oppression;[101] and you advisors may understand your-selves the King's many injustices, for nowhere, neither in Christian nor in Muslim states, is it proper to do this—to take such a Great Sovereign from his state by deception and violation of oath and hold him in great oppression and kill him with an evil and torturous death. And seeing his many injustices, how were we to take his son for the Moscow state? Even though we should all die for our Orthodox Christian faith we would not think that the son of King Sigismund would be the sovereign of the Moscow state or someone from any other state, it is not in our thoughts or understanding, and it is not ever proper to speak about it in the future."

And if King James or his close advisors or your conductors should ask by what manner did Tsar Mikhail Fyodorovich [ST] become sovereign Tsar and Grand Duke of all Russia in the Moscow state, and how close in blood relationship is he to the sovereign Tsar and Grand Duke Fyodor Ivanovich of all Russia? Then Aleksei Ivanovich and the Secretary Aleksei are to say:

"When, by the grace of the almighty God glorified in the Trinity, the Moscow state and the ruling city of Moscow were cleansed of the Lithuanian King Sigismund [p. 119] and of the Poles and Lithuanians, from their evil captivity, and made free, then the boyars and people of all sorts of ranks wrote to all districts of the whole great Russian tsardom—to the metropolitans, and archbishops, and bishops, and archimandrites, and hegumens, and to the whole holy council, and to the boyars, and generals, and gentlemen, and merchants, and townsmen, to all soldiers and gentlemen—that from all the districts of the whole Russian tsardom, from all ranks, they should send to Moscow for counsel about the land and for choosing a sovereign, the best and intelligent people.

"And from their counsel about the land they should choose for the Moscow and the Novgorod states, for the tsardoms of Kazan', Astrakhan', and Siberia, and all the Russian states, a Tsar and Grand Duke of all Russia, whomever God gives, so that in the future the Moscow state would not be without a sovereign, and our Orthodox Christian faith would not be completely ruined and insulted by the Polish King and the Pope's teachers.

"And when from all districts the authorities and the whole clergy in assembly, the boyars, the okol'nichie, the gentlemen, and gentry, and merchants, and all sorts of soldiers, and townsmen, and people from the provinces came together to the ruling city of Moscow to choose a sovereign for the whole Russian tsardom[102]; and our all-generous God glorified in the Trinity [p. 120] looked upon us, who were without a sovereign, with his gracious eye and sent his holy spirit into the hearts of all the Orthodox Christians of the whole great Russian tsardom, from small to great, not only adults but even to suckling babes, and [thereby] the unanimous unchangeable advice that for the Vladimir and Moscow states and for all the great and glorious states of the Russian Tsardom the Tsar and Grand Duke and Autocrat of all Russia should be the nephew of the

Tsar and Grand Duke Fyodor Ivanovich Autocrat of all Russia of blessed memory, from the noble family of Tsars of the previous great, noble, and pious, Russian sovereign Tsars, crowned by God, [that is,] Mikhail Fyodorovich Romanov-Iur'ev. And besides him, Mikhail Fyodorovich Romanov-Iur'ev, no one else from other states or other Moscow clans should be the sovereign in the Moscow state.

"And in the present year, 7121 [1613], on the 21st of February, by God's grace and by the common and well-united council of the whole community, and by the blessing of the metropolitans and archbishops and bishops, and the entire holy ecumenical council of the Moscow state, and all the districts of the great Russian tsardom, the Tsars and Tsarevich which serve in the Moscow state, the boyars and okol'nichie, chashniki, stol'niki and great gentlemen, and gentlemen of the provinces, and all sorts of chancellery officials, and gentry, and musketeer officers, and musketeers, and all sorts of soldiers, and merchants, and townsmen, and people from the provinces of the whole Russian state from small to great and even to suckling [p. 121] babes, chose for the Vladimir, Moscow, and Moscow states, and for the tsardoms of Kazan' and Astrakhan' and Siberia and for all the great and most glorious states of the Russian tsardom as sovereign Tsar and Grand Duke, Autocrat of all Russia, Mikhail Fyodorovich Romanov-Iur'ev, the nephew of the Tsar and Grand Duke Fyodor Ivanovich Autocrat of all Russia of blessed memory, from the Tsar's noble family of the previous great, noble, pious Russian sovereign Tsars crowned by God, since he [Mikhail], the Great Sovereign, is the son of Fyodor Nikitich Romanov-Iur'ev, the nephew of the Tsaritsa and Grand Duchess Anastasia Romanova-Iur'eva, mother of the Great Sovereign of blessed memory the Tsar and Grand Duke Fyodor Ivanovich, Autocrat of all Russia, and lawful wife of the Great Sovereign of blessed memory Tsar and Grand Duke Ivan Vasil'evich Autocrat of all Russia.

"And having chosen him, the Great Sovereign, as sovereign Tsar and Grand Duke of all Russia, for all the great Russian states, all the people with great joy kissed the cross to him, the Great Sovereign in Moscow and all other towns, swearing that they would serve and deal honorably with him, and stand firmly against his the sovereign's enemies and traitors, and fight even until death and, besides him, the sovereign, desire no one from any other states or from other Moscow clans for the Moscow state as sovereign. And now by the happiness and most wise understanding of the Tsar's majesty in the Russian states everything good is being built, and the people of the Russian state, seeing that the Great Sovereign is just, pious, intelligent, strong, [p. 122] brave, and mild, and gracious to the whole people, rejoice and pray God for his long life and health.

"Everyone strives to serve the Tsar's majesty with all types of service, people of all ranks, and with joy to stand against the sovereign's enemy the Polish King, Sigismund, and the lords councillors for their many injustices to the Moscow state and to avenge his injustice to the Moscow state, as much as the merciful God will help us. And the confusion, and dissension, and grief among men that was in the Russian state before him people have forgotten in their joy as if it never existed; and we all expect by God's grace in the state of our Great Sovereign that everything will be better and that there will be vengeance on the Polish King and his land for their injustice." [p. 122] And if King James or his advisors and the conductors ask about the age of Tsar Mikhail Fyodorovich [ST], how many years old he is? [Then] Aleksei Ivanovich and the secretary Aleksei are to say:

"Our sovereign the Tsar's majesty is only eighteen years old, and God has beautified the Tsar's majesty with strength and good looks, courage, intelligence and happiness, and he is mild and gracious to all people, and God has beautified him with all things, all good deeds and manner above all men."

And if King James should invite Aleksei and the Secretary Aleksei to eat, then Aleksei is to assert to the conductors that at that time at the King's table there should be no other ambassadors or emissaries of other sovereigns. And if there are ambassadors or emissaries of other sovereigns at the King's table, then they are not to go to the King's table. And if the King [p. 123] orders them to eat at his table with him, then Aleksei and the Secretary Aleksei are to go to the King to eat. And if at the King's table are the ambassadors or the emissaries of the Turk, the Pope, the Emperor, or the Spanish King or any other sovereigns, then Aleksei and the Secretary Aleksei are not to eat with the King in the presence of the ambassadors or emissaries and definitely not to go to the table. And if they should be seated at the table, and at the same time at the table there are the ambassadors or emissaries of other sovereigns, then Aleksei and the Secretary Aleksei are to rise from the table and return to their lodgings and say to the conductors and to assert to the King's advisors with the conductors: that when the ambassadors and emissaries of the English Queen Elizabeth of glorious memory were with our great sovereigns, the Tsar Ivan Vasil'evich [ST], and his son, Tsar Fyodor Ivanovich [ST], and Tsar Boris Fyodorovich, then at the audience with the Tsar's majesty and at the table there were no ambassadors or emissaries of other sovereigns.[103] And King James should order the same to be done, and that there be no ambassadors and emissaries with them at the table, so that the fraternal love with our great sovereign Tsar and Grand Duke Mikhail Fyodorovich Autocrat of all Russia not be broken.

[And if the King or his advisors say: that there was a rumor among them that they had chosen for sovereign the Swedish Prince Karl Philip,[104] and that the Novgorod Metropolitan, Isidor, and the boyar and general, Prince Ivan Odoevskii, had made a written agreement and oath with Jakob that they would take for the Moscow state Karl Philip the son of Charles. And [then] Aleksei Ivanovich and the Secretary Aleksei are to say:

"Someone has said something to you without knowing, and hiding something in vain. We know truly that this was in no one's thoughts to elect the son of Charles. We saw the great evil of the Polish Prince. About this we Russians have taken firm counsel and sworn an oath / no one from the Russian states / son not of the Greek faith to choose for the state. And if Jakob Pontusson de la Gardie ordered Metropolitan Isidor and Prince Ivan Odoevskii to write any paper and swear to it in prison, by force and under the sword, then we do not know about it. And they are to speak of the Swedish King's injustices / as in this instruction / such injustices / elect the Swedish Prince as sovereign for the Moscow state /]"[105]

And if the King or his advisors should ask: What now is the relationship of the Turkish Sultan and the Persian Shah with the Moscow state? [p. 124] Then Aleksei and the Secretary Aleksei are to say:

"From long past the previous Sultans were in communication about fraternal friendship and love and border matters with our previous Great Sovereigns the Russian Tsars. But the last communication was that of Tsar Fyodor Ivanovich [ST] with the Turkish Sultan, Mehmed.[106] And Sultan Mehmed died and in his place came the present new Sultan his son Sultan Ahmed. And now there has been no communication with him up to this time and none is expected in the future."

And on the Persians they are to say:

"From long past the Persian Shahs were in communication with our Great Sovereigns the Russian Tsars. And the present Shah, Abbas, has had frequent communications about fraternal friendship and love [p. 125] with our great sovereigns of blessed memory, with Tsar Fyodor Ivanovich [ST] and with the Tsar and Grand Duke Boris Fyodorovich, and with Tsar Vasilii Ivanovich. And now in the state of our great sovereign the emissaries of Shah Abbas, Amir Ali-Bek, and Murshikuli-Bek and the messenger Migip-Bek came to the Moscow state under Tsar Vasilii Ivanovich [ST]. And Tsar Mikhail Fyodorovich [ST] has seen off these emissaries and the messenger of the Shah and sends his own ambassadors with them to announce his sovereignty. And in the future our Great

Sovereign wishes to be in friendship and love and communication with the Shah just as the previous Moscow sovereigns were in friendship and love and communication with the Persian Shahs."[107]

And if the King and his advisors will ask: What now is the relationship of Tsar Mikhail Fyodorovich [ST] with the Crimean Khan? [Then] Aleksei Ivanovich and the Secretary Aleksei are to say:

"Before now the Crimean Khan was in friendship, and in the command of our Great Sovereigns Tsar Fyodor Ivanovich [ST], and after that with Tsar Boris, and finally with Tsar Vasilii. And the Khan died and a new Khan came to rule on the Crimean yurt. And now our Great Sovereign, having become the Great Sovereign Tsar and Grand Duke of all Russia in the Moscow state and all the great and most glorious states of the Russian tsardom, sent to the Crimean Khan his messenger the gentleman, Voin Purgasov, with a letter announcing his sovereignty [p. 126], and to the effect that the Tsar's majesty wishes to be with him, the Khan, in strong friendship and loving communication as before, as there was communication and love between the previous Great Sovereign Tsar and Grand Duke of Russia with the Crimean Khans, and with Khan Gazi-Girey[108]; and he should stand together with the Tsar's majesty against their common enemy the Polish and Lithuanian King Sigismund."

And if King James and his advisors and councillors should ask Aleksei and the Secretary Aleksei: How is the present relationship of the sovereign Tsar and Grand Duke Mikhail Fyodorovich of all Russia with the Roman Emperor?

Then Aleksei and the Secretary Aleksei Vitovtov are to say:

"You yourselves know that from long past the Roman Emperors of blessed memory were in fraternal love and communication and in agreement with our previous great sovereigns the Russian Tsars. And when by God's will and by blood relationship with our great sovereigns of Russia, and by the petition of people of all sorts of ranks of the whole Russian tsardom, our Tsar Mikhail Fyodorovich [ST] came to rule the Moscow state and all the great and most glorious states of the whole Russian tsardom, the Tsar's majesty sent his ambassadors to Matthias, the Roman Emperor, to announce his sovereignty and declare the injustices of the Polish King Sigismund and the lords councillors to the Moscow state, which they had committed in violation of oath. And before that, before the election of the sovereign [p. 127] by the boyars and generals and people of all sorts of ranks of the Moscow state the translator, Eremei Eremeev, was sent with letters about the injustices and violation of oath by the King and the lords councillors.[109] And now under our great sovereign the Tsar's majesty an emissary, Egeiuzuf Grigor'ev, has come from the Emperor to the Persian Shah, and he is to pass through the state of our Great Sovereign. And that imperial emissary by the command of our Great Sovereign was with the boyars of the Tsar's majesty, and told the boyars of the Tsar's majesty that: the Great Sovereign Emperor, Matthias, remembering fraternal love and communication of our Great Sovereigns the Russian Tsars with the Great Sovereigns the Roman Emperors, received the Moscow state's messenger Eremei Eremeev and quickly allowed him to see his eyes,[110] and took his letter, and heard him lovingly, and was well amazed at the injustices and violation of oath of the King and the lords councillors and the destruction of the great and most glorious Moscow state; and [he] sincerely grieved at the spilling of innocent Christian blood, and discussed the injustices of the King and the lords councillors and [p. 128] spoke of his injustices with great reproach; and [he] wrote about King Sigismund's injustices to his brother Maximilian, the Archduke of Austria and to the prince electors and all the appanage princes, and sent his own emissary to King Sigismund with a letter about it.[111] And he wrote to him and the lords with many accusations and reproach about the many injustices which he[112] had inflicted on the Moscow state in violation of oath and that he, remembering his previous oath, should do no evil to the Moscow state and make peace with the Tsar's majesty. And he released the messenger Eremei; and with him he will send his own emissary; and they went by sea, and we think they are already in the Moscow state with our great sovereign."

And if the King or his advisors ask about Kazan' or Astrakhan' or Siberia: Are Kazan' and Astrakhan', as before, in unity with the Moscow state? And [say] that they know that there was confusion in Astrakhan'. [Then] Aleksei Ivanovich and the Secretary Aleksei are to say:

"The Kazan' state did not waiver at all and was together with the Moscow state under the sovereigns and when there was no sovereign. And when the boyars and generals stood at Moscow then the Kazan' soldiers, Russians and Tatars, were with the boyars and generals up to the final capture. And [p. 129] Astrakhan', when for the sins of the whole Russian state there was confusion in the Russian state, and the thieves, the unfrocked monk Grishka Otrep'ev, took on the sovereign's name, calling himself falsely Tsarevich Dmitrii, and after him another such thief [calling himself] by the same name[113]; and when the Poles and Lithuanians were in Moscow, then at that time Astrakhan' wavered.

"And now, since Tsar Mikhail Fyodorovich [ST] has come to rule the great states of the Russian tsardom, and Astrakhan' people from Astrakhan' were at his election to sovereign, the Astrakhan' people elected him sovereign together with the Kazan' state and all Russian states. And when he became our Great Sovereign in his great states, he favored the Astrakhan' people with his Tsar's favor, released them back to Astrakhan' and sent a governor to Astrakhan'. And the Governor of the Tsar's majesty sent to the Tsar's majesty the best people of Astrakhan' so that all sorts of people of Astrakhan', gentlemen and officials, and musketeers, and cossacks, and all sorts of civilians would kiss the cross with joy to him, the sovereign. And the Tatars, according to their own faith—the Muslim law—swore that they would serve and take care of him the sovereign, and stand against any enemy of the sovereign, and did not want any sovereign besides him; and they serve him, the sovereign, with joy. And now by the command of the Tsar's majesty Kazan' and Astrakhan' armies [p. 130] go to war against the Polish and Lithuanian lands in number more than a hundred thousand."

And if the King or his advisors should ask about Siberia: What now is the relationship of the Siberian state with the Moscow state? Then Aleksei Ivanovich and the secretary Aleksei are to say:

"The Siberian tsardom is an ancient eternal inheritance of our great sovereigns the Russian Tsars, and Tsar Ivan Vasil'evich [ST], the great grandfather of our Tsar Fyodor Ivanovich [ST], took Siberia more than a hundred years ago, and placed tribute on them in sables and black fox.[114] And not long ago the Siberian people fell away from our sovereign. And Tsar Ivan Vasil'evich [ST], the father of Tsar Fyodor Ivanovich [ST] sent to Siberia his generals with a great army. And the generals who went with the sovereign's army defeated the Siberian Khan, Kuchum, and drove him from Siberia, and took Kuchum's brother Mahmetkul and after that killed Khan Kuchum and took his children and wives and brought them to Moscow.

"And now in Siberia there are many people of the Tsar's majesty: Russian boyars, and generals, and all sorts of soldiers and civilians. And many towns have been built by the river Tura and the great Ob' and the Irtysh, and by many other places, and churches of the Greek law have been built, and an archbishop appointed for the strengthening of the Christian faith. And much tribute comes to our sovereign from the Siberian land: sables and black fox and all sorts of other animals. And the Siberian land is two [p. 131] thousand versts along the great Ob' river to China. And when in the Moscow state by our sins there was confusion and dissension, the Siberian state was unshakable, and the Siberian people joined no confusion or thieving, and served the sovereign Tsars— Tsar Boris, and Tsar Vasilii and, after, Tsar Vasilii with the Moscow state together."

And if the King's advisors should ask: Are the Nogais beyond the Volga in the sovereign's will as before?[115] Then Aleksei Ivanovich and the Secretary Aleksei should say:

"The Nogais beyond the Volga of old served our great sovereigns the

Tsars and Grand Dukes of Russia, and until Tsar Vasilii left the Tsardom. And when Tsar Vasilii left the Tsardom, and they elected to the Russian states the son of the Polish King, Prince Władysław, at that time the Nogais wavered, for they did not like [it] that [a] Polish Prince had been elected to the Moscow state. And when the boyars and generals and people of all sorts of ranks of the states of Russia made a council and stood against the King for his injustices, then the Nogais returned again to the Moscow state and obeyed the boyars. And when by God's grace Tsar Mikhail Fyodorovich [ST] came to rule his great states of Russia, then the Nogai Prince, Ishterek, with his brothers and nephews sent to [p. 132] the Tsar's majesty his ambassadors to greet him, the sovereign, and petition him that the Tsar's majesty should hold them under his Tsar's hand as before; and they, the sovereign's slaves, were inseparable for ever, and prepared to go against the sovereign's enemies and rebels where he should command them. And the Tsar's majesty favored them, and praised them and sent to them his Tsar's charters of grant, that they should be hopeful for the Tsar's grace and that they should serve him, the Great Sovereign, and stand against any of his enemies as before."

And if the King or his advisors ask: [That] it has happened that they have heard from emissaries of the previous sovereigns and from the merchants who have come to the Moscow land under Tsar Fyodor and Tsar Boris, and who said that some new states had been added to the Russian state—Iberia with the Georgian Tsars, the Khan of the Kazak and Kolmak horde, the land of Kabarda, the mountain Circassians, the land of Shevkal and other lands of that area; and what is the relationship of these lands with the sovereign and the Moscow states now? And [then] Aleksei Ivanovich and the Secretary Aleksei are to say:

"The land of Iberia, the Georgian Tsars, Konstantin and Simon, and the Kazak horde, and the Kolmaks, and the Circassian and Kabarda land, and the Shevkal land and the Kumyks, and other small lands in that area, which under Tsar Fyodor Ivanovich [ST] and Tsar Boris came under the sovereign's hand to the Moscow state, have not [p. 133] fallen away from the Russian state. And for a short time, when there was dissension in the Russian state and thieves called themselves the children of the sovereign, at that time these small lands were in doubt and they did not send their ambassadors and emissaries because of the interference from the thieves. And when after the election of the Polish prince as sovereign of our Russian states, the boyars and people of all ranks made a council and stood against the Poles and Lithuanians, then from these newly added lands there were ambassadors and messengers about counsel with the boyars and generals and the whole Russian state. And now all these lands are joyful at the Tsar's majesty, that God has given him, the sovereign, [to them] from the family of the previous Great Sovereigns our Tsars of Russia, and they wish to serve the Tsar's majesty with joy as before."

And if the King or his advisors ask about the thief of Kaluga[116]: How [did] he meet his end? Then Aleksei Ivanovich and the Secretary Aleksei are to say:

"When the boyars who were in Moscow with Hetman Stanisław Żółkiewski made a treaty and ratified it about the election of Prince Władysław, then that thief left Moscow with Marinka Mniszech, to make war in the Sever towns with the Lithuanians by the King's command. And there Ian, the son of Arslan, of the Great Nogai Horde, Prince Petr Urusov, killed him; and that thief in accord with his evil thievish deeds ended his life evilly."

And if they should ask about Ivashka Zarutskii: That it was known that at Moscow [p. 134] Zarutskii stood against the Poles and Lithuanians, but now supposedly he has become a thief and is bringing towns of the Moscow state to thievery. Then Aleksei and the Secretary Aleksei are to say:

"Zarutskii was a thief, first he was a thief under the unfrocked monk Grishka Otrep'ev[117] and the general's daughter, the unfrocked monk's wife Marinka Mniszech. And when the whole Moscow state, reproving the thief, the unfrocked monk, killed him, that thief Zarutskii left Moscow for the Don. And when the King sent another thief with the same name, calling him the Tsarevich Dmitrii,[118] as if that thief had escaped Moscow alive, and the General gave his daughter Marinka to that second thief, then Zarutskii ran to that second thief and was with that thief and his wife, the General's daughter Marina, and did all sorts of evil to the Moscow state and together with the Poles and Lithuanians spilled Christian blood, and with that thief escaped from the camp to Kaluga. And when Prince Petr Urusov killed that second thief, then Zarutskii took for himself the General's daughter Marinka and came with the cossacks to Moscow supposedly to help against the Poles and Lithuanians, but did all manner of evil when he was at Moscow, and communicated with the Poles and Lithuanians for all manner of evil. And in that form the boyars and generals wanted to catch him and punish him for his thievery and treason. And he escaped from Moscow and the boyars and generals together with Marinka, the General's daughter. And that Marinka lived with him after the thief. And now he runs about in the border areas and has nowhere to go and no one with him; for all people now in the state of Russia are glad about the sovereign and have left off their evil deeds. And Zarutskii, when we were there, had sent to the Tsar's majesty [p. 135] to petition and ask for grace for his guilt—that the Tsar's majesty should show grace to him, forgive his guilt, and he would bring his guilt and Marina to the Tsar's majesty. And we think that he truly succeeded in his petition. And if he did not succeed, then he is caught, for he has nowhere to go." And if they do not ask about Zarutskii, then do not talk about him.

[Memorandum: in the case of the death of the English monarch]

And a memorandum to Aleksei Ivanovich and the Secretary Aleksei: If God decides that they come to England and by God's judgment King James has died, and his son or someone of royal family from another state has taken his place in the English kingdom and become King, then Aleksei Ivanovich and the Secretary Aleksei are to say, to the advisors and the conductor:

"That the Great Sovereign Tsar and Grand Duke Mikhail Fyodorovich of all Russia has sent them to his loving brother King James to announce his sovereignty, and about brotherhood and love and other great matters. And by God's judgment King James has died, and our Great Sovereign, the Tsar's majesty, did not know about their new sovereign the new King, that he had become King. And in this matter we have the instruction of the Tsar's majesty: if by God's judgment King James has died and someone has become the new King in the English kingdom in his place, then our Great Sovereign Tsar and Grand Duke Mikhail Fyodorovich of all Russia has ordered us to go to that new [p. 136] King and make a bow, and give the letter, and make a speech. And they, the advisors, should inform their sovereign so that he might order them to come to him."

And when the new King orders them to come to him for the audience then Aleksei Ivanovich and the Secretary Aleksei coming from the sovereign Tsar and Grand Duke Mikhail Fyodorovich of all Russia to the new King who is in King James's place, they will make a bow and give the letter according to the sovereign's instruction. And after that Aleksei is to say to the new King:

"The Great Sovereign Tsar and Grand Duke Mikhail Fyodorovich Autocrat of all Russia has sent me, his ambassador, to his loving brother King James to announce his sovereignty and with his loving letter. And by God's judgment King James has died, and in his place you, Great Sovereign, have come to rule his states, and you, Great Sovereign, should be in fraternal love and in strong friendship and unity and [in] an agreement with our Great Sovereign the Tsar's majesty as were the Great Sovereign English Kings of glorious memory with the previous Great Sovereigns our Tsars and Grand Dukes of Russia. And he should send to our Great [p. 137] Sovereign, the Tsar's majesty, his ambassadors or emissaries to announce his sovereignty and [to discuss] how you, Great Sovereign, should be in the future in fraternal love and strong friendship and unity with our Great Sovereign, the Tsar's majesty."

And Aleksei Ivanovich and the Secretary Aleksei are to do the sovereign's business, about which they were sent to King James, with the new King according to this instruction of the sovereign.

And if they choose someone in the place of King James as sovereign, and he does not quickly come to rule the state, then Aleksei Ivanovich and the Secretary Aleksei are to wait until the new King comes to rule the state. And then they are to go to the new King, after communicating with the advisors, and from Tsar Mikhail Fyodorovich [ST] to bow to him and give the letter, do the sovereign's business according to the instruction of the sovereign Tsar and Grand Duke Mikhail Fyodorovich of all Russia.

And if there they do not soon choose a new King for the state, and the advisors begin to rule, and the advisors send to them that they should come to the royal court or to some particular great advisor, and say to them that without the King they cannot do the business with which they were sent; then Aleksei Ivanovich and the secretary are to say:

"That Tsar Mikhail Fyodorovich [ST] had sent them to his loving brother King James to announce his sovereignty and about fraternal friendship and love. And by God's judgment King James has died and in his place in the kingdom [p. 138] a new King has not been chosen, there is no one with whom to have an audience; and the advisors should send them back to the Tsar's majesty; and [then] they should ask to go to Tsar Mikhail Fyodorovich [ST] as soon as the sea road should be possible."

And if Aleksei and the Secretary Aleksei find out truly that the English advisors are going to do the business for which they have been sent even without a King, then Aleksei and the Secretary Aleksei are to go to them and give the sovereign's letter and make the speech, and do the business by this instruction of the sovereign.

[Memorandum: on Baron Freiger of Flodorf, Arthur Aston, etc.]

A memorandum to the Ambassadors Aleksei Ivanovich Ziuzin and the Secretary Aleksei Vitovtov: When, if God grants, they are in England at the audience with the King, and after the audience the advisors begin to ask them about the Germans of the Empire and the English, about Baron Adrian Freiger and about Arthur Aston, and about James Hill who, with mercenaries, came on ships to Archangel in the year 7120 [1611/12]; that their sovereign King James, knowing the injustice and violation of oath of King Sigismund to the Moscow state and remembering the strong friendship and fraternal loving communication of the previous Great Sovereign Tsars and Grand Dukes of Russia with the Great Sovereign Queen Elizabeth of glorious memory, showing his love for the Tsar's majesty, allowed soldiers of his state to come to the Moscow [p. 139] state and serve the Moscow state for hire and stand against the Poles and Lithuanians. And in the past year, 7120 [1611/12], with the knowledge of their sovereign King James, Baron of the Empire Adrian Freiger and James Hill and the Englishman Arthur Aston and about a hundred soldiers, went from England on ships to Archangel to help and to serve the Moscow state for hire, and they had a pass given into all states by the King's hand and seal. And the rumor about these soldiers is that they came safely to Archangel. And the boyars of the Moscow state held those soldiers in Archangel for unknown reasons and gave them no food, nor any honor, and held them cruelly in the Moscow state until now like slaves, and they are honorable soldiers and true in their service in many states. Then Aleksei Ivanovich and the secretary Aleksei are to say:

"In the past year 7120 [1611/12] some men came from England on ships and said they were soldiers and that their leaders were Baron Adrian Freiger of the town of Flodorf in the Empire, and James Hill, and the Englishman Arthur Aston, and with them about a hundred soldiers. And they said that they had come with the knowledge of your sovereign King James and the dignitaries of the Netherlands to serve the Moscow state for hire and stand together against the Poles, and they showed the governors a pass into all the states of the Tsar's majesty with the King's signature and seal.[119] But letters from your sovereign King James [p. 140] or from any other states to the boyars of the Moscow state were not with them, they said. And before their arrival they sent to the boyars from Hamburg the Captain James Shaw,[120] and with him they sent a letter announcing their arrival, in their own hand; and in that letter is the hand of Jacques Margeret, and it is written about him that he will hire mercenaries, and they will be in the Moscow state early in spring.[121]

"And that Jacques is a known enemy of the Moscow state, and the whole Moscow state knows about him: he came to the Moscow state from the Empire with the Secretary Afanasii Vlas'ev under Tsar Boris to serve the sovereign's name[122]; and Tsar Boris favored him with estates and money grants. And he was a captain with the foreigners. And under Tsar Vasilii he petitioned to be allowed to return home. And Tsar Vasilii favored him, and let him go home with all the property that he had accumulated in the Moscow state.[123] And that Jacques, forgetting the Tsar's favor to him, came to Moscow with Hetman Żółkiewski and after Żółkiewski remained in Moscow as a lieutenant of the Pole, Borkowski, and ruined the Moscow state together with the Poles and Lithuanians and spilled Christian blood and stole riches in the Moscow state and went to Poland and for this received honor and favor from the King.[124] And why should someone like this want good for the Moscow state?

"And in addition Adrian Freiger and his associates said that Jacques Margeret communicated with the thief and traitor of the Moscow [p. 141] state, Ivan Zarutskii. And he wanted to hire men and help him, supposedly against the Poles and Lithuanians. And that Jacques, in the advice and intention of the present mercenary soldiers, declared himself and wished to go to Archangel with the mercenary soldiers and be with them together.

"And into our cities and to our generals the Swedish King's General Jakob Pontusson de la Gardie wrote, saying that those captains, Adrian Freiger and associates, with the German soldiers, came into the Moscow state by the design and mission of King Sigismund for the sake of all sorts of evil and their own profit, wherever they might fight and rob, and that in the Moscow state they should beware of them wherever they appeared, so that they did not lull people's guard and by deception and stealth do any evil to the Russians; and whatever they say should not be believed, for they speak falsely and with guile. He, Jakob de la Gardie, knows truly that they have come on the King's errand by deception for all sorts of evil, and they should definitely not be believed in anything, and [be] expelled from the state before any harm befall the Moscow state from them.

"And because of their friendship and counsel with Jacques Margeret and the letter of Jakob Pontusson de la Gardie there was no reason to believe them and let them come to the town of Archangel. And the Governor of Archangel received them honorably for the sake of their sovereign King James and gave them enough food, and wrote about their unannounced arrival to the boyars of the Moscow state.[125] And the boyars of the Moscow state, [p. 142] knowing the fraternal love and strong friendship of our Great Sovereigns the Tsars of Russia with your Great Sovereigns the English Kings and with your present Great Sovereign King James, ordered that the Germans, Adrian with his associates, and the soldiers be honored in all things and given enough food, but [that] care be taken against them in all things and that they not be allowed home by the winter route. And those Germans told the Tsar's majesty's boyars that they brought great matters that would be pleasing to the Tsar's majesty and the whole Moscow state, and they would announce these matters to no one but the great boyars, and they lived in the Moscow state in great honor.

"And when by God's grace Tsar Mikhail Fyodorovich [ST] came to rule the Vladimir and Moscow and all the great states of the Russian state as Great Sovereign Tsar and Grand Duke of all Russia, and our Great Sovereign the Tsar's majesty, remembering the previous fraternal love and friendship of our Russian Tsars with your Great Sovereign Queen Elizabeth, and for the sake of your sovereign King James, showing him, the Great Sovereign, fraternal love and goodwill, and putting aside all that, that there was counsel between them and Jacques Margeret and [p. 143] what the Swedish General Jakob Pontusson de la Gardie wrote about them, by his Tsar's mercy and most wise reason decided that Adrian and his associates had taken counsel with Margeret not knowing his thievery and hostility to the Moscow state, and that Jakob Pontusson de la Gardie had written about them to sow confusion, ordered Arthur Aston and James Hill and the captains and the best people with them to be taken from Kholmogory to Iaroslavl'.

"And Aston and Hill with their associates by the merciful command of the Tsar's majesty were in Iaroslavl' with the Tsar's majesty's boyars the near boyar Fyodor Ivanovich Sheremetev and they said to the Tsar's majesty's boyars, to Fyodor Ivanovich, that, hearing the injustice of the Polish King Sigismund against the Moscow state they came to the Moscow state for good things with the knowledge of the Great Sovereign King James and the rulers of the land of Holland to serve the Moscow state with mercenaries and to stand against the Poles together with the Russians. But they had not letters from King James or any other sovereigns to the boyars of the Moscow state; they only reported a pass from your Great Sovereign King James.[126] And the boyars, the boyar Fyodor Ivanovich, of the Tsar's majesty, hearing their speeches about their arrival, reported to the Tsar's majesty. And the Tsar's majesty favored those soldiers, ordered them to be granted enough food and to be honored, and in all [p. 144] care to be taken of them until they left the Moscow state. And now these soldiers live in the state of our Great Sovereign, in the towns, in quiet and honor, freely, and await the ships on which they may go beyond the sea. And when the ships come their release will be swift by decree of the Tsar's majesty according to the King's pass.[127] And there has been no holding them or dishonor or slavery in the state of our great sovereign anywhere."

And even if the King's advisors do not ask about these Germans, then Aleksei Ivanovich and the Secretary Aleksei are themselves to talk nonsense and declare by what manner they came to the Moscow state, and whether it was with King James's knowledge [that] they came to the Moscow state or by themselves.

[Memorandum: on English Foreign Policy]

And a memorandum to Aleksei Ivanovich and the Secretary Aleksei: when they are in England with King James they are to find out secretly what is the relationship between King James and the Emperor, the Turkish, Spanish, French, Venetian, Danish, Swedish sovereigns and those of the sea—with whom King James is in communication and peace, and with whom he is not in peace. And what ambassadors and emissaries were with King James in the past year and now again? And if there were, from what sovereigns, and why did they come, and what did they leave with, and to what states [p. 145] did King James send ambassadors and emissaries and about what matters?[128] And were there any communications recently or now with the Polish King Sigismund before this?[129] And if there were, how long ago, and what did King Sigismund send about and in what measure is King Sigismund with King James? And what is now the relationship of the Danish King Christian with the Swedish King: are they at peace? And if they are at peace, on what did they make peace and who brought them to peace?[130] Or are they at war, and who is the stronger, and how many towns did the Danish King take from the Swedish King and what are the names of the towns; and this year was there a battle of the Dane with the Swede, and if there was, where, and who was the winner? And what is to be expected between them in the future, peace or war? And what is the relationship of the Swede with the Polish King, Sigismund? And this year was there any communication about peace of the Swede with the Polish King Sigismund or is there war between them? And in what places do the Poles and Lithuanians fight in the Swedish land or in Livonia, and who is the stronger? And in the future what is to be expected between them, peace or war? And is there not between them again communication and designs about unity against the Moscow state? And if there is any design against the Moscow state, are the Pope and the Emperor and the Spanish and the French and other maritime sovereigns and free cities helping the Polish King Sigismund or the Swedish King with people and treasure against the Moscow state? And if they are helping, then what sovereigns and with what? And what in England and in [p. 146] other states do they say about the Polish King Sigismund and the Swedish King, about their injustices and violation of oath and about the Moscow state?[131] And whom do they more justify, the Moscow state or the King? And have there been any ambassadors or emissaries from the Emperor or other Christian sovereigns to King James again about unity against the Turk?[132] And if there were, of what sovereigns were they the ambassadors, and is there any treaty among them on that? And for the future what is the King's design: with which sovereigns does he wish to be in peace and with which to make war, and which sovereigns does he wish to help against which states, and with what sort of aid?

And Aleksei Ivanovich and the Secretary Aleksei are to find out in England about the German soldiers who came in 7120 [1611/12] on a ship from England to Archangel to serve for hire, about the Baron of the Empire, Adrian Freiger, and James Hill and the Englishman Arthur Aston: did they come from England to the Moscow state with the King's knowledge or by themselves? And if with the King's knowledge, then by what measures and was there some design against Archangel?[133] And now is there not some sort of design on the part of the Lithuanian King Sigismund or the Swedish King or some other maritime sovereigns against Archangel? And if there is a design by someone, by what measures is the design [to be realized]? And are the Pole or the Swede hiring soldiers in any states, and should the arrival of mercenaries of King Sigismund and the Swedish King be expected now or in the future in Archangel? [p. 147] And they are to find out strongly and surely by all means which sovereigns are favorable to the Moscow state and which are making evil designs against the Moscow state? And does King James want to stand together with the Moscow state against the Polish and Swedish Kings and help, and with what aid will he help?

And they are to find out secretly about all matters which need to be known in the Moscow state. And what news they learn about in England the Secretary Aleksei is to write down himself and keep the writing on himself secretly and with great care, so that no one of the English or the Russians would know about it besides them, and when they come to Moscow they are to tell it to the sovereign Tsar and Grand Duke Mikhail Fyodorovich of all Russia.

[Memorandum: on the Russian youths]

[p. 147] And a memorandum to Aleksei Ivanovich and the Secretary Aleksei: In the past year, 7111 [1602/3], under Tsar Boris Fyodorovich [ST], Grigorii, the son of Alferii Grigor'ev, and associates—four men—were sent from the Moscow state to England to learn Latin and English and other languages and writing of the various German states.[134] And Aleksei Ivanovich and the Secretary Aleksei are to say to the King's advisors:

"In the past year 7111 [1602/3] under the sovereign Tsar Boris Fyodorovich [ST], of blessed memory, and the Great Sovereign of glorious memory, Queen Elizabeth, were sent into England [p. 148] subjects of our Great Sovereign for a time to study Latin and English and other German

languages and writing, Grishka, the son of Alferii Grigor'ev, Fedka Semenov, and associates—four men.[135] And these subjects of the Tsar,
since they were learning, have studied all that for which they were sent
and now they are needed for the ambassadorial business of the Tsar's
majesty, and they have been in England for a long time, while in the
Moscow state for our sins evil people have caused confusion and disorder.[136] And now by God's grace and the most careful and wise reason and
happiness of graceful attention of our Great Sovereign the Tsar's majesty
to all the subjects of the Tsar's majesty, the Moscow state is in order and
all good is being done. They, the advisors of his royal majesty, should
return all the subjects of the Tsar's majesty who lived in England for
learning to him, the Tsar's majesty's Ambassador Aleksei Ivanovich, and
[to] the Secretary Aleksei Vitovtov; and they should take them with
them and bring them before the Tsar's majesty."

And when the royal advisors give Grisha Alfer'ev and associates to
them, then Aleksei Ivanovich and the Secretary Aleksei are to order
them to stay with them and take them with them to the sovereign in
Moscow.

And if the King's advisors do not want to give up the sovereign's
people, Grisha Alfer'ev and [p. 149] associates, and say about some that
they have died or by their own will have gone somewhere for learning
with the merchants into some far state, and they do not know if he is
alive or not, and if alive, then he will be awaited a long time.

And [then] Aleksei Ivanovich and the Secretary Aleksei are to say:
"That they should give them those who are now in England.[137] And if
someone has died by God's judgment, that was God's will.[138] And whoever is away in a faraway state, then they should do something about that
for the Tsar's majesty: write so that he should be quickly taken from
there; and having found out who is alive, they should give them to them.
And the fathers and mothers of those subjects are petitioning with great
insistence to the Tsar's majesty that the Tsar's majesty should favor them
and order them taken from England to Moscow, so that they, being a
long time in foreign states, should not leave the Christian faith of the
Greek law and should not part from them. And the Tsar's majesty has
given them an order in his name that it is ordered to take them and bring
them to Moscow. And we speak about these subjects of the Tsar's majesty
by order of our sovereign, and you should definitely seek them out and
give them to us."

And if the King's advisors should begin to say that they do not dare to
give over the subjects of the Tsar's majesty without the King's knowledge
because they have been here a long time, and none of them want to leave
for the Moscow state because they have grown accustomed to all sorts of

local customs; and some serve at the King's court or with some [p. 150] great man. And since they themselves do not wish to, how can they force them and give them into slavery; and even if they give them now into slavery, they will not be held in the future.

And Aleksei Ivanovich and the Secretary Aleksei are to say to the King's advisors: "Those subjects of the Tsar's majesty are native of the Moscow state and not foreigners, and they are of the Christian faith of the Greek law, and their fathers and mothers and brothers are still living. And under Tsar Boris they were sent for study and were all given into the hands of your sovereign's distinguished English merchant John Merrick.[139] And since the time that there was established fraternal love and strong friendship and unity between our past Great Sovereign of glorious memory and the sovereign Queen Elizabeth, from this country and until now, young boys [illegible] for study of the Russian language with English merchants. And there has been no holding or dispute about them, they study for six or ten years and come and go as they please.[140] And his royal majesty will not want to hold the subjects of our sovereign in his country, for his royal majesty has many native subjects who know the Russian writing and tongue. And in response to the statement that the boys do not want to go from the English land to the Moscow state, who will believe that? It is impossible [p. 151] that they want to abandon the Orthodox Christian faith of the Greek law, their native state and sovereign, and forget their fathers and mothers and family and clan. It is improper to say such things of them, who are intelligent and honorable men."

And Aleksei Ivanovich and the Secretary Aleksei are to speak about these people of the sovereign strongly, by all means, so that they might find those that are alive and give them to them; so that there should not be lack of love between the sovereigns for so small a cause. And if they say that one has died or is far away on a journey, then Aleksei Ivanovich and the Secretary Aleksei are to inquire of the English translators and all sorts of people, and even if something must be given by someone to someone, they must truly find out who died and who is far away on a journey. And if one of them has died, then how long ago, at what time and where is he buried? If one is on a journey, then in what state and with whom and how long ago and why did he travel, and is there any news of him that he is alive, and did he go for a time or to live, and are any of them at the royal court or with any great man? And when they find out the truth they are to discuss it with the King's advisors.

And if the King's advisors do not want to give up all of those people of the sovereign, and start to deceive and say that those sovereign's people have left England by their own will for various foreign states for study and are not expected back soon, but they have learned that they are alive in England.

[p. 152] Then Aleksei Ivanovich and the Secretary Aleksei are to speak about these sovereign's people to the King himself, when they see him after the audience. And they are definitely to speak about the sovereign's people to the King and his close advisors, and also to John Merrick, that he should take care of this for his own interest. For they were given into his hand for study, and he should definitely hand over those who live here and should send for or write to those who are away, that they should come to London.

And Aleksei Ivanovich and the Secretary Aleksei will do the business of the sovereign and the land according to this instruction of the sovereign, and considering the affairs there, as God will direct them, and however is more profitable to the affairs of the sovereign and the land and to the honor and advancement of the sovereign's name. And between them there must definitely be no disagreement, so that their disagreement should not harm the affairs of the sovereign and the land.

[Memorandum: on a Russian Embassy to the Emperor]

And a memorandum to Aleksei Ivanovich Ziuzin and the Secretary Aleksei Vitovtov: If they meet the King's advisors and the King's advisors begin to ask them, that [because] in England there is a rumor from the merchants of the Empire, from those through whose imperial cities passed the emissary of the Moscow state to the Emperor[141] in the year 7120 [1611–1612], when in the Moscow state was the courier of the Emperor, Iusuf Grigor'ev, who came from the Persian [p. 153] Shah with the Persian emissary. And when that imperial courier was departing from the stol'nik and general, Prince Dmitrii Mikhailovich Pozharskii, and Prince Dmitrii said that now in the Moscow state there was great Christian bloodletting and war from the Polish King Sigismund, and the King had not given his son to the Moscow state, and betrayed his oath, and now in the Moscow state there was no sovereign and it was unknown how to remove the blood and make peace with the Polish King. And the Emperor's subject said to Prince Dmitrii: as soon as they want for the Moscow state the Emperor's brother, Maximilian, the Emperor would give the Moscow state his brother Maximilian and reconcile them with the Polish King in an eternal peace, and Christian blood would cease to flow.[142]

And Prince Dmitrii is supposed to have said, that if their sovereign the Emperor would give his brother to the Moscow state then they would much petition the Emperor and take his brother to the sovereignty with great joy. And Iusuf supposedly returned home and quickly told his sovereign the Emperor of Prince Dmitrii Pozharskii's words. And the Emperor hearing this was supposedly joyful and praised Prince Dmitrii Pozharskii and all the people of the Moscow state, that they had sought the family of his imperial majesty, and wrote about this to his brother Maximilian. And Maximilian supposedly replied that he was old and wanted to be in peace and pray to God and wanted to go nowhere to any sovereignty. And the Emperor supposedly ordered his subjects to tell Prince Dmitrii that the Emperor's father's [p. 154] brother had a son Philip,[143] and if they would like him for the Moscow state then he would give him. And for this matter the Emperor sent to the Moscow state his near advisor, also to the Polish King for the same purpose.

And is it true that Prince Dmitrii Pozharskii had sent to the Emperor in this manner? And if he did send, was this at the advice of the whole land of the Moscow state or from himself alone, or was it cast away to make trouble? And what is the situation now and is there any command about this?

And Aleksei Ivanovich and the Secretary Aleksei are to say to King James's advisors: "We know that Emperor Matthias's emissary Iusuf came to the Moscow state and by the order of the Tsar's majesty met the boyars of the Tsar's majesty. But we have heard nothing to the effect that Prince Dmitrii Pozharskii spoke with him, Iusuf, or that he spoke to him about inviting the Emperor's brother, Maximilian, to assume the Moscow sovereignty. And there was no thought in the minds of the boyars and generals of the Moscow state or of any people of the whole great Russian tsardom that they might choose a sovereign not of the Greek faith from another state.[144] And since your great sovereign King James and you accurately know about the injustice and violation of oath by the Polish King Sigismund toward the Moscow state, how he in violation of his oath burned and destroyed the Moscow state and wrecked God's churches and monasteries and desecrated the healing relics of many [p. 155] saints, and did much insult to our Orthodox Christian faith of the Greek law and spilled numberless quantities of Christian blood.

"And afterward, when by God's grace the boyars and gentry and soldiers of the Moscow state had assembled, and saw the great injustice and violation of oath and destruction of the Moscow state at the hands of the Polish King, they resolved to oppose him and with God's help cleansed the Moscow state of him. And all the people of the whole Russian tsardom made a strong compact of union and took an oath that they did not want the Polish King's son for all the Moscow state and all the great and most glorious sovereignties of the whole great Tsardom, nor any

Kings or Princes from any other states and that they would neither think nor take counsel about this.

"And that they would elect for the Moscow state a sovereign from the Russian clans which were related to our Great Sovereigns the Russian Tsars. And now by the grace of God by the election and petition of all the people of the whole great Russian state a sovereign Tsar has been created for the Moscow state and all the great and most glorious sovereignties, one from the family of our previous great just and noble sovereigns the Russian Tsars, of our Great Sovereign the Tsar and Grand Duke Fyodor Ivanovich Autocrat of all Russia of blessed memory.[145] And before his election as Tsar the boyars and generals and people of all sorts of ranks had no thought of Maximilian or of any other sovereign Kings or Princes besides him, the sovereign. [p. 156] If Prince Dmitrii Pozharskii without the advice of the whole land of the Moscow state spoke with the Emperor's subject about this, or if that imperial emissary or the translator, Eremei, who was sent from the land from the whole Russian tsardom to the Emperor with a letter, initiated all this from the desire of some reward from the Emperor, then you, councillors, may understand yourself that such great matters are not done without the advice of the whole land; and such great matters are not conducted by Prince Dmitrii Pozharskii alone without the advice of the whole land; and if the boyars and generals and all the soldiers had heard of such words of Prince Dmitrii Pozharskii to the effect that he had made such a proposal to the Emperor, then no one would tolerate this from him. This idea is impossible, and there is nothing here to believe, and it is indecent not only for you to speak of it but even to listen to it. And there is no reason for the Emperor to send his emissaries to our sovereign about this, for it is an impossible idea, unless there is some enmity between the sovereigns in such improper discussions. And it is improper that you councillors believe such ugly and seditious talk.

"And it is proper that you exert yourselves to take care that there be fraternal friendship, love, and unity between our Great Sovereigns—our Great Sovereign Tsar and Grand Duke Mikhail Fyodorovich Autocrat of all Russia and your Great Sovereign King James. And that we stand together against the enemies [p. 157] of the cross of Christ, the Muslims and other common enemies, so that the enemies of our sovereigns should be afraid, seeing strong fraternal love and loving communication between the sovereigns. And it is improper for us to speak about this."

And there is nothing more that should be said about this [by the Alekseis] with them.[146] And whatever the King's councillors say about this with them, Aleksei Ivanovich and the Secretary Aleksei are to write down secretly, so that none in their embassy should know about it; and when they return to Moscow they are to inform the sovereign Tsar and Grand Duke Mikhail Fyodorovich of all Russia. And if [the councillors] do not bring this up, then they are not to talk about it themselves.

[The safe conduct for English Ambassadors to Russia][147]

For the mercy of our God's grace, and in them may Christ visit us from above, in which to direct our feet to the path of peace, by the grace of our God glorified in the Trinity, from the Great Sovereign Tsar and Grand Duke Mikhail Fyodorovich Autocrat of all Russia, of Vladimir, Moscow, Novgorod, Tsar of Kazan', Tsar of Astrakhan', Tsar of Siberia, sovereign of Pskov and Grand Duke of Smolensk, Tver', Iugra, Perm', Viatka, Bulgaria, and others, sovereign and Grand Duke of the Novgorod of the lower land, of Chernigov, Riazan', Rostov, Iaroslavl', Belozero, Livonia, Udora, Obdora, Konda, and commander and sovereign of the whole northern land and [p. 158] sovereign and possessor of the Georgian and Kartli Tsars of the Iberian land and of the Circassian mountain Princes of the land of Kabarda and of many other states, to our beloved brother James King of England, Scotland, France, Ireland and others. And to us, the Great Sovereign Tsar and Grand Duke Mikhail Fyodorovich, Autocrat of all Russia, you our beloved brother should send your great ambassadors or emissaries; and your ambassadors and emissaries will come to our Tsar's majesty and return home freely with all their people and goods without any hindrance or delay by this our Tsar's letter; and this is our Tsar's letter of safe conduct for the ambassadors of our brother.

Written in the court of our sovereignty in the ruling city of Moscow in the month of June, in year from the creation of the world 7121 [1613].

[Letter: To James I from Tsar Michael, introducing Ziuzin and Secretary Vitovtov]

For the mercy of our God's sake, and in them may Christ visit us from above, in which to direct our feet to the path of peace, by the grace of our God glorified in the Trinity from the Great Sovereign Tsar and Grand Duke Mikhail Fyodorovich Autocrat of all Russia [ST] [p. 159] to our beloved brother King James of England, Scotland, France, Ireland, *et cetera*. We have sent to you, our beloved brother King James, our ambassadors, our gentleman and Governor of Shatsk, Aleksei Ivanovich Ziuzin, and the Secretary, Aleksei Vitovtov, to announce our sovereignty and speak about other good and great matters; and whatever the ambassadors might say in our name, believe that these are our words.[148]

Written in the court of our sovereignty in the ruling city of Moscow in the month of July in the year 7121 [1613] from the creation of the world.

The beginning, God's name in full and the sovereign's name and title up to Vladimir, and the border with figures, and the King's name and title, written on large Alexandrian paper in gold, the great seal in red wax [p. 160] under a cover. The secretary's signature on the back, "To our beloved brother King James, King of England, Scotland, France, Ireland, et cetera."

[Letter: To Christian IV from Tsar Michael regarding passage through Denmark]

For the mercy of our God's grace, and in them may Christ visit us from above, in which to direct our feet to the path of peace, by the grace of God glorified in the Trinity from the Great Sovereign Tsar and Grand Duke Mikhail Autocrat of all Russia [ST] to the Great Sovereign our beloved brother Christian, King of Denmark, Norway, Vandalia, and Gothia, Archduke of Schleswig, Holstein, Stormarn, and Dithmarschen, Count of Oldenburg and Delmenhorst, et cetera. We have sent to our beloved brother James, King of England, our ambassadors the gentleman and Governor of Shatsk, Aleksei Ivanovich Ziuzin, and the Secretary Aleksei Vitovtov, about various matters of interest to us, great Christian sovereigns, and to the quiet, peace, and profit of all Christendom. And if it happens to our [p. 161] ambassadors to travel from us or back to our Tsar's majesty through your Danish land or by your land by water, you should allow our ambassadors Aleksei Ivanovich and the Secretary Aleksei to pass through your land without hindrance, and to be escorted. And whatever people of your land might also happen to be in our states or if it happen that they travel through it, we will favor them and also allow them to pass without any hindrance. Written in the court of our sovereignty in the month of June in the year 7121 [1613] from the creation of the world.[149]

The beginning, God's name in full and the sovereign's name, and the King's name, and the border with figures written in gold, the great seal in red wax under a cover, and the secretary's signature on the back.

[Letter: To English and Scottish doctors and apothecaries from Tsar Michael]

For the sake of the mercy of our God's grace, in which may Christ visit us from above, and direct our feet on to the path of peace, by the grace of our God glorified in the Trinity, from the Great Sovereign Tsar and

Grand Duke Mikhail Fyodorovich Autocrat of all Russia, [ST] [p. 162] to doctors and apothecaries of the English and Scottish Kingdoms, whoever are experienced in the business of doctors and apothecaries. If they should wish to come to us, the Great Sovereign Tsar and Grand Duke Mikhail Fyodorovich Autocrat of all Russia, to serve by their trade in our state, then those doctors and apothecaries are to come to our states to the Tsar's majesty and return home freely, without any hindrance with all their servants and goods; and this is our Tsar's pass for them.[150]

Written in the court of our sovereignty in the ruling city of Moscow in the month of July of the year 7121 [1613] from the creation of the world.

The beginning, God's name and the sovereign's name, title up to Vladimir, and the border without figures written in gold on average paper, the great covered seal under a cover in red wax.

[Reference to a Letter to the English silversmiths from Tsar Michael]

The letter about the silversmiths to be the same.[151]

[Letter: concerning Ziuzin's salary]

[Memorandum: To Secretary Begichev concerning an order regarding Ziuzin's salary]

[Copy to Ziuzin]

On 22 June of the year 7121 [1613] by the order of the sovereign Tsar and Grand Duke Mikhail Fyodorovich of all Russia, a memorandum to the Secretary, Mikhail Begichev.[152] The sovereign Tsar and Grand Duke Mikhail Fyodorovich of all Russia ordered Aleksei Ivanovich Ziuzin to be sent to the English King, James, for the business of the sovereign and the land; and for that embassy he ordered him to be given his sovereignly yearly salary from the quarters [p. 163] for two years, for the present year 7121 and for the future year 7122 in full, according to the scale.

And by the order of the sovereign Tsar and Grand Duke Mikhail Fyodorovich of all Russia to the Secretary Mikhail Begichev the sovereignly salary from the quarters for the two years, the present year 7121 and ahead for the year 7122 is to be given to Aleksei Ivanovich for the English embassy, [and] is to be given according to the scale and in full ahead of all others so that he will not be waiting in Moscow for it and will meet the ships in the harbor on which he must sail. And he will soon have a release from the Sovereign from Moscow.

A like memorandum was given to Aleksei Ziuzin himself.

[An addition to the above memorandum:
To the Secretary of the Duma on an order
regarding Vitovtov's salary]

On June 28 of the year 7121 [1613] by the order of the sovereign Tsar and Grand Duke Mikhail Fyodorovich of all Russia, a memorandum to the Secretary, Petr Tret'iakov.[153] In the Galich quarter in the salary list for the past year '120 [1612–1613], in a memorandum signed by the Secretary Mikhail Novokshchenov, it is written: "By the order of the boyars a salary of one hundred and ten rubles has been established for the secretary Aleksei Vitovtov." An addition to the memorandum of the Secretary Mikhail Begichev.

[Letter: To the Governor and Secretary of Archangel from Tsar Michael, 3 July 1613]

From the sovereign Tsar and Grand Duke Mikhail Fyodorovich of all Russia to the town of Archangel on the Dvina, to the Governor Nikita Mikhailovich Pushkin and to our secretary Putilo Grigor'ev: We are sending our ambassadors and emissaries to announce our sovereignty to Denmark, to King Christian, Prince Ivan Boriatinskii and the Secretary Gavrilo Bogdanov; to England to King James, Aleksei Ziuzin and the Secretary Aleksei Vitovtov; to the Roman Emperor, Stepan [p. 164] Ushakov and the Secretary Semoi Zaborovskii. And they are to go from Archangel to those states by sea on ships.

And we have written to you before about the ships several times: when the merchant ships come from abroad, from the Empire, Denmark, England, and other lands near them, then you are ordered to tell the merchants of those lands that we, the Great Sovereign, are sending our ambassadors and emissaries to Matthias, the Roman Emperor, to King James in England, and to the Danish King Christian to announce our sovereignty.[154]

And the merchants of those lands or of neighboring lands are to prepare three ships for our ambassadors and emissaries so that they can sail to those lands and thereby serve our Tsar's majesty. And at the same time it is definitely ordered to you to take care of commandeering a ship from English merchants for the ambassador to England, a Danish ship for the ambassador to Denmark, and for the ambassador to the Emperor an imperial ship or ships from merchants of other lands which will go to those lands or near them. And you are to take care of the ships without delay so that our ambassadors and emissary will not be waiting in Archangel.

And you are ordered to write to us quickly and tell us from which merchants you have commandeered the ships for the ambassadors and the emissary.

And you have not written up until July 4 in reply to our one previous letter to tell us how many ships of what states have come, and if there are in Archangel any Danish or imperial ships or ships of any neighboring states [p. 165] and what has been your action about the ships. And our ambassadors and emissary to England, Denmark, and the Empire have left us and are now on the road and will arrive in Archangel soon. And when you receive this letter, and if any Danish or imperial ships have come to Archangel then, in accord with our previous letter as well as this one, you should look after three ships for our ambassadors and emissaries: for the ambassador to England, a ship from the English merchants; for Denmark, a Danish ship; and for the Empire, an imperial ship or ships from merchants of other lands that will sail to those lands or by them.

And you should definitely not show neglect of this matter; and you should look after the three ships and commandeer and prepare them soon so that the ships are commandeered and prepared for the arrival of the ambassadors and are ready so that our ambassadors will not wait in Archangel or miss the navigation[155] and there will not be any damage to our business and that of the land.

And you must write to us in Moscow telling us from which merchants and traders of which states you have commandeered ships for the ambassadors and the emissary, and what are their names and on what terms, and you are to send the report to the Ambassadorial Office to our secretary, Petr Tret'iakov.

Written in Moscow 3 July in the year 7121 [1613].

Sent with Afanasii Tolochanov.

[Letter: To Tsar Michael from the Governor and Secretary of Archangel, 9 June 1613]

And on the 9th day of June, 7121 [1613], the Governor Nikita Push-kin, and the Secretary, Putilo Grigor'ev, wrote from the Dvina from Archangel to the Sovereign Tsar and Grand Duke Mikhail Fyodorovich of all Russia that they called to themselves the ambassadors of King James of the English land, [p. 166] John Merrick and William Russell, and the merchant, Fabian Smith, and said to them that the sovereign Tsar and Grand Duke Mikhail Fyodorovich of all Russia is sending his sovereignly ambassadors and emissaries to announce his sovereignty to England to their sovereign King James and to Denmark to King Christian and to the Roman Emperor.[156] And they are to go to those states from Archangel by sea. And the merchants of those lands or of such lands as lie on their borders are to prepare three ships for the ambassadors and emissaries so that the ambassadors and emissaries may go to those lands and by this they may serve the Tsar's majesty.

And the English emissaries, John Merrick and associates, petitioned the sovereign Tsar and Grand Duke Mikhail Fyodorovich of all Russia and said to them that they wanted to show their service to the Tsar[157]; when the sovereign's ambassadors and emissaries come to Archangel, then their ship will be ready for the sovereign's emissary who will go to their sovereign King James. And for those the sovereign's emissaries who will go to the Danish King and the Roman Emperor, their ship will also be ready. And if the sovereign's emissaries to the Empire and Denmark will go on different ships, then they will give a ship each to the emissaries to the Empire and Denmark. And the sovereign's emissaries can go to Hamburg in the same ship, since there is no way for either of them to avoid Hamburg. And from Hamburg the road is on land to both states, to Denmark and to the Roman Emperor, and Hamburg is a city of the Empire. And from Hamburg to the Dane is three days travel. And in the past [p. 167] the sovereign's ambassadors and emissaries went to those states on their English ships.

And in their same report it was written to them in the sovereign's letter: that it has become known to the sovereign that the Danish King's soldiers have gone to fight against the land of Sweden; and that they should find out from anyone who comes to the Dvina, from the Germans and other sorts of people who come to the Dvina, and they should be on purpose sent from Archangel to those places to find out what is heard of the Dane and the Swede. Where now is the Swedish King [Gustav] Adolf and his brother? Do the Danish troops war in Sweden, and if they do, in what places? And is the Dane stronger than the Swede and what is to be expected between them? And when they have found this out they are to write quickly to the sovereign with an express courier. And they asked them, John Merrick and his associates about the Dane and the Swede.[158]

And John Merrick and his associates told them that in the present year, 7121 [1612–1613], the Swedish King [Gustav] Adolf sent, petitioning their sovereign King James that their sovereign King James should make peace between the Swedish King and the Danish. And in response to the Swede a nobleman was sent from their sovereign King James to the Dane with mercenaries. And that nobleman with all the mercenaries had returned to England, they knew truly about it. And whatever soldiers the Swede had collected against the Dane were still assembled, and those soldiers had not been disbanded; and they do not know why they were not disbanded and where they will campaign. And John Merrick and his associates told them in conversation that they had heard that the Danish King seeks to marry [p. 168] the Swedish King, [Gustav] Adolf's, sister.[159]

[Letter: To Ziuzin and Secretary Vitovtov
from Tsar Michael, July [no day] 1613][160]

From the Tsar and Grand Duke Mikhail Fyodorovich of all Russia to Aleksei Ivanovich Ziuzin and to our Secretary Aleksei Vitovtov. In the present year, 7121 [1613], on July 9, the Governor, Nikita Pushkin, and the Secretary, Putilo Grigor'ev, together with Griaznoi Ershovskii wrote to us from Archangel that the English King James's merchants, John Merrick and associates, told them that in the present year, 7121 [1613], the Swedish King, [Gustav] Adolf, sent to petition their sovereign King James that their sovereign King James should make peace between him, King [Gustav] Adolf, and the Danish king, Christian. And supposedly their sovereign King James had made peace between the Swedish King and the Danish.[161] And in response to the Swede's request a gentleman was sent from their sovereign King James with mercenaries. And their sovereign's gentleman and the mercenaries had all returned to England, and they know all this for a fact. And the soldiers whom the Swede had collected against the Dane have not been disbanded. And they do not know why they have not been disbanded and against whom they will campaign. And in Archangel they should live cautiously. And John Merrick and his associates in conversation said that they had heard that the Danish King seeks to marry the sister of the Swedish King.

And we knew nothing of this news before your departure. And in our instruction to you it is written: When you come [p. 169] to England find out truly if the English King James and the Danish King Christian have made peace with the Swedish King for many years and ratified a treaty with their oaths, and at the audience and after the audience in conversation with the councillors list the injustices of the Polish and Swedish Kings.

And that King James, remembering the fraternal loving communications of the previous Great Sovereign Russian Tsars with his ancestors, the English Kings and Queen Elizabeth, and now wishing to be in fraternal friendship and love and communication with us, the Great Sovereign, he should help against the Polish King Sigismund with treasure, money and gold, and goods, and all sorts of artillery. And King James should write to the Swedish King [Gustav] Adolf that he should cease his injustices; and he should return to our Tsar's majesty the towns of our Novgorod state which he has taken in violation of his oath after exchanging ambassadors and emissaries. And he should be in friendship and communication with our Tsar's majesty, according to the peace treaty under our uncle of blessed memory the Tsar and Grand Duke Fyodor Ivanovich Autocrat of all Russia with the Kingdom of Sweden.[162] And he, the Swedish king, should stand with us, the Great Sovereign against the Polish king and be with us in peace and quiet.

And about this in our instruction to you it is [p. 170] written: If the King's advisors and councillors begin to say to you, have you any instructions from us how their sovereign King James is to help us with treasure against the Polish King, and what kind of treasure, and in what manner we are to stand together against him, and how are you instructed about treaties and unity and how are you to do all these things and establish and strengthen them.

And when, if God grants, you will see King James in England, or somewhat after the audience you chance to see King James or his councillors and advisors, and to speak with him about help about the Polish King Sigismund and the Swedish King [Gustav] Adolf, then you will speak according to our instruction and John Merrick's news, after finding out truly if the Swede has made peace with the Dane, and on what terms they have made peace and if John Merrick's news is accurate.

And adapting to the terms of the peace between them, you are to speak to the King or his councillors about aid so that King James, knowing the injustice of the King and lords councillors and the Swedish King, should show us fraternal heartfelt love and good wishes and help us against the Polish King Sigismund with his royal treasure, with gold and money and dollars and all sorts of artillery, whatever he has that would be useful in our state. And he should send to the Swedish King, [Gustav] Adolf, ambassadors or emissaries, and about his injustices which were inflicted on the Moscow state by his father, King Charles, and himself, [p. 171] King [Gustav] Adolf, he should write in a letter so that he, King [Gustav] Adolf, should cease his injustices and correct himself before us, the Great Sovereign, and send to our Tsar's majesty his own ambassadors or emissaries. And he should return the ancestral towns of our state, Novgorod and Korela and others, which his father, King Charles, and he himself, King [Gustav] Adolf, have taken unjustly, to our Tsar's majesty in their entirety. And he should order all his people to leave Novgorod and the Novgorod district and all our towns and he should look for something better for himself. And we, the Great Sovereign, will order our boyars to speak with King [Gustav] Adolf's ambassadors about all the things that have been done from his side, and how in the future things should be between us and our states, and to establish however is best in each case. And what is ordered to you in the instruction to say to the King's men about help against the Polish King Sigismund, then King James should stand together with us against the Swedish King [Gustav] Adolf because of his many injustices and should not communicate with the Polish and the Swedish Kings to harm us and our state. And he should write to the

Danish King Christian, that the Danish King Christian should stand together with us against the Swedish King.[163]

And you should speak to the royal councillors and advisors about help against the Polish King according to the articles [p. 172] that are written in our instruction and you should ask about help against the Swedish King, so that King James should help against him and stand with us together against him. And you should not talk about other things that are against the Swedish King [Gustav] Adolf, their peace treaty with the Danish King Christian, but you should speak about the Swedish article, so that King James, knowing the many injustices of the previous King, Swedish King Charles, and the present King, [Gustav] Adolf, against us and our states, should send to him his emissary.

And he should write in his letter truly about all his injustices so that he will cease all his injustices and correct himself before us, the Great Sovereign, and our states and send to us his ambassadors or emissaries. And we, the Great Sovereign, will order our boyars to speak with his ambassadors and establish peace between us, the Great Sovereign, and the Swedish King [Gustav] Adolf and our Great Sovereignties and the Swedish kingdom and bring quiet and be in friendship and love and stand together against all our enemies. And if the King's people start to talk to you about other articles, about the Swedish matter, then you, knowing that the Danish King has made peace with the Swedish, are to speak depending on the peace terms between the Dane and the Swede; [p. 173] and if King James has reconciled them, then this must not be displeasing to King James, depending on the state of affairs there, as God will suggest to you. Written in Moscow on July [nd] of the year 7121 [1613].

[Memorandum: To the Duma Secretary from Tsar Mikhail Regarding the English Doctor, Baldwin Hamey]

On July 29 of 7121 [1613] by decree of the sovereign Tsar and Grand Duke Mikhail Fyodorovich of all Russia a memorandum to the Duma Secretary Petr Tret'iakov. He is to send a letter to England to the doctor, Baldwin Hamey, that the sovereign Tsar and Grand Duke Mikhail Fyodorovich of all Russia, remembering his previous service to himself and his father and mother,[164] if he wishes to come to the sovereign, then he should come. And the sovereign will favor him for his previous industry and service. And if he wants to return home to his own country, then the Tsar will favor him and let him go. And the Secretary, Petr Tret'iakov, is to send the letter immediately without delay. Signature of the Secretary Ivan Fyodorov.

[Safe Conduct for Dr. Hamey to travel to Russia]

For the sake of the mercy of our God's grace, in which may Christ visit us from above, into which may he direct our feet to the path of peace, by the grace of our God glorified in the Trinity, from the Great Sovereign Tsar and Grand Duke Mikhail Fyodorovich, Autocrat of all Russia [ST], [p. 174] to Baldwin Hamey, of the English and Scottish Kingdom, as you were before in the great Moscow state and we, the Great Sovereign, remembering your previous service to us and to our father and our mother, declare to you our Tsar's word of mercy. If you wish to come to us, the Great Sovereign Tsar and Grand Duke Mikhail Fyodorovich, Autocrat of all Russia, to serve in our state by your trade, then you may come freely to our Tsar's majesty to our states and return without any hindrance with your servants and goods. And this our Tsar's letter is your safe conduct. Written in the ruling city of Moscow of our state on July [nd], 7121 [1613].

August 1 the Secretary Petr Tret'iakov gave the safe conduct himself above to Boris Mikhailovich Saltykov.

The letter is written on average paper, God's name and the sovereign's title written in gold up to Vladimir. A covered seal under a cover on red wax.

And on 20 October of the year 7123 [1614] the ambassadors of Tsar Mikhail Fyodorovich [ST], Aleksei Ivanovich Ziuzin and the secretary Aleksei Vitovtov, who had been sent from the sovereign to the English King James, returned to Moscow. And they brought to the sovereign from King James a petition and they gave the sovereign [p. 175] a report of their embassy, how they did the sovereign's business with the King.

And the ambassadors, Aleksei Ziuzin and the Secretary Aleksei Vitovtov, gave the sovereign a letter from the English King James with the King's seal and said that King James had sent his loving letter to the Great Sovereign, the Tsar's majesty.

And this is the report of the sovereign's ambassadors, Aleksei Ziuzin and the Secretary Aleksei Vitovtov.

And a translation of the letter which they gave to the sovereign from the King is glued on after this report.[165]

[The Report]

[p. 175] On the 30th of June of the year 7121 (1613) the Sovereign Tsar and Grand Duke Mikhail Fyodorovich, Autocrat of all Russia, sent to England to his brother King James the ambassadors of his majesty the Tsar, the Gentleman and Viceroy of Shatsk, Aleksei Ivanovich Ziuzin and the Secretary Aleksei Vitovtov, for his sovereign's and the land's business.[166]

And according to the instructions of the Sovereign Tsar and Grand Duke, Mikhail Fyodorovich, of all Russia, the ambassadors, Aleksei Ivanovich Ziuzin and the Secretary Aleksei Vitovtov, came to the harbor of Archangel on the 22nd of August and spoke to the Governor and Secretary that they should, according to the sovereign's decree, and the letter (which sovereign's letter had been sent to them about their departure), that they should release them, the ambassadors, into England on English ships without delay.[167] And the ambassador sent to the English merchants, John Merrick and William Russell,[168] so that they might prepare the ship for them and at the same hour the Governor and Secretary told the ambassadors that the English merchants have the English ships ready for them. And the English merchants, with John Merrick, came [p. 176] to the ambassadors on the same day. And John Merrick said to the ambassadors: "We have prepared the English ship for you the ambassadors to sail upon according to the decree of Tsar Mikhail Fyodorovich [ST], and according to the letter which was sent about this matter to me, John; and it is for you to inspect the ship."[169] And the ambassadors themselves rode to the ship and inspected it and with them were the merchants John Merrick and William Russell, and the English merchant, Fabian Smith.[170] And they prepared a place for the ambassadors on the ship where there would be room for themselves, their servants, and supplies. And when the ambassadors rode from the ship to their residence the same merchants, John Merrick and his associates, accompanied them and were with the ambassadors in their dwelling. And the ambassadors released William Russell and Fabian Smith, and they kept John Merrick with them for news, because it had been ordered to the ambassadors according to Tsar Mikhail Fyodorovich's [ST] instruction, when they had come to Archangel to find out from anyone about the English King, James, and the Danish King, Christian, and the Swedish King, [Gustavus] Adolph[us]. And what now is the relationship between King James and the Swedish King?[171] And what is the relationship between the Danish King and the Swedish King? Are they at peace or not at peace? And what is expected in the future between them? And when they have found out it was ordered to write about it to Tsar Mikhail Fyodorovich [ST].

And the ambassadors asked John [Merrick] about the news and John Merrick said to the ambassadors: "In the past the previous Swedish King, Charles, had sent to their Great Sovereign King James asking King James to make peace between them and the Danish King, and in what year he sent to James he does not remember.[172] And the Swedish King entrusted himself to the will of their sovereign, King James, as he would decide between them. And King [p. 177] James had supposedly sent about this matter to the Danish King asking him to be in peace with the Swedish King. And at that time the Danish King did not want to be in peace with the Swedish King. And after King Charles [sent to James] supposedly the Danish King had sent to King James asking for help against Charles's son, the Swedish King Adolph, so that he [173] would permit Englishmen to serve [the Dane] for hire, and their sovereign, King James, permitted his people to fight against the Swedish King, and he released these soldiers with his[174] boyar, Lord Willoughby,[175] in the present year, 7121 [summer, 1613]. And the Swedish King, [Gustav] Adolph, and the Danish King, Christian, communicating between themselves, made peace by themselves, agreeing that the Swedish King should pay the costs of the Danish King, for the costs of the expedition where the Danish King fought against him with mercenaries and took cities. And they agreed among themselves in respect to the cities which the Dane took from the Swede that the Danish King should rule those cities until the Swedish King should pay him for the hire of troops and his expenditures.[176] And the boyar of the English King James who had been sent into Sweden, Lord Willoughby, and his mercenaries, came to England when John [Merrick] was there and he, John, heard this news about the Swedish and Danish Kings from these English mercenaries."

And John Merrick told the ambassadors: "And an Englishman called Vil'ianko,[177] of his, the ambassador John's service, came to Archangel and that Vil'ianko had been among the English mercenaries with the Danish King, and stayed behind with the Danish king and that Vil'ianko had come from the Danish King after the English mercenaries and that Vil'ianko told him, John, that the Danish King, Christian, was seeking to marry the sister of the Swedish King, [Gustav] Adolph, and he does not know for sure whether the Danish King succeeded in marrying [p. 178] the Swedish King's sister or not.[178] And he, John, knows no more news of the Swedish and Danish Kings."

And the ambassadors wrote to the Sovereign Tsar and Grand Duke, Mikhail Fyodorovich, of all Russia, in Moscow, at the same time from Archangel about the news that John had told them. And there were no other foreigners besides John to ask about news because all the ships had left Archangel for home before the arrival of the ambassadors.[179]

On August 29th the ambassadors boarded the ship and sailed from Archangel toward England on the same day. And with them there were on the ship the following Russians: the undersecretary, Andrei Semenov, and the translator taken in Archangel from among the interpreters who are Moscow Germans,[180] Andrei Andreev, who knows how to translate

English,[181] and the ambassadors' servants. And on the ship with the ambassadors were the following Germans: the Englishman Captain, the merchant, Ul'ian Ul'ianov Voi,[182] and with him altogether twenty-four companions [illegible]. And they came to the sea by the mouth of the Pudoga[183] on the 30th of August. At the mouth a contrary wind held them and they stood until the 4th of September of the year 7122 [1613].

And on another ship, together with the ambassadors' [ship] went the merchants, John Merrick and William Russell. And on the 4th of September, after the contrary wind passed, they went out into the open sea and sailed with a favorable wind in three days to Kildin Island; and on September 7th a contrary wind arose at sea and drove the ships of the ambassadors and merchants, John Merrick, and his companions, along the sea.

And on the 13th of September, on the eve of the Exaltation of the Cross,[184] the ships were driven apart and they sailed on separately. And they were driven at sea by great winds. Up until the 19th of September [p. 179] their voyage was with great difficulty and they did not see the shore on either side. And on September the 19th they saw, according to the ship's sign chart the North Cape, and from the North Cape they sailed through the open sea with a favorable wind four days, and then they met a great contrary wind and were carried about on the sea for three weeks. And at that time on many occasions on the ships there was great distress to the ambassadors and other people; and the ship was carried past Scotland.

On October 13th they saw the coast of England, Flamborough Head, and they barely made it to the coast. And the same day they came to the town of Whitby. And it was not possible to go on to London because of the contrary wind. And they stayed at that town for three days, and the officials of that town sent to the ambassadors with supplies. And the people there told the ambassadors about the merchant, John Merrick and his associates: that they had been carried on the ship to the same town of Whitby three days before the arrival of the ambassadors[185] and that at sea they supposedly had been carried toward Denmark. And at that town they had disembarked from the ship and rode on to London by land in carriages. And that to London from the town of Whitby it was 250 versts.[186] And John Merrick and his associates told them about the ambassadors and were distressed that they had been carried about at sea and that they yet had no news about them.

And on the 15th of October the ambassadors sent to London in carriages the interpreter whom John Merrick had given them on the ship, Richard Finch,[187] and they ordered him when he had come to London to announce the ambassadors' arrival [p. 180] to the King's advisors; that

they should announce to their Sovereign King James about the ambassadors.

And the ambassador sent him with this news because the merchants,
John Merrick and William Russell, when they came to land, would say
that the ambassadors had been carried about at sea and that they yet had
no knowledge of them and now they had no news of the ambassadors.
And it would be known to King James and his advisors that the ambassadors had arrived at the English coast.

And on October 16th the ambassadors sailed from the town of Whitby
[south] along the coast [which when looking at the map is] on the left,
and the coast was on the right, and they went passed the town of Scarborough and passed the settlements of Blakeney and Yarmouth. And
from the town of Whitby to the settlement at Yarmouth is about 200
versts. And opposite that settlement of Yarmouth, at night, the ship was
carried onto the sand, and was stuck on the sand a long time.[188] And the
Captain and the Germans told the ambassadors that these places are
unlucky and that whatsoever ships are carried to these places great harm
happens. And at that time the ambassadors and other people were in
great and horrible distress seeing such divine hindrance. And the Germans on the ship began to pull up the decks to lighten the ship, and the
all generous God showed his love and the ship sailed on and passed
the town of Orford and came against the town of Harwich. And from the
settlement of Yarmouth to Harwich is about 75 versts. And from Harwich to the mouth of the Thames is about 50 versts.

And all these towns which they passed are stone and their settlements
are large, and between the towns along the seacoast are many large and
small villages, estates of the King's boyars, and appanage princes, and
other advisors and [p. 181] gentlemen. And in these large and small
villages are built great and tall stone churches; and all the houses are
stone.

And on October 19th coming from the sea they entered the Thames,
and they passed the town of Queenborough going along the Thames 40
versts. And they stood 3 versts from the town of Gravesend across from
the settlement of Tilbury. And they stayed on the ship waiting for a
message from the King from London.

On October 21st the English interpreter, Richard Finch, whom they
sent to London from Whitby, came to the ambassadors on the ship and
said: "When I came from you, the ambassadors, to London our great
Sovereign King James was not in London. He is entertaining himself in
his royal village 40 versts from London, and his advisors are with him.[189]
And now in London is Sir Thomas (the son of Thomas Smith),
Okol'nichii of the inner Council to whom ambassadorial affairs are en-

trusted.[190] He was sent as an ambassador in Moscow by our Sovereign King James in the time of the Tsar and Grand Duke Boris Fyodorovich, of all Russia. And I told him about you the ambassadors and he, Sir Thomas, immediately, with industry, himself went on your behalf to his Royal Majesty and, having been with our Sovereign King James, and having returned to London, he sent me to you with news. And he ordered me to say that in accord with the royal instructions the merchant, John Merrick, will come to you tomorrow on the ship and he is to go with you to the town of Gravesend, and there will be a meeting for you from our Great Sovereign King James in the town of Gravesend."

[p. 182] And on the 22nd of October the merchant John Merrick came from London to the ambassadors on the ship in small boats, with him were six English soldiers, and he said to the ambassadors: "Our Great Sovereign King James, the son of Andrew,[191] has ordered us to do you honor and ask about your health and ask whether or not you have come by the sea to England, to his Royal Majesty, in good health." And the ambassador petitioned for the King's allowance for themselves.[192] And they said to John: "That by the grace of God we have come from the Great Sovereign Tsar and Grand Duke Mikhail Fyodorovich, Autocrat of all Russia, from the country of his Tsar's Majesty to these places, his Royal Majesty's country of England, in good health, as God has granted it. And as to the fact that there were certain difficulties at sea, that was God's affair that He had, according to His holy will, softened and granted His grace."

And John Merrick said to the ambassadors: "Our Great Sovereign King James, the son of Andrew, has ordered me to say to you that you should come to the town of Gravesend and be there for a time until the King sends for you, until he sends his near boyar or okol'nichii to meet you. And now it will not be possible to send to meet you quickly because our Sovereign is living in his royal villages for his entertainments 40 versts or more from London. And until that time our Sovereign has ordered me, John, to be with you in Gravesend and to satisfy you with all manner of food. And it is the order of our Sovereign that you should be honored and want for nothing."[193]

And the ambassadors said to John: "We hear of the allowance of your Great Sovereign King James to us. We carry out his orders and will go to the town of Gravesend and industriously await his royal [p. 183] allowance and message to us in the future."

And before John Merrick came, on the 21st of October, a great warship of the King came and anchored near the ambassadors' ship. And when John came and sat with the ambassadors, at that time there came from that royal ship the King's General, Captain Algerd,[194] and with him twelve soldiers, and he said to the ambassadors: "According to the decree of our Great Sovereign King James I have come to you with soldiers and artillery to defend you from thieves." And the ambassadors asked the General, the Captain and the merchant, John Merrick, "From whom are they being defended and what kind of thieves do they have?" And the Captain and John said to the ambassadors: "Thieves collect from various countries, wandering vagabonds who sail on the sea in ships, come into the Thames and attack trading ships, and sneak up at night and, without being noticed, they kill people and take their belongings. And for this reason our Sovereign sends his royal warships to defend against them and to go after them and we seek them out and fight them."[195] And the ambassadors feasted the General, the Captain, and the soldiers who were with him and released him with love.

And John Merrick said to the ambassadors: "It is time for you to leave the ships and go in small boats to Gravesend," and the ambassadors, descending from the ship, went in the boats to the town of Gravesend, and the merchant, John Merrick, and the English men with him. And at the same time from the royal warship and from the other ambassadorial ship there was a salute from all of the artillery.

And when they came to the town of Gravesend [p. 183] at the same time from the town and from the watchtowers which stand below the town on both sides of the Thames, there was a salute from a great multitude of artillery. And their watchtowers were constructed before the town of Gravesend (one on the edge of the settlement and the other across from it on the other side of the river) against the attack from soldiers of other lands. And the artillery on them is numerous and large, and around these towers, below, and along the parapet, is also a great deal of artillery. And when they came to the shore the commander of that town,[196] and with him two hundred or more soldiers and merchants and all sorts of local people with him, met the ambassadors at the boats. And bowing to the ambassadors they asked them about their health and they followed the ambassadors to their lodgings. And they put the ambassador in the town of Gravesend at the merchants' yard. And there was sufficient food and they remained there until the 25th of October.

And on the 25th of October the royal *Okol'nichii* of the near Council, Sir Thomas, the son of Thomas Smith,[197] came to the town of Gravesend from King James and with him the royal gentlemen: his brother (Sir Thomas's brother) the Knight, Richard,[198] and Sir John Davies,[199] and Sir George Hayward[200] and Sir John Woodward[201] and their associates, altogether twelve men besides servants. And there was a meeting for Sir Thomas from the local commander[202] and all the English, with honor. And having come, he remained in his lodgings.

And at the same time Sir Thomas sent to the ambassadors the King's gentleman, their knight, Lord Knyvet.[203] And having come he did honor to the ambassador from Sir Thomas and said: "Sir Thomas (the son of Thomas Smith), the *Okol'nichii* of the near Council of his Royal Majesty has sent me and ordered me to tell you that he has sent to you, the ambassadors of the Tsar's Majesty, from our Great Sovereign King James, and he wants to see you whenever it is convenient for you."

And the ambassadors ordered Sir Thomas, with the King's gentleman, their Lord Knyvet, to come to them to their lodgings.

[p. 185] And at the same time Sir Thomas, and with him the King's gentlemen, came to the ambassadors to the lodging and, having taken off their hats they greeted the ambassadors with their hands.

And Sir Thomas delivered a speech to the ambassadors from King James his Sovereign: "Our Great Sovereign King James, the son of Andrew, having heard about you the ambassadors of your Great Sovereign Tsar and Grand Duke, Mikhail Fyodorovich, Autocrat of all Russia, his Tsar's Majesty, that you were sent from his Tsar's Majesty to our sovereign, he was glad about it and, wanting to see the fraternal love and friendship to himself of his brother, your Great Sovereign Tsar and Grand Duke, Mikhail Fyodorovich, Autocrat of all Russia, his Tsar's Majesty, he sent to you the ambassadors, me, his *Okol'nichii*. And he ordered me to meet you and ask about the Great Sovereign Tsar and Grand Duke, Mikhail Fyodorovich, Autocrat of all Russia, about his Tsar's health."

And the ambassadors said to Sir Thomas: "When we left our Great Sovereign Tsar and Grand Duke, Mikhail Fyodorovich, Autocrat of all Russia and sovereign and possessor of many states, his Tsar's Majesty, by God's grace our sovereign, his Tsar's Majesty, in his own great and glorious states of the Russian tsardom, was in good health."

And Sir Thomas said: "Our sovereign his Royal Majesty King James, the son of Andrew, hearing about you the ambassadors, that your voyage was difficult and slow, ordered me to ask about your health. Have you arrived now in good health, [p. 186] or not? And how have you been in his Royal Majesty's town of Gravesend? And was there sufficient food and was there anything wanting? And now our sovereign has ordered you to come to his royal and great city of London, and has sent royal boats for you, and ordered me, Sir Thomas, to accompany you to London; and that I am to be in London with you until his royal decree, and to satisfy you in everything. And our sovereign is not in London, he is entertaining himself in his royal villages."[204]

And the ambassadors petitioned for the King's favor to themselves that he had been ordered to ask about, and their healths. And they said to Sir

Thomas: "That by the grace of God with the grant of the Sovereign Tsar and Grand Duke Mikhail Fyodorovich, Autocrat of all Russia, his Tsar's Majesty, when we came from the state of Moscow to these places of his royal Majesty of England, we have come, God willing, in health. And whatever grief there was at sea, that was in God's power and here we, being in the town of Gravesend, are all satisfied according to the King's favor and ready to go to London."

And having said their speech, they sat down according to their places. Aleksei Ivanovich sat on the right hand and Sir Thomas on the left, and across from Sir Thomas sat the Secretary, Aleksei, and below them the King's gentlemen, Sir Thomas's brother, Sir Richard, with his associates. And Sir Thomas, having sat a bit, said to the ambassadors that: "you should go to the City of London early in the morning, at high tide (when the water comes from the sea up river)."[205] And Sir Thomas spoke and greeted the ambassadors by their hands, and with him the King's gentlemen went [p. 187] to their lodgings.

And on October 26th Sir Thomas and his associates came to the ambassadors at their lodgings and said that it was time to go. And at that time the ambassadors went to the ships and with them as conductor[206] were Sir Thomas and the King's gentlemen,[207] and the merchant John Merrick. And Sir Thomas walked on the left hand of the ambassadors and the gentlemen and the commander of the town[208] and the merchant John Merrick walked behind the ambassadors. And on both sides stood soldiers and the local merchants and all sorts of traders and other people. And the ambassadors sat in the boats in the great place and with them sat Sir Thomas and the gentlemen and they went to London. And on the same day the ambassadors came to London, and as they began to come into the royal docks where the King embarks on the boats, and to come out of the boats, at that time from the town there was a great salute from numerous large cannons. And from all ships they fired from all guns for a long time.[209]

And when the salute ceased, Sir Thomas and his associates, and the merchant John Merrick said to the ambassadors: "Such a great salute was given according to royal command for the Great Sovereign Tsar and Grand Duke Mikhail Fyodorovich, Autocrat of Russia, his Tsar's majesty, our sovereign wishing to see the Tsar's fraternal love and friendship to himself; and to give honor to you the ambassador of the Great Sovereign. And besides you, the ambassadors of his Tsar's Majesty, in our memory there was no such honor given as this great salute for you to any ambassadors and emissaries from whatever state had come to England. Our Great Sovereign King James has ordered this honor to be done to you the ambassadors of the Tsar's Majesty above the ambassadors and emissaries [p. 188] of all states. And at the dock as you disembark from the boats our sovereign has ordered his royal highness' near boyar and Viceroy of Ireland, Sir William Lord Danvers, with the Knight [Sir Thomas], and the gentlemen,[210] and all the best people to meet you with great honor. And they are awaiting you now on the shore at the dock, and are awaiting your arrival."

And as the ambassadors came to the dock and disembarked from the boats at the Tower[211] on the shore the ambassadors were met by the King's boyar and Viceroy of Ireland, Sir William Danvers, and with him many knights, and gentlemen, and gentry, and aldermen in bright velvet and scarlet dress with gold chains, riding on fine horses and stallions,[212] and on foot stood the better and middle merchants, and the townspeople, up until the royal bodyguards [who were in] bright dress with gilded halberds, about one hundred and fifty men. And on their dress, on both sides, front and back, the royal insignias are impressed and the borders are gilded. And many people of all sorts were there at that time.[213]

And Sir William Lord Danvers descended and, having removed his hat, he greeted the ambassadors by their hands and spoke to the ambassadors from his sovereign King James, a speech, with the title [of the King]: "Our Great Sovereign James, son of Andrew, King of England, Scotland, France, Ireland, etc., loving his brother, your Great Sovereign Tsar and Grand Duke Mikhail Fyodorovich, Autocrat of all Russia, hearing about his Tsar's Majesty, rejoiced and, wanting to see the Tsar's fraternal love and friendship to himself and granting favors to you the ambassadors, sent me, his boyar, to you. And he ordered me to meet [p. 189] you with great honor and to ask you about the Great Sovereign Tsar and Grand Duke Mikhail Fyodorovich, Autocrat of all Russia, about his Tsar's health."

And the ambassadors said to Sir William, Lord [Danvers]: "When we left our Great Sovereign Tsar and Grand Duke Mikhail Fyodorovich, Autocrat of all Russia, our Great Sovereign his Tsar's Majesty, in his great and glorious states, God willing, was in good health."

And Sir William, Lord [Danvers], said to the ambassadors: "Our Great Sovereign King James, the son of Andrew, has ordered me to ask you, the ambassadors of the Tsar's Majesty, about your health, for hearing about you from his emissaries, John Merrick and his associates, that your voyage was very grievous—and did you come to his Royal[214] Majesty's state of England in health?" And the ambassadors petitioned for the King's grace to themselves[215] and they said to Sir William [Lord Danvers]: "That according to God's grace that since we left our Great Sovereign Tsar and Grand Duke Mikhail Fyodorovich, Autocrat of all Russia, sovereign and possessor of many states, by his Tsar's Majesty we have come to his Royal

Majesty's state of England in good health. And what grief there was at sea, that is God's affair."

And after that Sir William [Lord Danvers] said to the ambassadors: "Our sovereign his Royal Majesty wanting to do you honor for his beloved brother, the Great Sovereign the Tsar's Majesty, has sent to you his royal coaches and sledges, and he ordered me to accompany you to the lodgings where, according to his royal order, a yard has been constructed, and as the conductors [p. 190] he ordered to be with you the *Okol'nichii* of his royal near Council, Sir Thomas, the son of Thomas Smith, and you are to get into the coaches and go to their lodgings."

And the ambassadors petitioned for the King's favor. And they sat in the coaches in the great place and on their sides, at the doors, Sir William, Lord Danvers and Sir Thomas sat by Aleksei Ivanovich and on the other side by the doors sat the King's gentleman, Sir John Davies and John Merrick. And with the Secretary Aleksei, in the coach at the doors, sat the royal gentlemen, Sir Richard and the son of Thomas, the brother of Sir Thomas. And Sir George [Hayward], and the other Knight, John [Woodward], and the Under-Secretary and the translator[216] and the ambassadors' servants also rode in coaches. And before the coaches, by the ambassadors, and on both sides of the coaches rode knights[217] and gentlemen; and behind the coaches rode the lesser gentry and the aldermen. And the merchants and traders walked and accompanied the ambassadors to their lodgings.

And when they had come to the ambassadorial yard and entered the rooms, Sir William, Lord [Danvers] said to the ambassadors: "According to the order of the Great Sovereign our King James, the son of Andrew, his Royal Majesty's table has been prepared here for you. And his Royal Majesty has sent here all sorts of his silver vessels. And your conductor, Sir Thomas, is ready, and our sovereign has ordered the merchant John Merrick to be with you, and the order of our sovereign about you bears his name. He has ordered that you be honored and satisfied in good measure. And in the future whom do you prefer to cook for you? Would you order that the King's cooks be with you or would you order your own cooks to cook for you? In this his Royal Majesty has ordered that you have the choice, whatever you want."[218]

[p. 191] And having spoken to the ambassadors, Sir William Lord [Danvers] went to the King and Sir Thomas and his brother, Sir Richard, and the other best gentlemen and the merchant, John Merrick, remained with the ambassadors, and fifteen of the best merchants went to the yard to the ambassadors.

And the ambassadors sat at the table and at a small distance from them sat Sir Thomas and his brother and with them the King's gentlemen and the merchants. And Sir Thomas and his associates feasted the ambassadors with great honor. And as they began to leave the table the conductor, Sir Thomas, and the King's gentlemen, having removed their hats stood up and asked the ambassadors about their Great Sovereign Tsar and Grand Duke Mikhail Fyodorovich, Autocrat of all Russia. And they said: "We hear that your Great Sovereign, his Tsar's majesty, has begun to rule his great, glorious states of the Russian tsardom, given to you by God and [he is] maintained on his Tsar's throne by God. What is his age? How old is he?"

And the ambassadors said to Sir Thomas and the gentlemen and the merchants: "Our Great Sovereign Tsar and Grand Duke Mikhail Fyodorovich, Autocrat of all Russia, sovereign and possessor of many states, has begun to rule the great state of Moscow and all his glorious states of the Russian tsardom. Our Great Sovereign Tsar and Grand Duke Mikhail Fyodorovich Autocrat of all Russia, is of the family of our great Russian sovereigns, the native Tsars and Grand Dukes, Autocrats of all Russia by the Tsar's close relation to them. About all of this you, the King's advisors, will truly hear yourselves at that time when we will be with your Great Sovereign King James as ambassadors to give news about his Tsar's Majesty and his sovereignty.[219] [p. 192] And about his, the sovereign's age, we say to you that our Great Sovereign, his Tsar's Majesty is eighteen. However, God has endowed his Tsar's Majesty with strength, fair appearance, bravery, intelligence, luck, and he is merciful to all people and well conducted to all, and God has endowed him, the sovereign, with all sorts of good deeds and customs above all others."

And Ivanovich [Żiuzin] spoke a cup of health for his Tsar's majesty and for his sovereign's long lasting health to Sir Thomas, and the gentlemen, and the merchants, and to all sorts of people who were at that time in the room: "The cup of our Great Sovereign given by God and endowed by God, just and merciful Tsar and Grand Duke Mikhail Fyodorovich, Autocrat of all Russia and sovereign and possessor of many states, his Tsar's Majesty. May the Lord grant that our Great Sovereign, his Tsar's Majesty, should be healthy and happy in his great state of the Russian tsardom, and terrible to his enemies; and also we, his servants, pray our all generous God, glorified in the Trinity, that God should lengthen life to him the Great Sovereign, and give him victory over his enemies, and that he should finally complete his grace and establish the root of his just Tsar's descendants for the heredity of his sovereign family forever unmoved."[220]

And the conductor, Sir Thomas, and the royal gentlemen, and the merchants, and all sorts of people stood, having removed their hats. And when the ambassadors had spoken and drunk the sovereign's cup themselves, then Aleksei Ivanovich gave his Tsar's Majesty's cup to Sir Thomas, and the gentlemen, and the merchants, and all sorts of people who were at that time [p. 193] in the room.

And having taken the sovereign's cup, Sir Thomas said to the ambassadors: "We have heard from you about your Great Sovereign Tsar and Grand Duke Mikhail Fyodorovich, Autocrat of all Russia, that he, the great Sovereign, the heir of the great Sovereigns the native Tsars of Russia, has come to rule his great states. For all this reason we all rejoiced at his Tsar's Majesty and were glad to drink the cup of his Tsar's Majesty for the sovereign's long lasting health. And we want to see that the great sovereigns on both sides, both your Great Sovereign, his Tsar's Majesty and our Sovereign, his Royal Majesty, should have between them fraternal love and friendship and stand as one against their enemies. And let there be, by God's will, now and in the future between them, the Great Sovereigns, no disagreement. And we, the sovereigns' servants would like to be in their sovereign grace and in unity among one another. May the Lord grant that your Great Sovereign, his Tsar's Majesty, have health and long life, and to this we drink his Tsar's Majesty's cup." And the conductor, Sir Thomas, and the King's gentlemen, and the merchants, and all the English who were there drank the sovereign's cup with enthusiasm.

And after the sovereign's cup they all sat at the table as before. And the conductor, Sir Thomas, the gentlemen, and the merchants, began to drink the cup to their Great Sovereign, King James, sitting at the table, and only removed their hats but did not stand. And the ambassadors, at the King's name, stood to drink the cup for his health and they said to Sir Thomas, and the gentlemen, and the merchants that it is not proper to drink the sovereign's cup sitting. Not only [p. 194] for you, his royal Majesty's born servants, but for us the servants of his Tsar's Majesty, it is not proper to do that, that it does not give honor to your sovereign.

And Sir Thomas and the gentlemen said to the ambassadors: "Here in England it is the order and custom to drink the royal cup at table sitting, but we bring to his Royal Majesty our service and truth with our sincere enthusiasm just as you fulfill your service in truth with enthusiasm to your Great Sovereign his Tsar's Majesty."

[p. 194] And the ambassadors said to Sir Thomas and the gentlemen and the merchants: "Many children of sovereigns, Tsars and Tsarevichs of various states, serve our Great Sovereign Tsar Mikhail Fyodorovich [ST]; and all these sovereign children and the born slaves of the Tsar, princes and servants of great rank, and of other various ranks, and we too, the sovereign slaves and all people to the very lowest ranks, we fulfill our servile task and we always give a worthy honor and praise to his most bright Tsar's Majesty according to his sovereign's rank and condition. And we serve him, our Great Sovereign, with direct enthusiasm and we die for him, our sovereign, and we stand for him in all truth. This is our servile and dutybound task. So it has come to you to give honor and praise to your own sovereign. And it is necessary for us to ask from God grace from both sides that the Great Sovereigns, both our Great Sovereign his Tsar's Majesty and his Royal Majesty should be in fraternal love and strong friendship and in communication by former custom, when [p. 195] the state of Moscow was in peace and quiet with the English state.[221] And now in the future this should be firm forever. And it is your task, the King's advisors, yours, Sir Thomas, and the gentlemen, and the merchants to fulfill their efforts to strengthen everything good so that there should be between them, the Great Sovereigns, and between their states, all manner of good."

And Sir Thomas, and the gentlemen, and the merchants said to the ambassadors: "We are all glad of the fact that between them, our Great Sovereigns, there has been fraternal love and strong friendship according to the former custom.[222] As it was under the previous Great Sovereigns, let it be so now. And we expect from his Royal Majesty that he will give his fraternal love and strong friendship with joy to your Great Sovereign, his Tsar's Majesty, since he wants to see in the future the fraternal love and friendship of his Tsar's Majesty to himself." And when Sir Thomas and the gentlemen had spoken and greeted the ambassadors by their hand they left the house and the merchants left, bowing down very low. And Sir Thomas left with the ambassadors and the merchant John Merrick.

On October 27th the conductor, Sir Thomas, the son of Thomas, came to the ambassadors' house, and with him the King's gentlemen. And Sir Thomas, the son of Thomas, and with him the King's gentlemen, inquired. And Sir Thomas asked the ambassadors about their health and rest, were they satisfied in everything?

And the ambassadors said to Sir Thomas: "Your Great Sovereign King James's favor to us is honorable and sufficient in food. The only thing that is necessary for us is that for which we have been sent from our Great Sovereign, his Tsar's Majesty, to your sovereign King James. [p. 196] We are speaking about this so that you, Sir Thomas, and the other royal advisors should take care of the sovereign's affairs and report this to his Royal Majesty so that your Great Sovereign King James might order us to see him about the common affairs of sovereigns which stand between them the Great Sovereigns to the good and quiet of Christians; so that his Royal Majesty might put a beginning to his fraternal love and friendship to our Great Sovereign, his Tsar's Majesty, he should allow us to see his royal eyes soon."

And Sir Thomas said to the ambassador: "Our Great Sovereign and King, James, the son of Andrew, has not yet arrived in London but we expect his arrival soon. And we expect that he will quickly order you to see him as soon as we fulfill your request making it known to his Royal Majesty." And he left the ambassadors.

On the 28th of October the conductor, Sir Thomas, son of Thomas Smith, and his brother, Sir Richard, and the other royal gentlemen, and the merchant, John Merrick, having come to the ambassadors said: "To-morrow in London there will be a great ceremony. They are electing the City judges according to the cities from the best merchants. And these judges are called here, Lord Mayors. Their inauguration has great honor and in places in some years some of them are greater than all of the boyars who are first under the King. And our sovereign, King James, the son of Andrew, gives to these judges[223] his royal sabre to rule over all people, to acquit and to convict whoever is worthy of it. And he is free to act in truth and in punishment; and this year it is necessary to put a new Lord Mayor [in office], and he is to ride from his house to the royal palace and, having been in the palace for [p. 197] a while as the ceremony requires, he is to ride back home through the City on horseback and by water on the river Thames in ships and boats. And there is a great salute from muskets and from all sorts of artillery. And the previous Lord Mayor who sat out his year before him rides with him, and the old Lord Mayors who were judges beforehand. And now those people, knights and aldermen, elected people who will in the future be Lord Mayors, and many other people of various ranks, accompany him; and the whole City watches. And except for the King's coronation there is no other such great cere-mony in England.[224] And now there is a royal order by name to you, the ambassadors, that you should go tomorrow to see the ceremony. And his Royal Majesty has ordered his coaches and sledges to be prepared for you and his own royal house (to which he comes when he is in the City) to be prepared for you."[225]

And the ambassadors said to Sir Thomas: "It is not possible for us now to go see your ceremonies because your Great Sovereign King James has not yet come to London and we have not been to see his Royal Majesty; we have not seen his eyes[226] and there has been no beginning to the affair with which we were sent from the Great Sovereign Tsar and Grand Duke Mikhail Fyodorovich, Autocrat of all Russia, sovereign and pos-sessor of many states, from his Tsar's Majesty, to his Royal Majesty about their various good sovereign affairs. And this business is your King's and your country's. Whatever is your ceremony, so be it."

And Sir Thomas said to the ambassadors: "There is a royal order to you that he, his royal majesty, will soon be in [p. 198] London for you. And now it is not for you to disobey his royal order nor to anger him by this, but to obey his command and watch the ceremony. And we will be there tomorrow for you with the coaches."

And the ambassadors said to Sir Thomas: "In this is his royal will; we are the unfree slaves of the sovereign but there is no reason for your sovereign King James to be angry with us. If we have not been to see your sovereign it is not proper for us to go look at that ceremony first. And as to the fact that we hear from you the royal order that he, your sovereign, will be in London soon, we are glad for his royal arrival and we await him, your sovereign."

And Sir Thomas and his associates said to the ambassadors: "We tell you about this by communication of our sovereign. Only obey his royal command and this will be for our sovereign an honor to you, and there will not be at that time anyone with you besides us, and we will come for you early so that you get there before the crowd gathers." And having spoken, Sir Thomas and the gentlemen left the ambassadors.

And the same day, after Sir Thomas, two of the Lord Mayor's associates who had been judges[227] came to the ambassadors from the Lord Mayor, and in England they are called sheriffs.[228] And they said: "The new judge, the Lord Mayor,[229] has sent us to you, the ambassadors of his Tsar's Majesty, and he has ordered us to petition you and to ask about your health. And the Lord Mayor has ordered us to petition you and, having heard about the Great Sovereign, your Tsar and Grand Duke Mikhail Fyodorovich, the Autocrat of all Russia, his Tsar's Majesty, [p. 199] our Great Sovereign King James, is joyful. And we, his royal subjects, have rejoiced with the whole English state at the name and health of your sovereign, his Tsar's Majesty. And our Great Sovereign has ordered us to honor and satisfy you, the ambassadors, though he is not here. And when he arrives he, our Sovereign, will receive you honorably because of his Tsar's Majesty's fraternal love and friendship to him. And tomorrow, according to the King's grace and by our custom, it is our festival day and I have bread to grant you tomorrow."

And the ambassadors ordered these judges to say to the Lord Mayor with his associates: "This is the most necessary business, hearing about the Great Sovereign, our Tsar and Grand Duke Mikhail Fyodorovich, Autocrat of all Russia, about his Tsar's Majesty. The sovereign King James is joyful and showing his favor to us he has ordered us to be honored. He shows his original fraternal love and friendship to our Great Sovereign, to his Tsar's Majesty, wanting in the future to see the fraternal love and friendship of our Great Sovereign his Tsar's Majesty to himself.

And therefore we perceive your service and industry toward our Great Sovereign that you rejoice at his Tsar's Majesty, and that you do the best permanent business as is proper between our Great Sovereign his Tsar's Majesty and your Great Sovereign, and between their great states now and in the future for all sorts of good. And we accept what you have done, Lord Mayor, as love, and that you have shown us your virtue. But it is impossible for us to go to you because we have not seen your King, James."

And on the same day to the ambassadors came from King [p. 200] James, from the villages of his entertainments, his near royal gentleman, Sir Lewis Lewkenor,[230] and with him four royal gentlemen. And meeting the ambassadors, they removed their hats and greeted them by their hand, and Sir Lewis said to the ambassadors: "Our Great Sovereign King James has sent me to you, the ambassadors of his Tsar's Majesty, and ordered me to bow to you and to ask about your health and about your supplies and whether, being in London with his Royal Majesty are you satisfied with everything, and is there any shortcoming with the food? And our Great Sovereign has ordered me to say to you that he wants to see the fraternal love and friendship to himself of his beloved brother the Great Sovereign, your Tsar and Grand Duke Mikhail Fyodorovich, the Autocrat of all Russia, his Tsar's Majesty, and he, our Sovereign, will be in London soon for you, the ambassadors, on this Sunday.[231] And he orders you to see him immediately. And it was not because of you, the ambassadors of his Tsar's Majesty, that our Sovereign has not yet been in London. And his Royal Majesty orders us to tell you that tomorrow in London, according to his royal ceremony and custom, and according to the laws of the land as has been the case for many years, the City judge, the Lord Mayor, will be installed. And this great ceremony occurs once a year, and you should watch this ceremony and not disobey our Sovereign's command. And for the future our Sovereign has sent me to his near councillors who are now in London, and ordered me to tell you this and to accompany you honorably where you might watch the ceremony in his royal palace."[232]

And the ambassador said to Sir Lewis: "We hear the royal [p. 201] order that you have for us that your Sovereign King, James, shows his fraternal love and friendship to our Great Sovereign Tsar and Grand Duke Mikhail Fyodorovich, Autocrat of all Russia, to his Tsar's Majesty, that he wants to come to London for us soon. And at this we, seeing fraternal love and strong friendship between them, the Great Sovereigns, rejoice and expect to see the royal eyes. And insofar as your sovereign King James has ordered, showing his favor to us, that you ask about our health and food, we are grateful for his royal favor and until now we are in honor with him, your sovereign, and satisfied about everything. And insofar as Sir Thomas, the son of Thomas Smith, has come to us according to the royal command, and with him the King's gentlemen, and has told us the same thing as the royal order that we now hear from you, that we are to go to see your ceremony according to the royal command, the installation of the Lord Mayor, we have told Sir Thomas that until we have been with your sovereign King James, until we have seen his eyes, it is not possible for us to go to see your ceremony. And we tell you the same thing, Sir Lewis, that to the honor of his royal Majesty we will be with him, your sovereign, and we will see his eyes before [we see] your City and country ceremonies. This is our first business."

And Sir Lewis said to the ambassadors: "For your Great Sovereign, his Tsar's Majesty our Sovereign King James, wanting to see his Tsar's fraternal love and friendship to himself, and showing his favor to you, the ambassadors, even though he was not finished with his royal affairs, and leaving them, he is coming to London for you and wants to see you soon and to receive you honorably. And he has ordered you with care [p. 202] that you should see what happens in this state because another such ceremony will not happen while you are here.[233] And you are not to disobey our sovereign nor to anger him, but to go and watch." And having said this Sir Lewis left the ambassadors.

On October 29th, at the first hour of the day, conductor Sir Thomas, the son of Thomas, and his brother, Sir Richard, and four royal gentlemen and the merchants John Merrick and William Russell, (that William [who] comes to the Moscow state with John)[234] came to the ambassadors at their lodgings. And Sir Thomas and his associates said to the ambassadors: "So that you might obey the order of our sovereign, King James, and see the royal ceremony, the installation of the Lord Mayor, the royal coaches are with us ready for you, and it is time for you to go. And I am telling you this, taking care of the Sovereign's affairs, so that you should definitely not disobey the royal order and by this anger our sovereign, and so that you should not make any interference in his measures of state."

And John Merrick said to the ambassadors properly: "Just as is the case of his direct service to the Great Sovereign, his Tsar's Majesty, I tell you that our sovereign King James, the son of Andrew, orders you with care and you should definitely not disobey in this matter."

And the ambassadors did not dare to disobey the King's orders and, so that they would not by that harm the affairs of his Tsar's Majesty and not anger the King, they went to see their ceremony. And the ambassadors sat in the coaches in the great place and on the sides in the coach with Aleksei Ivanovich [Ziuzin], at the door, sat the conductor, Sir Thomas, and the royal gentlemen, [p. 203] and the merchant John Merrick. And with the Secretary with Aleksei in the coach near the doors sat Sir Richard, and the gentlemen, and the merchant William Russell.[235] And the undersecretary and the translator sat in a separate coach. And the ambassadors' servants also rode in coaches, and when the ambassadors came to the yard[236] and entered the building, at that time there were no people at the yard besides the conductors who came with the ambassadors and a few local servants in the rooms to arrange things. And they placed for the ambassadors fine places, chairs and tables, they honored the ambassadors. And at the same time the Lord Mayor[237] went up the river Thames to the royal palace and he sat in a ship, and it was a decorated ship, small, painted in all sorts of various colors. And it was rowed by oars. Under the ship were made boats, and on the ship, as is the case with a straight ship, the lower decks had windows and in these windows were rowers on both sides. And with him sat the previous Lord Mayor who had been Lord Mayor for the year before,[238] and other people of rank. And before the ship and behind and on the sides, over the whole river, sailed on many boats, the King's gentlemen, and knights, and aldermen, and merchants, and traders, and the bodyguard of the King's court, and all sorts of people of the land in bright costume. And there were banners and great decorated royal flags and many others. And the King's trumpeters trumpeted, and they beat the drums and they played on litavra and there were all sorts of various instruments. And they fired a great salute from the ship in which the Lord Mayor sailed and from other ships which were there and from big boats and from the City [p. 204] wall. And from all the small boats there was a great shooting of muskets.

And when the Lord Mayor came to the royal palace where the King lives[239] with the Queen and the Prince, at that time there was a great salute at the royal palace. And when the Lord Mayor had been at the palace for a short time he went back through the City riding on stallions and argamaks. And before him walked the bodyguards of the King's court, about one hundred and fifty men in bright clothes with gilded partisans, two by two, and after them walked the merchants and traders organized by livery companies and between them rode the King's trumpeters and drummers in decorated dress on royal horses and trumpeted while riding and played the drums and litavri. And all sorts of players walked and carried big royal banners and flags, bright colored, wide and long. And after them other men, walking, carried on themselves wooden [models of] towns, worked and painted.[240] And in the [model] towns were churches and on the towers and along the wall were constructed guns, and on the steeples of the churches and on the city ladder sat old and young people and boys and girls in bright dresses. And on them were masks like human faces and like all sorts of animals. And they carried two [model] places from the royal coronation ceremony like a dais, or plat-form, with high decorated steps on four sides and on the top and on the places sat one person in each place as if from the royal ceremony, and around on all sides, above, and below, sat small girls and boys and here they carried a variety of great beasts: elephants, and unicorns, and lions and camels, and boars, and other animals. And each one was made as if it was real. [p. 205] And there was a small decorated ship and all the people who carried it were draped from all sides to the ground. And around them went people in masks with palms, and they carried palms with fireworks, and they threw from them sparkling fire on both sides because of the great press of people, that they might give way.[241] And before them and behind them went soldiers, and on both sides, turning quickly and waving swords and sabers so that people would get out of the way. And after, rode many of the King's gentlemen and behind them, last before the Lord Mayor, rode the knights who had been Lord Mayors before, in decorated clothing and wearing gold chains.

And with the Lord Mayor rode side by side, at his left hand, the Lord Mayor whom he was replacing, and behind them rode the aldermen, elected people who would be Lord Mayors in the future. And many people, men, women, and children—the whole City—watched this cer-emony. And at the ambassadors' windows there were curtains and shut-ters, and when the Lord Mayor had passed, the ambassadors returned to their lodgings. And the conductors, Sir Thomas, the son of Thomas Smith, with his brother, Sir Richard, and with the royal gentlemen, and with those who were with them at first, and the merchant, John Merrick, accompanied the ambassadors to their lodgings.

And on October the 30th, in the evening, the merchant John Merrick, came to the ambassadors and said in conversation: "Our Great Sovereign King James has come to London today shortly before I, John, have come to you. And you should know of the King's arrival. And he, our Sover-eign, is in good health. And the ambassadors said to John: "We are happy at the King's health and at his arrival."

[p. 206] And on October the 31st the King's privy gentlemen and master of the hunt, Sir Lewis Lewkenor, and with him six of the King's gentlemen came with him from the King to the ambassadors, and, having taken off his hat, Sir Lewis gave a speech with the [King's] title, from the King to the Ambassadors: "Our Great Sovereign, James, the son of An-drew, King of England, Scotland, France, Ireland, etc., loving his brother, the Great Sovereign, your Tsar and Grand Duke Mikhail Fyodorovich, Autocrat of all Russia, sovereign and possessor of many states, and want-ing to see in the future his Tsar's Majesty's fraternal love and friendship to himself and showing his grace to you the ambassadors, his royal Majesty has sent me, Sir Lewis, to you. And he ordered me to say that he, our Great Sovereign, has come to London for you the ambassadors, leaving off his entertainment, and has ordered you to an audience on November the 7th. And our sovereign has ordered me to tell you that his direct royal care for his brother, your Great Sovereign, his Tsar's Majesty, is such that there has never been such honor to the ambassadors and emissaries of any states who have come to his royal highness from the Great Sovereigns of various states; that he has done honor to you, the ambassadors of his Tsar's Majesty, that he has come quickly for you, himself, and ordered you to come to the audience in a short time. And many other ambassadors and emissaries, when they have come to England do not see the King quickly, and wait a long time, and send to petition his Royal Highness that he should order them to be quickly at an audience with him. But our Sovereign, King James, the son of Andrew, only orders them to see him after a time, according to his royal will, and not quickly; but his Royal Majesty has done [p. 207] more for you than for the ambassadors and emissaries of other states."

And the ambassadors said to Sir Lewis: "We hear the order to us of your sovereign, King James, and we ourselves see that his royal, fraternal love and friendship is for our Tsar, Mikhail Fyodorovich [ST], to his Tsar's Majesty. We live always in his, your Great Sovereign's, royal care unforgettably, forever, and we are satisfied in our food. And now his royal grace is shown to us and still better that he, the sovereign King James, has come quickly to London for us and ordered us to be with him in a short time. And we petition him for his royal favor and we will be glad to see his eyes. And when God grants that we will return to the Moscow state, to our Tsar Mikhail Fyodorovich [ST], then we, the sovereign slaves, will report to his Tsar's Majesty everything that we see, to him the Great Sovereign, to his Tsar's Majesty, the direct fraternal love and strong friendship of his brother, your Great Sovereign, King James. And now our Great Sovereign, his Tsar's Majesty, will return his fraternal love and strong friendship to his brother, the Great Sovereign, your King James. And now our Great Sovereign has sent us, his slaves, as ambassadors to his beloved brother, King James, about the several good affairs of sovereigns which exist between them, the great sovereigns, for fraternal love and strong friendship between their great states to the peace of Christendom. And when your King James [p. 208] sends his ambassadors or emissaries to our Great Sovereign, then our Great Sovereign, his Tsar's Majesty, because of the King's fraternal love, will grant his Great Tsar's grace to those ambassadors and emissaries who will be sent and order honor and sufficiency for them, and they will be in his merciful care."

And the ambassadors said to Sir Lewis: "That at the time when they are to be with your Great Sovereign, King James, at the audience business there should be no other ambassadors and emissaries of other states."[242] And Sir Lewis said: "I will report to my Great Sovereign, King James, your ambassadors' request that there should be no other ambassadors or emissaries at that time. And I expect that there will be no other foreigners there at that time." And greeting the ambassadors by the hand, he went off to his sovereign, King James.

And the conductor, Sir Thomas, the son of Thomas, was not with the ambassadors that day, and John Merrick said that he, Sir Thomas, was ill. And the ambassadors said to John: "If Sir Thomas cannot be with us because of his illness someone else ought to be a conductor in his place, whomever your King James orders."

And on November 1st the merchant John Merrick came to the ambassadors and said: "I went to see Sir Thomas today, I went to visit him and Sir Thomas ordered me to greet you and to ask about your health. And Sir Thomas ordered me to say to you: I was very glad to be a conductor with you, for I wanted to serve the Great Sovereign Tsar and Grand Duke Mikhail Fyodorovich, Autocrat of all Russia, with my direct care [p. 209] however much I was able, but because of my sins[243] trouble has taken me, and as soon as God gives me relief, then I will immediately be with you." And the ambassadors ordered to be said to Sir Thomas that they praise him for his care and that he wants to show his service to our Great Sovereign, to his Tsar's Majesty, and seeing his care that they expect him to be the conductor in the future.

On the 5th of November in London there was a great ringing of bells in the whole City, in the day and night in all churches. And the ambassadors asked the conductors and other local people why are they having such a great ringing of bells. And the conductors and other local people said to the ambassadors:

"We have today a great day,[244] that God has saved from death our Sovereign, King James, and the princes and the knights and the royal boyars [Lords], and other of his privy people and elected people of all sorts of ranks of the whole English state and the Scottish and Irish land. In that manner in the past year, 7116[245] our sovereign had an assembly with his boyars and the whole land[246] about the affairs of the King and the land, and about the ordering of the state—how to live in the future and how to resolve old business. And at that very time the Pope of Rome, corrupting our faith by his malicious intentions and leading us to his corrupted faith, wanted to put to an evil death our sovereign King James, and the princes, and all of the men of rank. He taught twenty English distinguished royal gentlemen who had gone over to his papist faith. And the Pope gave them, because of that, much riches, so that they should act according to his orders. And these traitors, shortly before the assembly, [p. 210] bought a shop which was built nearby the royal rooms by the square and they kept in it, for sale, food and drink for the arrival of the boyars' servants, and they put in it their own man with this trade. And from the shop they began to run a tunnel under the royal palace to the building where the assembly takes place. And they carried out the earth at night and dumped it in the river Thames, and they brought in gunpowder. And on the last night, having prepared everything, they left one man with a lantern, and they made an agreement with him to light the fuse in the morning. And themselves, they left London. And having traveled 20 versts they stopped on a high hill so that they could see, for they expected an explosion according to their evil design.

"And one of them had a friend who was a royal boyar,[247] and he pitied that boyar and sent to him a letter with his usual servant. And he wrote in it that that boyar, if he wanted to live, should not go to the assembly with the King; and that servant gave the letter to another boyar, for he did not recognize him and the name was similar.[248] And that boyar, having taken the letter and read it, immediately told the King and the King sent his privy boyar, the Lord Chamberlain,[249] to search out that treason and sent many privy people with him. And they searched the King's palace and outside the King's palace for a long time but they did not find the tunnel. And they barely found the tunnel and took the man with the lantern,[250] for he had lighted the fuse and wanted to leave, and therefore he was found. They captured all these traitors and they searched out other Englishmen who were in the plot with them at the Pope's instruction, in London about fifty people. And for their [p. 211] evil deeds, as they began so they finished; and various punishments were done to them.[251]

"And the King did not set his disgrace upon that boyar to whom one traitor had written out of friendship, for he established that he was not in agreement with them. And even if they had given the letter to him, he would not have kept it quiet, but would have told the King, too. And seeing such an inexpressible grace of God, the King himself, with the Queen and the Prince, praise God and honor that day every year. And the boyars, and the gentlemen, and all sorts of people of all ranks, with their wives and children—the whole City with little children, to the last person—come to church according to our faith and pray God for our Great Sovereign and for the Sovereign Queen and for their children, every year, with fervor, that God saved the King from death and did not allow the whole state to be destroyed."[252]

And about the Pope and his supporter, they said to the ambassadors, "for their evil deeds and hostile snares they will receive vengeance from God at the hand of all the states along the sea. And we say about the Pope that he is the follower of Satan."

On November the 6th the merchant John Merrick came to the ambassadors and said: "I was at the royal court and saw the boyar of the King's Privy Council who controls and takes care of all the affairs of the King and country, the Lord Chamberlain.[253] And he ordered me to tell you that you should be with our sovereign King James tomorrow, on Sunday, November the 7th. And his Royal Majesty will send for you as conductors his privy gentlemen and master of the hunt, Sir Lewis Lewkenor. And his companions will be Sir Richard, the brother of Sir Thomas, and [p. 212] other royal gentlemen, and you are to go to our sovereign King James and be with him after he dines, for such has been our ceremony for many years from the time of our sovereign's ancestors. And you are not to be offended that you do not come to dine."[254] And the ambassadors said to John: "If this has not started with us, and was done before, and is the King's will, then we will be glad to be with him, the sovereign, at that time as is his royal ceremony."

And on November the 7th, after dining, the King's privy gentlemen, Sir Lewis Lewkenor, and Sir Richard, the son of Thomas, brother of Sir Thomas, and with them six good King's gentlemen came to the ambassadors from the sovereign King James and, having taken off their hats, Sir Lewis said to the ambassadors:

"Our Great Sovereign King James, the son of Andrew, loving his brother the Great Sovereign, your Tsar and Grand Duke, Mikhail Fyodorovich, Autocrat of all Russia, has ordered you to be with himself for an audience today, and has sent with us his royal coaches for you and has ordered us to be your conductors. And his Royal Majesty, giving honor and showing his fraternal love to your Great Sovereign, to his Tsar's Majesty, and favoring you, the ambassadors, has ordered his Queen, Anne, and Prince Charles[255] to sit with him at that time when you will be with him, the sovereign King James. And there will be no ambassadors or emissaries of any states at the time when you will be with his Royal Majesty."

And the ambassadors petitioned for favor and they said to Sir Lewis and to Sir Richard: "We are glad to see the eyes of your Great Sovereign King James, [p. 213] and his Royal Majesty's Queen, and Prince."

And they sat in a coach in the chief seat and on the sides by the doors there sat by Aleksei Ivanovich [Ziuzin], the conductor, Sir Lewis Lewkenor, and the gentlemen and the merchant, John Merrick. And by the Secretary Aleksei [Vitovtov], in the coach by the doors, sat the conductor, Sir Richard, son of Thomas, and the King's gentlemen; and the undersecretary and the translator were in a separate coach.[256]

And the royal court is beyond the City after you have passed through the suburbs.[257] And when the ambassadors came to the royal court and got out of the coaches, on both sides of the gates before the royal gate stood many people. And at the gates the King's boyar, Lord Gerard, greeted the ambassadors.[258] And in the middle of the royal court the boyar Lord Walden, the son of the Lord Chamberlain, met them.[259] And as the ambassadors walked through the courtyard on both sides from the gates to the stairway stood soldiers and merchants. And the whole courtyard was full of all sorts of people. And on the stairway the King's near boyar and appanage Prince, Lord Dorset,[260] met them. And on the staircase on both sides stood good gentlemen of the King and the best merchants. And meeting the ambassadors, the lords walked on the left hand.[261]

And Lord Dorset spoke to the ambassadors with a word from the King, "Our Great Sovereign, the King, James, the son of Andrew, has ordered me to tell you that you should sit for a short time in the royal duma chamber[262] where he comes for counsel with the boyars, and he will send for you at that time."[263]

And the ambassadors went into the King's duma chamber and with them the Lords who met them and the conductors and the other good gentlemen of the King. And when they came into the chamber in the chamber at the end of the table stands the King's throne covered with [p. 214] wrought silver and gilded. And from the King's place on both sides of the table are the places of the close boyars.[264] And the King's boyar, Lord Dorset, said to the ambassadors, "This is the place of our Great Sovereign, our King James, the son of Andrew. He sits there, his Royal Majesty, when he has a great duma with his close boyars. And his royal command now that is with me is that you, Aleksei Ivanovich [Ziuzin], should remain here in the chamber and sit in the King's place and not disobey our sovereign in this. And our Great Sovereign gives you such an honor with honest zeal, wanting to see the fraternal love and strong friendship to himself of his brother the Great Sovereign, your Tsar and Grand Duke Mikhail Fyodorovich, Autocrat of all Russia. And for other ambassadors, not only those who come from various states from great Christian sovereigns but also for Turkish ambassadors this is not done, that they sit on the King's place.[265] Only for the ambassadors of your Great Sovereign his Majesty, the Tsar."

And the ambassadors petitioned for royal favor for themselves. And they said to Lord Dorset, "Your Great Sovereign King James does this, showing his fraternal love and friendship to our Great Sovereign, to his

Majesty the Tsar, and favoring us, the ambassadors, that he ordered us to sit on the King's place; but it is not proper for us to sit in the King's place."

And Lord Dorset said to Aleksei Ivanovich [Ziuzin]: "There is a command in the name of our sovereign that he ordered you to sit on the royal place. And you should not disobey our sovereign, but do what pleases our sovereign." And Lord Dorset, taking [p. 215] Aleksei by the hand, sat him on the King's place. And the ambassadors sat at the end of the table where the King sits and the royal boyars, all the lords who were meeting them, and the conductors, and the great gentlemen stood on both sides of the table. And not one person sat down.

And at that time, according to the message from the King, Lord Dorset said to the ambassadors: "It is time for you to go to our Great Sovereign." And the ambassadors went through the corridors from the duma chamber to the royal chamber where the King himself sits.[266] And in the corridors on both sides stood bodyguards in bright cloaks with gilded partisans. And when the ambassadors were close to the royal chamber the boyar of the King's Privy Council and governor and appanage Prince of the county of Suffolk,[267] the Lord Chamberlain, came out of the chamber from King James and met the ambassadors. And having greeted the ambassadors by the hand, he said: "Our Great Sovereign King James has ordered you to come to his Royal Majesty." And the ambassadors went to the King into the chamber, and the Lord Chamberlain walked on the left hand of the ambassadors. And as the ambassadors came into the chamber the Secretary, Aleksei Vitovtov, took from the undersecretary and carried into the room the letter that was sent from the Great Sovereign Tsar and Grand Duke Mikhail Fyodorovich, Autocrat of all Russia, to King James.

And as the ambassadors came into the chamber they looked carefully at his Royal Majesty, King James, and at his Queen, Anne, and their son, Prince Charles [to see] how they sat on their sovereign thrones.[268] King James sat in his royal throne and with him, near him, on his left hand, the Queen on [p. 216] a separate throne. And the Prince was by his father King James, on his right hand, only a bit farther away from him. And under their royal thrones was made a dais for height, according to the custom of sovereigns. And when the ambassadors had come to the middle of the chamber, King James, and with him the Queen and Prince, stood up from their thrones. And as the ambassador came close to the thrones on the platform the King and Queen came forward from their thrones about a yard and stood on the edge of the platform. And the Prince came down from the first step to the second step. And, having taken off their hats, they bowed to the ambassadors, first the King, and then the Queen and Prince; and the ambassadors made a deep bow from the Great Sovereign Tsar and Grand Duke Mikhail Fyodorovich, Autocrat of all Russia, to King James, and to the Queen and the Prince.[269]

And Aleksei Ivanovich [Ziuzin] said: "By the grace of God glorified in the Trinity the Great Sovereign Tsar and Grand Mikhail Fyodorovich, Autocrat of all Russia, of Vladimir, Moscow, Novgorod, Tsar of Kazan', Tsar of Astrakhan', Tsar of Siberia, Sovereign of Pskov, and Grand Duke of Smolensk, Tver', Yugra, Perm', Viatka, Bulgaria, etc., Sovereign and Grand Duke Novgorod of the Lower Land, Chernigov, Riazan', Polotsk, Rostov, Iaroslavl', Belozero, Livonia, Udora, Obdora, Konda, and Ruler and Sovereign of all the Land of the North, Sovereign and Possessor of the Iberian Land, of the Tsars of Kartli and Georgia, and of the Land of Kabarda of the Circassian and Mountain Princes, and many other states, has ordered me to bow to you,[270] the Great Sovereign, our beloved brother James, King of England, Scotland, France, Ireland, etc., and your royal Majesties [p. 217] Queen Anne, and your son, Prince Charles."

And after that he said: "By the grace of God the Great Sovereign Tsar and Grand Duke Mikhail Fyodorovich, Autocrat of all Russia and sovereign and possessor of many states, has ordered me to communicate his health to you, our beloved brother, King James, and your Royal Majesty's Queen Anne, and Prince Charles, and to see your fraternal beloved health." And Aleksei Ivanovich gave King James the letter of the sovereign Tsar and Grand Duke Mikhail Fyodorovich, of all Russia.[271]

And King James received the sovereign's letter himself, with great honor and unsealed the letter, kissed it lovingly, and asked about the imperial health of the Great Sovereign Tsar and Grand Duke Mikhail Fyodorovich, Autocrat of all Russia.

And the ambassador said: "When we left our Great Sovereign Tsar and Grand Duke Mikhail Fyodorovich, Autocrat of all Russia, our Great Sovereign, his Tsar's Majesty, in his great glorious states, God grant, was in good health." And after King James [asked], the Queen, and Prince separately asked about the health of our Great Sovereign, his Tsar's Majesty. And the ambassador declared the Tsar's health to both the Queen and the Prince separately.

And after that Aleksei Ivanovich [Ziuzin], and the Secretary Aleksei gave speeches from the Great Sovereign Tsar and Grand Duke Mikhail Fyodorovich,[272] Autocrat of all Russia, sovereign and possessor of many states, to King James, declaring the design and sedition and [p. 218] frequent violation of oath and destruction of peaceful conditions by King Sigismund of Poland of Lithuania, and the lords council and the hetman Stanisław Żółkiewski and their destruction to the Moscow state and cruel bloodshed and all their evil injustices; [and he described] the battle where

they defeated, by God's grace, near Moscow, the hetman, Karol Chodkiewicz and King Sigismund himself near Volokolamsk, and in other
places[273] and in Moscow the Moscow people defeated the Poles and the
Lithuanians and took them prisoner; and the injustices of the Swedish
King Charles and his son [Gustavus] Adolph[us], in violation of their
oath, and the betrayal of the Moscow state in violation of oath, by their
Swedish General, Jakob Pontusson de la Gardie.

And the ambassadors spoke about the cities of Tsar Mikhail Fyodorovich [ST], about the capture of Great Novgorod, and Korela, and other
towns according to the sovereign instruction and according to the sovereign's letter which was sent about these matters to Aleksei Ivanovich
[Ziuzin], and to the Secretary Aleksei after their departure on the road to
Vologda.[274]

And the ambassadors said, according to the instruction of the sovereign
and Grand Duke Mikhail Fyodorovich, Autocrat of all Russia, to King
James about the Moscow state: "When, by the grace of our all powerful
and generous God, glorified in the Trinity, and of the most pure mother
of God, and of the great miracle workers of Moscow and of all the saints,
the Moscow state was liberated from the Poles and the Lithuanians, and
when our God-given Great Sovereign Tsar and Grand Duke Mikhail
Fyodorovich, Autocrat of all Russia [ascended to the throne of] the
Moscow state and all the great Russian Tsardom according to the family
of our Great Sovereigns, the Russian Tsars, of his grandfather, our Great
Sovereign of blessed memory, the Tsar and grand Duke Ivan Vasil'evich,
of all Russia, and [p. 219] his son, who was his Tsar's Majesty's uncle, our
Great Sovereign of blessed memory, the Tsar and Grand Duke Fyodor
Ivanovich, Autocrat of all Russia, and according to the sincere wish of all
sorts of people in the beginning following the prayer and request of the
metropolitans and archbishops, and the entire sanctified council of the
Moscow state, and following the petition of the Tsars and the Tsarevichi
of various states who served the previous Great Sovereign in the Moscow
state for many years and now serve his Tsar's Majesty, and of the boyars
and the Okol'nichie and the gentlemen and all the soldiers and officials
and of the merchants and of the multitude of the whole people of the state
of Moscow and of Novgorod and of the tsardoms of Kazan', Astrakhan',
and Siberia and of all the towns of the great Russian tsardom [and] he, the
Great Sovereign Tsar and Grand Duke, Autocrat of all Russia, having
accepted the blessing, our Great Sovereign, from the Great Sovereign his
Tsar's mother, the nun, Marfa Ivanovna, and taking pity on the people
he began to rule the great states of Vladimir, and Moscow, and Novgorod,
and the Tsardoms of Kazan', and Astrakhan', and Siberia, and all the great
most glorious states of the Russian tsardom. And now he, our Great

Sovereign Tsar and Grand Duke Mikhail Fyodorovich, Autocrat of all Russia, his Tsar's Majesty, remembering the previous strong fraternal love and loving communications between the Russian Tsars with their beloved Tsar's sister of beloved memory, with the Great Sovereign Queen Elizabeth, and after Queen Elizabeth the loving communications with him, the sovereign King James to the sovereign Tsar and Grand Duke Boris Fyodorovich of all Russia,[275] and the Tsar and Grand Duke Vasilii Ivanovich of all Russia, he has sent us, his slaves, to him his beloved brother as [p. 220] ambassador to announce his sovereignty and report his Tsar's health and to find out about his royal fraternal health and about other good and great things which exist between them the great sovereigns and between their great states to the good business and peace of Christians. And he, the Great Sovereign King James, remembering the previous fraternal love and strong friendship with our Great Sovereigns the Tsars and Grand Dukes, the Autocrats of all Russia, for this reason should now be in fraternal love and strong friendship with our Great Sovereign Tsar and Grand Duke Mikhail Fyodorovich the Autocrat of all Russia, and should stand with him against any enemy."

And King James asked of the ambassadors for all of these speeches in writing. And the ambassadors gave to King James the written speeches according to the instructions of the sovereign Tsar and Grand Duke Mikhail Fyodorovich, Autocrat of all Russia.[276]

And King James took the written speeches himself from the ambassadors and said to the ambassadors: "Having heard about your Great Sovereign our beloved brother the Tsar and Grand Duke Mikhail Fyodorovich Autocrat of all Russia, that he, the Great Sovereign has come to rule the great state of Moscow and all of the states of the great Russian tsardom chosen by God according to his natural close sovereignly affinity to the previous great Tsars and Grand Dukes of Russia[277]; and seeing his, the Great Sovereign's, his Tsar's Majesty's loving communication and fraternal friendship to me, the Queen, [and] the Prince and I rejoice at this. And I wish to return to his Tsar's Majesty our fraternal love and strong friendship. Not only was there with the previous Great Sovereign [p. 221] Tsars and Grand Dukes of Russia our royal fraternal loving communications and strong friendship, but beyond that I will be, with the Great Sovereign our beloved brother, with the Tsar and Grand Duke Mikhail Fyodorovich, Autocrat of all Russia, with his Tsar's Majesty, in fraternal love and strong friendship immovably forever."

And King James said about the Lithuanian King, Sigismund: "It is known to us and in all states the injustices and violation of oath of King Sigismund and the lord councillors to the Moscow state and their destruction and blood-shedding; and that they have committed all sorts of evil in the state of Moscow and we reproach him for this, and we have no communication with him about anything."

And King James spoke about the Swedish King, Charles, and about his son [Gustavus] Adolph[us] and about their injustices to the Moscow state: "That the treason of their Swedish General, Jakob Pontusson, and their seizure of cities is known to us, and that they with injustice violated their oath and broke an agreement of peace.[278] But I only order you to explain your written ambassadorial speeches to my duma boyars, and I will hear them personally.[279] And to you, the ambassadors, I give my command and I order them to speak with you about whatever business I will be able to conduct with your Great Sovereign, our beloved brother, his Tsar's Majesty."

And King James said to the ambassadors that they should put on their hats, and he reminded them about it twice and three times, and by his royal word he insisted strongly on it and bowed slightly that they put on the hats. And King James himself, and his son, Prince Charles, did not put any hats on themselves, [p. 222] and held them themselves and the Queen stood there according to her own queenly rule and custom.[280]

And the ambassadors petitioned James, the King, for his royal favor for them and in addition to that they said: "Our Great Sovereign the Tsar and Grand Duke Mikhail Fyodorovich, Autocrat of all Russia, and the sovereign and possessor of many states, his majesty the Tsar, sent us his slaves to you, the Great Sovereign, his beloved brother King James to announce his sovereignty and to declare his fraternal love and strong friendship. And now we see your fraternal love to show friendship toward our Great Sovereign the Tsar's Majesty. And your royal speeches were heard and the name of the Tsar our Great Sovereign is glorified. And we see your royal eyes from nearby, and it is for us your slaves to do that, to put the hats on ourselves at this time." And King James and the Queen and the Prince bowed slightly to the ambassadors and praised them for it and called them to [take] their hands.

And the ambassadors were at his hand, first at the King's, and then the Queen's and the Prince's and when they were at the hands they favored the ambassadors and they honored them kindly. And the undersecretary and the translator were at their hands. And the ambassadors bowed to his Royal Majesty, giving gifts and they bore in the gifts. Aleksei Ivanovich [Ziuzin] gave from himself to King James, forty black sables and a black fox; and to the Queen he gave forty sables and two pairs of black foxes; and to the Prince, forty sables and a pair of black foxes. And the Secretary, Aleksei Vitovtov, gave to the King forty sables, black; and to the Queen, two pairs of good black [foxes]; and to the Prince a black fox. [p. 223] And King James and the Queen and the Prince took the gifts from the ambassadors themselves, favoring them with care.[281] And they bowed to the ambassador for the gifts, and they released the ambassadors from themselves with honor. And themselves, they stood the whole time and did not put a single hat on themselves. And the ambassadors, to King James, and the Queen, and the Prince[282] of King James at her court. And you are to be at the Queen's court[283] with our sovereign in the rooms without superfluous people. And the ambassadors said to Sir Lewis: "That is the King's will. Wherever he, the sovereign, wants us to be with him we will go to him, your Great Sovereign, to the Queen's court as well."

And they went without delay so as to see the King at the present arrival. And the ambassadors went from the King's court to the Queen's court, about a verst and a half toward the City of London, for the Queen's court is closer to the City than the King's court. And on both sides of the Queen's court are the houses of boyars and merchants, the houses of all sorts of traders, and great markets with all kinds of goods on the same side and across the way from the court. And as they came to the Queen's court they descended from their horses by the gates and they entered the yard, and at that time by the gates and in the yard going from the gates stood on both sides women—wives and unmarried women. And the women were in bright fancy dresses and they honored the ambassadors, bowing according to their custom, and in the yard there were all sorts of people, men and women. And when the ambassadors came to the stairway [p. 224] the Queen's boyar and steward, the Lord Chamberlain,[284] met the ambassadors descending from the stairway to the yard.

And, having taken off his hat he greeted the ambassadors by the hand and said: "Our Great Sovereign King James has ordered me to meet you and bring you to his Royal Majesty." And he walked on the left hand of the ambassadors and they went through three rooms. In the first room stood on both sides guards with halberds, and in the second and third rooms stood the King's and Queen's boyars and other people of rank and many gentlemen and their wives and daughters, all parting to both sides as the ambassadors came. And they did honor to the ambassadors and bowed. And as the ambassadors came to the room where the King was to be, the King's boyar and Lord Lieutenant, the Lord Chamberlain,[285] came out of the antechamber of that room, met the ambassadors and walked with the ambassadors into the room; and in that room there were no other royal boyars, and the King's throne stands there, painted, on a dais, and below, on both sides, are chairs as well.

And the Lord said to the ambassadors: "It is good for you to sit, for our sovereign King James will come soon." And the ambassadors had just sat down when Sir Thomas, the son of Thomas, came from the King,[286] and he and the Lord Chamberlain spoke to one another and said to the ambassadors: "Our Great Sovereign King James, for the sake of his beloved brother, your Great Sovereign, his Tsar's Majesty, wanting to see his imperial fraternal love and friendship to himself and favoring you, the ambassadors, gives you an honor that has never been given to the ambassadors of any other states nor any other foreigners. No one besides you has ever been in the King's presence in these rooms."[287]

[p. 225] And the ambassadors said to the Lord and to Sir Thomas: "We see his Royal Majesty that he, your sovereign King James, as he is a just Christian sovereign, seeks out all good and carries out justice, wants to be in sincere fraternal love and friendship with our Great Sovereign, the Tsar and Grand Duke Mikhail Fyodorovich, Autocrat of all Russia, and so does this, and favors us, the slaves of his Tsar's Majesty. And we petition his Majesty for his favor to us. And our Great Sovereign, his Tsar's Majesty, in return for this will reward his beloved brother, your great sovereign King James, with his Tsar's fraternal, sincere love and friendship."

And at that time King James came out of the room from the Queen, and with him the Prince, and he came near to the ambassadors and when he stood in front of them he took off his hat to the ambassadors and went to his royal throne. And, standing on the step, he stopped on the edge on the dais and the Prince stood lower on another step and the ambassadors, coming up to the dais, bowed down to the ground to King James and King James, having taken off his hat, bowed to the ambassadors; and the King and the Prince did not put on the hats on themselves, and they held them themselves. And the ambassadors made a speech to King James:

"The Great Sovereign and Grand Duke by the grace of God, Mikhail Fyodorovich, Autocrat of all Russia and the sovereign and possessor of many states, wishing to announce to you, the Great Sovereign King James, his own Tsar's fraternal love, and remembering the previous loving communications and strong fraternal [p. 226] friendship according to the origin and family of his ancestors, the native Great Sovereign tsars and Grand Dukes, Russian Autocrats, the Tsar Ivan Vasil'evich [ST] and his son Fyodor Ivanovich [ST] and after these sovereigns, Tsar Boris Fyodorovich [ST], with the Great Sovereign of glorious memory Queen Elizabeth, and after that your King James, fraternal love and strong friendship and harmony with the Tsar and Grand Duke Boris Fyodorovich, and with the Tsar and Grand Duke Vasilii Ivanovich [Shuiskii] of all Russia, the Tsar's majesty has sent us, his servants, as ambassadors to you, Great Sovereign.

"And he has ordered us to announce his sovereignty and declare his Tsar's fraternal and friendly love to you, Great Sovereign, his beloved brother, King James, and to describe the injustices of the Polish King, Sigismund, and the lords councillors and the Swedish King to the Moscow state in great violation of their oaths. And this we have told you, Great Sovereign, at our audience and have given you our words in writing.[288] And now according to that we announce that we have been instructed by our Great Sovereign, the Tsar's majesty, to speak to you, Great Sovereign, about your other sovereignly matters, that Tsar Mikhail Fyodorovich [ST] wishes to be in fraternal love and strong friendship and agreement with you, Great Sovereign, his loving brother. And you Great Sovereign, King James, in this accord with our Great Sovereign, the Tsar's majesty [p. 227] should be in fraternal love and strong friendship and agreement and send to our Great Sovereign the Tsar's majesty your own ambassadors together with us and instruct them truly how you, the Great Sovereign, may be in loving and fraternal friendship and communication with our Great Sovereign for ever, unshakably.

"And for the completion of fraternal love now the Great Sovereign King James should show his original heartfelt loving friendship to our Great Sovereign, the Tsar's majesty, by this, that at the present time, because of the destruction of the Moscow state and his Tsar's majesty, he should help his Tsar's majesty against his enemy the Polish King Sigismund according to his fraternal love with treasure, money and gold, and all sorts of supplies, powder and lead, as is possible for you, great sovereign, so that the Great Sovereign, the Tsar's majesty might have something with which to favor his soldiers. And the Great Sovereign our Tsar and Grand Duke Mikhail Fyodorovich Autocrat of all Russia, seeing such fraternal friendship and love and aid from you, Great Sovereign, in response will return his own Tsar's love and stand with you against any enemy. And whomsoever you, Great Sovereign King James, send as ambassadors to our Great Sovereign, the Tsar's majesty, for those ambassadors a safe conduct has been sent with us from our Great Sovereign, the Tsar's majesty, to you Great Sovereign."[289]

[p. 228] And King James said to the ambassadors: "Before now, when you were before me at the audience,[290] I said to you and I now repeat: That I wish to be in sincere fraternal love and friendship and communication with the Great Sovereign my loving brother the Tsar and Grand Duke Mikhail Fyodorovich the Autocrat of all Russia, not only as with the previous Great Sovereigns, but even more than before."

And he asked the ambassadors for their speeches in writing. And the ambassadors gave their speech in writing to King James and the safe conduct for his ambassadors.

And King James took the speeches and the safe conduct himself, and looking at the documents he asked about them again, what was written in them, and was glad about them; and favored the ambassadors, bending over from the platform, and asked about [the ambassadors'] health and how God was looking after us and whether we had any needs or troubles.

And the ambassadors petitioned King James for his royal favor and said that by God's grace and your royal favor we need nothing more. And we were only sad that we had not seen your sovereignly eyes for so long. And all the business of our Great Sovereign, the Tsar's majesty, was not announced to you, great sovereign, all at once, because we had heard your royal order, that we should not announce all the business to you, Great Sovereign, at once because of pressing business. And now, Great Sovereign, you have ordered us to come to you and we, seeing your royal eyes and declaring all the business, are joyful. And when the ambassadors had finished speaking and bowed to the ground before King James they left.

And King James, as when they first arrived and before their departure, while the ambassadors were leaving, stood, having removed [p. 229] his hat, and held it himself. And in the same way the Prince stood having removed his hat.

And the King's boyar, the Lord Chamberlain, and the Prince's boyar and Lord Steward, also the Lord Chamberlain,[291] escorted the ambassadors in the same manner as they met them. And the ambassadors walked through the palace and sat in the coaches, and Sir Lewis Lewkenor and the merchant, John Merrick, escorted them to their lodgings. And when they had come to the lodgings Sir Lewis took them to their rooms and shook hands with the ambassadors and returned to his sovereign King James.[292]

And on the 5th day of February [1614] John Merrick came to the ambassadors and said that their sovereign King James had returned the ambassadors' speeches and the safe conduct yesterday to the Lord Chamberlain, and to Sir Thomas, and had ordered them to be translated. And Sir Thomas translated [them] to him, John.

And the ambassadors said to John [Merrick] that he should soon translate them and give them to Sir Thomas. And John Merrick translated the speeches for the letter and took it to Sir Thomas on the 6th day of February. And on the same day the ambassadors sent a translator[293] to Sir Thomas and ordered him to say that he had taken that translation to the sovereign King James earlier, before the King had left London.

And on February the 7th Sir Thomas sent to the ambassadors the English translator[294] so that he, Sir Thomas, might give the translation of the speeches and the letter to his Great Sovereign King James on that day in the morning. And our Sovereign left London for his royal villages at the third hour, and took the originals and the translations of the letter with him.

And on the 8th day of February Doctor Baldwin visited the ambassadors.[295] And the ambassadors and John Merrick had many times invited him to come. And John told him that only he had not gone to those places.

[p. 2] And the ambassadors spoke according to the instruction of the sovereign Tsar and Grand Duke Mikhail Fyodorovich of all Russia and according to the letters, which letters of the sovereign had been sent to them in Archangel, one to the ambassadors and the other a letter of grant to him, Baldwin.

And they said to Baldwin: "Our Great Sovereign Tsar and Grand Duke Mikhail Fyodorovich, Autocrat of all Russia, sovereign and possessor of many states, his Tsar's majesty when, by the petition and request of the whole Moscow state, and of all the towns of the Russian tsardom from the first ranks to the last, and of all sorts of people, and by the blessing of his mother, the Great Sovereign, the nun, Marfa Ivanovna, he became Great Sovereign Tsar and Grand Duke Autocrat of all Russia in all the great and most glorious states of the Russian tsardom, and by family relation to the previous Great Sovereigns our Tsars and Grand Dukes of Russia, as is known to you, then his Tsar's majesty remembered Baldwin Hamey, how you were in the Moscow state under his Tsar's majesty's uncle of blessed glorious memory, the Tsar and Grand Duke Fyodor Ivanovich, Autocrat of all Russia, and the sovereign's near relation. And you served the sovereign father of his Tsar's majesty, the Great Sovereign our Tsar and Grand Duke Mikhail Fyodorovich, Autocrat of all Russia, Fyodor Nikitich, when he, the sovereign, was among the boyars, and the sovereign mother of the Tsar's majesty, and you were honored and wished good to the sovereigns and afterward suffered for them, the sovereigns, [p. 3] and the Tsar's majesty ordered us, taking pity on you, to speak a word of the Tsar's favor so that you might hope for his sovereignly grace and would serve him as before.

"And now, hoping again for his Tsar's grace you might go to him, the Great Sovereign, our Tsar's majesty, to serve him with your trade together with us the ambassadors. And the Great Sovereign our Tsar and Grand Duke Mikhail Fyodorovich, Autocrat of all Russia will favor you with his great Tsar's favor and you will in his merciful Tsar's care, and he has sent you his Tsar's letter of favor and a safe conduct that you might freely come to his Tsar's majesty and return without any hindrance."

And they announced the sovereign's letter of favor and ordered it read out and did not give it to him, waiting for what he would say.

And Baldwin heard the sovereign's letters of favor and the ambassadors' speeches and said to the ambassadors: "I heard of the Great Sovereign Tsar and Grand Duke Mikhail Fyodorovich, Autocrat of all Russia, that he has become the sovereign of the Moscow state and seeing his great Tsar's love to me I am joyful at it, and though I have gotten old I would only wish with all my soul to go to his Tsar's majesty and serve him the Great Sovereign[296] and be honest and be glad to wish him good as much as I am able."

And he asked the ambassadors to give him the sovereign's letter of grant. And he spoke according to his custom: "That the very cover and the Tsar's letter of favor is dearly valuable and I will hold it with great honor and boast of the Tsar's favor; and I have the old [p. 4] letter of grant of the uncle of the Tsar's majesty, the Great Sovereign and Grand Duke Mikhail Fyodorovich, Autocrat of all Russia. And I will keep those sovereignly letters of grant together, for I and my children will remember their Great Sovereigns' Tsars' favor forever."

And the ambassadors said to Baldwin, seeing his care for the Tsar's majesty, gave him the letter and asked him to say whether he would go together with us to our Great Sovereign.

And Baldwin said to the ambassadors: "I said to you let me talk it over, for I am definitely glad to go to the Great Sovereign but I cannot say right now, give me time to talk to my near ones and I will let you know."

And the ambassadors said to Baldwin to come to them more often and assured him that he could without doubt go to our great sovereign to his Tsar's majesty hoping for his Tsar's grace.

And on February 28 Baldwin came to the ambassadors and the ambassadors asked him, has he Baldwin decided and is he ready to go together with them to our Great Sovereign his Tsar's majesty?

And Baldwin said to the ambassadors: "I was glad to go together with you to the Tsar's majesty; and when I told my mother and my other near ones that I would go to the Tsar's majesty with my whole family, with my mother, wife, and children, so as to go to serve the Great Sovereign his Tsar's majesty, and live in the Moscow state at his Tsar's command however much my service should be useful to him, the Great Sovereign. And my mother now does not allow [me] [p 5] to go because she is old and my wife is pregnant and now it is not possible for me to go."[297]

And the ambassadors said to Baldwin, that he should remember the previous favor of the Tsar's majesty, what sovereignly grace he enjoyed before in the Moscow state. And now he expected ever greater favor of the Tsar and he should go to serve our Great Sovereign hoping for his Tsar's grace even if he went alone because he could not do it with his whole family. "And when you will be in the Moscow state the Great

Sovereign our Tsar and Grand Duke Mikhail Fyodorovich, Autocrat of all Russia, by his Tsar's merciful custom, favoring you, he will not allow to be forced about how much you will serve with his Tsar's majesty. And when you want to go back to your own land then the Tsar's majesty will order you to be released without any hindrance whatsoever."

And Baldwin said to the ambassadors that: "I see the present favor of the Tsar's majesty to me and I remember the previous sovereignly grace and am glad at the future favor of the Tsar. But when I was then in the Moscow state I was not married and now I have a wife and children and have established a household and cannot part from my family. And in the future when my chance comes I will be glad to go to serve the Great Sovereign the Tsar's majesty."

And on March 5 the ambassadors spoke to the merchant, John Merrick, about doctors and smiths and in accord with the letters of the sovereign Tsar and Grand Duke Mikhail Fyodorovich of all Russia [that] spoke to him about doctors and smiths.[298]

And John Merrick said to the ambassadors that he would speak to doctors and [p. 6] smiths about this with care.

And on March 15 John Merrick said to the ambassadors the doctors and smiths do not want to go and they say that there is enough for them here.

And the ambassadors told John that you know how in the past under our Great Sovereigns the Tsars of Russia many willing people from other states and from England, doctors and smiths and many learned necessary artisans, knowing about the Moscow state, that it is abundant in everything and hearing of the Tsar's grace, came by themselves and were in honor and sufficiency and earned a great deal. And now our Great Sovereign the Tsar's majesty wants also to see in his country necessary foreigners, and wants to show his Tsar's grace to them more than before, and for that reason he has sent his sovereignly safe conduct to them and you, John, should, as in your previous service take care of finding doctors and smiths for the Tsar's majesty.

And John Merrick said to the ambassadors: "I will take care of it." And he took the Tsar's safe conducts with him so that they would trust him more.

April 24, on Easter, to the ambassadors from the Great Sovereign King James came his royal gentleman of the bedchamber, Edward Walgrave,[299] and got out of the coach outside the gates and came to the ambassadors having taken off his hat, and shook their hands and said to the ambassadors that our Great Sovereign King James has sent me to the ambassadors of the Tsar's majesty. And he ordered me to tell you that you are to/[300]

THE END

Notes

1. The page numbers in square brackets throughout the text refer to the pagination of the rotoprint edition, *Posol'skaia Kniga po sviaz'iam Rossii s Angliei*, edited by V. Buganov and N. Rogozhin (Moscow, 1979). The manuscript (fund 35, op. 1, d. 3) is part of the collection of English affairs documents (*Angliiskie dela*) originating in the Ambassadorial Chancellery (*Posol'skii prikaz*) at the State Archives for Ancient Documentation; see Preliminary Materials.

2. Probably the letter written in early June from Moscow that was referred to in the Tsar's letter of 3 July 1613 (see below, p. 139) and was responded to by the Governor and Secretary on 9 June 1613 (printed below, pp. 140–141).

3. In the interests of economy from this point forward where the designation [ST] (short title) is inserted into the translated text the full title of the ruler has been shortened to "Tsar," followed by the Christian name and patronymic, as Tsar Mikhail Fyodorovich. For a description of the customary full title, see the Editorial Conventions, above, pp. x–xi.

4. For a letter to the Governor and Secretary from Tsar Michael, 3 July, see below, pp. 139–140. According to that correspondence there were several letters sent from Moscow about the arrangements for the ships.

5. "Germans" was the name Russians gave in the sixteenth-seventeenth centuries to North European foreigners, including the English.

6. We have not found the letter to Tsar Michael from Ziuzin and Vitovtov. On 9 June Pushkin and Gregoriov had informed the Tsar that they had spoken with the English merchants in Archangel (see below, p. 140). According to Ziuzin's report, Merrick and company petitioned Michael, wanting "to show their service to the Tsar" (see below, p. 141). On 2 July 1613 the Tsar requested that John Merrick demonstrate his service by "commanding a ship to be prepared and made ready for the transporting of our ambassador into England. . . . [and] to go along with our ambassador to your great sovereign. . . ." HMC, *Buccleuch and Queensberry*, 1: 136–137.

7. Christian IV, King of Denmark, 1588–1648 (regency 1588–1596). For the letter to Christian from Tsar Michael, Moscow, June 1613, see below, pp. 137.

8. Michael Fyodorovich had been elected Tsar on 7 February 1613 but would not be crowned until 21 July of that year.

9. Prince Ivan Boriatinskii was sent as ambassador to Denmark with his secretary, Gavrilo Bogdanov. See below, p. 137, 139 and Introduction, p. 70. The new Russian government also sent ambassadors to Holland, the Empire, and Turkey. See V. A. Kordt, "Ocherk snoshenii Moskovskogo gosudarstva s Respublikoi Soedinennykh Niderlandov po 1631 g.," *SRIO* 116 (1902): CIII-CXI; Walter Leitsch, *Moskau und die Politik des Kaiserhofes im XVII Jahrhundert (1604–1654)* 1 (Graz, 1960), pp. 182–188; and idem, "Sultan Ahmed I und Michail Romanov im Jahre 1614," *Jahrbücher für Geschichte Osteuropas* 4 (1956), 3: 246–261.

10. At the time that Ziuzin and Vitovtov left Moscow for Archangel Tsar Michael did not know that James had negotiated the peace of Knaerød between the Danes and the Swedes (see below, p. 141 and n. 11). The news regarding Knaerød and the disposition of Lord Willoughby's mercenaries was brought by the English merchants when they landed

at Archangel and relayed to Moscow by the Governor (see below, pp. 140–141). As a result of the confirmation of the situation between England and Sweden Tsar Michael amended and expanded the original instructions to Ziuzin; see below, pp. 142–144.

11. James aided in the treaty negotiations between Sweden and Denmark to end the Kalmar war (see below, n. 12) at the initial suggestion of his ambassadors. See Sir R. Anstruther to T. Lake, 18 Jan. 1613, that "we fearing that their [the Danes and Swedes] meeting should be altogether without fruit, which to prevent we made offer of our labors in behalf of his Majesty of Great Britain, who had sent us, to procure so much as possible might be, a cessation of arms and a good peace between them. . . . the matter is so agreed that both the Kings of Denmark and Sweden to rest content, and are to send and give humble and hearty thanks to his Majesty of Great Britain. . . . You may be so persuaded that this treaty is so concluded that his Majesty of Great Britain only has the honor of it, and no other princes, for the beginning and ending thereof is in his name." SP 75/5, ff. 59–60. Same to same, 24 January 1613, ". . . for the condition is so betwixt them that they both shall sollicitate for his Majesty of Great Britain his confirmation, for next unto God the honor belongs only unto his Majesty." Ibid., ff. 61–61v. See also SP 84/68, ff. 111–112; HMC, *Downshire*, 4: 73. See below, p. 141.

12. Christian IV declared war on Sweden on 4 April 1611 (for the declaration, see SP 75/4, f. 247–247v; and see also SP 84/68, f. 44–44v, Sir R. Winwood to Salisbury from the Hague, 26 April 1611). Letters of challenge were exchanged on 12 and 13 August (SP 75/4, ff. 266, 267; see also BL Add. 15,939, f. 19). Charles IX accused Christian of violating the peace of Stettin and challenged him to a duel, which Christian refused (ibid., ff. 19v-20). For the duration of the Kalmar War the English were kept informed of events by newsletters from various sources. A major concern to the English was the resulting relationship between Sweden and Poland. Sir James Spens wrote to Salisbury, 8 November 1610, that the "assistance of the Poles against the Russes he will be compelled (although with hazard) to accept rather than to be in danger of the Danes" (SP 95/1, f. 177). See also rumors of a "secret" Polish-Danish contract against the Swedes. Sir R. Winwood to Salisbury, 19 March 1612 (SP 84/68, f. 260). Sir Henry Peyton (English adventurer in Holland) wrote on 7 March 1611 that "Poland and Sweden, the ancient enemies, knit in keeping off this blow [of Denmark] for one year more" (MS Eng. Hist. C 4, f. 9v); Sir R. Winwood to Sir T. Edmondes, 7 August 1611 (Stowe 172, ff. 152–153). See also A. Aidy to R. Salisbury, 15 April 1611 (SP 88/3, f. 17; Talbot, ed., *Elementa* 6: 101–102). T. Lake to R. Salisbury, 17 July 1611 (SP 14/65:38); same to same, 19 August 1611 (SP 14/65:79). See also Sir R. Winwood to Sir T. Edmondes, 12 April 1611 (Stowe 172, ff. 12–13v); same to same, 10 May 1611 (ibid., f. 130); CSPV 1610–1613, sub Sweden. The Swedish King did not live to see peace, for he died at Nyköping on 30 October 1611. The war ended successfully for the Danes with the Treaty of Knaerød, 20 January 1613 (for the "contract of peace," 12 May 1613, see SP 75/5, ff. 73–78; Rymer, *Foedera* 7: 189–191). James I was a guarantor of the treaty (SP 75/5, f. 63 and see SO 3/5, April 1613). See also the memo of Sir R. Anstruther, 1612 (SP 75/5, f. 55–55v); Sir R. Anstruther to T. Lake, 18 Jan. 1612/13 (ibid., ff. 59–60), same to same, 24 Jan., 1612/13 (ibid., f. 61–61v; CSPV 1610–1613, pp. 508–509, 519, 524). Complaints about the increase in tolls "raised higher in the last war" were sent to Denmark from the States General of Holland (SP 75/5, ff. 79–82; SP 84/69, ff. 72–73). See also HMC, *Downshire*, 4: 45, 141, 296.

13. Sigismund III, King of Poland, 1587–1632, had pleaded with King James in 1603 "to extend lawful favors" to Roman Catholics in England (SP 14/6:37); in 1606 James wrote to Sigismund supporting him against the Zebrzydowski revolt (SP 88/3, f.156;

Talbot, ed., *Elementa* 6: 26). In August 1616 the Venetian ambassador reported that the Swedes complained that James favored Poland by allowing shipping of English war material to Riga (*CSPV 1610–1613*, p. 26). Sweden subsequently sought an alliance with England against Sigismund but James refused, declaring he would neither assist the Poles nor make himself hostile to them (ibid., 31). More recently Sigismund had written personally to James on 23 February 1611 (SP 88/3, f. 9; ibid. 6: 97), and on 14 April 1613, regarding peace between Poland and Sweden (SP 88/3, f.62; ibid. 6: 130–131); and concerning trade, etc., see P. Gordon to R. Salisbury, 28 April 1611 (SP 88/3, f. 19; Talbot, ed., *Elementa* 6: 103).

14. MS.: *pod'iachii*. Andrei Semenov was the undersecretary; see below, p. 147.

15. See below, p. 170.

16. See below, p. 171.

17. For the reports of Ziuzin's and Vitovtov's speeches to James I, see below, pp. 171–173. According to Ferdinand de Boisschot, ambassador from the Archduke to England, "The ambassador harangued in his tongue for almost an hour." HHST, Abteilung Belgien, PC fz. 48.

18. Ivan IV, Tsar, 1547–1584. Privileges were granted to English merchants by Ivan in 1555 (*CSPD Addenda 1547–1565*, p. 439), 1567 *CSPD Addenda 1566–1579*, p. 39; Richard Hakluyt, *The Principall Navigations, Voiages and Discoveries of the English Nation* (London, 1589; reprt. Cambridge University Press), 1: 397–399 and 1569 (ibid., p. 81; *CSPD 1547–1580*, p. 338; Lansd. 11, ff. 50–55v; ibid., 141, ff. 278–284v). See Hakluyt, *Voiages*, 1: 292–293, 302–304. Anthony Jenkins went to Russia in 1557 (Hakluyt, *Voiages*, 1: 333–374). In 1568 Thomas Randolph traveled to Russia on behalf of the English merchants (see *CSPD 1566–1579*, p. 84 and Hakluyt, *Voiages*, 1: 399–406) and went again as ambassador in 1571 (ibid. 1: 426–436). Privileges were restored in 1572 (*CSPD 1572–1574*, p. 99). Daniel Sylvester went as envoy to Ivan in 1575 (for his instructions, see Cotton Nero B XI, f. 349; Egerton 2790, ff. 178–180; Harl. 36, ff. 194–196v); Pisemskii was ambassador from the Tsar to Elizabeth in 1582, and Sir Jerome Bowes was ambassador in 1583–1584 (for his instructions; see Cotton Nero B VIII, ff. 32–34v; SP 91/1, ff. 10–14). See also, Hakluyt, *Voiages*, 1: 491–496; and Robert M. Croskey, "Hakluyt's Accounts of Sir Jerome Bowes's Embassy to Ivan IV," *SEER* 61 (October, 1983): 546–564.

19. Fyodor Ivanovich, Tsar, 1584–1598. Privileges were granted by Fyodor in 1586/87 (SP 91/1, ff. 55–58); in 1597/98 (*CSPD 1595–1597*, p. 222; *CSPD Addenda 1580–1625*, p. 376; SP 91/1, ff. 118–119v; Hakluyt, *Voiages*, 1: 502–503). Jerome Horsey, a clerk in the Russia Company, went to Russia in 1573 and subsequently represented the Tsar to the English court. *D[ictionary] of N[ational] B[iography]*. Giles Fletcher went as envoy in 1588 (Hakluyt, *Voiages*, 1: 502–504) and Francis Cherry as a messenger in 1598.

20. Boris Fyodorovich Godunov, Tsar, 1598–1605. For the correspondence between Elizabeth and Boris, see SP 91/1, passim. Sir Richard Lee was ambassador to Boris from Elizabeth I, 1600 (for his instructions, see Cotton Nero B VIII, ff. 35–36; BL Dep. c. 544/4; SP 91/1, f. 137; HMC, *Salisbury*, 10: 169–172) and Gregory Ivanovich Mikulin was ambassador to Queen Elizabeth from Boris in 1600–1601 (see N. E. Evans, "The Meeting of the Russian and Scottish Ambassadors in London in 1601", *SEER* 55 [October, 1977]: 517–528; SP 12/175:89, 94). John Merrick went to Russia on behalf of Elizabeth in 1602/3 (for his account of the trip, see Cotton Nero B VIII, ff. 38–40v; for the instructions, see SP 91/1, ff. 177–178). Sir Thomas Smith was special ambassador to Boris from James in 1604 (for a draft of his instructions, see SP 91/1, ff. 196–198; 199–202). See also the account of his mission in Purchas, *Haklutys Posthumus*, 14: 132–157. Regarding Smith, see below, nn. 190 and 197.

21. Elizabeth I, Queen of England, 1558–1603. Aside from the embassies during her reign (see above note), there were in 1575/76 "Articles agreed upon on her Majesty's part for a league of amity between her Highness and the great Duke of Moscow." (SP 103/61,ff. 7–8). Article 9 provides for regular ambassadorial representation between the countries (SP 103/61, f. 1–1v). See Introduction, above, pp. 15–17. See also BL Cotton Nero B, VIII, f. 32, copies of the Instructions to Sir Jerome Bowes to treat of a league defensive and offensive and a treaty of amity (1583).

22. Vasilii Ivanovich Shuiskii, Tsar, 1606–1610.

23. MS: *Ivan Ul'ianov*, John, son of William; the patronymic is used throughout the manuscript. John Merrick was the son of William Merrick, a London Merchant Taylor. Geraldine M. Phipps, *Sir John Merrick, English Diplomat in Seventeenth Century Russia* (Newtonville: Oriental Research Partners, 1983), p. 1. The letter is printed in Purchas, *Hakluytus Posthumus* 14: 184–196.

24. I.e., his own, Sigismund's.

25. MS: *sekretar'*, evidently referring to the royal secretaries of Poland, officials of the King's chancery.

26. Sigismund III and Shuiskii signed a treaty in 1608 whereby Sigismund agreed to withdraw support from the second False Dmitrii. Robert O. Crummey, *The Formation of Muscovy* (New York: Longman), p. 224; Michael Roberts, *The Early Vasas, A History of Sweden, 1523–1611* (New York: Cambridge University Press, 1986), p. 453.

27. I.e., the first False Dmitrii. Claiming to be the youngest son of Ivan IV he was, in fact, Grishka Otrep'ev, a defrocked monk from the Chudov monastery in Moscow. His assassination in 1606 opened the way for Vasilii Shuiskii to take the throne. Crummey, *Muscovy*, pp. 217–219. For an account of the town of Pskov rendering itself over "to the Poles in the name of one Demetrius, whom they say is yet alive," see SP 75/4, f. 115.

28. I.e., the area to the northeast of Kiev, now lying partly in the Ukraine and partly in Russia.

29. I.e., the second False Dmitrii also known as the thief of Kaluga. After the overthrow of Shuiskii in early 1610 Patriarch Germogen rallied support against this second imposter who was murdered the same year. See Crummey, *Muscovy*, pp. 224–227.

30. Jerzy Mniszech and his daughter Marina Mniszech. Marina is referred to throughout the text in the somewhat derogatory diminutive, Marinka. In England she was described as "a daughter of a peer of Poland." See SP 91/2, ff. 66–66v, brief notices of Russian rulers endorsed, "The Succession of the Emperor of Russia," Appendix, below, p. 212.

31. The truce between Sigismund and Shuiskii was agreed to in 1608 but was ineffectual, "worth less than the parchment on which it was written." Crummey, *Muscovy*, p. 224.

32. Marina Mniszech married and had a child by the second False Dmitrii, who was identified in a newsletter from T. Chamberlayn to R. Salisbury, as "questionless a Jesuit." (SP 88/3, f. 42; Talbot, ed., *Elementa* 6: 116). See also, same to same, 22 January 1611, where it was reported in 1611 that, "Demetrius, the second Jesuit that married with the first Dmitrii's wife is cut in pieces by his own people." (SP 88/3, f. 7v; Talbot, ed., *Elementa* 6: 96). She had previously married the first False Dmitrii (Grishka Otrep'ev) in an Eastern Orthodox service on 8 May 1606, although he was known to have been secretly a Roman Catholic. It was reported, G. Bruce to Salisbury, 5 August 1606, that he was assassinated ten days later, on 27 May (SP 88/2, f. 143; Talbot, ed., *Elementa* 6: 15–16). Apparently the Moscoviters found both of "these Dmitriies to be but a popish statagem," G. Bruce to Salisbury (SP 88/3, f. 42v; Talbot, ed., *Elementa* 6: 13–14, 116). See the newsletter from Danzig, 2 Aug. 1605, HMC, *De L'Isle and Dudley*, 3: 187, and see

also Crummey, *Muscovy*, p. 219. After the second Dmitrii's death Marina took up with Ivan Zarutskii; see below, pp. 123–124.

33. Smolensk fell to Sigismund on 3 June 1611. Sigismund was in part retaliating from Shuiskii's signing of the Treaty of Viborg with Sweden on 28 February 1609, an act in violation of the four-year Polish-Russian truce (see above, n. 26). Roberts, *Early Vasas*, p. 453. Accounts of the siege had been sent to England as early October 1610. See P. Gordon to King James (SP 88/2, f. 242); T. Chamberlayn to Salisbury (SP 88/2, f. 246); J. M. Radziwiłł to King James (SP 88/3, f. 5). See also P. Gordon to Salisbury (SP 88/3, f. 19); A. Aidy to Salisbury (SP 88/3, f. 24); same to same (SP 88/3, f. 34); R. Winwood to Salisbury, 21 July 1611, from the Hague (SP 84/68, f. 91). T. Chamberlayn to Salisbury (SP 88/3, f. 42–45), printed in Talbot, ed., *Elementa* 6: 79–80, 81–82, 94–95, 101–102, 106, 111, 116–119, respectively. On 8 Dec. 1611, H. Bilderbeck reported to W. Trumbull that, "at the Diet of Warsaw, at which the King was present, it was decided to continue the Russian war for nine years" (HMC, *Downshire*, 3: 193). See also, CSPV 1610–1613, p. 57; and R. Engelsted to Salisbury, 25 October 1608 (SP 75/4, ff. 115–116).

34. Jakob Pontusson de la Gardie; see below, pp. 97–100.

35. Charles IX, King of Sweden, 1604–1611 (Regent, 1599–1604).

36. See above, n. 5.

37. I.e., the General Żółkiewski who was killed in battle in late 1620 (SP 88/3, f. 203; Talbot, ed., *Elementa* 6: 208–209).

38. I.e., Sigismund's son, Prince Władysław, who succeeded his father as Władysław IV, King of Poland, 1632–1648. He was formally chosen Russian Tsar on 17 August 1610 by a group of boyars. Roberts, *Early Vasas*, p. 455.

39. King Sigismund's letter to the boyars (12 November 1609). SRIO 142, 48–49. It was reported that Władysław was to succeed "provided that he puts no Poles into any of their strengths or ports, and not to bring in papistry, as in particular no Jesuits, priests, monks, or friars." T. Chamberlayn to Salisbury, n.d. (SP 88/3, f. 45; Talbot, ed., *Elementa* 6: 119). Furthermore a condition was that "Moschovitish empire . . . be no ways subject or annexed to the crown of Poland." P. Gordon to James I (SP 88/2, f. 242; Talbot, *Elementa* 6: 79); see also, P. Gordon to Salisbury, 28 April 1611 (SP 88/3, f. 19; Talbot, *Elementa* 6: 103–104). See also, CSPV 1610–1613, pp. 127, 152.

40. Shuiskii was deposed on 17 July 1610. A contemporary English account records that he was "shorn a friar and, with his two brothers, delivered up prisoner into the Poles' hand . . . his younger brother lives still in Poland, unmarried." SP 91/2, f. 66v. The Polish intervention was seen as Catholic. In November 1610 T. Chamberlayn writing to Salisbury announced that he had succeeded in getting a letter of introduction "to the Pope or any Catholic prince or state whatsoever." He then proposed, if England saw fit to employ him in that service, to go to Brussels and "to either poison or pistole" Hugh O'Neill, Earl of Tyrone (SP 88/2, f. 246; Talbot, ed., *Elementa* 6: 81).

41. See Crummey, *Muscovy*, pp. 226–227.

42. I.e., to offer Prince Władysław the crown. See Crummey, *Muscovy*, pp. 226–227.

43. On Patriarch Germogen, see above, n. 29 and see Crummey, *Muscovy*, p. 227. Germogen provided leadership against the Roman Catholic attempt to convert the Muscovites.

44. Sigismund chose now to put himself forward to be the Tsar rather than supporting his son for the title; see below, pp. 94–95. In theory and practice ambassadors represented the government they served and consequently were immune from prosecution from any other. See William Segar, *Honor, Military and Civill*. London: 1602, STC 22164, p. 32. "Ambassadors ought to be in all countries inviolable . . . and who so offered them

violence was thought to have done contrary to [the] law of nations . . . whosoever did strike an ambassador should be delivered unto that enemy from whom the ambassador was sent." An English translation of Jean Hotman's *The Ambassador*, appeared in London in 1603 (STC 13848). He wrote that ambassadors are "inviolable even in the midst of armies" (no page numbers). And see T.B. Howell, A *Distinct Treatise of Ambassadors, etc.* (London, 1664), pp. 187–189. See also G. Mattingly, *Renaissance Diplomacy* (New York: Dover edition, 1988).

45. T. Chamberlayn wrote to Salisbury about this incident: "Now the tyrannies which the Poles have used unto the Russians in these wars have made them so hateful that they had rather to be commanded by any other nation than by them, so in my duty and love I could wish that our noble Duke of York were there to decide this question" (SP 88/3, f. 45v; Talbot, ed., *Elementa* 6: 119).

46. The editors can only conjecture about the identity of Mark, the English merchant who remained in Moscow during the siege by the Lithuanians and Poles. See below, pp. 110–111 and n. 97.

47. These are court ranks: the *chashnik* took care of the Tsar's drinks, the *stol'nik* his table, and the *striapchii* was a sort of general adjutant. All three ranks were often honorific. See below, p. 93

48. I.e., the well-populated district of the city of Moscow to the east of the Kremlin.

49. I.e., the semi-rural part of the city of Moscow outside the walls erected in 1535.

50. The Russian army was led by Pozharskii with support from Prince Trubetskoi's cossacks.

51. I.e., the monastery town to the west of the city of Moscow.

52. See above, nn. 18, 19, and 20.

53. See below, p. 136. Ziuzin carried with him to England writs of safe conduct for English ambassadors traveling to Russia.

54. James did ask for the speeches in writing (see below, p. 173) and ordered them translated (see below, p. 178).

55. Russia had been cut off from Europe since the death of Boris Godunov in 1605. The Instructions to Ziuzin were written before the arrival of the English merchants in Archangel bringing news from the outside world and they were constructed to give latitude to the ambassador in responding to a variety of eventualities. Before the arrival of the English merchants the Tsar was obviously unclear about the Treaty of Knaerød, signed 20/30 January 1613. See above, n. 12. For the news brought by Merrick, see below, pp. 140–141.

56. In the previous version of the history (see above, p. 10), Jakob Pontusson bore the blame for breaking the oath rather than King Charles. In this case the responsibility is placed on the Swedish King, and as a countermeasure an Anglo-Russian-Danish alliance against Sweden is proposed. The issue of such an alliance was raised again in the amended instructions, see below, p. 143.

57. I.e., the Tsar's letter that accompanied the ambassadors to Denmark. See above, n. 9.

58. Printed edition: *our*.

59. I.e., Ziuzin and Vitovtov.

60. For the Tsar's instructions, see below, pp. 104–106.

61. I.e., the case wherein the Poles had already presented their interpretation of events to James.

62. Grishka Otrep'ev, the first false Dmitrii. See above, n. 27.

63. Charles IX had two sons by his second wife, Kristina of Holstein-Gottorp: Gusta-

vus (II) Adolphus who succeeded his father in 1611 and Karl Philip. A newsletter from Cracow, 28 January 1613, Anon. to Anon., announces that "Il vient confirme que le Moscovite avoit envoié une principale ambassade en Suède pour demander le second filz du feu Roy Charles pour estre leur Prince . . ." (SP 88/3, f. 61v; Talbot, ed., *Elementa* 6: 129–130). On 29 January 1613/14 Sir R. Winwood wrote to W. Trumbull, "We hear that Prince Charles [Philip], younger brother to the King of Sweden, is chosen by the Muscovite to be grand Duke." HMC, *Downshire*, 4: 29. See also, SP 84/69, ff. 16–17v, Sir R. Winwood to Rochester, 5 February 1613; *CSPV 1610–1613*, p. 163; *Moscovitica* 1 (Letters and Archives of Swedish Diplomatic Missions), vols. 17–19, Documents concerning Duke Charles Philip's election as Tsar of Russia, 1612–1616, Swedish National Archives, Stockholm. See Ziuzin, below, p. 00, where the story is denied as a rumor.

64. Gustavus (II) Adolphus, King of Sweden, 1611–1632.

65. The treaty of 11 March 1601 is to be found in *SRIO* 137; 58–73. For a brief description of Sapieha's embassy, see Jacques Margeret, *The Russian Empire and Grand Duchy of Muscovy*, ed. S.L. Dunning (Pittsburgh: Series in Russian and East European Studies), pp. 54–55.

66. See above, Introduction, n. 9.

67. According to Margeret (Dunning, ed., p. 67) on his march to Moscow Dmitrii himself daily dispatched letters admonishing the Russians to surrender. See also Purchas, *Hakluytus Posthumus* 14: 148–150.

68. Godunov died on 13 April 1605.

69. It was at the time of Boris's death that Jacques Margeret entered the Russian service. See Margeret (Dunning, ed.), *Russian Empire*, p. 69. See below, nn. 122–125.

70. An account of both the wedding and the assassination was sent to Prince Henry's tutor, Adam Newton. See G. Bruce to Salisbury, no month, 1605 (SP 88/2, f. 141; Talbot, ed., *Elementa* 6: 13–14). See also, same to same, 5 August 1606 (SP 88/21, f. 143; ibid., 15–16); and Margeret (Dunning, ed.), *Russian Empire*, pp. 68, 72–73.

71. See above, n. 70.

72. Witowski's embassy from Sigismund to Shuiskii: *SRIO* 137, 388–736.

73. I.e., the second false Dmitrii, also known as the thief of Tushino. See Crummey, *Moscovy*, pp. 222–226.

74. See above, n. 31. See Anon. to Anon., 30 October 1606 (SP 88/2, f. 147; Talbot, ed., *Elementa* 6: 19).

75. See above, n. 32.

76. See above, n. 39.

77. See above, n. 39.

78. In 1610. See above, n. 40.

79. See above, n. 29.

80. See above, n. 44.

81. See above, n. 33.

82. See above, nn. 48 and 49. Apparently it was in one of these battles that Mark, the Englishman, was killed. See below, n. 97.

83. See above, n. 51.

84. See above, n. 35.

85. The treaty of Tiavzino (Teusina) of 18 May 1595 recognized Swedish rule in Estonia and staples in Viborg and Reval for Russian trade with the West.

86. See below, pp. 171 and 172. James acknowledged that "the treason of their Swedish General . . . is known to us."

87. See above, n. 63.

88. Tsar Michael's hope was that James would send ambassadors to Russia qualified to carry out negotiations with the Tsar after he had been apprised of the political situation in England by Ziuzin. See below, n. 92.

89. Secretary Winwood said in parliament that Tsar Michael was looking for £50,000. See *Proceedings in Parliament 1614*, ed. Maija Jansson (Philadelphia: American Philosophical Society, 1988): 429, 433. According to Winwood, the Dutch offered the Russians £60,000 support in the expectation of favorable trade status; the information was conveyed by the secretary of the east country merchants. See SP 91/2, f. 58–58v. A ruble was worth 14 shillings (S. Konovalov, "Anglo-Russian Relations, 1620–4," OSP [1953], 4: 74). See also, Appendix, below, p. 211.

90. This was the 1595 Russian embassy to Emperor Rudolf: *Pamiatniki diplomaticheskikh snoshenii* 2, 202–373, and Introduction, pp. 44.

91. For the safe conduct, see below, p. 136.

92. Ziuzin's discussion of a Swedish-Polish peace in 1613–1614 was preliminary to the actual request for James's help in that regard in 1616–1617 by Michael's second ambassador to England, Stephan Evanovitch Volinskii. Sir J. Throckmorton wrote to W. Trumbull on 11 January 1613/14 that, "the King is now resolved to deal between the 'Russhes', Sweden and Poland for peace, thereby to bind the Russhes to him for the merchants' trade there." HMC, *Downshire*, 4: 286. See also, ibid., 274 and the report that the Emperor was sending an ambassador to arrange peace between the Poles and the Grand Duke elected in Moscow. Patrick Gordon would be sent by James to Poland in March 1614. See also, CSPV *1613–1614*, pp. 97–98. Volinskii's embassy resulted in the English negotiation of the Treaty of Stolbovo in 1617.

93. The following text was crossed out in the manuscript after the word "majesty": "his ambassadors or emissaries to the conference to them without delay. And he will send his Tsar's letter to your sovereign and to King Sigismund's ambassadors, saying where the ambassadors should meet. And they will arrange the meeting as the two sides will agree and find convenient. And we have not been instructed as to where the meeting will be."

94. A year and a half before the embassy from Tsar Michael English merchants were discussing plans for new routes for Eastern trade. A commission had been granted to Thomas Button for "the discovery of the northwest passage to Cathay and China, etc." (SO 3/5, April 1612). And see J. Chamberlain to Sir D. Carleton, 29 April 1613: "There be many far set projects on foot, how to draw all the traffic of Persia and the inland parts of the East Indies up the river Hidaspes into the river Oxus that falls into the Caspian sea, whence with certain small ships that shall be built the commodities are to be brought up the Volga to a strait of land not above forty miles and so into the river Dwina that comes to St. Nicolas or the town of the Archangell the ordinarie ports and stations of our shipping in those parts: these I doubt are but discourses in the air, and yet Sir Henry Nevill has been much employed in them . . ." (SP 14/72:120; printed in Chamberlain, *Letters*, 1: 445). Chamberlain reported to Sir R. Winwood in May that the merchants' idea of a route through Russia grew out of "certain speeches of some of the nobility to an English merchant about two years since, but *tempora mutantur . . .* these be goodly specious discourses of things not so easily done as spoken" (Winwood papers, vol. 9, printed in Chamberlain, *Letters*, 1: 448). See also Cotton Nero B XI, ff. 381–384, where the argument for a presence in Russia is related to the supply of naval stores.

95. English merchants wanted no competition from the Dutch in the Russian ports. The Venetians reported on 12 April 1614 that the States and Prince Maurice receive letters from Tsar Michael offering free commerce (CSPV, *1613–1614*, p. 110). On 23 May they reported the arrival of a Russian ambassador at the Hague to discuss trade (ibid.,

p. 121). This was also reported in England two weeks earlier (9 May) by Sir Henry Peyton, who described him as "a person of great quality, his train 20 in number. He was honorably received by his Excellency, so lodged and defrayed by the States" (MS Eng. Hist. c. 4, f. 23; see also SP 91/2, f. 58–58v, "Reasons to induce his Majesty to the loan of monies unto the great Emperor of Russia now required by his ambassador Alexsey Ivanov, etc." Appendix, below).

96. Privileges had been granted from the Tsars to English merchants in 1555 (Lansd. 141, f. 262–262v; printed in Hakluyt, *Voiages* 1: 302–304); in 1569 (Lansd. 141, ff. 278–284v; printed ibid., 1: 402–406); in 1586 (SP 91/1, ff. 55–58); in 1598 (Cotton Nero B VIII, f. 29–31); in 1602 (printed in N. Aleksandrenko, "Materialy po smutnomu vremeni na Rusi XVII v.," *Starina i novizna* 14 [1911]: 235–238); and in 1602 (Queens College MS 384). For copies of trading privileges, 1555, 1567, 1569, 1586, 1620, see also BL Add. 30,571, ff. 234–263v (French). See above, nn. 18–20.

97. Mark the Englishman was apparently connected with the merchant community in Moscow. We have been unable to identify him further although we find reference to one Mark Brewster who was Merrick's deputy agent in Moscow (SP 91/1, f. 144v) and who was caught in the siege (see Purchas, *Hakluytus Posthumus* 14: 225–226). There were, however, also English mercenaries in Russia at that time fighting against the Poles. See Lord Stuart's letter from Moscow, 17 August 1611, to the Lord Treasurer (SP 91/1, f. 222). See also the letter of Charles I to Tsar Michael, 1631, requesting monies owed for English soldiers who had fought during the Time of Troubles [USSR archives] and the Tsar's response, 4 March 1631 (in Russian, SP 102/49; printed in OSP 8: 140–142; also ibid., pp. 122–123), and see above, n. 46.

98. Russian cossacks entered the fighting in the autumn of 1612, allied with Prince Trubetskoi, Minin, and Pozharskii. They defeated Hetman Chodkiewcz and the Poles and took the Kremlin on 26 October 1612 (Crummey, *Moscovy*, pp. 230–231; see also, HMC, *Downshire*, 4: 16, 19, 21, 26, 34, 42, 61, 274).

99. See above, n. 38.

100. After the defeat of the Poles in October 1612 (see above, n. 98) delegates were called to a zemskii sobor that assembled in January 1613 for the purpose of electing "a native Muscovite" Tsar (Crummey, *Muscovy*, 231). See Introduction, p. 61.

101. It was reported on 20 April 1612, P. Gordon to King James, that "the late Duke, Suski, is kept captive within the castle of Marieburg in Prussia" (SP 88/3, f. 55; Talbot, ed., *Elementa* 6: 126).

102. I.e., the zemskii sobor. See above, n. 100.

103. See below, n. 276.

104. See above, p. 85 and n. 63.

105. The text between brackets was not included in the final version of Ziuzin's report.

106. Mehmed IV was Sultan of Turkey 1595–1603 and Ahmed I, 1603–1617. On 6 July 1605 the English commissioned Thomas Glover ambassador to Sultan Ahmed. Rymer, *Foedera* 7, pt. 21 155.

107. Shah Abbas of Persia (1587–1629) showed repeated interest in an alliance with Russia against Turkey. This led to the separate missions of Amir Ali-bek and Migip bek in 1608. Both seem to have been caught by the Time of Troubles and able to return only in 1613. Tsar Michael sent M. N. Tikhanov to Persia in 1613. All the activity produced friendship indeed, but little more for the Russians were not interested in a confrontation with the Ottomans. See Bushev, *Istoriia posol'stv, 1588–1612*, 422–432, and Bushev, *Istoriia posol'stv, 1613–1621*, 13–88.

108. The Khan of Crimea Gazi Giray II (1588–1608) did make peace with Russia in

1594, but in 1607 allied with Sigismund, a fact the Russians may not have known, for little came of it. His successor Djanibek Giray (1610–1623, 1624, and 1627–1635) was occupied in his first reign mainly with internal challenges to his power.

109. Eremei Eremeev, originally Hermann Westermann, came as a courier to the Emperor in 1612: Leitsch, *Moskau*, pp. 63, 66–70.

110. Egeiuzuf Grigor'ev was the Lwow Armenian Josef Gregorowicz sent by the Emperor on a mission to Persia in 1607 or 1608 to announce the Imperial-Ottoman peace of 1606. He stopped in Iaroslavl' on the way back in 1612, where he joined Westermann (Eremeev) for the rest of the journey: Leitsch, *Moskau*, pp. 64–87.

111. The reference is presumably to the brief war between Sigismund and Maximilian in 1587–1589, following the election of both princes to the Polish throne. Archduke Maximilian's defeat was followed by a brief imprisonment in Poland until he conceded the victory to King Sigismund.

112. I.e., Sigismund.

113. See above, nn. 27 and 29.

114. The cossack Iermak began the conquest of Siberia in 1579 or 1581.

115. English merchants were concerned about the dangers of passing through Nogais territory in order to reach Persia. The issue of travel by way of the Volga into Persia persisted in Anglo-Russian affairs through the end of the decade. See S. Konovalov, "Anglo-Russian Relations, 1617–1618," *OSP* (1950–1951): 70–71.

116. I.e., the second false Dmitrii. See above, nn. 29 and 32.

117. I.e., the first false Dmitrii. See above, nn. 27 and 32.

118. I.e., the second false Dmitrii. Zarutskii led the cossacks against the Poles and Lithuanians but refused to join Pozharskii's army. See above, n. 98.

119. James Hill (Hyll), a mercenary (see R.B. Wernham, ed., *List and Analysis of State Papers. Foreign Series, Elizabeth I* [London, 1984], 1: 391–393) was at the court of the Elector of Brandenburg in October 1611 waiting a command in the Russian wars. He wrote to Salisbury that "if I can get no command in these wars here, [then] do I determine to come in the spring . . . to my native soil again" (SP 88/3, f. 36; Talbot, ed., *Elementa* 6: 112). The same letter relates the arrival of Arthur Aston "with letters of recommendations unto my Lord Elector from his Majesty's highness." Aston left the Elector's court sometime in April 1612 (SP 88/3, f. 55; Talbot, ed., *Elementa* 6: 125), after Hill had reported in his letter from Königsberg to Salisbury, 16/26 February 1611/12, that they both "will take ship at Hamburg 5 weeks after Easter and land at St. Nicholas" (SP 81/11, f. 210 [Germany]). Adrian Baron Flodorf wrote from Archangel to James, 10 September 1612, concerning the "*injuste invasion des Polonnois (enemys et oppresseurs de la vraye chrestienne) sur les Moscovites*" (SP 91/1, f. 224). See also a memorandum on the requests of the Russian ambassador, Appendix, below.

120. We are unable to identify James Shaw.

121. For a letter written by Margeret from Hamburg, 29 January 1612, to John Merrick, in England, indicating the Russians' need for mercenaries to use against the Poles, see Purchas, *Hakluytus Posthumus* 14: 225–226. The Russians by now mistrusted Margeret and forbade him entrance into the country. Margeret (Dunning, ed.), *Russian Empire*, p. xxii.

122. Jacques Margeret had served the Holy Roman Emperor, Rudolf II, in Hungary before taking command of a company of foot soldiers for Sigismund III. In 1599, Afanasii Vlas'ev, Boris Godunov's ambassador, met Margeret in Europe and persuaded him to enter Russian service for the Tsar (Margeret [Dunning, ed.], *Russian Empire*, p. xvii). Vlas'ev's mission to the Imperial Court at Prague at this time was interpreted by con-

temporaries as "directly menacing" to English commercial interests. N.E. Evans, "The Anglo-Russian Royal Marriage Negotiations of 1600–1603," *SEER* 61 (1983): 365.

123. Margeret left Russia in September 1606 but returned in 1609 in the entourage of the second false Dmitrii (Margeret [Dunning, ed.], *Russian Empire*, pp. xix–xx).

124. After the overthrow of Shuiskii, Margeret fought with the Poles and supported Władysław's candidacy for Tsar. He left Russia for Poland in 1611, never to return (Margeret [Dunning, ed.], *Russian Empire*, pp. xxi–xxii). Margeret joined the Protestant Prince Janusz Radziwiłł, at Danzig and served as an envoy from him to James as late as 1620 (SP 88/2, f. 173; Talbot, ed., *Elementa* 4: 192).

125. We are unable to find the letter from the Governor of Archangel to the boyars of the Moscow state.

126. We are unable to find evidence that Aston and Hill had any credentials from the English government. Regarding Aston, see Appendix, below, pp. 209–210.

127. Apparently the Tsar provided Aston with a writ of safe conduct out of Russia in April 1614 (Harl. 214, ff. 149–150). However, it was not until a letter of 22 December 1617 from James reached Tsar Michael on 4 August 1618 that Aston (and his son) were released, with the provision that they not join the Poles or assist the Polish King (SP 102/49, in Russian; printed in OSP 7: 127–129, and ibid., 119–120, and n. 1). By 1618, however, the Astons were both in the service of Poland fighting the Turks and were considered traitors by Russia. See ibid., 4: 82–83, 109–111. Aston, however, claimed that he never took arms against Russia (SP 91/2, f. 85–85a; and see also ibid., 84–84v).

128. The marriage of James's daughter Elizabeth to Frederick, Count Palatine, in spring 1614 brought various embassies to England. In November of that year the Venetian ambassador reported that "the King has lately been giving audience to all the ambassadors. On Saturday to France and myself, Sunday to him of Muscovy and Monday to those of Spain and Flanders" (*CSPV 1613–1614*, p. 67). Anthony Shirley's embassy to the Emperor in 1600 had been to solicit a league against the Turks (SP 12/175:89; printed in Chamberlain, *Letters*, 1: 107). He returned traveling from Germany to Turkey and through Russia as an envoy of Shah Abbas where he was badly received by Boris Godunov. See below, n. 132. In 1611 Sir Robert Shirley arrived in England as ambassador from the King of Persia to offer silk trade in exchange for an alliance against the Turks (*CSPV 1610–1613*, pp. 109, 166, 195, 226). The English expressed interest in the trade but not in the alliance, the Turkish threat believed by many to exist in rumor only; see below, n. 132.

129. See above, n. 13.

130. See above, nn. 11, 12.

131. See above, nn. 45, 86.

132. See Sir Stephen Lesieur to James I, 6 September 1613, Regensburg: "A Polonnian ambassador (by profession an ecclesiastical man) is lately arrived here . . . about a league against the Turk and to remember the Emperor of his promise to help to compose matters between that King and the Muscovites" (SP 80/3, f. 29v). It was remarked on at the Emperor's court that "the States have stirred up the Turk against Christendom by supplying him with munitions and merchandise" (HMC, *Downshire*, 4: 23; see also, ibid., 31, 60, 111). There was concern among some Protestants that weakening Spain would destroy Europe's bulwark against the Turks (ibid., 357), but the degree of the threat was questionable. D. Buwinckhausen wrote to W. Trumbull that "much is said about the threat from the Turks but I do not know if it is genuine or merely to get money" (ibid., 60). Regarding the Turkish threat in Transylvania, see ibid., 175, 183, 211, 319, 466.

133. See above, n. 119.

134. See SP 91/2, f. 46, Appendix, below. See also *OSP* 4: 80–82, 110; SP 12/285 (Chamberlain, *Letters*, 1: 168–170).

135. The youngest of the four, Grishka, styled himself Mikepher Alphery in England. He matriculated at St. John's College, Cambridge, in 1609 and later moved to Clare College, receiving there a bachelor's degree in 1611/12 and a master's in 1615, being the same year ordained as a priest in the Church of England. See Ralph Cleminson, "Boris Godunov and the Rector of Wooley: A Tale of the Unexpected," Marginalia, *SEER* 65, no. 3 (July 1987): 399–403 and S. Konovalov, "Anglo-Russian Relations, 1620–4," *OSP* 4 (1953): 80–82.

136. I.e., have caused the Time of Troubles.

137. Mikepher Alphery was apparently the only one left in England. See above, n. 135.

138. Two of the boys, Sophone Mychalove and Cazaren Davidove, became factors for the East Indies Company and died in that service sometime between 1617 and 1621. Their names are spelled variously. See SP 91/2, f. 46, Appendix, below, and see S. Konovalov, "Anglo-Russian Relations, 1620–4," *OSP* 4 (1953): 80–82; 105–111.

139. The boys had been entrusted to John Merrick in June 1602. See Cotton Nero B, VIII, ff. 40–41. Part of the instructions were that the boys were "not to be drawn to forsake their religion."

140. Apprentices were sent from the Russia Company to Moscow although their names apparently disappeared with the other Company papers. In 1557 ten young men were sent abroad "into the notable cities of the country for understanding and knowledge" (Willan, *Russia Company*, p. 38).

141. Matthias, Holy Roman Emperor, 1612–1619.

142. See nn. 109–110.

143. Phillip IV, who would be King of Spain 1621–1625.

144. Religion was the issue when Władysław had been offered the throne. See above, p. 80.

145. See above, p. 82.

146. I.e., the councillors.

147. John Merrick would be sent as ambassador to Russia in June 1614 (SP 14/77:53; printed in Chamberlain, *Letters*, 1: 540–543). For other contemporary copies of the writ of safe conduct, see SP 91/1, ff. 232–234. Ziuzin reports that on 5 February James ordered the safe conduct writ translated. See below, p. 178.

148. A copy of the credential letter (in Russian) is printed in *OSP* 7: 122 from SP 102/49, no. 6. For a translation, see SP 91/1, f. 238.

149. Relations between Russia and Denmark were amicable as a result in part of the earlier conflict between Sweden and Denmark. See above, nn. 11–12. Christian IV was the brother-in-law of James I; Christian's father, Frederick II, had granted a patent to English merchants trading in Muscovy, to pass through Norway and Denmark, 22 June 1582 (BL, Cotton Nero B, III, f. 184).

150. A tradition of English doctors and apothecaries serving the Tsar began in 1557 during the reign of Ivan IV, although little has been written on the arrangement before the 1660s. See John H. Appleby, "A Survey of some Anglo-Russian Medical and Natural History Material in British Archives from the Seventeenth Century to the Beginning of the Nineteenth Century," in Janet M. Hartley, *Guide to Documents and Manuscripts in the United Kingdom Relating to Russia and the Soviet Union* (London, 1987), pp. 107–131. See also Tsar Boris's letter to Elizabeth I, 1598, SP 91/1, ff. 112–113 (printed in *SRIO* 38: 261–265; contemporary translation, SP 91/1, ff. 112–113). Baldwin Hamey had served in

Fyodor's household and then returned to England; Tsar Michael was inviting him to back to Moscow; see below, p. 144 and n. 164.

151. Ivan IV had earlier requested that craftsmen be sent from England to Russia. See Harl. 296, f. 189. See also Charles C. Oman, *The English Silver in the Kremlin 1557–1663* (London, 1961).

152. Secretary of the King's Chancery in Poland.

153. Tret'iakov was a secretary in the ambassadorial office (see below, p. 140) and also a secretary of the Duma (see below, p. 144).

154. See above, p. 72 and n. 9.

155. The early onset of winter storms in the northern latitudes made navigation difficult by the end of August.

156. See above, p. 72 and n. 9.

157. See above, n. 6.

158. See above, n. 10.

159. See above, n. 10, and below, n. 178.

160. I.e., wherein Tsar Michael officially relates to Ziuzin what the Governor and Secretary of Archangel have learned about the Scandinavian alliances from the English merchants.

161. See above, n. 12.

162. The peace of Teusina promulgated on 18 May 1595 ended the protracted Livonian wars. It provided that Russia keep Viborg and Reval and Estonia be recognized as Swedish. Roberts, *Early Vasas*, pp. 271–272.

163. See above, n. 56.

164. MS: *Baldwinus Ameus*. Baldwin Hamey served Tsar Fyodor, Michael's uncle, from 1594 to 1597. See J.J. Keevil, *Hamey the Stranger* (London, 1952), pp. 30–63; and see below, pp. 179–181.

165. I.e., a translation from English into Russian. The letter from King James to Tsar Michael is no longer attached to the report. For a memorandum for the drafting of the letter, see Appendix, below.

166. See above, p. 71. The order from the Tsar was made on 20 June.

167. See above, pp. 71–72 and nn. 2 and 4.

168. MS: *Ivan Ulianov* and *Ulian Ulianov*. John, son of William Merrick (see above, n. 23) and William, son of William Russell. Russell was a free brother of the East India Company and in 1612 director of the Company of Merchants of London. A member of the Muscovy Company, he brought suit against it (jointly with Sir Richard Smith, see below, n. 198) for the Company's plan to assess members for accumulated debts owed to investors who were strangers not free of the Company. See *Lord Proceedings 1628*, ed. by R.C. Johnson, et al. (New Haven: Yale University Press, 1977–1983), pp. 668–671.

169. See above, n. 6.

170. Fabian Smith was a member of the Muscovy Company and King's agent in Moscow, ca. 1613. He was described in an undated memorandum from the Company, probably later than 1613–1614, as "a professed merchant by his trade which is not only against his Majesty's honor but also against the general good of the Company which some of the merchants that have lived at the Moscow lately will aver. As also they will justify that he has forestalled their markets by bribing their customers and their men in Russia to let him know when such and such commodities should come to such and such places, whereby it will plainly appear he is unfit for the place. . . ." (SP 91/2, f. 150).

171. See above p. 72 and nn. 10 and 11. See also SP 14/67 (docquet), letter to Sir R. Stuart, 8 December 1611, signifying James's refusal to become involved in the Danish-

Swedish business until he understood the disposition of the King of Sweden. James's concern may have been to protect a possible Protestant marriage match for Princess Elizabeth with Gustavus Adolphus, even though he told the Danes otherwise (SP 75/5, ff. 191–195). Although some Englishmen found Gustavus's claim to the Swedish crown "specious, as being *testa cornata*," the Swedish court was believed to be more prestigious than some of the lesser German principalities. An anonymous memorandum on the subject of a Protestant marriage alliance (SP 14/67:83) concludes that "any of these courses will so bind the allies and confederates of England as that the greatness of it may run in balance with whatsoever other in Christendom."

172. See SP 75/5, f. 3; see also, ibid., f. 55–55v.

173. I.e., James.

174. I.e., James's.

175. MS: *Ulibei*. Word of the Swedish-Danish conflict reached London by July 1611 (SP 14/65:38). The English began raising mercenary troops to support the Danes as early as 13 November 1611 (SP 14/67:25; Chamberlain, *Letters*, 1: 336–341). See also HMC, *Montagu of Beaulieu*, p. 87. By 25 March 1612 Robert Bertie, twelfth Lord Willoughby of Eresby, was raising 4,000 men for Denmark, and in August of that year was troubled that as a result of fighting and sickness barely 200 remained alive (SP 14/68:83, 70:38; Chamberlain, *Letters*, 1: 341–343, 375–378). Peace was concluded in 1613 (see above nn. 11 and 12) and the troops were released.

176. Regarding the "contract of peace" (Treaty of Knaerød) between Denmark and Sweden, see above, n. 12.

177. We are unable to identify the mercenary Vil'ianko.

178. Christian IV had married Anna Catharine, daughter of Margrave Joachim Frederick who became Elector of Brandenburg in 1598. Anna Catharine died in 1612 (CSPV 1610–1613, p. 367) and Christian did not remarry. Rumors circulated regarding him and the daughter of the Duke of Savoy (SP 14/72:115) as well as the sister of Gustavus Adolphus (CSPV 1610–1613, p. 458).

179. See above, n. 6.

180. See above, n. 5.

181. Merrick gave the ambassadors an English translator by the name of Richard Finch; see below, n. 187.

182. We are unable to identify this William, the son of William.

183. I.e., by the Pudozhemskoe ust'e, or the "old bar," in the estuary of the Dvina at Archangel. By 1629 this entrance was considered hazardous because of the shallowness of the water and the English merchants petitioned for permission to use the new bar (Berezovske ust'e). See S. Konovalov, "Seven Letters of Tsar Mikhail to King Charles I, 1634–8," OSP 9: 35–36.

184. I.e., 14 September. *Exaltatio sancte crucis* or Crouchmas day.

185. On the first ship were the Russian ambassadors, the undersecretary (Andrei Semenov), the translator from Archangel (Andrei Andreev), the ambassadors' servants, the English captain, the merchant, and twenty-four of his companions. John Merrick, William Russell, and their associates followed on the second ship that had reached Whitby three days before the ambassadors' ship was becalmed there on 13 October. Merrick and Russell disembarked and went by coach to London. There are no extant records in the Whitby archives (Whitby Museum) relating to this incident.

186. A verst is equal to 0.6629 miles or about 1.067 kilometers. The distance from Whitby to London by the old road was about 243 miles.

187. Richard Finch had been employed in the Muscovy Company office in Moscow

and knew Russian. S. Baron, "Thrust and Parry: Anglo-Russian Relations in the Muscovite North," *OSP*, New Series 11 (1988): 23 n. 10. Perhaps a son of John Finch, a servant to Sir Jerome Bowes on the 1583 embassy to Russia (see T.S. Willan, *Early History of the Russia Company* [Manchester: At the University Press], pp. 165, 233 n. 4) and the same Richard Finch who was sent out of Russia by order of the Tsar as a "hinderer of the said country's trade" (i.e., because he was an interloper), but through some misinformation to James received credentials to continue trading (SP 91/2, f. 5, undated, calendared as 1614).

188. The sands off Yarmouth were treacherous. Even in recent times "temporary shoaling is liable to occur in the harbour entrance during strong easterly winds when depths of 3 ft. less than [normal]" can be expected. *The Cruising Association Handbook* (London: 1975).

189. James was at Royston, Hertfordshire, when the ambassadors arrived. Nichols, *Progresses* 2: 678.

190. I.e., some matters of protocol relating particularly to this embassy were assigned to Sir Thomas Smith and John Merrick (see Appendix, below). Generally ambassadorial audiences were under the direction of the Master of Ceremonies. Sir Thomas Smith, free of the Company of London Haberdashers, and a member of the Skinners' Company (son of Thomas Smith who was also a Haberdasher and grandson of Sir Andrew Judd, one of the founders of the Muscovy Company) had been sent by James I to Boris Godunov in June 1604. The account of the embassy was subsequently published as *Sir T. Smithes Voiage and Entertainment in Rushia* (London, 1605), STC, no. 22869. Smith was governor of the East India Company for fifteen years and held that position for shorter periods in the Russia, French, Levant, Virginia, and Sommers Islands Companies. See Alfred B. Beaven, *The Aldermen of the City of London*, 2 vols. (London: Published by the Corporation of the City of London, 1908), 2: 47, 175.

191. James VI and I was the son of Henry Stewart, Lord Darnley. Secretary Vitovtov apparently wrote *Andrei* in his report rather than *Henri* or *Henry*. The clerk compiling the record then transliterated Andrei as *Andrew*. Henry Carey (Lord Hunsdon) is transliterated *Andrei Carey* in the Russian account of Fyodor Andreevich Pisemskii's embassy to England in 1581. *SRIO* 38: 52. See also, ibid., 38: 343, where Sir Henry Lee is given as Sir Andrei Lee. And see below, p. 152, where there is an account of the Englishman, Sir Thomas Smith, using the same phrase.

192. It was customary for the expenses of extraordinary ambassadors to the English King to be assumed by the crown. See Albert J. Loomie, *Ceremonies of Charles I* (New York: Fordham University Press), pp. 30–31. Regarding the Ziuzin embassy, see below, n. 215.

193. On this day (22 October 1613) Sir John Swinnerton, Lord Mayor of London, having received news of the arrival of the ambassadors from the Lord Chamberlain, sent a precept to the masters and wardens of the livery companies instructing them about the arrival of the embassy the following Tuesday (26 October) at Tower Wharf. London MS Journal, no. 29 (1612–1614); see Appendix, below. A copy of the precept is also included in the records of the Grocers' Company, MS 1115 88/2, f. 783 (Guildhall Library).

194. We are unable to identify the captain.

195. A little more than a month before the arrival of the embassy complaint had been made by merchant strangers and others to the Privy Council about great losses "sustained by pirates that have adventured to set upon them within the rivers as they pass to and fro, and to rob and spoil them of such goods and merchandizes as they[y] find aboard" (*A[cts] of the P[rivy] C[ouncil] 1613–1614*, pp. 194–195).

196. Probably Henry Pinock, the Portreve of Gravesend, 1613–1614. See R.P. Cruden, *The History of the Town of Gravesend in the County of Kent and the Port of London* (London, 1843), p. 539.

197. MS: *the royal Okol'nichii of the near duma.* Sir Thomas Smith functioned as a spokesperson for the crown to this embassy (see above, n. 190, and below, Appendix, p. 203). He was a respected and trusted advisor to King James on shipping and naval affairs. Never formally a privy councillor, he consulted with that body on numerous occasions until his death in 1625 (see, for example, SP 14/90:115 and 97:117). He was appointed a commissioner of the navy in 1618 (C66/2165, 23 June; *CSPD 1611–1618*, p. 547).

198. Sir Richard Smith, brother of Sir Thomas Smith. Richard was one of the investors who later brought suit against the Muscovy Company for its assessment of members to pay accumulated Company debts. See SP 14/97:138; *Lords Proceedings 1628*, pp. 668–671; William R. Scott, *The Constitution and Finance of English, Scottish, and Irish Joint Stock Companies to 1720*, 3 vols. (Cambridge, Eng.: The University Press, 1912), 2: 56, n. 6. See also above, n. 168.

199. MS: *Dodvyz.* Probably Sir John Davies, Attorney General of Ireland and King's Serjeant.

200. Probably Sir George Hayward of London (Shaw, *Knights* 2: 135). Hayward was the son of Thomas Smith's daughter, Katharine, and her first husband Sir Rowland Hayward, merchant. See Chamberlain, *Letters*, 1: 579, and P. Hasler, ed., *House of Commons, Elizabeth I* (London: Stationery Company, 1989), 2: 283–285.

201. Sir John Woodward had been Gentleman Extraordinary of the Privy Chamber to Prince Henry. Nichols' *Progresses*, 2: 608 n. 5; *Ordinances and Regulations of the Royal Household* (London: 1790), p. 324.

202. Probably one of the commanders of the Blockhouses at Tilbury or Gravesend.

203. MS: *Rytsar'netleia*, meaning either "knight" or "Richard" Netley. Possibly Sir Thomas Knyvet, Lord Knyvet of Escrick, Gentleman of the Privy Chamber to James and Privy Councillor. *Dictionary of National Biography.*

204. See above, n. 189.

205. The Muscovites were unaccustomed to tidal rivers.

206. MS: *pristav*, a conductor of ambassadors.

207. See above, nn. 198, 199.

208. See above, n. 196.

209. J. Chamberlain wrote to Sir D. Carleton, 27 October 1613, that "yesterday here arrived an ambassador from the newly elected emperor of Moscovy. He had a peal of ordnance at his landing at Tower Wharf" (SP 14/74:89; Chamberlain, *Letters*, 1: 482).

210. MS: *Darvis.* Sir Henry (not William), Lord Danvers, was Lord President of Munster. See LC 5/1, the Master of Ceremony's account of foreign ambassadors in England, f. 23v, "26 October 1613, An ambassador from the Emperor of Russia landing at Tower Wharf was there received by the Lord Danvers."

211. MS: *Vishegorod.* This was probably the Tower, as the same name was often given to similar structures near Russian towns.

212. The Vinters record a payment of 6d. "To the ostler of the inn where the horses were set when they met the Russian ambassador." Vintners' Company Register of Accounts from the year 1582–1617, MS 15,333/2, p. 602 (Guildhall Library).

213. The ambassadors were "received by a 100 citizens on horseback in velvet coats and chains of gold and most of the aldermen in scarlet and about twenty coaches furnished with courtiers and gallants; the Spanish, the Archdukes and Savoy ambassadors stood in windows not far asunder to see him pass." J. Chamberlain to Sir D. Carleton, 27

October 1613 (SP 14/74:89; Chamberlain, *Letters*, 1: 482). Boisschot described the reception as "extraordinary." See HHST, Abteilung Belgien, PC fz. 48, f. 61. See also, HMC, *Downshire*, 4: 235, 242 and Introduction, above, n. 30. According to Finet the reception of ambassadors at Tower Wharf was regularized in 1627, "not only for the present but for the future." John Finet, *Finetti Philoxensis*, (London, 1656), p. 228.

214. MS: *Tsar*.

215. I.e., the ambassador's allowance, see above, n. 192. The Muscovy Company had assumed the costs of earlier embassies, establishing the custom that the expenses of Russian missions be defrayed for the length of the embassy. It is not clear who paid Ziuzin's expenses. Vinogradoff, ("Russian Missions to London, 1569–1687," OSP, New Series 14 [1981]: 38) suggests that by this time the crown paid the allowance. However, a memo of 22 April 1615 regarding Company business suggests that the Company owed £5,000 for, "the great charge of ambassadors falls upon them." And Finet notes that in 1627 the crown established that it would not defray the costs of ambassadors except at "conclusions of peace, marriages, or baptisms of his [the King's] children and such extraordinary occasions." Finet, *Finetti Philoxensis*, p. 228. According to the French ambassador Ziuzin *"est logé et defrayé par le corpe de cestes ville, et y doit ses journier jusquelle au caresme [carême] prochain."* S. Spifame to Mon. de Puysieux, 8 Nov. 1613, Bib. Nat., MS 15,987, ff. 153–154.

216. Andrei Semenov (see above, pp. 73 and 147) and Andrei Andreev, the translator from Archangel (see above, p. 147).

217. The rules of coach etiquette are written in a later letter of John Finet to Lord Viscount Scudamore, ambassador of the English King in Paris, 22 February 1636. PRO, C115/n8/8802. See also, PRO, LC5/1, a copy of Finet's *Philoxensis*, including "Reasons for masters of ceremonies to sit in the same coach with the ambassadors."

218. Customarily the King supplied at least part of the daily provisions of the ambassador and his entourage. These provisions, called "specie" were then "disposed of and dressed by the ambassador's own cooks," if such there were. This support, provided by the Cofferer of the King's Household, was phased out under Charles I. On royal hospitality, see Loomie, *Ceremonies of Charles I* (New York), pp. 30–32.

219. See below, pp. 170–174.

220. See below, n. 277.

221. I.e., during the Elizabethan period, before the Time of Troubles.

222. See above, nn. 18–21.

223. I.e., the Lord Mayor. See Sir Edward Coke, *The Fourth Part of the Institutes of the Laws of England* (London, 1797), p. 247, regarding mayoral judicial responsibilities.

224. I.e., the Lord Mayor's festival.

225. I.e., Whitehall.

226. Observing the Russian embassy of 1617–1618, Sir John Finet recorded that, "it was the custom of their country that whensoever an ambassador was to have an audience of the Prince's council they were to see the Prince's eyes first." See Finet, *Finetti Philoxensis*, p. 470.

227. I.e., the previous Lord Mayors.

228. MS: *shry*. Edward Rotheram and Alexander Prescott were sheriffs, 1612–1613. PRO, *Lists and Indexes* 8: 205.

229. Sir Thomas Middleton.

230. MS: *Kniaz' Lev Liutorin*. Sir Lewis Lewkenor was first to hold the newly created office of Master of Ceremonies, granted to him for life on 7 November 1605. PRO, C66/1676 (MS Cal. Pat. Rolls, 3 Jac. I, pt. 14, f. 30; printed in Rymer, *Foedera* 7: pt. 2, p. 144).

231. I.e., Sunday, 31 October, and see p. 165.

232. I.e., Whitehall. See above, p. 159.

233. The Lord Mayor's festival occurred once a year in October at the swearing in of the new Lord Mayor.

234. I.e., William Russell who had accompanied Merrick to Russia the previous June.

235. See above, n. 217.

236. I.e., the courtyard at Whitehall. Probably in this case the Pebble Court that opened to the ordinary chamber of attendance for audiences. Nichols, *Progresses* 3: 456.

237. Sir Thomas Middleton, the new Lord Mayor, elected on Michaelmas Day, 29 September, and installed this day, 29 October 1613.

238. Sir John Swinnerton.

239. I.e., Whitehall.

240. These were floats in the Lord Mayor's procession for which was "paid to John Grynkyn, painter-stainer for the making of the pageant Senate House, ship, error's and truth's chariots, with all the several beasts which drew them, the five islands, and for all the carpenter's work, painting, gilding, and garnishing of them with all other things necessary ready for the children and players to sit in, and also in full for the greenmen, devils, and fireworks, with all things thereunto belonging, according to his agreement, the sum of 310 pounds." MS 11,1590, Guildhall Library (Grocer's Company). The pageant at the installation of the Lord Mayor in 1613 was sponsored by the Worshipful Company of Grocers. An account of the pageant was printed contemporaneously, *The Triumphs of Truth. A Solemnity at the Establishment of Sir Thomas Middleton, Lord Maior* (London, 1613), STC, 17903; reprinted in Nichols, *Progresses* 3: 679–701.

241. I.e., Roman candles used to disperse the crowd from the path of the parade.

242. It was customary for the Russian ambassadors to request that no other emissaries be present. See Mikulin's instructions in "The Meeting of the Russian and Scottish Ambassadors in London in 1601," N.E. Evans, *SEER* 55 (October, 1977): 518.

243. MS: *skorb'*.

244. I.e., Guy Fawkes day. For contemporary accounts of the plan to blow up the King and parliament, see T. Birch, ed., *Court and Times James I* (London, 1849), 1: 36–38; E. of Salisbury's letter of 9 November to Sir C. Cornwallis, and Sir E. Hoby's letter to Sir T. Edmondes, Nichols, *Progresses* 1: 578–584, 584–588. See also *Lucta Jacobi: or a Bonfire for his Majesties Double Deliverie*, etc. (London, 1607), STC, 14426. John Gerard published a narrative of the plot from the Catholic perspective, printed in Morris's *Conduct of the Catholics*.

245. The date in the MS (1607/1608) is erroneous; the Gunpowder Plot occurred in 1605.

246. The ambassador conceived of the English parliament as comparable to the *zemskii sobor*, i.e., an assembly with the boyars and the whole land about the affairs of the kingdom.

247. William Parker, Lord Mounteagle.

248. Henry Percy, Earl of Northumberland; see *Court and Times James I*, 1: 38.

249. Thomas Howard, Earl of Suffolk. See below, n. 253.

250. John Johnson, the assumed name of Guy Vaux, alias Faux, or Fawkes.

251. See Howell, *S[tate] T[rials]* (London: 1816), 3: 159–358.

252. By statutory law the day was to be remembered. *SR*, 3 Jac. I, An *act for a public thanksgiving to almighty God every year on the fifth day of November.*

253. Thomas Howard, Earl of Suffolk, Lord Chamberlain 1603 to July 1614, when he was appointed Lord Treasurer (SP 14/77:63). It was rumored in London that Ziuzin had been invited to hold audience the previous week but "excused himself upon the death of

one of his servants, it being the custom of his country not to come abroad in certain days after such an accident." SP 14/75:4 (Chamberlain, *Letters*, 1: 485). We find no other reference to the servant's death.

254. There is no evidence in Ziuzin's account that Russian ambassadors were accustomed to dining with James I. See Igor Vinogradoff, "Russian Missions to London, 1569–1687," OSP, New Series 14 (1981): 43–45. Finet records the changed policies of Charles I in this regard, ibid., 48–49. See below, n. 300.

255. Anne of Denmark, Queen of James I, and Prince Charles, Duke of York (created Prince of Wales, November 1616).

256. See above, n. 217.

257. I.e., Whitehall.

258. Perhaps Thomas Lord Gerard.

259. Theophilus Howard, eldest son of Thomas Howard, Earl of Suffolk, who was summoned as Baron Howard de Walden in 1610.

260. Richard Sackville, third Earl of Dorset, Lord Lieutenant of Sussex. Boisschot reported that, "on the seventeenth day of this month there was a public audience granted by the King to the Ambassador of Muscovy. He was ushered in by the Earl of Dorset and accompanied by other gentlemen to the main chamber of the palace where the King and Queen were to greet them" (HHSA, Abteilung Belgien, PC fz. 48, f. 68; see also Foscarini to the Doge, etc., 8 Nov. 1613, CSPV 1613–1615, p. 65; HMC, *Downshire*, 4: 246). The custom was "that the ambassador of a King is to be brought in by an Earl at least" (T.B. Howell, A *Distinct Treatise of Ambassadors*, p. 208).

261. One on the right hand is always more honored than one on the left. Segar, *Honor, Military and Civil* (London: 1602), p. 211.

262. MS: *duma*, i.e., the Council Chamber.

263. See Editorial Conventions for "boyars" and "duma".

264. MS: *blizhnie boiare*, Russian for "close boyars," in this case equivalent to privy councillors. See Editorial Conventions.

265. See Loomie, *Ceremonies of Charles I*, p. 29. By the 1630s the Presence Chamber was customarily used for the first and last public audiences of ambassadors.

266. I.e., the new Banqueting House. J. Chamberlain wrote to Sir D. Carleton that for the audience, "there was a great presence in the new banqueting room" (SP 14/75:4; Chamberlain, *Letters*, 1: 485).

267. I.e., Thomas Howard, Earl of Suffolk.

268. Boisschot reported that "the ambassador was preceded by sixteen servants, carrying each in his hands a crest, then followed his secretary who carried his credentials waved in the air. These were the size of an unfolded sheet, and a very large seal hung from them" (HHST, Abteiling Belgien, PC fz. 48, f. 68). For Ziuzin's credentials (in Russian), see SP 102/49, f. 6; for a contemporary translation, see SP 91/1, ff. 236–239 (printed in OSP 7: 122). See above, pp. 136–137.

269. According to Boisschot, Ziuzin brought his sons aged eleven and fourteen to England and to this audience with the King. They followed Secretary Vitovtov in the procession, "all dressed according to their custom, except that they wore high pelt bonnets instead of turbans" (HHST, Abteilung Belgien, PC fz. 48, f. 68).

270. Boisschot reported that Ziuzin, "at twelve steps distance from the King, took off his bonnet and, instead of making reverence, lay prostrate—all of his body—on the floor. Then the King and Queen rose to their feet and the King took off his hat" (HHST, Abteilung Belgien, PC fz. 48, f. 68).

271. Regarding the letter, see above, n. 148. For a memorandum of James's answer to Tsar Michael, see Appendix IV, below.

272. For the speeches, see above, pp. 73–83. See also HMC, *Downshire*, 4: 260.

273. See above, pp. 81–82.

274. See above, pp. 142–144.

275. See above, nn. 20 and 21.

276. See above, p. 83. Regarding the speech, see also n. 272, above. According to Boisschot, "The ambassador harangued in his tongue for almost an hour, presenting the King his credentials, and sables to the King, and some to the Queen and Prince. The interpreter related the substance of the speech. Once finished, he bowed twice, as in the beginning, and was from there taken to the Council Hall where supper was served" (HHSA, Abteilung Belgien, PC fz. 48, n. 69). The supper was for the ambassadorial party only; see above, n. 254.

277. James acknowledged Michael's "affinity to the previous great tsars and grand dukes of Russia" but made no response to the matter of his election. This was a touchy issue with James. In 1610 he had declared in parliament that, "the King takes himself to be beholding to no elective power, depends upon no popular applause, that he derives the lines of his fortunes and greatness from the loins of his ancestors . . ." (Elizabeth Read Foster, *Proceedings in Parliament 1610*, 2 vols. [New Haven: Yale University Press, 1966], 2: 49).

278. See above, and n. 56.

279. Boisschot noted that, "the businesses he brings with himself have been forwarded to the Council, with whom up to now he has not met. Neither have any of the resident ambassadors visited him" (HHSA, Abteilung Belgien, PC fz. 48, f. 69; see also HMC, *Downshire*, 4: 389).

280. A year and a half later it was reported that an envoy of Tsar Michael had been imprisoned for demanding an explanation "with an insolence which may cost him his life" of why the Emperor did not bow or bare his head at the mention of the Grand Duke of Muscovy (HMC, *Downshire*, 5. 199). Boisschot reported that Ziuzin "never covered himself in front of the King, even when commanded to do so" (HHSA, Abteilung Belgien, PC fz. 48, f. 69).

281. Foscarini reported that "he presented sixteen bundles of sables and some knives of good workmanship. He caused the letter to be read and fulfilled his office, which was to express the friendship of his master and to render thanks to his Majesty for his goodwill" (CSPV 1613–1615, p. 67; see also SP 14/75:4 [Chamberlain, *Letters*, 1: 484–487]). For a description of presents exchanged between England and Russia, see Charles Oman, *The English Silver in the Kremlin, 1557–1663* (London, 1961). See also, *English Silver Treasures from the Kremlin*, the catalogue of a loan exhibition sponsored by Sotheby's and others, January 1991.

282. At this point a small break occurs in the manuscript text.

283. I.e., Somerset House.

284. Robert Sidney, Viscount Lisle, Chamberlain to Queen Anne.

285. I.e., Thomas Howard, Earl of Suffolk.

286. I.e., Thomas Howard, Baron Howard de Walden.

287. We find no record of other ambassadors being entertained by the King at Somerset House.

288. See above, p. 173. For a contemporary translation of this speech, see SP 91/1, f. 242.

289. See above, p. 136.

290. I.e., on 7 November. See above, pp. 170–174.

291. We have been unable to identify the Lord Steward and Lord Chamberlain of Prince Charles's court.

292. The text from this point forward to the end of Ziuzin's report was separated at some time during the past from the rest of the account and was believed lost. In 1988 Nikolai Rogozhin found the quire erroneously bound in with a Polish relation, TsGADA, fund 79 (Polish Relations), opis' 1, bk. 29, 732–739v; it was not included in the Russian rotoprint edition (see above, n. 1). On 4 January 1614 Foscarini reported that "the ambassador of Muscovy continues here always surrounded by merchants" (CSPV 1613–1614, p. 81). Again on 18 January he wrote that "the Russian ambassador has been successful in his negotiations . . . and in the matter of commerce he has given the greatest satisfaction" (ibid., p. 84).

293. I.e., Andrei Semenov. Purchas notes that he "saw him also presently after the running at tilt at Whitehall the four and twentieth of March, admitted to his Majesty's presence, performing that Russian rite of bowing with his face down to or near the ground" (Purchas, Hakluytus Posthumous, 14: 225).

294. Richard Finch; see above, n. 187.

295. See above, pp. 144–145.

296. Baldwin Hamey, born in Bruges in 1568, was forty-six in 1614 (Keevil, Hamey the Stranger, p. 1).

297. Sarah Hamey, née Oeils, gave birth to a son, Charles (named for the Prince), on 8 May 1614 (Keevil, Hamey the Stranger, p. 118).

298. For the letters, see above, pp. 137–138.

299. Possibly Edward Waldegrave, the agent of the Elector Palatine in England. See HMC, Downshire, 14: Index.

300. The extant manuscript text ends here. It is conceivable that the remaining folios will eventually come to light. Ziuzin was not invited to dine with James until Eastertime when "the King dined in public with the Moscovian ambassador . . . and during the dinner [James] toasted twice with very big goblets to the health of the great lord of Moscovy and to the state. On each occasion the ambassador rose from the table and lay prostrate on the floor until his servant notified him that the King was finished drinking . . . later the King sent the same vessels [goblets] with the leftover wine, which was not a little, and gave them all away as a present" (HHST, Abteiling Belgien, PC fz. 48, f. 111). The Master of Ceremony's accounts (LC5/1) record that the dinner took place on 25 April (see Appendix, below). Foscarini reported that the meal was held on Monday, 2 May 1614, shortly before Ziuzin was to leave England (CSPV 1613–1615, p. 120). The dinner was also reported by Don Diego Sarmiento de Acuña, Count of Gondomar, to Philip III in a letter of 9 May (Documentos Ineditios para la Historia de España [Madrid, 1945], 4: 107–108; see also, HMC, Downshire, 4: 431). E. Waldegrave wrote from London to W. Trumbull that, "the Emperor of Russia's ambassador, having been royally feasted and entertained by H[is] M[ajesty] at court . . . took his leave on the 1st." Foscarini reported in his dispatch of 4 July 1614 that "the ambassador of Muscovy has left to return to his master after a very successful mission." News subsequently arrived by way of Denmark of the death of the Duke of Muscovy. "This has postponed the departure of the King's ambassador to those parts until more certain news arrives" (CSPV 1613–1614, p. 144). The report of Tsar Michael's death was incorrect and John Merrick, recently elevated to knighthood (Shaw, Knights, 2: 154), departed for Russia at the end of June 1614 (APC 1613–1614, p. 470; SP 14/77:33 [Chamberlain, Letters, 1: 542–543]), arriving in Archangel on 23 July (SP 91/2, f. 1, see Appendix, below).

Appendixes

I. *Sir Thomas Smith to Lord Viscount Rochester, 28 August 1613, SP 91/1, f. 240.*

Right Honorable,

I have received letters lately out of Moscovia (by a ship that is now returned from those parts) directed from Mr. Merrick and Mr. Russell (lately sent thither as your Lordship knows), which do import that at their arrival they understood of a new election made for their emperor of a young gentleman of the age of 18 years, son unto the metropolitan of that land. Whereupon they directed a message unto him, signifying that they were sent from the King's majesty of England about the settling of a peaceable trade for his subjects in those countries, and procuring some privileges for the better managing of their affairs (but discovered no other business) and understood (by letters sent directly back again unto them) from his Highness that he had a purpose to send an ambassador into England and was desirous of his Majesty's friendship, as may appear by that letter unto them, a copy whereof I have herein sent enclosed unto your Lordship, which news I do desire that your Lordship would be pleased to signify unto his Majesty for the present, and upon return of Mr. Merrick and Mr. Russell (which we expect within a month or six weeks) your Lordship shall be further made acquainted with the success, and so humbly taking my leave do rest,
Ever ready to be disposed at your Lordship's service,
Thomas Smith
London, August 28th

II. *Thomas Howard, Earl of Suffolk to Sir John Swinnerton, Lord Mayor of London, 21 October 1613, Remembrancia, III, 1610–1614, f. 58 (no. 48).*

[f. 58] My Lord,

I have received notice of the coming to Gravesend of an ambassador to his Majesty from the Emperor of Muscovy who I know the King's desire is to have him as well entertained in all respects as his predecessor who was sent to the old Queen. The particulars whereof your Lordship may receive knowledge from Sir Thomas Smith and Mr. Merrick, who have a record of all the former entertainment to that ambassador. That which belongs to your part I assure myself you will see well performed. That which shall remain for me to do him honor in, as his Majesty's officer, I will look unto. The rest that belongs to Sir Thomas Smith as Governor of the Muscovy Company, I know he will be careful of; so as upon conference between you and Sir Thomas Smith I shall presume all things will be well accommodated, to whom I leave the care thereof as,

Your Lordship's
loving friend,
T. Suffolk

Whitehall,
xxi October 1613

III. *Precept to the Livery Companies, Journal no. 29 (1612–1614), f. 46v.*

By the Mayor[1]
To the Master and Wardens of the Company of ＿＿＿ For the entertainment of the Muscovian ambassador.

For as much as I have received intelligence from my Lord Chamberlain that the Muscovian ambassador will land here on Tuesday next and propose that my brethren the aldermen shall receive him on the Tower wharf and from thence conduct him to his lodging, these are therefore to will and require you that you give special direction, order, and commandment that eight persons of the chiefest of your company do meet and attend my brethren the aldermen at Guildhall on Tuesday next by eight of the clock in the morning, apparelled in velvet coats with chains of gold, well mounted on horseback in comely and decent order to accompany and ride with the aldermen to the Tower wharf for the more graceful entertainment of the said ambassador; and hereof to be very respective and careful as you will answer the contrary, given the xxii of October 1613.

Weld[2]

1. A copy of the precept was written in to the Orders of the Court of Assistants for the Grocers Company, MS 11588/2, f. 783, 19 July 1591 to 14 July 1616. At the end of the precept was written: "The execution whereof was by this court referred to the consideration of Mr [Master] Wardens."

2. John Weld. He was admitted town clerk in March 1609. *London Letter Books*, FF, f. 119v.

IV. *The Master of Ceremony's Account of Foreign Ambassadors in England 1612–1618, LC5/1, f. 23v.*

26 October 1614 [sic]
An ambassador from the emperor of Russia landing at Tower wharf was

there received by the Lord Danvers. I, and other gentlemen, his Majesty's servants attending his Lordship thither.

1614. The 25 of April following, he having been invited to dine with his Majesty at Whitehall was seated on his left hand toward the corner of the table, and a secretary that came in commission with him at the table's end. He had two of his own servants attending at his elbow, but with little service (the King's servants supplying) and his other followers bestowed elsewhere in the court apart. It was first ordered the Prince should have dined there also, seated at the King's right hand towards the other end of the table. But this considered to be somewhat short, the dishes many, and doubted, besides, whether the ambassador would have accepted of the place at his Majesty's left hand if the Prince should have had the right. His Highness dined not with his Majesty.

V. *An Account of the Russian Youths Sent to England, 23 March 1618, SP 91/2, f. 46.*

In the year 1600, in the time of the reign of the Lord Emperor and Great Duke Boris Fyodorovich of all Russia, and in the blessed and happy time of the late reign of Queen Elizabeth of England of famous memory, were sent into England four Russe youths of our Lord and Emperor his subjects to be trained for a time to learn Latin, English, and other languages as their capacities would give them leave to attain unto. The names of those said youths, vizt., Mechefor Olferiovsm-Gregoriove, Pheodor Semonove, Sophone Mychalove, and Cazaren Davidove who, having been absent a long time before they were demanded by reason of the troubles of our countries of Russia by foreign enemies, which God sent unto our princes' dominions for our sins, the said youths being now sufficiently entrusted and serviceable for our Lord and Master his use for interpreters of those languages they have learned, it is given us in special charge to entreat the King's Majesty they may be returned with us unto their own country.

Our Lord and Emperor his former ambassador Alexey Ziuzin and Secretary Alexey Vitovtov had the same charge concerning them and dealt with your Lordships therein. And presently after Sir John Merrick did deliver unto our Lord his said ambassador, one of them named Mechefor Alferiov Sin-Gregorie, who continued in the House with them three days, after which Sir John Merrick did dismiss the said youth to the university again from whence he came, answering the ambassador that when they had their dispatch to go from thence both he and another of the youths, Pheodor Simonove, should be ready to go in company with them.

But for the other two, namely Sophone Michalove and Cazaren Davidove, was answered they were in the East Indies. And at the time the King's majesty was pleased and did dispatch from hence our lord his forsaid ambassador.

His Majesty did then answer them that they should be sent to our Lord the Emperor by his own ambassador who should in short time after follow them. And when the King's Majesty's ambassador, Sir John Merrick, was with our Lord the Emperor his Privy Council they did earnestly entreat him to move the King's majesty to be pleased to send those youths unto our Lord the Emperor affirming that they were delivered unto him by the Emperor Boris with promise to be sent again when they should be demanded, who gave answer unto our Lords councillors the King's Majesty would not detain them but would cause them to be sent to his Majesty.

Now, your Lordships may be pleased to order all the said Russ youths sent hither to be delivered unto us his Majesty's ambassadors to be transported into their own countries, unto their parents who are continual suitors to our Emperor for them to be returned again.

[Endorsed] The translation of the scroll touching the Russ youths delivered to the honorable lords of his Majesty's Privy Council by the Russ ambassador. 23 March 1617 [1618].

VI. King James's answer to the Russian Ambassador Regarding the Four Youths, [undated]. SP 91/1, f. 246.

The King's Majesty's answer to the former Russian ambassadors, Alexis Ivanovich Ziuzin and Alexis Vitovtov,[1] touching the four Russian youths sent long since into England.

His Majesty was content so as the youths themselves were willing that they should return for Russia, but they having already refused the same, committing themselves under his Majesty's protection, it stood not with his honor and dignity to enforce them against their wills.

The answer touching the said youths the King's Majesty's ambassador, viz., John Merrick, in his commission was commanded to deliver to the great Duke and his Council:

And for the Russian youths which the great Duke desires to have returned, your majesty gave them to understand that it agrees not with the course of our royal proceedings to banish any strangers out of our kingdoms that desire there to inhabit, much less by violence to force them thither, whither they have no will to go. But if at any time the said youths or either of them shall have any disposition to return, we will not only be content to let them freely pass, but also to afford them our royal furtherance for their transportation.

[Endorsed] The answer heretofore given concerning the Russian youths.

    1. MS: *Olexsey Evanovich Hzuzine* and *Olexsey Wettove*. Regarding the youths, see above, pp. 130–133.

VII. *Memorandum for a Letter to the Emperor of Russia, SP 91/1, f. 244.*

[Memorandum] A letter to be framed from his Majesty unto Michael Fyodorovich, Emperor of all Russia (his whole style remembered). And therein to answer his letter written to his Majesty as also to signify that according to his ambassador's request his Majesty has sent a messenger into Sweden who is returned, and that his Majesty purposes to send his own ambassador forthwith into Russia who shall have order both to treat of those businesses and those other affairs demanded by his ambassadors.

    [Endorsed] Information for a letter to the Emperor of Russia from his Majesty.

    1. The memorandum is undated; cf. *CSPV 1613–1614*, p. 97.

VIII. *Memorandum of the Requests of the Russian Ambassador, 1614.*
SP 91/2, f. 3.

[1.] He craves an answer of the business upon which his Majesty sent unto the King of Sweden. The messenger he understands is returned from thence.

    [2.] He desires his Majesty's pleasure for the sending an ambassador unto Russia according to the Emperor's request. And that they may go in company together.

    [3.] Further to understand his Majesty's pleasure for the request of the Emperor for borrowing monies to supply his present wants.

    [4.] He demands the two Russ youths, the one in Cambridge (but at present out of the way and is not willing to return into Russia), the other in Ireland, and is sent for by the Lord Deputy. The ambassador has commission to return them again and will not be willing to depart without them.

    [5.] He expects at taking his leave of the King's Majesty that his Highness will be pleased to remember his princely love and affection unto the Emperor by him; the like he expects to the pleasure of the Queen's Majesty and the Prince. The same affection he performed by commandment from the Emperor, his Lord and Majesty.

    The ambassador being in presence before the King's Majesty it may please his Majesty to touch unto him the injury done by a Frenchman in Russia against his Majesty's subjects, Sir Arthur Aston, Knight, and

James Hill, Colonel, who has accused them to have plotted many great treasons against that country and people by which means they have and do endure much trouble and disgrace. And that also it might please his Majesty to let the ambassador understand that those gentlemen are men merely wronged, their repair thither being only to perform some honorable service to that country, as partly has been already affected by them, whereof the King's Majesty has received knowledge.

And further it may please his Majesty to touch unto the ambassador that whereas it pleased his highness to send his princely letters the last year by his servants John Merrick and William Russell unto the state of Russia, the same Frenchman[1] raised up a most slanderous report affirming that those letters were merely deceitful, wherein the honor of his Majesty is nighly touched. And that his Majesty does expect satisfaction by inflicting punishment upon him worthy such deep dishonor.

[Endorsed] Muscovy, 1614.

1. Presumably Jacques Margeret.

IX. *John Merrick to Sir Ralph Winwood, Archangel, 7 August 1614.*
SP 91/2, f. 1.

Right Honorable Sir,

Your worthy expectation of our safe arrival I cannot but answer at present. The 23th of the last month, praised be God, we came hither well and in health. The currents as they here pass I gladly present.

And first, if it please you, upon the return of the Russ ambassadors from divers parts. The same out of England arrived here the third of July and was gone up to the Mosco before my coming thither. He left in this place (as worthily he had cause), many honorable reports of our King's majesty and country, and of his gracious bounties toward him.

The second, out of Denmark, arrived but, it seems by some harsh speech, but ill contented. There came in company with him a messenger from the King and [they] are gone up together to the Mosco. The third, from Germany, who returned by the way of Holland, the States have sent home well fitted with a ship of war. He gives very great commendation of his entertainment in Holland. By him the States have written their letters and sent a present unto the Emperor for £2,000 value. And that further (for so is the secret report) they have largely promised his Majesty by their letters to furnish him with what monies and munition shall be required in these his present wants, and so have desired his Majesty to be pleased to send his ambassador unto them to treat with them of those business[es]. These things come very nigh unto us and I doubt will too soon be embraced. Might it have pleased the King's majesty to have engaged his princely word by his letters to the Emperor in his loans of money it had mightily preferred the business in hand and have been a great curb to the Hollanders in their violent courses which they carry with great boldness against our state. We cannot deny but this people of Russia have ever well deserved of us. And hitherto in this his Majesty's employment I receive from them all things to my content.

This winter is expected here ambassadors from the Emperor of Germany and others from the King of Poland.

This year, praised be God, the Emperor has had a good hand upon his enemies. Smolensk, a key town bordering on the Pole, and now possessed by them, is besieged by the Russe and greatly distressed of victual, so that they have good hope in short time to become masters again thereof.

Astracan, a great province of this empire which was lately held by one Zarutsky, sometime a great commander among the Russe and a man much favored of the Cossacks is now rendered up to the Emperor and the traitor with Marina, wife of a counterfeit Dimitri, and her son, delivered prisoners. Their practice was to have given that whole province into the Persians' hands.

Pontus de la Gardie, General for the King of Sweden, still holds the town of Novgorod and now is certain news of a supply of 2,500 soldiers come to him out of Sweden. These are the latest and truest reports. If further were offered I should right gladly advise you hereof in that favorable acceptance of these. I wish unto your honor chiefest welfare and happiness. Your honors truly affected,

John Merrick
Archangel, 7 August 1614

X. *Translation of Sir [sic] Arthur Aston's Pass from the Emperor of Russia, Harl. 2149, ff. 149–150.*

The Emperor of Russia his pass to Sir Arthur Aston, the original in that language and in the custody of Colonel Aston. Translated out of the Russian language under the hand of the secretary to the Russia merchants.

Glorying in the Almighty, the omnipotent working, and all-knowing God, filling all places, instructing all people in the way of blessedness and giving them strength to persist therein. The sole lover of mankind and supplier of all their wants, the same trinity in unity we glorify through and by his mercy, power, will and holy commandments, the same dreadful God confirmed unto us forever, the upholding and keeping with all circumspection and justice, the scepter of the truly famous and most potent empire of Russia, adding many other new kingdoms unto the same, and that by his mercy and power we may govern the same in peace and tranquility without interruption of evil-disposed persons from the most mighty Emperor, Lord, and Great Duke Michael, the son of Theodore, of all Russia, sole commander of Volodemer, Moscow, Novgorod, Emperor of Kazan, Emperor of Astrakan, Ugorske, Permskee, Watrckee, Bolgorskee, and others, etc., to the most mighty kings, princes, curhursts (?), etc.,

We are pleased to make known unto you that there arrived within our great empire of Russia, with a desire to serve us against our common enemy Sigius Mundus [sic], King of Poland, from our loving brother the great and mighty prince James of England, Scotland, France, and Ireland, King, one Sir Arthur Aston, Kt., with a certain number of men, captains, and commanders, and being within our great empire he did perform all service that has since appeared to our lying [sic], and did make his abode in the empire during the vacancy of our imperial seat, and at what time, by the mercy and assistance of God and the devout prayers of the people of our several kingdoms, the archbishops, bishops, archdeacons, deacons, priests, and all the princes and commons of this empire and several kingdoms in the same, as also by the blessing of our dear mother, we were elected and established by all lawful rites and orders as lawful successor to our predecessors, emperor and sole commander of all the sole empire of Russia and all the several kingdoms, principalities, and dukedoms in the same.

We then the great prince for and in respect of our brother, King James, as also we seeing that the said Sir Arthur Aston, his readiness and willingness to do us service in our empire, we therefore are now graciously pleased to confer on him our gracious princely favor in permitting of him to repair home into his native country, the kingdom of England, with all his servants and goods, and when or wheresoever into any kingdom, principality, dukedom, or free state town, the said Sir Arthur Aston, Kt., shall arrive, our princely request is that they the said kings, princes, dukes, marquesses, and free states, in request of us, and for our sake, be pleased to suffer him the said Sir Arthur Aston, Kt., to pass freely without any let or stay, and that they be pleased to suffer no wrong or disgrace to be done unto him, but to afford him all lawful favor according to the writs beseeming a person of his rank and quality.

Given in our palace within our imperial city of Moscow, in the year of the world seven thousand one hundred twenty and two, in the month of April, the first day, and in the eleventh year of our imperial reign.[1]

1. There is confusion about the dates, perhaps a result of the translation. The eleventh year of Tsar Michael's reign would be 1624, however the year 7,122 was 1614.

XI. *Reasons to induce his Majesty to the loan of monies unto the great Emperor of Russia now required by his ambassador Alexsey Ivanov, etc., SP 91/2, f. 58–58v.*[1]

First, the ancient entire amity continued now above threescore years, between the princes and subjects of both nations who have ever reputed us their best and chiefest friends and, as a testimony of their loves to the princes of England have confirmed unto the English merchants trading Russia large privileges free from all customs throughout their dominions which are continued to this day.

Secondly, the benefit of trade in the vent of English commodities chiefly dyed and dressed cloth as much as any country in Christendom.

Thirdly, the maintenance of shipping and increase of mariners, the safety and wealth of this island, are much strengthened by keeping this trade.

Fourthly, the needful and serviceable commodities of those countries, especially materials for shipping cordage, masts, etc., brought from thence, the best in Europe, which since their wars have been raised to eight and ten shillings per centum of cordage, yet not so good as that brought from Russia by five shillings the hundred, from whence has formerly been yearly had 1,000 or 2,000 tuns besides great quantities of hemp, flax, tallow, hides, furs of all sorts, wax, and many other worthy and rich commodities transported by us unto the Levant seas, to the great employment of ships and mariners. Iron may be made there, being quantity of ore and wood plenty for the cutting.

Fifthly, the hopes of getting the trade down the river Volga into Persia, which will be a great benefit in venting thither our English cloth and tin. From whence we shall return great store[s] of raw and wrought silk, indigo, and many other rich commodities now brought out of Turkey at a high price by reason of many customs it pays the great Turk which may be brought at an easier rate by the river Volga, being the nearest way into those countries, to the great benefit of his Majesty by increase of his customs in England and enrichment of his subjects which will be more easily obtained by reason most of the Russia merchants and counsellors of state are murdered and consumed by their wars. And we by some of the principal now alive, the last year were invited to solicit that trade who promised to join with us in procuring the same.

Sixthly, the advantage the Hollander will take if content be not given to the Emperor of Russia, the Hollanders purposing to send an ambassador into Russia who will without question make large [f. 58v] offers to obtain privileges to expel us and make England and all Christendom beholding to them for materials for shipping and those country commodities which is the rather to be doubted. For they conceiving the Pole likely to prevail in Russia wrought with him and proffered £60,000 per annum for sole trade, which information we received from the Secretary of the East Country merchants who lay at the King's court and was informed thereof by one of the Secretary of State there, who advised to signify so much into England besides their late working with the Emperor of Russia's ambassador sent the last year to the Emperor of Germany in his return to Hamburg where the English merchants had provided shipping to send him into his own country. The States of Holland sent for him to come to the Hague promising to receive him with honor and presents and convey him home with ships of war for his better safety, and an ambassador with him, from their state, which motion was by him entertained and he received by Grave Maurice and the rest, with great magnificence at the Hague. Whereby easily may be discerned their diligence in procuring trade. And some more experience may be gathered by them in prosecution of the fishing voyage for the whale by us discovered, who set forth this year 12 great ships and four men of war to convey them to King James his new land. And have procured of the state of France forty Biscaynors for the killing of the whale (it being death to serve us or any other) upon promise to assist the French that shall come thither to fish against the English nation, so that we cannot expect less than the like measure in Russia, if it lie in their power.

Lastly, if content be given there may be some hope to prevent the Dutchman's coming into that country further than the Archangel, which will be a great hinderance to their trade; and this has been affected heretofore by Mr. John Merrick, who was the English agent in those parts at that time.

1. A copy of the Reasons is in the Hastings Collection, MS 1608, Huntingdon Library, San Marino. S. Konovalov dated the Reasons March 1618 and printed them as Appendix III to his article, "Anglo-Russian Relations, 1617–18," *OSP* (1950–1951): 99–100.

XII. *The Succession of the Emperor of Russia [ca. 1619], SP 91/2, f.66–66v.*

1. Ivan Vasillievich dying left issue two sons, Fyodor and Demetrius. This Demetrius, being not above a year old when his father died, was murdered when he came to the age of eight years.

2. Fyodor succeeded his father and reigned fourteen years not leaving any issue behind him. In this prince the whole race of the emperors ended.

3. After him Boris Fyodorovich Godunov was elected emperor. He was a gentleman but of mean rank, only advanced to dignities by the means of his sister who was Queen to Fyodor. Boris reigned about six years and

a half, died suddenly supposed by a poisoned potion which he took. He left issue a son of the age of eighteen years and a daughter of two and twenty years.

4. His son succeeded him in the kingdoms. He was never crowned emperor, but within three months after his father's death he and his mother were both of them (by command from the following emperor, named Demetrius) smothered to death. The daughter of Boris was never married but shorn a nun.

5. In the later years of Boris's reign rose up that Demetrius who named himself the son of Ivan Vasillievich. He, by the revolt of the Russe army, gained the kingdom and was crowned emperor. His wife, a daughter of a peer of Poland, was likewise crowned Queen. He reigned one year and was murdered in the Mosco and left no issue behind him. His wife died afterwards in the Mosco.

6. The chiefest of the conspirators of his death was a principal noble-man of Russia, named Vasily Ivanovich, whose ancestors (many years before) had been great Dukes of Russia. This nobleman was chosen emperor and reigned five years and was deposed and shorn a friar, and with his two brothers delivered up prisoner into the Poles' hand. Himself and his eldest brother died in Poland leaving no issue, but his younger brother lives still in Poland unmarried.

Władisław, the King of Poland's eldest son, was elected emperor but after five months the Russe revolted.

The whole land, then carrying a special love to Fyodor Nikitich, nobleman of an ancient house (the Patriarch that now is, at that time prisoner in Poland) fell to a new election and settled the crown upon his son, Michael Feodorovich, that now is Emperor, then of seventeen years of age. He has reigned about six years and remains yet unmarried. Neither has he any brother or sister, or near kinsman but one Uncle by the father's side. His great grandfather's sister was Queen to Ivan Vasillievich by whom he had two sons, Ivan and Fyodor. Ivan died before his father and Fyodor succeeded him, as [written] formerly, leaving no issue.

Select Bibliography

Bibliographic Works

Baron, Samuel H. "A Guide to Published and Unpublished Documents on Anglo-Russian Relations in the Sixteenth Century in British Archives." *Canadian-American Slavic Studies* (Fall, 1977): 354–386. [CASS]

Bell, Gary M. *A Handlist of British Diplomatic Representatives 1509–1688.* Royal Historical Society Guides and Handbooks, no. 16. London: Royal Historical Society, 1990.

Hartley, Janet M. *Guide to Documents and Manuscripts in the United Kingdom Relating to Russia and the Soviet Union.* London: Mansell Publishing, 1987.

Historical Manuscript Commission. *Eighteenth Report.* London: Stationery Office, 1917. Appendix II, Materials for English Diplomatic History, 1509–1783.

Phipps, Geraldine M. "Manuscript Collections in British Archives Relating to Pre-Petrine Russia." *Canadian-American Slavic Society* (Fall, 1979): 400–415.

_____. "Britons in Russia: 1613–82." *Societas—A Review of Social History* 7 (Winter, 1977): 19–45.

_____. "Britons in Seventeenth-Century Russia: an Archival Search." In *The Study of Russian History from British Archival Sources*, edited by Janet M. Hartley, pp. 27–50. New York: Mansell Publishing Limited, 1986.

Manuscripts

Bibliothèque Nationale, Paris
  MS 15,987 (Spifame correspondence)
Bodleian Library, Oxford
  Eng. hist. C 4
British Library, London
  Additional 15,939; 30,571
  Cotton Nero B, II, III, VIII, XI,
  Cotton Vesp. F. III
  Egerton 2790
  Harleian 36, 247, 296, 1217, 2149

Lansdowne 10, 11, 12, 141, 1422
Stowe 172
Danish Rigsarkivet, Copenhagen
Guildhall Library, London
City Remembrancia III (1610–1614)
Grocers' Company, MS 1115 88/2
Vinters' Company, MS 15,333/2
Haus-, Hof- und Staatsarchiv, Vienna
Abteilung Belgien, Fz. 61, 76, 77
Huntington Library, San Marino, California
Ellesmere MSS 1608, 1620, 1621
Marquis of Bath
Whitelocke Papers, Volume I
National Library of Scotland, Edinburgh
MS 2912
Public Record Office, London
C66 (Chancery)
PRO 31/3/41 (Transcripts from the French archives, Paris)
SO 3/5 (Signet Office)
SP 12 (State Papers, Elizabeth I)
SP 14 (State Papers, James I)
SP 75 (Denmark)
SP 80 (German Empire and Hungary)
SP 81 (Germany, States)
SP 84 (Holland)
SP 88 (Poland)
SP 90 (Spain)
SP 91 (Russia)
SP 95 (Sweden)
SP 102 (State Papers Foreign, Royal Letters, Russia)
SP 103 (Treaty Papers)

Printed Sources

A Complete Collection of State Trials and Proceedings for High Treason . . . compiled by T.B. Howell. 21 volumes. London: 1816.

Acts of the Privy Council of England. London: Stationery Office, 1921—.

Bestuzhev-Riumin, K. N., ed. Pamiatniki diplomaticheskikh snoshenii Moskovskogo gosudarstva s Anglieiu: S 1581 po 1604 god. SRIO 38, St. Petersburg: 1883.

[Birch, Thomas], ed. *Court and Times James I.* 2 vols. London: Henry Colburn, Publisher, 1849; reprint, AMS Press, 1973.

Calendar of State Papers: Domestic Series. London: Stationery Office, 1857. [CSPD]

Calendar of State Papers and Manuscripts Relating to English Affairs, Existing in the Archives and Collections of Venice and in the Other Libraries of Northern Italy. London: Stationery Office, 1900——. [CSPV]

Calendar of State Papers Foreign . . . Preserved in the Public Record Office. London: Stationery Office, 1900. [CSPF]

Calendar of State Papers Relating to Ireland . . . Preserved in the Public Record Office. London: Stationery Office, 1900. [CSPI]

[Chamberlain, John]. *The Letters of John Chamberlain,* ed. N.E. McClure. Philadelphia: The American Philosophical Society, 1939.

[Cherry, Francis] *A Declaration of the proceedinge of me Fraunces Cherry, sente as Messenger by her Majesty to the Emperour of Muscowia. . . .* The Egerton Papers, Camden Society. London: 1840 (pp. 292–301). Cherry's account is preceded by a letter from Tsar Fyodor Ivanovich to Elizabeth I, 1598.

Documentos Ineditos para la Historia de España. 20 vols. Madrid: 1945.

Elementa ad Fontium Editiones 4. *Res Polonicae Elisabetha I Angliae Regnante Conscriptae ex Archivis Publicis Londoniarum,* Ed. C. H. Talbot. Rome: Institutum Historicum Polonicum Romae, 1961.

_____ 6. *Res Polonicae Iacobo I Angliae Regnante Conscriptae ex Archivis Publicis Londoniarum,* Ed. C. H. Talbot. Rome: Institutum Historicum Polonicum Romae, 1962.

_____ 13. *Res Polonicae ex Archivo Musei Britannici I pars,* Ed. C. H. Talbot. Rome: Institutum Historicum Polonicum Romae, 1965.

_____ 17. *Res Polonicae ex Archivo Musei Britannici II pars,* Ed. C. H. Talbot. Rome: Institutum Historicum Polonicum Romae, 1967.

Elizabethan England and Europe: Forty Unprinted Letters from Elizabeth I to Protestant Powers, Ed. E.I. Kouri. *Bulletin of the Institute of Historical Research,* Special Supplement no. 12 (November 1982).

[Finet, Sir John]. *Finetti Philoxensis: som choice observations of Sir John Finett, Knight, and Master of Ceremonies to the two last Kings, Touching the Reception, and Precedence, the Treatment and Audience, the Puntillos and Contests of Forren Ambassadors in England.* London: 1656.

[Finet, John]. *Ceremonies of Charles I, The Note Books of John Finet, Master of Ceremonies, 1628–1641,* Ed. Albert L. Loomie. New York: Fordham University Press, 1987.

Fletcher, Dr. Giles. *Of the Russe Commonwealth.* London: 1591. STC no. 11056 (reprinted in Hakluyt Society, First Series, Ed. Edward A. Bond, 1856).

Hakluyt, Richard. *The Principall Navigations, Voiages and Discoveries of the English Nation*. London: 1589; reprint, Cambridge, England: Cambridge University Press, 1965.

Hakluyt Society, First Series, Ed. Edward A. Bond. London: 1856.

Historical Manuscripts Reports. London: Stationery Office. *Buccleuch and Queensberry*, 1 (1899–1926); *Downshire*, 3, 4 (1940); *Montagu of Beaulieu* (1900).

Horsey, Sir Jerome. *Travels* . . . See Hakluyt, Richard, ed.

[Howell, T.B.], ed. A *Discourse Concerning the Precedency of Kings* . . . *whereunto is also adjoyned A Distinct Treatise of Ambassadors, etc*. London: 1664.

Jenkinson, Anthony. *Early Voyages and Travels to Russia and Persia by Anthony Jenkinson and other Englishmen, with some account of the first intercourse of the English with Russia and Central Asia by way of the Caspian Sea*, Ed. E. Delmar Morgan and C.H. Coote. Hakluyt Society, First Series. London: 1886.

Kordt, V. A., ed., *Doneseniia poslannikov Respubliki Soedinennykh Niderlandov pri Russkom dvore*, SRIO 116: St. Petersburg: 1902.

Letters of King James VI and I, Ed. G.P.V. Akrigg. Berkeley: University California Press, 1984.

Lapteva, L. P., ed. "Donesenie avstriiskogo posla o poezdke v Moskvu v 1589 godu," *Voprosy istorii* 6 (1978): 95–112.

Larkin, J. F. and Paul Hughes, eds. *Stuart Royal Proclamations*. 2 vols. Oxford: Oxford University Press, 1983.

Likhachev, D. S., ed. *Puteshestviia russkikh poslov XVI-XVII vv.: Stateinye spiski*. Moscow and Leningrad: 1954.

Loomie, Albert, see Finet, John.

Margeret, Capitaine Jacques. *Un Mousquetaire a Moscou, Mémoires sur la première révolution russe 1604–1610*, Ed. Alexandre Bennigsen. Paris: La Decouverte/Maspero, 1983.

Margeret, Jacques. *The Russian Empire and Grand Duchy of Muscovy*, Trans. and ed. by Chester S. L. Dunning. Pittsburgh, Series in Russian and East European Studies, no. 5. Pittsburgh: 1983.

Nichols, John, ed. *The Progresses, Processions, and Magnificent Festivities of King James the First*. 4 vols. London: 1878.

Papers Relating to the Scots in Poland, Ed. A. Francis Steuart. Edinburgh: Scottish History Society, 1915.

Piot, Charles, ed. "Une mission diplomatique des Pays-Bas espagnoles dans le nord de l'Europe en 1594." *Bulletin de la commission royale d'histoire* 4 ser., 11 (1883–1884): 437–520.

Proceedings in Parliament 1610, Ed. Elizabeth Read Foster. 2 vols. New Haven: Yale University Press, 1966.

Proceedings in Parliament 1614, Ed. Maija Jansson, Philadelphia: American Philosophical Society, 1988.

Purchas, Samuel. *Hakluytus Posthumus or Purchas his Pilgrims*. 20 vols. Glasgow: Hakluyt Society, 1905–07.

Rymer, Thomas, ed. *Foedera, Conventiones, Literae et cuisucunque generis Acta Publica inter Reges Angliae*. 10 vols. [n.p.]: Joannem Neaulme, 1739–1745.

Selden, John. *Titles of Honor*. London: 1972.

[Smith, Sir Thomas]. *Sir T. Smithes Voiage and Entertainment in Rushia*. London: 1605.

Tolstoi, Iurii. *Pervye sorok let snoshenii mezhdu Rossieuiu i Anglieiu 1553–1593*. St. Petersburg: 1875; reprinted, New York: Burt Franklin, nd.

Wernham, R.B., ed. *List and Analysis of State Papers. Foreign Series, Elizabeth I*. Vol. 1, May 1592-June 1593. London: Stationery Office, 1984.

[Winwood, Sir Ralph]. *Memorials of the Affairs of State in the Reigns of Q. Elizabeth and K. James I Collected (chiefly) from the Original Papers of the Right Honorable Sir Ralph Winwood, Kt.* 3 vols. London: 1725.

Printed Secondary Works

Adams, Simon. "Spain or the Netherlands? The Dilemmas of Early Stuart Foreign Policy." In *Before the English Civil War*, ed. Howard Tomlinson, pp. 79–102. London: Macmillan Education, Ltd., 1983.

Almquist, Helge. *Sverge och Ryssland 1595–1611*. Uppsala: Almquist and Wiksells Boktryckeri A.B., 1907.

Attman, A. "Freden i Stolbova 1617." *Scandia* 19 (1948–1949): 36–47.

_____ . *The Russian and Polish Markets in International Trade 1500–1650*. Publications of the Institute of Economic History of Gothenburg University 26. Göteborg: 1973.

_____ . *Den ryska marknaden in 1500-talets baltiska politik*. Lund: Carl Bloms Boktryckeri, 1944.

Baron, Samuel H. "Herberstein's Image of Russia and its Transmission through Later Writers." In Gerhard Pferschy, *Siegmund von Herberstein, Kaiserlicher Gesandter und Begründer der Russlandkunde und die europäische Diplomatie*, pp. 245–273. Graz: Akademische Druck- und Verlagsanstalt, 1989.

_____ . "Ivan the Terrible, Giles Fletcher and the Muscovite Merchantry: a Reconsideration." *Slavic and East European Review* 56, 4 (October, 1978): 563–585.

_____ . "The Muscovy Company, the Muscovite Merchants and the Problem of Reciprocity in Russian Trade." *Forschungen* 27 (1979): 133–155.

_____ . "Osip Nepea and the Opening of Anglo-Russian Commercial Relations." *Oxford Slavonic Papers*, New Series 11 (1978): 42–63.

_____ . "Thrust and Parry: Anglo-Russian Relations in the Muscovite North." *Oxford Slavonic Papers* 21 (1988): 19–40.

Berg, Tor. *Johan Skytte: Hans ungdom och verksamhet under Karl IX:s regering.* Stockholm: Alb. Bonniers, 1920.

Bushkovitch, Paul. *The Merchants of Moscow 1580–1650.* Cambridge: Cambridge University Press, 1980.

Cleminson, Ralph. "Boris Godunov and the Rector of Wooley: A Tale of the Unexpected." *Slavic and East European Review* 65, no. 3 (July, 1987): 399–403.

Croskey, Robert. "The Composition of Sir Jerome Horsey's 'Travels'." *Jahrbücher für Geschichte Osteuropas* 26, no. 3 (1978): 362–375.

Cruden, Robert Peirce. *The History of the Town of Gravesend in the County of Kent and the Port of London.* London: 1843.

Crummey, Robert O. *The Formation of Muscovy 1304–1613.* New York: Longman Inc., 1987.

Dukes, Paul. "The Leslie Family in the Swedish Period (1630–5) of the Thirty Years' War." *European Studies Review* 12, no. 4 (October, 1982): 401–424.

Dunning, Chester. "James I, the Russia Company, and the Plan to Establish a Protectorate Over North Russia." *Albion* 21, no. 2 (Spring, 1989): 206–226.

_____ . "A Letter to James I Concerning the English Plan for Military Intervention in Russia." *Slavic and East European Review* 67, no. 1 (January, 1989): 94–108.

Ehrenberg, Richard. *Hamburg und England im Zeitalter der königin Elisabeth.* Jena: 1896.

Evans, N. E. "The Anglo-Russian Royal Marriage Negotiations of 1600–1603." *Slavic and East European Review* 61, no. 3 (July, 1983): 363–387.

_____ . "Doctor Timothy Willis and his Mission to Russia, 1599." *Oxford Slavonic Papers*, New Series 2 (1969): 39–61.

_____ . "The Meeting of the Russian and Scottish Ambassadors in London in 1601." *Slavic and East European Studies Review* 55, no. 4 (October, 1977): 515–528.

_____ . "Queen Elizabeth I and Tsar Boris: Five Letters, 1597–1603." *Oxford Slavonic Papers* 12 (1965): 49–68.

Fedorowicz, J. K. *England's Baltic Trade in the Early Seventeenth Cen-*

tury: A Study in Anglo-Polish Commercial Diplomacy. Cambridge: Cambridge University Press, 1980.

Floria, B. N. *Rossiia i cheshskoe vosstanie protiv Gabsburgov*. Moscow: 1986.

_____. *Russko-pol'skie otnosheniia i baltiiskii vopros v kontse XVI—nachale XVII v*. Moscow: 1973.

_____. *Russko-pol'skie otnosheniia i politicheskoe razvitie Vostochnoi Evropy vo votroi polovine XVI—nachale XVII v*. Moscow: 1978.

Forstreuter, Kurt. *Preussen und Russland von den Anfängen des Deutschen Ordens bis zu Peter dem Grossen*. Göttinger Bausteine zu Geschichtswissenschaft 23. Göttingen: 1955.

Garstein, Oskar. *Rome and the Counter-Reformation in Scandinavia*. 2 vols. Oslo: 1964–1980.

Hassø, Arthur G. *Rigshofmester Kristoffer Valkendorf til Glorup (1525–1601)*. Copenhagen: 1933.

Heiberg, Steffen. *Christian 4*: Monarken, mennesket og myten. Copenhagen: Gyldendal, 1988.

Hildebrand, Emil. "Johan III och Filip II: Depescher från det spanska sändebudet till Sverige kapten Francisco de Eraso 1578–1579." *Historisk Tidskrift* 6 (1886): 1–50.

Hildebrand, Karl. *Johan III och Europas katolska makter 1568–1580*: Studier i 1500-talets politiska historia. Uppsala: 1898.

Huttenbach, Henry R. "Anthony Jenkinson's 1566 and 1567 Missions to Muscovy Reconstructed from Unpublished Sources." *Canadian-American Slavic Studies* (Summer, 1975): 179–203.

_____. "New Archival Material on the Anglo-Russian Treaty of Queen Elizabeth I and Tsar Ivan IV." *Slavic and East European Studies Review* 49, no. 117 (October, 1971): 535–549.

_____. "The Search for and Discovery of New Archival Materials for Ambassador Jenkinson's Mission to Muscovy in 1571–72: Four Letters by Queen Elizabeth I to Tsar Ivan IV." *Canadian-American Slavic Studies* (Fall, 1972): 416–425.

Jensen, Bergit Bjerre. "Jakob I's Østersøpolitik 1603–25." *Historie: Jyske samlinger* Ny raekke 12 (1977): 1–26.

Keevil, John J. *Hamey the Stranger*. London: 1952.

Konovalov, S. "Anglo-Russian Relations, 1617–1618." *Oxford Slavonic Papers*, Series 1, 1 (1950): 64–103.

_____. "Anglo-Russian Relations, 1620–4." *Oxford Slavonic Papers*, Series 1, 4 (1953), pp. 71–131.

_____. "Seven Russian Royal Letters (1613–1623)." *Oxford Slavonic Papers*, Series 1, 7 (1957): 118–134.

_____ . "Twenty Russian Royal Letters (1626–1634)." *Oxford Slavonic Papers*, Series 1, 8 (1958): 117–156.

_____ . "Two Documents Concerning Anglo-Russian Relations in the Early Seventeenth Century." *Oxford Slavonic Papers*, Series 1, 2 (1951): 128–144.

Lausten, Martin Schwarz. *Religion och politik: Studier i Christian IIIs forhold til det tyske rige i tiden 1544–1559*. Copenhagen: 1977.

Liubimenko, Inna. *Istoriia torgovykh snoshenii Rossii s Angliei*, part 1, *XVI-i vek*. Iur'ev (Dorpat/Tartu): 1912.

_____ . "A Project for the Acquisition of Russia. . . ." *English Historical Review* 114 (April, 1914): 246–256.

_____ . *Les Relations Commerciales et Politiques de l'Angleterre avec la Russie avant Pierre le Grand*. Bibliothèque de l'École des Hautes Études: Sciences philologiques et historiques 261. Paris: 1933.

_____ . "The Correspondence of the First Stuarts with the First Romanovs." *Royal Historical Society Transactions*, Fourth Series, 1 (1918): 77–91.

_____ . "The Struggle of the Dutch with the English for the Russian Market in the 17th c." *Royal Historical Society Transactions* (1924): 27–51.

Lur'e, Ia. S. "'Otkrytie Anglii' russkimi v nachale XVI v." *Geograficheskii sbornik* 3 (1954): 185–187.

_____ . "Russko-angliiskie otnosheniia i mezhdunarodnaia politika vtoroi poloviny XVI v." In *Mezhdunarodnye sviazi Rossii do XVII v.*, ed. A. A. Zimin and V. T. Pashuto, pp. 419–443. Moscow: 1961.

Mierzwa, Edward Alfred. *Anglia a Polska w pierwszej połowie XVII w.* Warsaw: 1986.

Oman, Charles C. *The English Silver in the Kremlin 1557–1663*. London: 1961.

Page, William Samuel. *The Russia Company from 1553–1660*. London: 1911.

Palme, Sven Ulric. *Sverige och Danmark 1596–1611*. Uppsala: 1942.

Perrie, Maureen. "Jerome Horsey's Account of the Events of May 1591." *Oxford Slavonic Papers*, New Series 13 (1980): 28–49.

Phipps, Geraldine M. "Britons in Seventeenth-Century Russia: A Study in the Origins of Modernization." Ph.D. dissertation, University of Pennsylvania, 1973. Ann Arbor Microfilms, 72-17, 411.

_____ . *Sir John Merrick, English Diplomat in Seventeenth Century Russia*. Newtonville, Mass.: Oriental Research Partners, 1983.

Roberts, Michael. *The Early Vasas, A History of Sweden, 1523–1611*. Cambridge, England: Cambridge Paperback Library, 1986.

Skilliter, S. A. *William Harborne and the Trade with Turkey 1578–1582:* A Documentary Study of the First *Anglo-Ottoman Relations.* London: Oxford University Press, 1977.

Tandrup, Leo. *Mod triumf eller tragedie: En politisk-diplomatisk studie over forløbet af den dansk-svenske magtkamp fra Kalmarkrigen til Kejserkrigen med saerligt henblik på formuleringen af den svenske og isaer den danske politik i tiden fra 1617 og isaer fra 1621 til 1625.* Skrifter udgivet af Jysk Selskab for Historie 35. 2 vols. Aarhus: 1979.

Thyresson, B. *Sverige och det protestantiska Europa från Knäredfreden till Rigas erovring.* Uppsala: 1928.

Uebersberger, Hans. *Osterreich und Russland seit dem Ende des 15 Jahrhunderts.* Veröffentlichungen der Kommission für neuere Geschichte Osterreichs 2. Vienna: 1906.

_____ . "Das russisch-österreichische Heiratsprojekt von Ausgang des XVI Jahrhunderts." *Beiträge zur neueren Geschichte Osterreichs.* Vienna: 1906.

Vinogradoff, Igor. "Russian Missions to London, 1569–1687." *Oxford Slavonic Papers,* New Series 14 (1981): 36–72.

Wiese, Ernst. *Die Politik der Niederländer während des Kalmarkriegs (1611–1613) und ihr Bündnis mit Schweden (1614) und den Hansestädten (1616).* Heidelberg: 1903.

Willan, T. S. *The Early History of the Russia Company 1553–1603.* Manchester: Manchester University Press, 1956.

Zins, Henryk. *England and the Baltic in the Elizabethan Era,* trans. H. C. Stevens. Manchester: Manchester University Press, 1972.

Index
England and the North:
The Russian Embassy
of 1613–1614

[The names of the Tsars of Russia and the Kings of England are indexed in relation to events; the names are not listed below each time they are mentioned in the repetition of titles and toasts. Preliminary Material is not indexed.]

Abbas, Shah of Persia (1587–1629), 190n107, 192n128

Adrian, Baron of Flodorf. See Frieger, Adraian.

Ahmed I, Sultan of Turkey (1603–1617), 190n106

Aidy (Ady), Andreas, mercenary, 183n12, 186n33

Ali-bek, Amir, Persian Ambassador to Russia, 118, 190n107

Alphery, Mikepher (spelled variously), Russian youth, 130–131, 193nn135 & 137, 205

Altmark, 42n116

Ambassadors
expenses of, 196n192, 198n215
provisions for, 155, 198n218, 200n254, 202n300
seating for, 117–118, 153, 154, 155, 168, 178, 205

Amity, articles for, 185n21

Amsterdam, 56

Andreev, Andrei, Russian translator, 195n185, 189n216

Anglo-Russian league (c. 1570), 13–14

Anna Catharine, Queen of Denmark (d. 1612), 195n178

Anne, Queen of England, 1, 7, 168, 170, 171, 173, 200n255

Anstruther, Sir Robert, diplomat, 55, 183n11

Antwerp staple, 9

Archangel, vii, 44n120, 45, 59, 65, 69, 71, 72, 109, 179, 183n1, 187n55, 189n94, 191n119, 192n25, 212

Archduke Karl (brother of Maximilian), 12, 14

Archduke Maximilian, 35, 68n203

Archdukes, the of the Netherlands, 6, 40, 66

Armada, Spanish, 21

Arslan, of the Great Nogai Horde, 123

Aston, Arthur (Ktd. 1641), 67, 125, 126, 130, 191n119, 192nn126 & 127, 207, 209–210

Astrakhan' (Astracan), 120, 121, 209

Barne, George, Muscovy Company, 27, 28

Barnekov, Christian, Danish nobleman, 22, 37

Baron, Samuel, vi

Batory, Gabor, 63

Batory, Stefan, 23, 24, 27, 35, 63

Beckman, Reinhold, 34

Bel'skii, Bogdan, 29, 30, 31
Bertie, Peregrine, Lord Willoughby, 18, 19
Bertie, Robert, Lord Willoughby of Eresby, 147, 182n10, 195n175
Bethlen, Gabor, Prince of Transylvania (1613–1629), 5
Bilderbeck, Henry, Dutch agent at Cologne, 186n33
Biscaynors, 212
Bodley, Thomas, 19, 20, 21
Bogdanov, Gavrilo, Secretary to Prince Boriatinskii, 182n9
Bohemia, 64n185
Boisschot, Ferdinand de, Ambassador from the Archdukes to Eng., 6, 68, 184n17, 198n213, 200n260 & 268 & 269 & 270, 201nn276, 279
Bomelius, Elisaeus, German physician, 33n103
Boriatinskii, Prince Ivan, 182n9
Boris Godunov, Tsar (1598–1605), 1, 7, 35, 46, 119, 188n69, 192n128, 193n150
    daughter (Kseniya) of, 7
    and England, 3, 33, 47, 184n20
    his election, 86
    and the Horsey mission, 36–37
    joins imperial faction, 35, 36
    and marital interests, 44, 45
    and treaty with Poland, 185nn26 & 31. See also Sigismund III Vasa, King of Poland.
Bowes, Sir Jerome, English Ambassador to Russia, 23, 27–34, 36, 37, 184n18, 185n21, 196n187
Brabazon, Edward, 63
Brahe, Magnus, Count of Visingsborg, 22
Brandenburg, Johann Sigismund, Elector of, 4n15, 65
Brandenburg-Ansbach, Frederick, Margrave of, 195n178
Brandenburg-Ansbach, Joachim Ernst, Margrave of, 4n15
Bremen, 39, 41, 43
Brewster, Mark, English merchant, 190n97
Bromley, Sir Thomas, Lord Chancellor of England (1579–1587), 28

Bruce, Guillelmus (William), mercenary, 185n32, 188n70
Bukhara, 109
Button, Thomas, 189n94
Buwinckhausen, Daniel, Sieur de Walmerode, Privy Councillor of the Duke of Württemberg, 192n132
Byngley, Colonel, 50

Calvin, John, 65
Calvinists, 3
Carew, George, 43, 45
Carey, Henry, Baron Hunsdon, 26
Carisius, Dr. Jonas, 41, 53n149
Carleton, Sir Dudley, English Ambassador to Venice, etc., 2, 189n94, 197nn209 & 213
Caron, Noel de, States General Ambassador to England, 20
Carr, Robert, Viscount Rochester, 70n212, 203
Casimir, Johan, of the Palatinate, 31n99, 33
Cathay, 189n94
Catholic(s), Roman, 1, 2, 5, 25n84, 48, 54, 60, 183n13, 186n40
    and Catholic church(es), 78, 79, 80, 89, 183n13
    Catholic League, 3, 5
Cecil, Robert, Earl of Salisbury, 42n117, 49n131, 50nn134 & 135 & 139, 52, 53n145, 55nn156 & 157, 62, 64, 67nn197 & 198, 183n12, 184n13, 185n32, 186nn33 & 39, 187n45, 191n119, 199n244
Cecil, Sir Edward, 67n198
Cecil, William, Lord Burghley, 12, 13, 16, 19nn66, 67, 20n72, 21, 38, 40, 45
Chamberlain, John, newsletter writer, 189n94, 197nn209 & 213
Chamberlayn, Thomas, mercenary, 62, 185n32, 186n33, 189nn39 & 40, 187n45
Chancellor, Richard, navigator, 9, 11
Charles I, King of England (1625–1649), 190n97
Charles IX, King of Sweden (1604–1611), xi, 4, 49, 59, 68n203, 76, 85

death of, 52, 73n12
employed Irish soldiers, 50. And see
 Ireland, soldiers from.
injustices of, 104, 118, 172, 177,
 187n56
marriage rumors about, 195n178
and mercenaries, 97
and Shuiskii, 60
sons of 68n203, 99, 187n63. See also,
 Sweden.
Charles V, Holy Roman Emperor
 (1519–1556), 11
Charles, Prince, Duke of York, 4, 62,
 168, 170, 171, 173, 187n45,
 200n255
Cherry, Francis, English Ambassador to
 Russia, 34, 44, 184n19
Chichester, Arthur, Baron, 63
China, 121, 189n94
Chodkiewicz, Karol, hetman of the
 Grand Duchy of Lithuania, 81, 96,
 97, 113, 172, 190n98
Christian IV, King of Denmark
 (1588–1648), 1, 2, 4, 22, 37, 46, 51,
 68, 72, 182n7, 193n149
 and Charles IX, 51
 Dutch mercenaries for, 55
 and England, 38, 53, 54, 72
 and Habsburgs, 54
 and Kalmar war, 52, 54–57, 73n12,
 183n12
 majority of, 37
 marriage rumours about, 141, 142, 147
 offers to mediate, 37
 regency of, 21, 22n77. See also,
 Denmark.
Christian states
 to stand against Muslims, 111–112
Church of England, 3
Cichocki, Gaspar, author, 61
Cikowski, Stanisław, Polish calvinist,
 48n128
Circassians, 122
Cleve, 66
Cobham, Henry, 22, 28
Company of Merchants of London,
 194n168
Cornwallis, Sir Charles, 199n244
Correr, Marc' Antonio, 1

Cowell, Dr. John, 62n176
Cracow, 188n63
Crimean Khan, 119. And see Gazi-Girey,
 Khan.

Dançay, Charles, French Ambassador to
 Denmark, 18, 20
Danvers, Henry, Lord, President of
 Munster, 197n210
Danzig, vii, 9, 10, 11, 12, 24, 25, 42,
 64n183, 65, 192n124
Davidove, Cazaren (spelled variously),
 Russian youth, 205, 193n138
Davies, Sir John, Attorney General for
 Ireland, 5, 197n199
de la Gardie, Jakob Pontusson, Swedish
 General, 2, 59, 60, 70, 76, 77, 84,
 85, 92, 97, 98, 99, 100, 118, 172,
 174, 187n56, 209
Denmark, 2n4, 4, 9, 10, 37, 39, 147, and
 conflict with Sweden. See Knaerød,
 Treaty of and Kalmar War.
 England, 18–22, 37–41, 53–57
 Spain, 5, 6, 20, 21, 38, 56
 War of Three Crowns, 9
 Holland, 38. See also, Christian IV;
 Sound, Danish
Deulino, Truce of (1618), 70
Dmitrii Ivanovich (son of Ivan III), 35,
 36
Dmitrii of Uglich, Tsarevich, 87, 88
Don, River, 88, 90, 123
Drake, Sir Francis, 21
Dudley, Robert, Earl of Leicester, 26
Dun, Daniel, commissioner at Bremen
 (1602), 41
Dutch, the, 4, 39, 56, 65, 66
 at Kholmogory, 30
 naval strength of, vi, 37
 solvency of, 5
 and Sweden, 51, 53. See also, Nassau,
 Count Maurice, Prince of Orange;
 Netherlands.
Dvina River, 9, 26, 71, 189n94, 195n183
Działyński, Paweł, 42, 43

East India Company, 194n168
East Indies, 189n94
Eastland Company, 10, 24, 25

Editorial conventions, x
Edmondes, Sir Thomas, 199n244,
    183nn2 & 12
Edward VI, King of England
    (1547–1553), 47
Elbing, 24, 25, 65
Elizabeth I, Queen of England
    (1558–1603), vi, 1, 12, 13, 25, 37,
    38, 40, 73, 83, 103, 108, 185n21,
    193n150, 203
  death of, 41
  favored harmony, 43
  and the Hanse, 9
  and Ivan IV, 12, 15
  letter of (1576), 13
  offended by Poles, 42, 48
  and Pisemskii embassy, 26–29
  and relations with Russia, 8–18
  and Russian youths, 132, 205. See also,
    Russian youths.
  treaty (league) with Russia (c. 1570),
    13, 14
  treaty of 1576, 17
Elizabeth, Princess, daughter of James I,
    192n128, 195n171
Emden, 9, 18, 39, 40
Empire, The Holy Roman, vi, 37,
    119–120, 182n9, 133–136
  shifts against England, 40
  and war against Turks, 40. See
    also, Ferdinand I; Rodulf II;
    Matthias
Engelsted, R., 50n139, 53n145, 186n33
England, 8, 9, 18n62, 37, and,
  Denmark, 10, 18–22, 37–41, 53–57
  the Empire, 13
  the northern powers, 8–11, 18, 47–49,
    59
  Poland, 23–26, 41–43
  the Pope, 28
  Russia, 11–18, 26–37, 44–47, 59–71.
    See also, Chancellor, Richard; Boris
    Godunov; Ivan IV; Jenkinson,
    Anthony; Randolph, Thomas;
    Michael, Tsar.
  Spain, 37, 47
  Sweden, 22–23, 41–43, 49–53
  treaty (league) with Russia, 13–14, 17.
    See also Elizabeth I; James I;

Mikulin, Gregory Ivanovich;
    Pisemskii, Fyodor, Andreevich.
English "project" in Russia, 66–69
Eraso, Francisco de, Spanish emissary to
    Sweden, 22
Eremeev, Eremei (Hermann Wester-
    mann), 119, 120, 191n109
Erik XIV, King of Sweden (1560–1568),
    10, 23n79
Essex affair (1601), 46
Estonia, 42, 54, 188n85, 194n162
Eure, Robert, commissioner at Bremen
    (1602), 41
Evans, Norman,

Ferdinand I, Holy Roman Emperor
    (1556–1564), 9
Ferrers, Thomas, English Ambassador to
    Denmark, 39
Finch, Richard, English translator,
    195nn181 & 187
Finet, John, author, 198nn213 & 214 &
    217 & 226
Finland (and Finns), 53, 54, 60
First False Dmitrii. See Otrep'ev,
    Grishka.
Fisk, Thomas, 69
Flabäck, 54
Fletcher, Giles, English envoy to Russia,
    34, 36, 58n168, 184n19
Foscarini, Antonio, Venetian
    Ambassador to England, 67,
    201n281, 202nn292 & 300
France (and French), 4, 30, 37, 111, 112,
    212
Frederick II, King of Denmark
    (1559–1588), 9, 18, 193n149
  as intermediary, 20
  Dançay's report on, 18
  opposes Russian trade, 19
  and promise to Spain, 20, 21
  receives Order of the Garter, 30. See
    also, Denmark.
Frederick, Count Palatine, 3, 4n15, 5,
    192n128
Frieger, Adrian, Baron of Flodorf, 66, 67,
    125–128, 191n119
Frolov, Savva, 29, 30, 31
Fyodor I, Tsar (1584–1598), xi, 33, 37,

59, 73, 83, 86, 97, 105, 108, 115, 121, 179, 184n19, 194n150, 212, 213

Georgian Tsars, 122
Gerard, John, author, 199n244
Gerard, Thomas Lord, 169, 200n258
"Germans" (foreigners), 76, 77, 79, 80, 81, 92, 94, 95, 98, 110, 182n5
Germogen, Patriarch of Moscow, 79, 80, 94, 185n29, 186n43
Giray II, Gazi, Khan of Crimea (1588–1608), 190n108
Giray, Djanibek, Khan of Crimea (1610–1623, 1624, 1627–1635), 191n108
Glover, Thomas, English Ambassador to Turkey, 190n106
Godunov, Boris. See Boris Godunov.
Golitsyn, Prince Andrei Vasil'evich, 80, 95
Golitsyn, Prince Vasilii Vasil'evich, 78, 94
Gondomar, Don Diego Sarmiento de Acuña, Count of, 7, 202n300
Gordon, Patrick, 63, 64, 65, 70, 71, 184n13, 186nn33 & 39, 189n92, 190n101
Gorge, Thomas, English emissary to Sweden, 22
Gosiewski, Aleksander, Starosta of Wieliż, 75, 85, 88, 90
Grand Vizier, 5
Gravesend, 6, 149, 150, 151, 152, 197n202, 203
Great Stone City, 81, 96
Greek Orthodox Church. See Orthodox Church, faith.
Greenwich, 27
Greep, Andrew, 49, 50
Gregory XIII, Pope
and Russian affairs (c. 1582), 28. See also, Pope, the.
Gregorowicz, Josef. See Egeiuzuf Grigor'ev.
Grigor'ev, Egeiuzuf, Imperial emissary to Persia, 119, 191n109
Grigor'ev Grigorii. See Alphery, Mikepher.

Grigor'ev, Putilo, Secretary to the Governor of Archangel, 71, 182n4, 182n6
Grocers, Worshipful Company of, 196n193, 199n240, 204n1
Grynkyn, John, Painter-Stainer, 199n240
Guildhall, 204
Gunpowder plot, 49. See also, Guy Fawkes Day.
Gustavus I Vasa, King of Sweden (1523–1560), 10n41
Gustavus II Adolphus, King of Sweden (1611–1632), 42n116, 52, 68, 71, 86, 101, 172
injustices of to Russia, 86, 142–143, 174
and marriage rumours, 147, 195n171
succeeds Charles IX, 59, 187n63. See also, Charles IX; Sweden.
Guy Fawkes Day, 166–168, 199n244

Habsburgs, vi, vii, 1, 10, 23, 25, 35, 48, 51, 54
Hadersleben, 20
Hamburg, 9, 18, 191nn119 & 121, 212
Hamey, Baldwin, English Doctor, xi, 179–181, 193n150, 194n164, 202n296
Hamey, Sarah, 202n297
Hanse, the, 9, 24n83, 40, 41, 56
Hastings, Mary, daughter of Earl of Huntingdon, 26, 28, 29, 30, 33
Hatton, Christopher, 26
Hayward, Sir George, 197n200
Heinzken, Bertold, 43
Henrietta Maria, French Princess, 54n150
Henry IV (of Navarre), King of France (1589–1610), 5, 20, 54
Henry, Prince of Wales, 3, 4
Herberstein, Baron Sigismund von, author, 58n168
Herbert, John, English Ambassador to Poland, etc., 24, 25, 41
Herle, William, 20n72
Hill, James, mercenary, 43n118, 64, 65n187, 67, 191n119, 192n126, 208
Hoby, Sir Edward, 199n244
Hoddesdon, Christopher, 22

Holland (and Hollanders), 182n9, 209, 211

Holy Roman Emperors. See Empire, the Holy Roman.

Horsey, Jerome, English Ambassador to Russian, xi, 33, 184n19

Howard, Charles, Baron Howard of Effingham, 21

Howard, Henry, Earl of Northampton, 52

Howard, Rowland, 34

Howard, Theophilus, Baron Howard de Walden, 169, 200n259

Howard, Thomas, Earl of Suffolk, Lord Chamberlain, 168, 175, 176, 178, 199nn249 & 253, 203, 204

Huguenots, 4

Huitfeldt, Arild, Chancellor of Denmark c. 1596, 37, 38, 41

Hunsdon, Lord, see Carey, Henry.

Iam Zapol'skii, treaty of (1582), 23, 26

Ian, son of Arslan of the Great Nogai Horde, 123

Iberia, 122

Iermak, and conquest of Siberia, 191n114

Imperial Mandate of 1582, 40

Imperial Mandate of 1596, 42

Imperial Mandate of 1597, 38, 39, 40, 44

Ireland,
    soldiers from, 2, 49, 50, 63, 64. And see Greep, Andrew; and Byngley, Colonel.
    and Spain, 5

Irtysh river, 121

Ishterek, Nogai Prince, 122

Isidor, Metropolitan of Novgorod, 118

Italy, 58

Iur'ev-Zakharin, Nikita (Romanov), 29, 30, 32, 33, 35

Ivan III (the Great), Grand Duke (1462–1505), 35

Ivan IV Vasil'evich (the Terrible), Tsar (1547–1584), 11, 12, 26, 36, 44, 47, 73, 83, 121, 193n150, 194n151, 212
    comments on English merchants, 13
    and England, 13–14, 17, 23, 26, 32
    martial interests of, 26, 30, 32. See also Hastings, Mary.
    signs truce with Poland, 14

was "English Emperor", 32
    his letter to Elizabeth I, 13

Ivangorod, Castle of, 50

Ivanov, Andrei, Secretary to Prince Volkonskii, 74, 89

Ivanovich, Prince Dmitrii, 88

Ivanovna, Marfa, 82, 111, 172, 179

Jacob, Robert, Dr., 26

James, I, King of England (1603–1625), vi, viii, 1, 8, 47, 4, 48, 49, 51, 57, 66, 72, 83, 85, 103, 110, 111, 210
    accession of, 145
    audience of at Whitehall, 166, 168
    an author, 51
    and Catholics, 48–49
    children's marriages, 54
    and Christian IV, 51, 56, 72
    has speeches translated, 178
    heredity of, 61, 201n277
    interest of in northern alliance, 3, 68
    letter of to Tsar, 145
    marriage of, 1, 20, 46
    memorandum of to Tsar, 207–208
    on progress, 196n189
    peacemaker, 4, 8, 43, 47, 48, 53, 65, 141, 142, 146. And see Knaerød, Treaty of.
    and policies regarding Sigismund III, 3, 8, 43, 48, 100
    receives credential letter, 171
    son of Andrew, xii, 150, 152, 154, 155, 159, 162, 165, 168, 169, 196n191
    to send ambassador to Russia, 105–106
    speech of to Ziuzin, 173–174

Jenkinson, Anthony, English emissary to Russia, etc., 11, 12, 14, 15, 17, 18n62, 159, 160, 161, 164, 184n18

Jesuits, 5, 22, 40, 62, 66, 69, 186n39

Johan III, King of Sweden (1568–1592), 10, 15, 22, 23

Johan, Prince of Denmark, 7

Johann, Count of Pfaltz-Zweibrücken, 4n15

Johnson, John or Guy Fawkes, 199n250

Johnson, Robert, author, 58n168

Judd, Sir Andrew, 196n190

Juliers (and Cleves), 3, 67n198

Kabarda, 122
Kalmar War (1611–1613), 42, 43, 52,
    54–57, 183n11. See also, Knaerød,
    Treaty of.
Kaluga, 76, 77, 79, 91, 94, 99
Kaluga, thief of. See Second False
    Dmitrii.
Karl Philip, Prince of Sweden, 68n203,
    85, 118, 188n63
Karl, Duke of Södermanland, 23, 25, 37,
    42, 43, 45, 46
Karnkowski, Stanisław, Primate of Poland
    (1583–1603), 25
Kashtanov, Sergei, viii
Kazan', 120, 121
Keith, Andrew, Jr., 51
Keith, Sir Andrew, English Ambassador
    to the Emperor, 22
Kholmogory, 30
Kitaigorod, 81, 96, 97, 110
Klushino, victory at (1610), 52, 60
Knaerød, Treaty of (1613), 53, 55, 56,
    58, 59, 146, 182n10, 183n12,
    187n55, 195n176. See also, James I,
    peacemaker; Kalmar War.
Knibbe, Paul, 22
Knoppert, Dr. Albert, 10
Knyvet, Sir Thomas, 197n203
Kola peninsula, 26, 30
Komulović, Alessandro, 44n120
Konstantin, Georgian Tsar, 122
Korela, 172
Krag, Nils, 38
Kremlin, 81, 96, 97
Kseniya, daughter of Boris Godunov, 7
Kuchum, Siberian Khan, 121

La Rochelle, 4
Lake, Sir Thomas, 62, 69n210, 183n11
Lapland, 54
Lee, Sir Richard, English Ambassador to
    Russia, etc., 43, 45, 184n20
Lesieur, Sir Stephen, English Ambassador
    to the Emperor, etc., 1, 2n3, 3, 39,
    41, 192n132
Lewkenor, Sir Lewis, Master of
    Ceremonies, 161, 164, 165, 168,
    175, 178, 198n230, 204
Liapunov, Prokopii, 61

Lichfield, Thomas, 50
Liechtenstein, Karl von, 41
Linköping, treaty of, 43
Lithuania and Lithuanians, 72, 74, 75,
    76, 78, 79, 80, 81, 85, 87, 90, 91,
    93, 94, 95, 96, 97, 99, 101, 110,
    113, 115, 120, 122, 123, 172,
    191n118
Livonia, 10, 15, 32, 42n116, 46, 50
Livonian Order, 8n38
Livonian Wars (1558–1583), 8, 11, 23,
    194n162
London, Livery Companies of, 204. See
    also, Grocers, Worshipful Company
    of; Vintners, Company of.
Lord Chamberlain. See Howard, Thomas,
    Earl of Suffolk.
Lord Mayor of London. See Middleton,
    Sir Thomas and Swinnerton, Sir
    John.
Lord Mayor's Festival, 159, 161, 162–164,
    199n233
Lorraine, Duke of, 63
Louis XIII, King of France (1610–1643),
    6
Low Countries, 66
Lübeck, 21, 40
Lubimenko, Inna, vii, viii, 68n202
Lur'e, Ia. S., vii
Luther, Martin, 65
Lutherans, 3, 23, 25

Magnus, Prince of Denmark, 15
Mahmetkul, brother of Kuchum, Siberian
    Khan, 121
Marfa Ivanovna. See Ivanovna, Marfa.
Margeret, Jacques, 188nn65–68,
    191nn121–124, 208
Marinka. See Mniszech, Marina.
Mark the Englishman, 80, 110, 187n46,
    188n82
Marsh, Anthony, 34, 36, 44
Mary I, Queen of England (1553–1558),
    10
Matthias, Holy Roman Emperor
    (1612–1619), 17, 64, 119–120,
    193n141. See also, Empire, the Holy
    Roman.

Maurice of Orange. See Nassau, Count
    Maurice.
Maurice, Prince, 189n95
Maximilian II (1564–1576), 9, 12, 16,
    17
Maximilian, Archduke of Austria, 120
Maximilian, Duke of Bavaria, 3
Medina Sidonia, Alonso Pérez de
    Guzmán el Bueno, Duke of, 21, n75
Mehmed IV, Sultan of Turkey
    (1595–1603), 190n106
Memoranda (for Ziuzin embassy),
    124–145
  in case of the death of the English
    king, 124–125
  Letter concerning Ziuzin's salary,
    138–139
  Letter of introduction for Ziuzin,
    136–137
  Letter regarding Baldwin Hamey (and
    safe conduct), 144–145
  Letter to apothecaries from Tsar,
    137–138
  Letter to Christian IV from Tsar, 137
  Letter to the Governor, etc., of
    Archangel, 139
  Letter to Tsar from Governor, etc., of
    Archangel, 140–141
  Letter to Ziuzin, etc., 142–144
  on Baron Freiger of Flodorf, Arthur
    Aston, etc., 125–128
  on English foreign policy, 129–130
  on a Russian embassy to the Emperor,
    133–136
  on Russian youths, 130–133
  reference to a letter to English
    silversmiths, 138–139
  safe conduct for English ambassadors to
    Russia, 136
Mendoza, Francisco de, Admiral of
    Aragon, 42
Merchant Adventurers, 9, 39, 42, 44
merchants, English, 6, 24, 25, 34, 39, 64,
    65, 70, 109, 187n55, 189nn94 & 95
Merrick, John, 3, 43, 44, 150, 158, 159,
    162, 163, 164, 166, 168, 178, 179,
    181, 184n20, 185n23, 190n191,
    193n139, 194n168, 203–204, 205,
    206, 208

  ambassador to Russia (1614), 193n147,
    202n300
  in Archangel (1613), 58, 140, 142,
    143, 146, 182n6, 187n55, 203,
    208–209
  carries letters, 73
  commission to (1613), 68
  letters of, 71n217, 208–209
  receives knighthood, 71, 202n300
  and Russian youths, 132, 133, 140, 205
  spokesman for English project, 68
Metropolitan Filaret of Rostov and
    Iaroslavl', 78, 94
Metropolitan Isidor, 100
Michael, Tsar. See Mikhail (Michael),
    Tsar.
Middleton, Sir Thomas, Lord Mayor of
    London (1613–1614), 6, 199n237
Migip-bek, 118, 190n107
Mikhail (Michael), Tsar, viii, xi, 7, 58,
    59, 109–110, 128
  age of, 117, 156
  coronation of, 2, 182n8
  election of, 61, 69n209, 82, 116,
    182n8, 203, 213
  title of, x–xi, 82–83, 171
  instructions of to Ziuzin, 71–84,
    84–124
  invites ambassadors from England,
    106–107, 187n53 189n88
  legitmacy and sovereignty of, 7,
    115–116, 140
  reasons to loan money to, 211–212
  requests of, 84, 101, 103, 104,
    105–106, 143, 177. And see Ziuzin,
    Aleksei, instructions to.
  rumor of death of, 171
  sends ambassadors, 70, 72, 182n9. See
    also, England; Russia.
Mikulin, Gregory Ivanovich, Russian
    ambassador to England, 184n207,
    199n242
Minin, Kuzma, 190n98
Minkwitz, Ehrenfried von, emissary of
    Rudolf II, 39, 40–41, 45
Mniszech, ———, son of Jerzy Mniszech,
    91
Mniszech, Jerzy, Governor of Sandomierz,
    75, 76, 85, 87, 88, 89, 91

Mniszech, Marina, daughter of Jerzy
    Mniszech, 75, 87, 88, 89, 91, 94,
    123, 209
Moldavia, 63
Montagu, Sir Edward, 66
More, John, 67
Murshikuli-Bek, 118
Muscovy Company, vi, vii, viii, 9, 13, 14,
    27, 32, 34, 35, 36, 44, 46, 51, 57,
    66, 67, 68, 69, 193n140, 194n168,
    197n198, 198n215
Muslims, 108, 111, 112
    Muslim law, 121
    Muslim states, 114
Mychalove, Sophone (spelled variously),
    Russian youth, 205, 193n138

Narva, 9, 10, 11, 12, 15, 64
Nassau, Count Maurice, Prince of
    Orange, 6, 52, 212
Nepeia, Osip, 11
Netherlands, 18, 20, 40. See also, Dutch,
    the; States General, the; United
    Provinces.
Newsletters, 62
Newton, Adam, tutor to Prince Henry of
    England, 188n70
Nilsson, Peder, 43n118
Nogais, 121–122, 191n115
Nonsuch, treaty of (1585), 19
Norvegus, Nicolai, Laurentius (Jesuit),
    22n78, 23
Norway, 19, 39
Novgorod (Great Novgorod), 59, 60, 70,
    77, 92, 97, 98, 99, 100, 115, 172,
    183n12, 209
Nyköping, 183n12

O'Neill, Hugh, Earl of Tyrone, 186n40
Ob' river, 121
Odoevskii, Prince Ivan, 100, 118
Ograrev, Postnik, emissary of Boris
    Godunov, 87
Mikołaj Oleśnicki, Castellan of
    Malogoszcz, 75, 76, 85, 88, 90, 91
Orthodox Church, faith, 3, 78, 79, 80,
    81, 89, 93, 95, 99, 111, 113, 114,
    115, 118, 121
Ostroróg, Jan, 25

Otrep'ev, Grishka, the First False Dmitrii
    (d. 1606), 59, 74, 87, 90, 97, 120,
    123, 185nn27 & 32, 187n62, 213
Otrep'ev, Smirnoi, Uncle of Grishka
    Otrep'ev, 87
Ottomans, the, 44, 46

Palavicino, Sir Horatio, 21n75
papists, 66, and see Catholics.
Parker, William, Lord Mounteagle,
    199n247
Parkins, Christopher, English Ambassador
    to Denmark, etc., 21, 24, 25, 38
Parliament, English, Lower House of, 61
Parsberg, Manderup, delegate to Bremen
    (1602), 41
Pechenga, 26
Percy, Henry, Earl of Northumberland,
    199n248
Persia, 35, 65, 109, 118, 119, 189n94,
    191n115, 209, 211
Peyton, Sir Henry, English adventurer in
    Holland, 183n12, 190n95
Philip II, King of Spain (1556–1598), 6,
    11n44, 20, 24. See also, Denmark;
    Spain.
Philip III, King of Spain (1598–1621),
    53n147, 66, 202n300
Philip IV, King of Spain (1621–1665),
    193n143
Phipps, Geraldine M., vi
Pindar, Sir Paul, English factor and
    diplomat, 5
Pinock, Henry, Portreve of Gravesend,
    197n196
pirates, 196n195
Pisemskii, Fyodor Andreevich, Russian
    Ambassador to England, xii, 26–28,
    30, 31, 184n18
Poland-Lithuania, vi, viii, 2, 4, 9, 11, 17,
    25, 51–52
    and England, 9, 23–26, 41–43, 47–49
    and the Hanse, 9
    and the Livonian War, 8, 42. See also
    Mniszech, Jerzy; Mniszech, Marina;
    Poles; and Sigismund III Vasa.
Poles, 60, 64, 69, 72, 74, 75, 76, 78, 79,
    80, 81, 85, 87, 90, 91, 93, 94, 95,
    96, 97, 99, 101, 110, 113, 115, 120,

122, 123, 172, 186n39,
190nn97–100, 191n118, 212. See
also, Lithuanians.
Pope, the, 2n7, 27, 30, 49, 86, 111, 112,
117, 166, 167
Possevino, Antonio, papal mediator, 26,
28
Pozharskii, Prince Dmitrii, 69, 61,
187n50, 190n98, 191n118
Prague, 25, 35, 40, 41, 44n120
Prescott, Alexander, Sheriff of London,
198n228
Privileges to English merchants, 184nn
18 & 19, 190n96. See also, Russia.
Protestant Union, 49, 65, 64
Protestants, Protestantism, vi, 2, 3, 4, 10,
19, 25, 38, 48, 51, 52, 54, 57, 64,
66, 192n132
Prussia, 64
Pskov, 77, 92, 185n27
Pudozhemskoe ust'e, 195n183
Purchas, Samuel, 6n30
Purgasov, Voin, 119
Pushkin, Grigorii, Governor of Vologda,
71
Pushkin, Nikita Mikhailovich, Governor
of Archangel, 71, 182n1, 182n6

Radziwiłł, Prince Janusz, 186n33,
192n124
Ramel, Henrik, Chancellor to Frederick
II, 20
Randolph, Thomas (Muscovy Company),
12, 13, 27, 28, 184n18
Reval, 15, 188n85, 194n162
Riazan', noblemen of, 61
Riga, blockade of, 52n140
Rogers, Daniel, English Ambassador to
Denmark, etc., 20, 21, 23
Rogers, Dr. John, English Ambassador to
Denmark, etc., 18n62, 24
Romanov, Metropolitan Filaret, 61
Romanov, Mikhail Fyodorovich, Tsar.
See Mikhail (Michael), Tsar.
Romanov, Nikita. See Iur'ev-Zakharin,
Nikita.
Romanov-Iur'ev, Fyodor Nikitich, 116
Romanova-Iur'eva, Anastasia, 116
Rome, 3, 49

Rotheram, Edward, Sheriff of London,
198n228
Rozrażewski, Hieronym, Bishop of
Kujawy, 25
Różyński, Prince Roman, 74, 90
Rudolf II, Holy Roman Emperor
(1576–1612), 22n77, 40, 44, 45, 64,
105, 189n89, 191n122. See also,
Empire, the Holy Roman.
Rumpf, Wolfgang von, councillor of
Rudolf II, 41
Russell, William, English merchant and
diplomat, 68–69, 162, 163, 194n168,
195n185, 199n234, 203
Russia, 11–18, 35, 36, 63
    and England, 8–18, 26–37, 44–49,
    59–71
    imperial faction in, 32, 33
    poverty in, 101, 104
    and treaty with Denmark (1516). And
    see, Boris Godunov; Gustavus II
    Adolphus, injustices of; Ivan III; III;
    Ivan IV; Lithuanians; Mikhail
    (Michael), Tsar; Poles; Shuiskii,
    Tsar Vasilii; Sigismund III, injustices
    of.
Russian news in England, 57
Russian youths, 130–133, 93nn135–139,
205–207. See also, Alphery,
Mikepher; Davidove, Cazaren;
Mychalove, Sophone; Semonove,
Pheodor.

Sackville, Richard, Earl of Dorset, 169,
200n260
Saltykov, Gleb, 79
Saltykov, Mikhail (Mikhailo), 77, 79, 92,
94
San Clemente, Guillén de, 25, 40,
44n120
Sapieha, Jan Piotr, 74, 77, 78, 90, 91, 94,
99
Sapieha, Leon, Chancellor of Grand
Duchy of Lithuania, 86
Scarborough, 26
Schomaker, Georg, 21
Scotland (and Scots), 5, 21n73
Scudamore, John Viscount, 198n217
Second False Dmitrii, 60, 62, 74, 90, 120,

123, 185nn26 & 29 & 32, 188n73, 192n123, 209
Selbie, John, 49n131
Selden, John, xin2
Semenov, Andrei, Russian undersecretary, 184n14, 195n185, 198n216, 202n293
Semonove, Pheodor (spelled variously), Russian youth, 205
Sever, land of, 74, 75, 79, 87, 90, 94, 123
Shah Abbas, 118
Shaw, James, 191n120
Shchelkalov, Andrei, 30, 31, 32, 33, 35, 36
Shchelkalov, Vasilii, 45
Shevkal, 122
Shirley, Anthony, English adventurer and diplomat, 192n128
Shirley, Sir Robert, emissary from Persia to England, etc., 192n128
Shuiskii, Prince Dmitrii Ivanovich, 76, 77, 92, 98
Shuiskii, Prince Ivan Ivanovich, 114
Shuiskii, Tsar Vasilii Ivanovich (1606–1610), 42n116, 59, 60, 62, 63, 73, 74, 75, 76, 77, 78, 79, 80, 83, 85, 89, 91, 93, 94, 97, 119, 185n27, 186n40, 192n123
Siberia, 93, 120, 121
Sidney Robert, Viscount Lisle, Lord Chamberlain to Queen Anne of England, 175
Sigismund August, King of Poland (1548–1572), 10
Sigismund III (Vasa), King of Poland (1587–1632), 35, 42, 45, 46, 66
as King of Sweden (1592–1604), 23, 37. And see Karl, Duke, of Södermanland.
Catholic, 51, 60, 64, 86
defeat of, 66, 69
election of, 23, 24
injustices of, 73, 80, 83–85, 89–94, 100, 104, 111, 114, 118, 120, 125, 171–172, 173, 177
invited to Russia, 60
marriage of, 25, 53n147
Muscovites stand against, 80–81

and relations of with England, 24–26, 43, 65, 73
and Smolensk, 61, 69, 70
Swedish revolt against, 41–42, 43
treatment of ambassadors by, 79, 94–95
truce with Russia, 75–76, 86, 91, 185
and wars with Archduke Maximilian, 191n111. See also, Elizabeth I; England; Poland.
Simon, Georgian Tsar, 122
Sinclair, A., 54
Skene, John, Scottish Ambassador to Denmark, later Lord Curriehill, 48
Skopin-Shuiskii, Prince Mikhail Vasil'evich, 97, 98
Skytte, Johan, Swedish Ambassador to England, etc., 51, 52
Smith, Fabian, English merchant, 194n170
Smith, Sir Richard, 162, 168, 169, 194n168, 197n198
Smith, Sir Thomas, Conductor of the Russian Ambassadors, Governor of the Muscovy Company, 46, 58n168, 70n212, 156, 157, 158, 159, 162, 166, 175, 184n20, 196nn190 & 191, 197n197, 203, 204
Smith, Thomas, 197n200
Smolensk, 61, 63, 64n184, 70, 76, 78, 79, 80, 92, 94, 98, 186n33, 209
Söderköping, Diet of (1595), 25, 42
Sokoliński, Prince Jan z Drucka, Secretary to Stanisław Witowski, 74, 75, 90
Somerset House Conference, 48
Somerset House, reception at, 7, 175–177
Sonnenburg (Estonia), 54
Sound, Danish (and tolls for), 8, 19, 20, 22n77, 39, 53, 183n12
Sovin, Andrei Grigor'evich, Russian Ambassador to England, 13, 14
Spain, 4, 66, 111, 112, 192n132
navy of (and stores for), 19n67, 22n78
and Sweden, 22
and Denmark, 5, 6, 20, 21, 38, 56
Spanish Armada, vii
Spanish Netherlands, 1, 22n77
Spens (Spence), Sir James, English envoy

to Sweden, etc., 50, 52nn141 and
142, 53, 183n12
Speyer, Peace of (1544), 10
Spifame, Samuel, 6
St. Nicholas (Nicolas), 67, 189n94,
191n119
Stade, 9
Staritsa, 14
States General, the, 56n161, 57
Steelyard, 9
Stenbock, Gustav, Swedish Ambassador
to England, etc., 51, 52
Stepan Tverdikov, 11
Stettin, negotiations in (1615), 62n176
Stettin, peace of (1570), 15, 183n12
Stewart, William, Scottish Ambassador
to Denmark, etc., 48
Stolbovo, Peace of (1617), 70, 71,
189n92
Strale, Olof, 52
Mikołaj Strús, *Starosta* of Chmielnik and
Lubecz, 81, 97
Stuart, Lord, 190n97
Stuart, (Steward, Stewart), Sir Robert,
49, 194n171
Stuart, Sir William, 64, 50n134
Suarez, Francisco, 49
Sultan Ahmed, 118
Sultan Mehmed, 118
Sultan, the, 4
Sweden, 11, 69,
    and England, 10, 22–23, 41–43, 49–53,
    73
    and the Hanse, 10
    and Irish soldiers. See Ireland, soldiers
    from.
    and Livonian War, 8, 42
    and pro-Catholic policy, 22
    revolts against Sigismund, 41–42, 51
    signs truce with Russia (1595), 97, 142
    and War of Three Crowns, 9
Swinnerton, Sir John, Lord Mayor of
London (1612–1613), 196n193, 203
Sylvester, Daniel, English envoy to
Russia, 15–16, 17, 184n18

Tarło, Zygmunt, 76, 91
Tarnowski, Jan, Vice-Chancellor of
Poland (c. 1591), 25

Tartar Khanates of Kazan' and
Astrakhan', 11
Temkin-Rostovskii, Prince Mikhail,
Governor of Vologda, 71
Teusina, Treaty of. See Tiavzino, Treaty
of.
Tenneker, Thomas, 23
Thames, River, 159, 163, 167
Thirty Years' War, vii, 3, 42
Thomas Tenneker, 23
Throckmorton, Sir John, Lieutenant-
Governor of Flushing, 66, 189n92
Tiavzino (Teusina), Treaty of (1595), 41,
45, 188n85, 194n162
Tikhanov, M. N., Russian Ambassador to
Persia, 190n197
Tilbury, 197n202
Time of Troubles, 8, 16, 37, 58, 59, 62,
190n107, 190nn97 & 107
Titles, of office and rank, x, xii
Tottenham High Cross, 26
Tower of London and Tower Wharf, 6,
154, 197n211
Translations of speeches, 178–179
Transylvania, 23, 25, 192n132
Trautson, Count Paul Sixt von,
councillor of Rudolf II, 41
Treaty of London (1604), 48
Tret'iakov, Petr, 194n153
Trubetskoi, Prince, Dmitrii, 187n50,
190n98
Trumbull, William, English agent in
Brussells, 66, 188n63, 192n132,
202n300
Tura river, 121
Turkey (and Turks), 4, 5, 22n77, 28, 40,
42, 45, 46, 112, 117, 118–119,
182n9, 192nn 127 & 128 & 132,
211
Tylicki, Vice-Chancellor of Poland
(c. 1598), 43
Tyszkiewicz, Jan, 74, 90
Tyszkiewicz, Samuel, 90

Ukrainian cossacks, 90
Ulfeldt, Jakob, Chancellor of Denmark
(1609–1630), 56
Ulster Plantation, 49, 63

United provinces, English agreement
    with (1603), 48
Uppsala, and declaration of (1593), 2, 25
Urusov, Prince Petr, 123

Valkendorf, Christoffer, 19, 20n73
Vanegas, Captain Alonso, 21n75
Vasilii III, Grand Prince (d. 1533), 11,
    35
Vasilii, Tsar. See Shuiskii, Tsar Vasilii
    Ivanovich.
Vel'iaminov, Mikhail Ivanovich, 105
Velikii Novgorod, 92
Venice, Doge of, 111, 112
Viborg, and Treaty of (1609), 186n33,
    188n85, 194n162
Vil'ianko, 195n177
Vintners' Company of, 197n212
Virgina, 5, 65
Vitovtov, Aleksei, Secretary of Aleksei
    Ziuzin, 200n269
  carries credential letter, 170, 171
  letter to, 142
  presents gifts, 174
  speeches of, 74–77, 79–82, 85–100,
    101–102, 103–117, 118–124,
    172–173, 174, 176–177
Vlas'ev, Afanasii, Russian Ambassador to
    the Emperor, 105, 191n122
Volga, River, 88, 121, 189n94, 211
Volinskii, Stephan Evanovitch, 189n92
Volkonskii, Prince Grigorii, 74, 89
Vologda, 71, 72
Volokolamsk, 82, 97, 114, 172

Waad William, 19
Waldegrave, Edward, 202nn299 & 300
Wale, Jan de, Netherlander, 28, 29, 30,
    33n103
Walgrave, Edward, Gentleman of the
    Bedchamber, 181. See Waldegrave,
    Edward.
Wallachia, 64n184
Walsingham, Sir Francis, 21, 23, 26
War of the Three Crowns (1563–1570),
    8
Wardo, 29
Warkocz, Nicholas, 35n106, 44n120, 105
Warsaw, 64, 65, 66

Weld, John, Clerk of the City of
    London, 204
Wernham, R.B., vi
Westermann, Hermann. See Eremeev,
    Eremei.
Whitby, 195n185
Whitehall, 1, 3, 6, 49, 199n236,
    202n293, 205
Willan, T.S., vi, 12, 16
William the Silent, 19
Willis, Dr. Timothy, English envoy to
    Russia, p. 45
Willoughby, Lord. See Bertie, Robert.
Wilno, 64
Winwood, Sir Ralph, English agent to
    States General, 2, 5n24, 62, 189n89,
    208
  letters of, 2n7, 4n17, 6n29, 53n147,
    54n153, 55nn156 & 157 & 159,
    56n162, 57nn165–167, 71n217,
    73n12, 182n12, 183n12, 186n33,
    189n94
  report of, 2
Wiśniówiecki, Prince Adam, 74, 87, 89,
    90
Wiśniówiecki, Prince Konstanty, 87, 89
Witowski, Stanisław, Wójski of Parcew,
    emissary to Russia, 74, 75, 90,
    188n72
Wladyslaw, Prince of Poland, 60, 68n203,
    186n38
  and proposal to rule Russia, 77–78, 80,
    85, 93–94, 99, 113–114, 122–123,
    133, 186nn39 & 42, 192n124,
    193n145, 213
Wilhelm, Wolfgang, Duke of Neuburg,
    65
women, 175
Woodward, Sir John, 197n201

Yarmouth, 196n188
Youths, Russian. See Russian youths and
    Alphery, Davidove, Mychalove, and
    Semonove.

Zamoyski, Chancellor of Poland
    (c. 1594), 25, 43
Zarutskii (Zarutsky), Ivashka, 123, 124,
    188n32, 191n118, 209

Zborowski, Alexander, 74, 90

Zebrzydowski revolt (1606), 183n13

zemskii sobor, xii, 61, 190n100, 199n246

Ziuzin, Aleksei, Ivanovich, Gentleman
and Viceroy of Shatsk, Ambassador
to England
arrival in England, 6, 57
audience for at Whitehall, 7, 166, 168,
170
briefed by Merrick, 69. And see
Merrick, John.
credentials of, 73, 136–137, 170, 171
English report on, 57
expenses of, 6. And see Ambassadors,
expenses of.
and Guy Fawkes day, 166–168
instructions to in case of death of
James I, 124–125
instructions to, 58, 71–124
James I's speech to, 173–174
leaves England, 71
no power to conclude treaty, 101, 102,
105

and other ambassadors, 111
presents gifts, 174, 201n281
protected from thieves, 151
provisions for. See ambassadors,
provisions, for.
reception for at Somerset House, 7,
175–177
report of, 145–181
see Lord Mayor's festival, 70. And see
Lord Mayor's Festival.
speeches of, 73–74, 77–79, 82–83,
85–100, 101–102, 103–117,
118–124, 171, 172–173, 174,
176–177
success of embassy, 70
to discover English policies, 129–130
travels up to London, 153
Tsar's letter to, 142–144

Stanisław Żółkiewski, Polish hetman, 60,
62, 77, 78, 79, 80, 92, 93, 94, 98,
99, 113, 114, 123, 171, 186n37

Zouche, Edward La, 38

www.ingramcontent.com/pod-product-compliance
Lightning Source LLC
Chambersburg PA
CBHW080923100426
42812CB00007B/2348